CRADLES
of POWER

The Mothers and Fathers
of the American Presidents

HAROLD I. GULLAN

Skyhorse Publishing

10 9 8 7 6 5 4 3 2 1

Library of Congress Cataloging-in-Publication Data is available on file.

Cover design by Rain Saukas
Cover photos: John F. Kennedy Presidential Library and Museum; George Bush Presidential Library and Museum; Franklin D. Roosevelt Presidential Library

Print ISBN: 978-1-5107-0533-3
Ebook ISBN: 978-1-5107-0534-0

Printed in the United States of America

This book is dedicated to
Grace Elizabeth Gullan
and
Winston Lakin Gullan,
either of whom might one day be elected president.

Contents

⟋⟍

Where I'm Coming From

Harry Truman once said that the only new thing in the world is the history we don't know. I'm reputed to be a historian. Yet when I embarked on this remarkably neglected subject, I readily realized just how little I knew. Yes, Washington didn't get along with his mother and Lincoln with his father, Sara Roosevelt and Joseph P. Kennedy were domineering, "Miss Lillian" Carter was a character, Abigail Adams was (thankfully) given to recording her thoughts, and Gerald Ford and Bill Clinton had stepfathers who couldn't have been more different.

But what of all the others? Why have we had so many books about first ladies and so few about first parents? Indeed, to my knowledge, this is only the second one ever to tell the stories of both our first mothers and first fathers all within a single set of covers. And what stories many of them are! No, not every parent provided the earliest inspiration to a favored son who eventually became president, but many did. And just as many were remarkable in their own right. Consider the heroic mother of Andrew Jackson, who literally saved his life. Or the senior Theodore Roosevelt, who seemingly founded and funded every worthwhile charity in New York. The parents of our presidents have been as varied as American parents generally, and their stories form a compelling component of American history—the history so few of us know very much about.

John F. Kennedy once said that every American mother wants her son to be president. She just doesn't want him to be in politics. Actually, he was wrong on both counts. The only American mother who, at least near the end of her life, wanted her son to be president was Abigail Adams. She simply felt that the nation needed him. His father, John, who *had* been president, preferred to see John Quincy return to join him in a law firm so the family could finally make some money.

Rose Fitzgerald Kennedy came from a family steeped in politics and campaigned vigorously for all her sons, but she had also hoped that Bobby would enter the priesthood. The only first mother who specifically wanted her son to be in politics was Rebekah Baines Johnson, but she intended that Lyndon should run for Congress and nearly drove him crazy promoting it. By the way, note how many of our presidents have had their mothers' maiden names as their middle names, indicating their importance. In Woodrow Wilson's case, after he abandoned "Thomas" as being too undignified, his mother's maiden name became his first name, as was the case with Millard Fillmore.

Well, what did all the mothers of our presidents really want for their sons? Simply, like all mothers, that they should lead fulfilling lives. However, if pressed for a specific profession, they would have chosen the ministry. "Mother" McKinley (popularly called that throughout the nation) even had a particular goal in mind—that William should one day become a Methodist bishop. Alas, she had to settle for the White House. The only president who actually studied for the ministry was Woodrow Wilson, and he changed his career goals after his freshman year in college.

What of the first fathers? Except for those with inherited wealth, they were all ambitious, although only about half were successful in their business ventures. Many hoped their sons would join them in expanding these enterprises; but barring that, the preferred profession was the law—and *not* as a way to enter politics. Of our forty-three presidents, only a dozen haven't pursued a legal career, although not all proceeded to practice the profession. Yes, Joseph P. Kennedy Sr. wanted one of his sons to be president, but his first choice had been himself.

What I have tried to do, in so necessarily brief an account, is not to dwell on the detailed biographies of each individual parent or the policies of each future president. My concern is less with precisely what they did than with *why* they did it. Theirs is a shared story combining many separate stories of parents and children. Only these particular children became presidents. Who and what most influenced each of them during his vital formative years? Growing up, how did each interact with his parents? How did their own experiences, values, and character influence his? Of course, we know much more about some families than others. Hopefully, this book of intertwined stories will add some modest insight into the American story we all share.

Please join this voyage of discovery. Consider, for example, the inspiring Ida Eisenhower and Martha Truman, the resourceful Lucy Hayes and Eliza Garfield, the supportive John Coolidge, and the venturesome Samuel Polk—just to name a few. Even some parents not so highly esteemed by their sons made critical decisions affecting their lives and ultimately the nation. For example, suppose Ulysses S. Grant's father had not insisted that his son, against his will, attend West Point to find some focus for his life? Would we have ever heard of him?

It's all a part of the history we *should* know. Thank you for sharing your own conclusions, and enhancing mine.

CHAPTER 1

Foundations of Independence— Mary and Augustine Washington

———✦———

"I was early denied of a father," the adult George Washington reflected. He had also been denied the educational opportunities his half-brothers had received. His father, Augustine, had died too young to specify them in his will. George was only eleven. All his life, the father of our country felt deeply his lack of intellectual attainments, an opinion shared by the other founders, however much they esteemed Washington's importance in unifying their fragile new nation.

Miriam Ann Bourne suggests that even given so few years together, it is inconceivable that so energetic a man as Augustine Washington "would not have had some influence on his best-known son." Whatever the extent of that influence, Paul Longmore concludes, "Perhaps we can see in the loss of his father" George Washington's "extraordinary drive for public fame." In either case, the public image Washington crafted for himself came out of both what he'd lost and what he'd sought. The tall, dignified silent figure wearing his old uniform at the Continental Congress was the picture of resolve, in itself a call to action and an offer to lead.

1

The private George Washington was far less austere. He enjoyed entertaining, had an eye for a trim ankle, was known to indulge in coarse conversation, operated the largest distillery on the continent, and was acquisitive almost to the point of excess. H. L. Mencken called him "the Rockefeller of his time." He poured out his emotions in a constant stream of letters, both official and personal. Throughout the War for American Independence he castigated Congress for its lack of support, and throughout his life he conducted a candid correspondence with many relatives.

There was one notable exception—his mother, Mary Ball Washington. To her, his letters were few and formal. What to make of this perplexing woman has long challenged historians. As Bourne puts it, "Nineteenth-century sentimentality created a virtuous myth; twentieth-century revisionism has created a nagging monster." Of one quality there is no doubt. In an age of male domination, Mary Ball Washington was a woman of immense will, which she constantly sought to exert on her oldest son, and which, in a protracted contest, he sought to escape.

Much has been made of the patrician origins of our first six presidents, four of whom were the sons of Virginia planters and the other two from a well-established Massachusetts family. In the saga of the Washingtons, however, there are humbler themes and a dramatic mobility akin to that of later generations of immigrants. For generations, the Washington family had lived in the Essex region of England, rising to become landed gentry, just below the aristocracy. Their estates were prosperous enough to enable young Lawrence Washington to answer a call to the Anglican priesthood. However, he wound up on the wrong side of the English Civil War of the 1640s, and the ascendant Roundheads found this heavy-drinking minister too cavalier for their tastes and expelled him for "immorality."

Before long, his high-spirited son, John, decided it prudent to go to sea. In 1657 he landed in the Colony of Virginia and wasted little time in finding himself a prosperous bride, the most direct form of upward mobility. Soon they had a son, another Lawrence, who would be George Washington's grandfather. As James Thomas Flexner points out, "The

Wild West was then on the Atlantic seaboard, and John Washington was a turbulent spirit well suited to so violent a world." Sued by his captain for desertion, he responded by accusing the captain of murder on the high seas.

Energetic John Washington became a self-taught lawyer, rising to become both advocate and judge, ultimately sitting on both the county court and his church vestry. Most important, he indulged in what Flexner calls a "passion for acreage," a quality to be emulated by his successors. In short, this first Washington in Virginia soon restored his family to the level it had enjoyed in the old country, his success exemplifying the ambivalence of a colonial society overlaying raw acquisitiveness with a veneer of English sensibilities.

Not surprisingly, John's son, Lawrence, a respectable, introspective lawyer, chose to overlook some of the foundations of his father's prosperity. Lawrence's second son, Augustine, the father of George Washington, enjoyed the benefits of an education in England, no longer at war with itself, and also married the daughter of a well-to-do Virginia planter. By the time he came of age in 1715, he was the master of some 1,750 fertile acres.

The descriptions that have come down to us about Augustine Washington have almost a mythic quality. Douglas Southall Freeman quotes young George as describing his father as a gentle, genial giant: "tall, fair of complexion, well proportioned, and fond of children." Flexner notes that Augustine, called "Gus" by his friends, was "blond, of fine proportions and great physical strength . . . standing six feet tall in his stockings. His kindly nature matched his towering strength." Adding to this, his possession of a spacious plantation at Pope's Creek made him at twenty-one as attractive a catch as his popular teenage bride, Jane Butler.

Only three generations removed from the arrival of tempestuous John Washington in Virginia, Augustine would be an acknowledged leader in each of the three localities where he and his family would reside. Apparently, he always had a profound love of the land. Eventually, he built a handsome home called "Wakefield" at Pope's Creek. By then Jane had given birth to four children, three of whom survived. The two boys bore familiar family names—Lawrence and another Augustine.

What changed their father's life was the discovery of a rich deposit of iron ore on his plantation. It also eventually changed the senior Augustine's cheerful disposition, turning him from a gentleman farmer to an overburdened entrepreneur. Having entered into a partnership with English investors to form the Principio Company, Augustine was often away from home. While he was in England in 1729 to meet with his increasingly contentious partners, Jane, his devoted wife of fourteen years, passed away.

Despite profound feelings of guilt and grief, Augustine was obliged to find a new mother for his children. It took him two years, although amiable widows were hardly in short supply even in sparsely populated Virginia. But Augustine, then a mature thirty-seven, settled on an "old maid" of twenty-three named Mary Ball. The source of his attraction is uncertain. Flexner describes Mary Ball as "a healthy orphan of moderate height, rounded figure, and pleasant voice." Not everyone was to find her voice so pleasant in future years. She brought to the marriage in 1731 a substantial inheritance of her own, few emotional ties, and a strong will more than a match for her obliging husband's.

Eleven months into their marriage, on the morning of February 22, 1732, Mary gave birth to a boy large enough to seem a proper son of the robust Augustine Washington. He was christened George, not a traditional Washington name, for George Eskridge, who had been Mary's devoted guardian after the death of her parents. By the time he learned to walk, George had a sister named Betty. They were followed by another sister and three brothers. That five of these six children survived to adulthood, an unlikely percentage in that time and place, testifies to the vigor of both parents. Growing up, George hardly wanted for playmates, black as well as white. At Pope's Creek, the natural world was just outside his door, supplemented by a menagerie of dogs, chickens, calves, pigs, and horses. Throughout, Augustine was the parent on the move; Mary, the parent in place.

When George was only three, Augustine moved his family from Westmoreland County to a much larger plantation further up the Potomac in what is now Fairfax, Virginia. A few years later, in 1738, the family moved for the final time to be closer to Augustine's principal iron mine and furnace, at Accokeek Creek in present-day Stafford County, on the Rappahannock River, near the new town of Fredericksburg. Called "Ferry Farm," it was truly George's childhood home. If, indeed, he cut down that cherry tree, it was likely there. A precocious, lively child, George loved to hunt in the nearby woods and to fish, swim, and sail in a river narrow enough for a sturdy youth to hurl a coin across. Some of this activity had to be in the company of his nature-loving father, although by then Augustine was not only immersed in the iron business, but was also still farming tobacco and other crops and buying, selling, and leasing land to others. He also fulfilled community obligations, from church vestryman and high sheriff to trustee of Fredericksburg.

With his half-sister deceased and his two half-brothers away at the Appleby School in England, George was the oldest child at home. For a time he was enrolled in a small school operated by an Anglican clergyman, but his education was largely in the hands of tutors. He learned to write in a fine, flourishing hand, became a proficient draftsman, and was good at arithmetic. His studies included moral and natural philosophy. However, his classical education was intended to come later, like his half-brothers' across the sea at Appleby, followed by college at William and Mary.

It was particularly George's half-brother Lawrence who joined with their father as an example to emulate. When George wrote down with such care in his notebook all 110 maxims of the "Rules of Civility in Decent Behavior in Company and Conversation," devised by Jesuits for European nobility, they seemed equally to apply to Virginia gentry. When Lawrence at twenty returned as a dashing young captain from a British expedition against Spain in the Caribbean and became engaged to lovely Anne Fairfax, whose family stood at the pinnacle of Tidewater society, George shared in his own family's satisfaction.

Only a few months later, in the spring of 1743, while playing with nearby cousins, George was visited by a messenger with an urgent summons to return home. His overburdened father was dying. Augustine Washington died on April 12, 1743, at only forty-nine. The official cause was "gout of the stomach," although it may have been exacerbated by pneumonia. The usually thorough Augustine had neglected to specify in his will that George, then only eleven, was to receive the same classical education as his older half-brothers.

In other respects, Augustine tried to provide equitably for everyone. To Lawrence, the older son of his first marriage, went the house at Little Hunting Creek, which he would rebuild and rename Mount Vernon in honor of English Admiral Edward Vernon, under whom he had served. To George, to be kept in trust for him until he came of age at twenty-one, went Ferry Farm and its surroundings. Mary Washington was to be in charge until that time, yet it would be twenty-eight years until she finally left.

In 1743, however, she faced daunting challenges. Even so self-reliant a widow, now thirty-six and determined not to remarry, was obliged to maintain substantial property and to raise the five children still at home. She would need a good deal of help. Since George at eleven was the oldest, he would have to stay at home by her side, become the titular head of the household, and look after his siblings, all under her relentless supervision.

It is hardly surprising that George preferred the more congenial company at Mount Vernon, which he came to see as his true home, with access to the palatial neighboring Belvoir estate of the Fairfax family. Soon Colonel Fairfax himself began to see in this younger Washington a potential conspicuously lacking in his own weak-kneed sons.

Back at Ferry Farm, Mary worked as best she could with and through her often-absent son, a tug-of-war she was bound eventually to lose. George admired his mother's determination without wanting to share in its application. Moreover, Mary Ball Washington's undoubted strengths as a manager were compromised by difficulties in setting priorities. As

Freeman notes, "A thousand trivialities were her daily care to the neglect of larger interests." One of George's contemporaries relates, "Of the mother I was ten times more afraid than I was of my own parents. She awed me in the midst of her kindness." Indeed, Mary Ball Washington could be kind, and she was genuinely devoted to her restless son, making her later concerns that he never contributed sufficiently to her welfare all the more puzzling.

Lawrence's extensive land holdings had encouraged George's interest in surveying and exploring, just as his half-brother's military prowess inspired George's dreams of his own future success. "My inclinations," he declared, "are strongly bent to arms." When he was sixteen, his mother reluctantly permitted him to accept Colonel Fairfax's offer to join an expedition surveying western lands. At seventeen he gained his first paying job as surveyor for the county of Culpepper, affording him ample opportunity, in the family tradition, to acquire land for himself in the fertile Shenandoah Valley. By his later teens, George Washington was already physically a man, at six-foot-two taller than his imposing father had been, and developing something of that commanding public persona. In one respect, however, young George was typically vulnerable. He fell in love with a dazzling young lady of eighteen, Sally Cary. Unfortunately, she was already betrothed—to a Fairfax—and had the good sense to eventually end the relationship with Washington, saving both parties from scandal and preserving for him the patronage of the powerful. When he finally did marry, it was to the sensible, amiable, very wealthy, and widowed Martha Dandridge Custis.

Lawrence Washington had returned from a session at the House of Burgesses in Williamsburg with a serious problem of his own. His chronic cough had escalated to "consumption," likely a form of tuberculosis. Seeking a cure in the beneficent climate of Barbados, he was accompanied by nineteen-year-old George, on the only ocean voyage of his life. The tropical locale enthralled him, but unfortunately George contracted smallpox and had to return home. One can imagine a likely maternal refrain of "I told you so." Lawrence went on to Bermuda. George recovered, but Lawrence did not. He died at the age of thirty-four, fourteen years younger than had his father, Augustine. By the time he was twenty, George Washington had lost both of the male role models from his own family.

Lawrence's will gave his half-brother "in love and affection" several lots in Fredericksburg, and in the event of contingencies, the ultimate possession of Mount Vernon, with its 2,000 acres. On the verge of his majority, beyond the restraint of his mother's hand, Washington embarked on his true vocation, military adventure. Assuming Lawrence's position as adjutant of the Virginia militia, he undertook a dangerous mission from the provincial governor to convince the French to abandon their plans for expansion in the Ohio Valley. The ultimatum failed, the French and Indian War followed, and Washington was engaged in periodic combat for the better part of the next eight years.

Returning home as a full colonel who had commanded all of Virginia's forces, Washington had important decisions to make. He had suffered setbacks but had accumulated vast experience. Despite this, he had been denied a commission in the regular British Army, which was to be a source of enduring resentment. He resigned his commission (but kept his uniform), comparing the valor of his Virginia militia to the "cowardice" of the British regulars.

He married Martha and set about to become the country squire his mother had envisioned. By then George had inherited both Mount Vernon and a new family to inhabit it. Martha had brought her own immense resources and her two surviving Custis children, a son and a daughter. George lavished attention on them and their eventual offspring, as well as a host of nieces and nephews, although it would be a profound disappointment that he and Martha were unable to have any children of their own.

Throughout his campaigns, as he would later, George had found time to write letters of warmth and candor to his remaining half-brother and his siblings. To his terrified mother he wrote little, although he once asked that she not be told of a "shameful defeat." Apparently, he still valued her grudging favor, even after she left Ferry Farm to move to her modest new home in Fredericksburg.

Near her daughter Betty's family, Mary Washington saw little of her oldest son and avoided sharing in his subsequent success. Flexner's view that "she was clearly a powerful woman, but all her power was centered on herself" seems excessively harsh. Her moral and religious beliefs may have been "strictly orthodox," as Doris Faber writes, but she sincerely tried to impart them to all her children throughout their time together, particularly dwelling on the grandeur of nature as embodying "the majesty of the Creator of all things." She had settled on a location near "meditation rock," her favorite retreat for reading and prayer, as her final resting place.

Mary had now to rely on her children for support, particularly George, who, she felt, never contributed quite enough. The complexity of her character emerges from these complaints. It reached the point where, in 1781, her want and discontent became so public that the Virginia House of Delegates proposed to raise a pension for her, the mother of the commanding general of the Continental Army. An embarrassed and infuriated Washington protested, "Before I left Virginia, I answered all her calls for money; and since that period, I have directed my steward to do the same. Whence her distresses can arise therefore I know not." Only the preceding year, in a letter to "My dear George," she thanked him for the "2 five ginnes" he had sent, regretting that she had been unable to see her preoccupied son when he happened to go through Fredericksburg, noting, "I am afraid I never shall have that pleasure again." Washington used his patient younger brother, John, as an intermediary. Waiting anxiously for the peace treaty to be signed in 1783, he wrote John about yet another plea for funds from their mother: "It is too much while I'm suffering in every other way . . . to be saddled with all the expense of hers." Yet she kept imploring, "I am going fast, and . . . the time is hard . . . I never lived so poore in my life."

Consider how similar was the tone of George Washington's own complaints to Congress about its parsimonious lack of support. In the very first year of the conflict he wrote his stepson, "Jacky" Custis, "I do not think that any officer since the creation had such a variety of difficulties and perplexities to encounter as I have." Moreover, there is much of his mother's

stubborn strength in his reliance throughout on his own judgment, however much he departed from her plans for him. That childhood friend who
had been so impressed, even frightened, by Mary Washington looked back
from the perspective of time and concluded, "Whoever has seen that awe-
inspiring air and manner so characteristic in the father of his country, will
remember the matron as she appeared when the presiding genius of her
household, commanding and being obeyed."

After his brother John died in 1787, George turned his attention
back to the parent who by then must surely be "aged and infirm." In a
letter to his mother of unaccustomed length, he advised her to wind up
her own affairs and come to "live with one of your own children." Of
course, Mount Vernon, with life so lively it might be "compared to a well
resorted tavern," would "never answer your purposes." He also finally
managed to visit her in Fredericksburg, on his way to the Constitutional
Convention. She seemed as mentally alert as ever, but "reduced to a skeleton." Perhaps each viewed this final meeting as a sort of reconciliation.
Two years later, on September 1, 1789, Mary Ball Washington passed
away, probably from some form of cancer. Whatever the size of her
estate, she had named George as her executor. He would outlive her by
only a decade.

The amiable father of George Washington became increasingly overburdened when he immersed himself in a business venture he pursued so
vigorously that it probably shortened his life. The mother of George
Washington was a complex, dominating enigma whose affection for her
oldest son was framed in fear for his future path and the desire to direct
it. The message both lives imparted, tempered by the time granted to
each, and despite their own shortcomings, was simply the importance of
will: the will to decide, the will to prevail, and most of all, the will to
persevere.

CHAPTER 2

Revealing Just Enough—Jeffersons, Madisons, and Monroes

Jane and Peter Jefferson

Thomas Jefferson conveyed his limitless interests to an extent unequaled by any other president. Merrill Peterson refers to the "vast corpus" of public and private papers Jefferson left for posterity. Yet his personality remains "elusive." Biographers like Joseph Ellis keep trying to explain how this icon remains an enigma. Of course, Jefferson's immense achievements speak for themselves. John F. Kennedy once told a group of visitors to the White House that they were its most gifted guests since Thomas Jefferson had dined there alone.

Jefferson's conflicted feelings extended to his parents. He wrote just enough about his father, Peter, to express a measure of admiration. Of his mother, he wrote next to nothing. Jefferson seems to have most valued the traditional domestic virtues of "modesty and diffidence" in women, represented by both the mother he ostensibly ignored and the wife to whom he was utterly devoted. Of their children, only two daughters lived to adulthood. When his wife, Martha Jefferson, died on September 6, 1782, at the age of thirty-three, Thomas Jefferson had something akin to a nervous breakdown. Although he burned the private correspondence with both his mother and his wife, in letters to others Jefferson refers to "the catastrophe" that closed the last summer of his marriage.

Later, he would be attracted to at least two highly independent women, neither of whom he could marry. One would not leave her husband. The other was at least technically black. However, this did not prevent him from having six children with her, four of whom survived, establishing a parallel line of mixed-race Jefferson descendants. Sally • Hemings could have been freed in France, but she chose to remain with Jefferson as his "domestic servant."

Jefferson's earliest memory was as a child of three being carried on a pillow from one home to another. Like Washington, he would be "early deprived of a father"—in Jefferson's case, at the age of fourteen. But unlike Washington, Jefferson was denied neither the education nor the travel both had anticipated. What he most missed was spending more time with a father who died too soon.

By his mid-twenties, Peter Jefferson stood over six feet tall, and his strength was legendary. For example, he was reputed to have lifted two hogsheads of tobacco simultaneously, each weighing a thousand pounds. Such superhuman strength was put to the test as Peter explored and expanded the land he had inherited, much of it still a wild domain. Thomas Fleming writes, "He had fought his way through the winter wilderness, sleeping in hollow trees while wolves and wildcats howled around him." When his mapping was done, he found his way back to the humble hut he had built to read Addison, Swift, Pope, and Shakespeare.

In his autobiography, written sixty-three years after Peter Jefferson's death, Thomas Jefferson notes rather blandly, "My father's education had been quite neglected; but being of a strong mind, sound judgment, and eager after information, he read much and improved himself." He was the obvious inspiration for his son's vision of the new nation, to be governed by an agrarian-based self-made aristocracy not of birth, as in Europe, but of authentic achievement.

Of his mother, Jane Randolph Jefferson, Thomas volunteered only that she came from a family tracing "their pedigree far back in England & Scotland, to which let everyone ascribe the faith and merit he chuses (sic)." It is uncertain why he said so little. Did he resent her aristocratic background as failing to conform to the more egalitarian new society he had envisioned? Fawn Brodie proposes a more likely scenario. After his early schooling and the death of his father, Jefferson lived with his mother, excepting the years at William and Mary, until he was twenty-seven. His avoidance of even mentioning her at any length "seems evidence rather of very great influence which he deeply resented, and which he struggled to escape." It sounds like Mary Ball Washington. Yet family recollections, as quoted by Brodie, describe Jane Randolph Jefferson in invariably favorable terms: a lady of "amiable and affectionate disposition," lively, sensible, cheerful, and humorous, yet refined and elegant.

When her home was destroyed by fire in 1770, Jefferson wrote a friend bemoaning the loss of his papers and books rather than voicing concern for his mother's welfare. It took him two months to inform an uncle in England of his mother's death on March 31, 1776. Of course, this was a tumultuous year for England's American colonies. It implies a good deal more that Jefferson fell so ill, with six weeks of agonizing headaches, following his mother's death that it took him away from the Continental Congress at a most pivotal juncture. He would have such debilitating headaches again in future years, most severely after the death of his wife, where there was no doubt of his affection.

At least Jefferson's recollections of his father imply strength and judgment. However, for all his resourcefulness, some argue that sturdy Peter Jefferson was not quite as self-made as his son suggested. Although Dumas Malone writes of Peter, "The enhancement of his fortunes, like the improvement of his mind, must be chiefly attributed to his own exertions," Peterson notes that there had been Jeffersons in Virginia since its earliest settlement. The youngest son of a moderately successful planter, Peter Jefferson was born to neither wealth nor privilege, but he had inherited a good name, his forebears' energy, and property ripe for development. He would improve it as he improved himself. In his equally brief account of his lineage, Thomas seems more interested in natural than familial history. "The tradition of my father's family was that their ancestors came to this country from Wales and from the mountain of Snowden, the highest in Great Britain." By the 1680s his grandparents had acquired abundant farmland to the west of tidewater Virginia.

Although described by Brodie as "grave and taciturn," Peter Jefferson had a "faculty for friendship." He took people as they came, making friends readily, to his great advantage, whether with the resident Indians, not yet alarmed by an excess of interlopers, or with his few neighboring plantation owners, intrepid pioneers like himself. The most prominent was wealthy young William Randolph, whose 2,400 acres adjoined Peter's smaller property. The Randolphs would be to the Jeffersons what the Fairfaxes had been to the Washingtons, a connection helping to vault them within one generation from little more than yeoman farmers to community leaders of high standing. At the age of thirty-two, Peter Jefferson won the hand of Randolph's beguiling nineteen-year-old cousin, Jane.

Together, they established a plantation named Shadwell after her ancestral home in England. Shadwell was situated by the Rivanna River in the foothills of the hazy Blue Ridge Mountains. They were among the earliest settlers in the region, as Peter rounded out a larger tract to develop. His basic crop was tobacco. Working hand-in-hand with his slaves, Peter erected a remarkably spacious edifice rising a story and a half. Its grounds included a terraced garden for Jane, who also loved the outdoors. However isolated from polite society, it was a healthier environment than the lowlands. Eight of the ten children born to the Jeffersons survived infancy. When Peter and Jane moved to Shadwell, they already had two daughters. It was there, on April 13, 1743, that their first son was born and given the recurring family name of Thomas.

A widower with two children, William Randolph died at only thirty-three. His will stipulated that upon his death the Randolph plantation, its mansion at Tuckahoe fifty miles east of Shadwell, and the Randolph children would be under the care of his "dear and loving friend," Peter Jefferson. For the next seven years the Jeffersons resided mainly at Tuckahoe, with dutiful Peter and Jane raising two sets of children and managing both plantations. At least young Tom didn't want for playmates.

From the age of five he was taught by a tutor in a little schoolhouse on the Tuckahoe grounds, but his most valued lessons—from surveying to mathematics—came from his self-educated, self-sufficient father. As Henry Sterne Randall writes, Peter made certain that Tom could ride, swim, shoot, survive in the wilderness, and "boldly stem the Rivanna" when it turned treacherous. Tom never enjoyed hunting, but he thoroughly absorbed his father's love of the natural world. Peter gave him a canoe of his own, for which a local Indian chief provided a cherished hand-carved paddle.

The merged families sang and celebrated together. Tom learned to play the fiddle. Peter encouraged his son to delve into his modest but well-worn library of some forty books. He would not have a second son until Tom was twelve. Peter and Tom even began to think alike, sharing a rather measured, serious approach to things, as well as a calm demeanor. Tom's facial features, rather delicate and small, favored his father's, although his pale face was more freckled and his hair was a bright red. He was growing up to be as tall as his father, six-foot-two, and strong, even if not quite the equal of Peter in this regard. Tom was gangling and lanky, more slender. Between them there developed a bond of evident affection, even if it was rarely voiced.

In 1752, with things well established at Tuckahoe, the Jeffersons finally returned to Shadwell, but Tom felt abandoned. At only nine he was sent to study and board at the classical school of the Reverend William Douglas. Even though he was able to return from time to time, Tom was terribly homesick and was bound to blame Peter for such a sudden separation. As Page Smith observes, "Even though his later references to his father are respectful and admiring, there is about them an unmistakable reserve."

Meanwhile, Peter Jefferson had emerged as the first citizen of Albemarle County. He was named to chancery court and was a justice of the peace, church warden, county surveyor, and chief officer of the local militia. For a time he served as a member of the House of Burgesses. He had accumulated an estate of some 7,500 fertile acres. His meticulous care in maintaining it would also be transmitted to Tom, as was his example of egalitarianism. On the frontier, Peter had run into all manner of men and learned to judge them only by their deeds. Even what

Tom had seen of slavery firsthand was relatively benign; his parents taught their slaves useful skills, from carpentry to housekeeping, as part of an interdependent extended family. Yet Thomas Jefferson had already absorbed enough to sense the challenges ahead, a fundamental dilemma with the "moral depravity" of slavery itself that he would never be able to resolve through his proposals of gradual emancipation.

On August 17, 1757, Peter Jefferson died, abruptly terminating his son's reluctant tenure with the Reverend Douglas. Although he had been feeling rather poorly throughout the summer and had been frequently visited by his friend Dr. Thomas Walker, his death came as a sudden shock to everyone. He was only forty-nine. Perhaps the accumulation of all those forays into the forests had overtaxed even his robust constitution and legendary strength.

What did he endow to Thomas in tangible terms? "My mulatto fellow Shawney, my Books, mathematical instruments & my Cherry tree Desk and Bookcase." When he came of age, Thomas would be given his choice of either Peter's "lands on the Rivanna River and its branches" or his other major property. But there was more. Unlike Augustine Washington, Peter had specifically spelled out in his will that his son's "thorough classical education" be continued and completed. Beyond Peter's love of learning, his own personal example inspired the future president's conception of a new nation governed by such self-made men of merit.

Yet Thomas's immediate reaction to his father's death, beyond inevitable sadness, seems peculiarly self-centered. Even a lifetime later he recalled, "At fourteen years of age the whole care and direction of myself was thrown on myself entirely." What of his five devoted guardians and his mother? Instead, after three years of study with the Anglican Reverend James Maury, Thomas complained of distractions at home. He wrote to one of his guardians, "As long as I stay . . . the Loss of one-fourth of my Time is inevitable, by Company's coming here and detaining me from School."

He was ready to move on to the College of William and Mary and was enrolled at the age of sixteen. Malone concludes that the loss of

Peter Jefferson "created a chasm" in his son's life "which remained unfulfilled until his years in Williamsburg." Although Jefferson's effusive tributes to mentors such as William Small and George Wythe are in contrast to the relatively few praising the father who had made it all possible, the influence of Peter Jefferson is palpable. At college, while his classmates caroused, Thomas was known to study as long as fifteen hours at a stretch, the mental equivalent of his father's physical energy.

When he built Monticello on his mountaintop, characteristically never ceasing to expand it, Jefferson was only four miles from the site of Shadwell, the land still beautiful and wild. He remained at least symbolically close to his family and its heritage. That he would die in debt is a sad tribute to the cost of his own creativity.

The sudden losses Thomas Jefferson sustained during his lengthy lifetime he suffered largely in silence. Smith suggests that Thomas's "silence about his mother, like his silence about his dead wife, may have been the consequences of a dependence too profound for him to speak of." His father indeed had left him even sooner but had endowed him with an estate, an education, and the opportunity to enhance them both. As Peterson concludes, "The pathway to power had been blazed for his son."

Nelly and James Madison Sr.

Five generations before the birth of James Madison Jr., the first of his family arrived in the Virginia Colony. John Maddison (the extra *d* would be dropped as extraneous) possessed the same sort of innovative energy that had launched the earliest Washingtons and Jeffersons who had reached the New World. A ship's carpenter by trade, he was even more proficient as a salesman. Under the "headright" system, he recruited others to make the perilous journey across the Atlantic. For every immigrant he brought over, he was enabled to "patent" fifty acres of land for himself. By the time he died in the late 1600s, he had amassed over 1,300 acres and was deemed a self-made success.

His sons and grandsons fared even better and married well. By the time James Madison Sr. was born, his family possessed considerable acreage in the piedmont of the Shenandoah Valley beyond the Blue Ridge. James Madison, an only son with two younger sisters, was obliged, in the words of Virginia Moore, to "be a man before he was a boy."

His father, Ambrose, died when James was only nine. Their plantation was a self-contained community, its modest main house surrounded by outbuildings—slave family cabins, barns and sheds for cattle, sheep, hogs, and horses. Pasture land had to be maintained, apple and peach trees planted. Wheat, corn, and especially tobacco had to be marketed. Relied on by his mother, it fell to James to keep it all going.

Despite his relative isolation, Madison's father had established warm relationships with the surrounding planters. One of them, Francis Conway, was made an executor of his will. The Conways had a daughter named Nelly whom James had met when she was only nine. As James grew into manhood, one of his tasks was to transport great hogsheads of tobacco for storage to a warehouse owned by the Conways. The main attraction was Nelly, now a lovely and lively teenager. Acquaintance ripened into affection, and they were married in September 1749, when she was seventeen and he a mature twenty-six.

Their first child, named James for his father, was born on March 16, 1751. Called "Jemmy," he would be followed by eleven more children. In the sad demographics of the time, only seven of the twelve were to survive to maturity. Unlike George Washington and Thomas Jefferson, sturdy sons of sturdy fathers, "little Jemmy" would reach only somewhere between five-foot-three and five-foot-six. Moreover, he was always sickly. Somehow he survived to eighty-five, and, as he put it, not only outlived most of his contemporaries but "may be thought to have outlived myself."

The Conways were reputed to have been descended from Scottish nobility, indeed from Robert the Bruce himself, but family pride born of lineage was no more a preoccupation of young James Madison than it had been of Thomas Jefferson. As an adult, James Jr. ignored genealogy, writing that the forebears he knew something of, "In both the paternal and maternal line . . . were planters and among the respectable, though not the most opulent, class." Pride of place was another matter. The elder

James Madison was already planning a most impressive replacement for the modest wooden home his father had erected.

The harmonious, graceful mansion named Montpelier was completed when Jemmy was eight. He expanded the house as an adult and particularly enjoyed its setting of fields, lawns, and forests, opening out to the vista of the Blue Ridge Mountains. Madison's was a more settled, emotionally secure childhood than that of Washington or Jefferson—his mother solicitous, his father busy but not so often away. Montpelier would always be his true home.

The major event each Sunday, both social and liturgical, was attending services at the Brick Church, erected in the 1750s. Since the Anglican faith was officially sanctioned in Virginia, as a vestryman, James Madison Sr. played a role in the colony's government, as well. Ultimately, Madison was convinced to take on more tasks, becoming a justice of the peace, presiding magistrate of Orange County, and a colonel in the militia. Like Augustine Washington and Peter Jefferson, he became, in effect, the first citizen of his community.

Jemmy enjoyed nothing more than following his father around his domain, exploring its wonders on foot or horseback. His lifelong hatred of slavery derived from this rural childhood. His earliest playmates were largely the children of his father's slaves. As with Jefferson, he saw little of slavery's overt brutality firsthand, but the inherent inequity of such a system was self-evident. Like Jefferson, Madison would struggle throughout his career to evolve a solution, only to pass on any implementation to future generations.

The elder Madison, now often called "Squire," was a more scientific farmer than many of his neighbors, expanding and rotating his acres of wheat and tobacco to other crops less dependent on the vagaries of nature. Over the vagaries of man he had less control. In his thirties, during the French and Indian War, Madison headed what amounted to a home guard. The entire area was terrified by the possible results of English General Edward Braddock's crushing defeat. It may be that young Jemmy actually saw Virginia rangers commanded by the young George Washington protecting Braddock's straggling survivors.

Taught reading, writing, and computation at home, Jemmy had demonstrated great promise. His parents, loath to send him too far away, enrolled him from the ages of eleven to fifteen at the nearby classical boarding school of Donald Robertson, and then with the Reverend Thomas Martin to help prepare him for college. James Madison Sr. was none too happy about what he had heard of the licentiousness then reputedly prevailing at William and Mary, the customary choice for the sons of Virginia planters. Martin induced him to consider his own alma mater, the College of New Jersey at Princeton, then headed by a distinguished new president, John Witherspoon, and located in a relatively healthful area.

It proved a fortuitous choice, broadening Jemmy's horizons. As Oscar and Lilian Handlin point out, Witherspoon linked civil morality with clerical mission, insisting that "all people possessed the capacity for reason, just as all possessed souls to save." Squire Madison's venturesome step, Merrill Peterson adds, would pay off "not simply in the standard currency of education but in the education of a man whose personal identifications were neither Virginian nor Anglican [Witherspoon himself was a Presbyterian] but American." As young Madison noted, at commencement he and his classmates wore only "American cloth." He would insist on the same some forty years later at his presidential inauguration.

His mother, so supportive through all the years, witnessed it all, immensely gratified. As Doris Faber writes, the picture of Nelly Conway Madison that emerges is simply one "of an unpretentious lady who sewed shirts for young James while he studied at Princeton, who sent tubs of butter to him when he went on the public's business at Richmond," and who ultimately enjoyed the private quarters her son constructed for her in his expansion of Montpelier. Favored guests looked forward to visiting her, none more than her admiring daughter-in-law, Dolly Madison. Nelly Conway Madison didn't require any reassurances. She knew she had been appreciated. A year before she died on February 11, 1829, at the remarkable age of ninety-eight, she proclaimed, "I have been a blest woman all my life and blest in this my old age."

Both father and son had been moving in the same political direction, concerned by the implications of the Stamp Act and later alarmed by news of the bloodshed at Lexington and Concord. Although instinctively conservative, when the American Revolution finally came to Orange County, Virginia, James Madison Sr. joined his son in organizing a local committee of public safety and mobilizing and arming its militia. Both would hold the position of colonel. According to Jeff Young, despite their difference in height, both the "Old Colonel" and the "Young Colonel" even looked a bit alike, with a distinctively long upper lip, and shared a reserved manner. They didn't sound much alike, however, because Jemmy's voice was so soft it could scarcely be heard. He didn't make an actual public address until he was thirty. And yet somehow he bested the eloquent Patrick Henry in their dramatic debate over Virginia's adoption of the Constitution and managed to be elected to the highest office in the united land it defined. As Robert Rutland attests, he often turned to his father for advice during these critical days. In old age, the lonely "last sentinel" of the founders, James Madison Jr., modestly declined the title of "sage," insisting that the Constitution was "the work of many heads and hands."

If, despite the warm relationship between them, young Madison would never quite credit his father's inspiration, perhaps it was more due to the tradition of the times. To the missing mothers of Virginia, one might add the marginalized fathers. Why would James Madison Jr., echoing Jefferson, say not of his father but of his schoolmaster, "All I have in life I owe largely to that man"? It was always his father who not only paid his bills but paved his way. If Madison's gratitude to his parents is difficult to discern, it is probably because he didn't view his private life as anyone else's business. When finally induced to dictate an autobiography of sorts, he provided only the "merest skeleton," some two hundred words, to describe his first eighteen years.

"Little Jemmy," however, reached a poignant eloquence when he wrote on February 28, 1801, to an anxious President Thomas Jefferson awaiting the overdue arrival of his new secretary of state, of the death of seventy-seven-year-old James Madison Sr.: "Yesterday morning rather suddenly, tho very gently, the flame of life went out." Torn between his family and his friend, Madison stayed with his father to the end.

Elizabeth and Spence Monroe

If James Madison was "the last of the founders," James Monroe came close behind, completing the cycle of four favored Virginians who, in concert with a remarkable Massachusetts family, transformed a collection of colonies into unique nationhood. Of his father, Andrew Spence Monroe, we know just enough to validate at least some similarities with the first fathers who preceded him. His fortunes were advanced by an advantageous marriage, and his fondest wish was to ensure the education of particularly his oldest son, James. Born on April 28, 1758, James was the first of five children, four of whom survived.

Of his mother Elizabeth, often called "Eliza," James Monroe's belated biographical sketch, even more spare than Madison's, affirms that, predictably, she was "amiable and respectable," lively, well educated for that time and place, and possessing "the best domestic qualities of a good wife and a good parent." It was her family's status, however, that enhanced Spence Monroe's expectations for their children. She was the daughter of an "undertaker in architecture," and her father had married the sister of a prominent lawyer. Her brother, Judge Joseph Jones of Fredericksburg, presided over the Virginia General Court, later served in Congress, and became a confidant of Washington, Jefferson, and Madison.

His forebears, the "Munroes" of Scotland, had emigrated to Virginia after siding with the losing Royalists in the English Civil War. A Captain Andrew Munroe was the first to depart in 1647. Oliver Cromwell certainly had an influence in developing the American colonies. Over time, Munroes became Monroes and major landholders around what became known as Monroe's Creek in Westmoreland County.

Unfortunately, there were so many Monroes that young Spence, in their third American generation, inherited only a little more than 500 acres. His subsequent pursuits didn't fit into any clearly defined category.

He was both a carpenter and a modest landowner. In the evolving interior of the colony, that still made him at least marginally a gentleman. James recalled his father as a "worthy and respectable citizen possessed of good land and other property." Spence's carpentry was not nautical, like John Maddison's, but domestic. As a craftsman, he was technically a "joiner." It seems likely that his unpretentious two-story frame house was largely constructed through his own efforts. Such a humble dwelling, on sandy soil near a virgin forest, represented little cachet to aristocrats in their 60,000-acre estates, largely English-emulating proprietors in the "Northern Neck" of Virginia. Here, the gentry consumed their abundant fare on fine china in the elaborate luxury of elegant dining rooms. The Monroes ate in the same area in which they lived, using wooden bowls, their food cooked in pots and pans hanging over a slow-burning flame in their central fireplace, more like our conception of pioneers.

The sons of the planter elite were educated by tutors often imported from abroad. They would then go to Oxford or Cambridge in England or, after its chartering in 1693, to the College of William and Mary in Williamsburg. The best Spence Monroe could manage was to send his son trudging through several miles of deep woods to the schoolhouse of stern Parson Archibald Campbell. The travel, if not the course of study, wasn't all that challenging for vigorous young Monroe.

Even at the age of eleven he seems as solemn a youth as James Madison, but there the comparison ends. Monroe was tall and strong, skilled at every outdoor pursuit. He loved riding, hunting, and any form of exercise. A crack shot, he carried a rifle over one arm and his schoolbooks over the other. On his way home he would often bag game for his family's dinner table. His congenial daily companion was future Chief Justice John Marshall, whose personality was as lighthearted as Monroe's was somber.

Parson Campbell may have stressed discipline but, more significantly, he valued constancy and character. As William Penn Cresson writes, Monroe gained "a solid foundation in the classics, a respect for the factual exactness of mathematics, and an understanding of such words as loyalty, honesty, honor, and devotion"—from an exceptional teacher. At home, as Harry Ammon notes, both of Monroe's parents allowed their children unusual freedom to pursue their own interests.

James's father had provided an example of courage. At the behest of Richard Henry Lee, Spence Monroe in 1766 was one of those bold Virginians who drafted and signed resolutions opposing the Stamp Act and encouraging a boycott of English goods to back up their demands. In this way, as George Bancroft writes, "Virginia rang the alarm bell for the continent." Whatever Monroe had to risk, he risked it all.

At sixteen, James Monroe went off to William and Mary, at least initially financed by his father, however hard-pressed, and carrying with him the expectations of both his parents. Apparently divested of the excesses Madison's father had decried, under an inspiring new president, the college seethed with excitement. The War for American Independence was at hand. As Cresson writes, serious young James Monroe was already "solid at sixteen." After only two years, he left William and Mary to serve in the Continental Army. His notable bravery in a number of engagements won General Washington's personal commendation. At scarcely twenty years of age, Monroe became a lieutenant colonel and would soon be launched on both his legal and political careers.

Neither parent lived to see it. Both Spence and Eliza Monroe died in 1774. Their modest homestead, inherited by James, only made him more responsible for the welfare of his siblings. However, his mother's most tangible gift was posthumous. At his death, her influential brother, Judge Joseph Jones, directed that his sizable estate be divided among the children of his late sisters, "allowing my nephew Colonel James Monroe the first choice." The bequest proved critical to his future success.

By the measure of prior first fathers, Spence Monroe was not notably successful. We know even less about his wife Eliza than of the other missing mothers of Virginia, renowned as the mother of presidents. But even if their means were meager, so much greater was the example provided by Spence and Eliza Monroe.

Meanwhile, six hundred miles to the north, the first potential political dynasty of the new nation had already begun to take shape. There would be no missing mothers of Massachusetts. Abigail Adams would see to that.

CHAPTER 3

Examples to Emulate—Adamses

Susanna and John Adams Sr.

Augustine Washington was at home on two continents. "Deacon" John Adams rarely strayed from the town of Braintree, in the Massachusetts Bay Colony, but the scope of his ambition was no less. It was not so much for himself as for his firstborn son. The goal was less high office than high achievement. John's strong-willed wife, Susanna, was equally intent on education as the means to elevation.

The Adamses had been among the first to settle in the town. They came from another Braintree, across the sea in Somersetshire. Had they stayed for the English Civil War, they would have been on opposite sides from the Royalist Washingtons. To the Church of England and King Charles I, still in possession of his head, these dissenting Puritans were a royal nuisance. Some twenty thousand emigrated in the 1630s and later, intent on building their City of God in a new land.

The neighboring towns of Braintree and Weymouth were a world removed from the western reaches of Virginia, representing a harsher if healthier environment. Hard-worked farmland extended outward from tight-knit communities at the core. The resulting sense of living in such close proximity to one's neighbors could be comforting but also claustrophobic. Originally it had been based on a Puritan ethic foreign to the more permissive Anglicanism of the decentralized South. As Page Smith writes, "A good Puritan . . . kept a kind of daily audit of his soul's state of grace and submitted the account to God in private prayer and public meeting."

By the time the senior John Adams was born on February 8, 1691, only the residue of such rigidity remained. He was the second son of Joseph Adams, the grandson of distiller Henry Adams, a descendant of John and Priscilla Alden of fabled lore, and a cousin of future patriot Samuel Adams. Henry had been both a farmer and a "maltster," who processed barley into beer. Apparently, the Calvinists had always accepted imbibing, but circumstances were now so relaxed that taverns dotted the village of two thousand; increased social contact between young people had led to an alarming increase in illegitimate births; and a "Great Awakening" was calling people back to their theological roots. The senior John Adams had come to be called "Deacon" as affirmation of his devotion to both church and community. At Sunday services, with the elders seated in front, Adams's central place faced the pulpit. For fourteen years he was selected for this honor, man and mission seeming to merge in public consciousness.

John had always seemed bright, but in the tradition of the times, only his older brother would be granted the opportunity for higher education. He would become a respected Congregational minister in New Hampshire. Although John was disappointed, perhaps the seed was planted in his mind that one day he might find fulfillment in a first son of his own.

With so many small farms surrounding Braintree, and soil so stony that only the most strenuous labor could yield much bounty, virtually every household required an additional occupation to get through the rigorous winters. The Deacon supplemented growing wheat, corn, oats, and barley on his modest acreage with learning to become a "cordswainer," making shoes and other leather goods. From mid-March to early autumn Adams tended to his fields. At the end of the growing season he would fashion his shoes, working on a low bench in a tiny room off the kitchen of his modest home.

Despite his apparent unobtrusiveness, he had firm opinions and little hesitation in voicing them, and people were drawn to his company for advice. He was as short in stature as his namesake would be, but sturdy and sound. He served as Braintree's tax collector and a lieutenant in the militia and was nine times elected a selectman, second only to his tenure as church deacon. Yet this senior John Adams viewed himself neither as gentry nor even as the town's first citizen. That distinction went to Colonel of Militia Josiah Quincy, a glass manufacturer who was Braintree's representative to the Governor's Council and speaker of the Massachusetts Assembly. The town would eventually be renamed for him. If it mattered, Adams was surely the second citizen of this modest realm.

Yet he remained unfulfilled. In his forties, an age many of his neighbors might have been happy simply to reach, he decided he must get married. The object of his affection seems as surprising as her agreement to the match. Sophisticated, socially superior, and equally strong willed, Susanna Boylston came from Brookline, near Boston, and was member of a family noted for its medical practitioners. Called Sarah by her friends, even at the cusp of spinsterhood at twenty-six she didn't want for suitors. What could she see in stolid, stocky, sober, short, rural-rooted forty-three-year-old John Adams? Perhaps it was some of the same qualities that had endeared the reliable deacon to his neighbors. And in truth, Adams was as intelligent as he was industrious, loving to read as avidly as she did. In any case, on November 23, 1734, they were wed, and she was introduced to all the amenities Braintree could offer.

On October 19, 1735, as John Ferling writes, Deacon John awoke "nervous and excited," about to become a father for the first time. While he sat uneasily tinkering at his bench, Susanna, assisted by a midwife, gave birth to a healthy son, also named John. Reportedly, Susanna and John, equally outspoken and stubborn, bickered throughout their lives together, but of the future of their son they were of one mind. He was destined for Harvard and then, they hoped, to a career of distinction. His father preferred that it might be the ministry, but it was the goal that mattered.

That family would soon grow, although by modest dimensions compared with many of their neighbors. John Jr. would have two younger brothers, Peter Boylston and Elihu. They lived in a typical village house, a compact two-story frame "saltbox" that still exists at a picturesque spot near Penn's Hill, adjacent to Adams's fields, the town, and the salt marshes of Boston Bay. Their home was often crowded with overnight visitors, relatives, and townsfolk who simply came to consult with Deacon John. Susanna's prior lifestyle little inhibited the range of her new activities. As Ferling writes, "Both parents worked diligently," however they differed on details: the father toiling inside and out; the mother tending their garden, managing the home, and teaching each child to read by the age of five.

At six, young John was sent to school at a neighbor's, where the regimen was largely reading and recitation. Along with the town's other more promising scholars, he was then advanced to Braintree's Latin School, presided over by Joseph Cleverly, a gentleman late of Harvard. It was only the deacon's belated recognition of Cleverly as "the most indolent man I ever knew" that helped explain how so bright a child as his son had turned away from the pursuit of knowledge as a source of stimulation.

Not that the boy needed much incentive. He loved the outdoors and delighted in simply roaming and spending his hours as "idly" as possible. Writing years later, he recalled his pleasure in "making and sailing boats . . . in making and flying kites . . . in driving hoops" and in games and sports of all kinds—marbles and quoits, wrestling, swimming, and above all, shooting the abundant game. His fowling piece was rarely from his side. Such bounty might be welcome at his family's dinner table, but it was hardly Deacon John's priority when he had sent his oldest son off to school.

An increasing source of concern was also young John's active social life, "running around to quiltings and frolics and dances among boys and girls." A hint of potential trouble is indicated by John's recitation of his preferences: "Girls, girls, cards, flutes, violins . . . laziness, languor, inattention are my bane." How totally at variance with the somber symbol he would become.

When he was only ten, his father had asked him what he proposed to do with his life. Although he had already been at primary schools for five years, the boy replied, "Why, be a farmer like you." The deacon responded with some vehemence, "A farmer! I'll show you what it is to be a farmer!" The next morning he took his son out with him to the marshes to cut thatch, a particularly laborious task. They didn't return until dark. "Well," asked John Sr., not unkindly, "are you satisfied with being a farmer?" His son persisted, "I like it very well, sir." His father's tone grew sterner, "Aye, but I don't like it very well, so you shall go back to school." It took four years for John Adams Sr. to find out the truth. "Sir, I don't like my schoolmaster!" his son blurted out. The next day, he had a new one.

Joseph Marsh, although the son of Braintree's former minister, had little use for organized religion and was a nonconformist generally. But Marsh genuinely appreciated the cadence of a Latin sentence, the elegance of mathematics, and the glories of English history—and he could impart that enthusiasm to others. Under his tutelage young John Adams had his personal Great Awakening. The intensive year and a half he spent with Marsh refocused his life.

Still, at sixteen, would he be ready for the challenges of Harvard? Marsh exuded confidence and prepared to ride with his charge to Cambridge. Unfortunately, at the last moment the schoolmaster fell ill. John would have to face the formidable Harvard elders alone. It turned out, however, that they were also benign, allowing the apprehensive young scholar to use a dictionary in translating a difficult Latin passage into English. After reviewing a theme they had allowed John to write over the summer, he was accepted on the spot, an admissions process that certainly compares favorably with today's. He was even granted a partial scholarship, although his father would be obliged to sell the only ten acres of ground that ever passed from his possession in order to help pay for his tuition. Young John all but floated home, a hero to his friends and the pride of his parents.

In one respect, however, he had to disappoint the deacon. John Adams would not be the learned minister that was his father's career preference for him. After graduating from Harvard, Adams took some time in reviewing his alternatives. He was not inclined to be a teacher or preacher. Physicians, in his view, were as likely to take life as to save it.

Government service was more a commitment than a career. The law was dry, "a rubbish of writs" and quarrelsome discourse, but it could be lucrative and lead to many other opportunities.

In 1756, just short of his twenty-first birthday and still wracked by doubts, Adams decided to begin an apprenticeship with his friend James Putnam, only twenty-eight but already the leading attorney in Worcester, some sixty miles west of Braintree. After all, John reasoned, perhaps for his father as much as himself, "The Practice of the Law . . . does not Dissolve the Obligations of Morality or of Religion."

He lived with the Putnams, a most hospitable couple. To pay his way he taught in a local school, finding it as little to his liking as he had surmised. Poring over precedents and accompanying Putnam on his rounds, Adams was reassured to discover a decided affinity for the law. It was not easily mastered, but it would definitely be his future. After his apprenticeship was completed in 1758, the Putnams wanted him to stay and start his practice in Worcester. However, Adams longed to return to the healthful sea breezes and "the pure zephyrs from the rocky mountains of my native town." He had begun to have severe headaches, an affliction he would share with Jefferson.

Adams had already started his daily diary—during an earthquake. Visiting at home, he had suffered a severe jolt. Suddenly, he recalled, "The house seemed to rock and reel and crack as if it would fall in ruins around us." The quake, so unusual for New England, was one of a series of seismic shocks felt on both sides of the Atlantic. To Adams it had a kind of symbolic significance. As Lyman Butterfield writes, "it 'jolted' him into starting his diary. With this record of a young schoolmaster's daily thoughts and experiences, the family's records may be said to begin," as would the productive years of John Adams's life.

He had left Braintree a boy of sixteen; he returned a man of twenty-three. A room in his parents' home became his office. John Adams would never reach a height of more than five feet six or seven, but he could hardly stand taller than he did now to John Sr. and Susanna. For a time he lived where his father had, amidst the familiar people and places he would always view as home. His old friends still called him "Johnny" or

"Jack," while acknowledging his more serious demeanor. Adams also set out for Boston, where most of Braintree's legal business was conducted. It took time, but under the sponsorship of such leaders of the bar as Jeremiah Gridley, the fledgling attorney was admitted to practice before the Superior Court, equivalent to passing the bar today. Already in 1760, Adams was considering cases concerning the legality of writs of assistance, the sort of questions that would imperil relations between England and its American colonies.

Then there was another, more personal shock—and everything changed. No colony was immune from periodic epidemics. In the spring of 1761 an attack of influenza throughout the Massachusetts coastline put half the citizens of Braintree to bed. Only seventeen died, but among them was seventy-year-old Deacon John Adams. He expired only a few days after falling ill, on May 25, 1761, his three sons by his bedside. His wife, Susanna, who had also been stricken but survived, was too weak to attend his funeral. She would live into her eighty-ninth year, the first of her son's presidency. The ministers at the meeting house, so familiar to all the Adams family, celebrated the deacon's life, stressing that those taken in the fullness of years should be more appreciated than mourned. That was scant solace to young John, who for some time sank into a deep depression.

Deacon John left a relatively substantial estate, carefully expanded over the years. As in life, he sought to distribute it equitably. A nearby farm he owned in Randolph went to Elihu and the Adams homestead to Peter Boylston. His oldest son and namesake, his executor, inherited the smallest share in that he alone had received a "liberal education," but it included a small house and some thirty acres. What this did, however, was enable John, once he had recovered emotionally, to be established as a landowner, however modest, and a taxpayer. He could now take part in town meetings and gain a responsible place in the community. He was elected a freeholder and even for a time was named surveyor of highways. In his final gift, the deacon had provided his favored son with the means to launch his legal practice in the most direct way possible.

Aristocratic Charles Francis Adams would characterize his great-grandfather, the senior John Adams, as "merely a 'typical New England' yeoman." John Adams Jr. knew better. As David McCullough details, he could hardly find adequate words to sufficiently praise his father, this stalwart citizen who for twenty years had managed "almost all the business of the town." He venerated Deacon John as "the honestest man I ever knew. . . . In wisdom, piety, benevolence, and charity in proportion to his education and sphere of life I have never seen his equal." In geographical terms that "sphere of life" was minute. In terms of influence on his first son, it was immense. No less significant had been his mother's supportive stress on education. Her own family's social standing surely hadn't hurt his admission to Harvard.

Abigail and John Adams Jr.

Overlaid with serious concerns for the future, there was still some trace of the youthful John Adams's passionate nature. His father's generosity had also endowed him with a bit more substance when it came time to bring suit for the affections of a young lady.

While John Adams was discovering the wonders of Harvard, seven-year-old Abigail Smith of Weymouth was already displaying what Lynne Withey cites as a "certain stubbornness of spirit." Small, sickly, and initially very shy, "Nabby" Smith was the daughter of a minister less doctrinaire than those the Adamses were acquainted with. However, even in Braintree it was customary for young girls as well as boys to learn rudimentary reading and writing. Reading the Bible reinforced the primacy of their religion. As she grew, Nabby would not only read but also reflect on every book she could lay her hands on. She would not stay shy very long.

Her father, Congregational Parson William Smith, was the son of a prosperous Boston merchant. Called to Weymouth and the North Parish Church, where his equanimity enabled him to enjoy a notably extended tenure, he had the means to buy not only its parsonage but also acres of surrounding farmland. His wife, Elizabeth Quincy Smith, daughter of the distinguished John Quincy of Braintree, added more than additional wealth and cachet to their union. Of a more practical bent than her affable, intellectual husband, she helped assure the success of their forty-five-year ministry, despite the religious turmoil of the times, in the oldest town of the original Massachusetts Bay Colony. All three of their girls grew up to be lively and bright.

Expected to lead narrowly circumscribed lives, the Smith daughters, particularly Abigail, were determined to expand their horizons, which, as Withey recounts, "delighted her father." Nabby devoted every available hour to devouring not only Scripture but also Shakespeare, Milton, Pope, Swift, and even John Locke, and then discussing them with him and his astonished friends. Unlike John Adams, Abigail provided her own motivation. It was not, however, a form of rebellion. To Nabby Smith, exploring the realm of the mind did not need to be at the sacrifice of her expected domestic diligence. It supplemented it. Abigail's perplexed mother, however, without loving her any less, became inclined to focus her attention on her less challenging children. Still, the slights Nabby felt at being deprived of a formal education were never quite forgotten. Nearly a lifetime later she lamented, "I never was sent to any school."

Although something less than a classic beauty, Abigail at fifteen had grown into a striking, slender, dark-haired, and quite popular young woman. Her proclivity for argumentation and her wit were generally taken as tokens of a distinctive personality. The young residents of Weymouth and Braintree mingled frequently, and the three vivacious Smith sisters enjoyed a wide acquaintance. In the late 1750s, a solemn young lawyer was introduced into the midst of their bustling household. He was equally free with his opinions yet seemingly ill at ease. Abigail was less attracted than intrigued by this odd combination. It was her lovely and flirtatious cousin, Hannah Quincy, however, who was the object of Adams's attentions. They were not reciprocated. As for the senior Smiths, John was not impressed. He viewed the father as rather worldly and crafty for a parson, concealing his wealth under a veneer of piety. As for his three daughters, they were "not fond, not frank, not candid."

Two years later, however, when Nabby and John were reintroduced by a mutual friend, somehow something clicked. Now a spritely seventeen, had she been transformed into someone more fond, frank, and candid? When she stood up to him in amiable contentiousness, he discovered that he had actually come to like it, and her. Whatever it was that appealed to Nabby, however, it cannot have been John Adams's looks. Although he was once described as a handsome child, as a young man his short frame was already thickened to the stocky figure prevalent in his family. His baldpate was surrounded by a halo of unkempt hair. As Stephen Hess writes, "The Adams face from top to bottom had a tendency to baldness, a broad forehead, finely arched eyebrows, penetrating eyes, a slightly aquiline nose, and a bulldog jaw."

Opposites physically, they balanced each other temperamentally. Mutual curiosity had grown into affection, then transformed into something more—the start of a unique partnership. Her counsel is what he would always seek, her sunnier nature what he needed. Many of his contemporaries, while admiring Adams's talents, viewed him as something less than lovable. As Hess enumerates, throughout his long career Adams would often be described as rude, tactless, humorless, introspective, preachy, arrogant, austere, and unsocial. Only Abigail might have added "passionate."

However smitten, Adams remained frugal enough to carefully calculate his professional prospects before taking on a wife. Yet it was Abigail's parents who delayed the wedding. They probably felt she could do better. Finally, on October 25, 1764, Nabby's father did the honors. She was nineteen, Adams twenty-nine.

Their first child, born in the summer of 1765, was a girl they named Abigail, a miniature Nabby. And then, on June 11, 1767, the Adamses had a son. They named him John Quincy, which immensely pleased Abigail's mother. On the day the child was christened, old Colonel Josiah Quincy, much loved by both sides of the family, passed away. John Quincy's parents would always call him "Johnny." He would grow up with the American Revolution. John and Abigail were to have two more sons, Charles and Thomas, but a second daughter, Susanna, died in infancy.

It is to their subsequent separations that we owe the documentation of the Adamses' remarkable relationship. During their first thirty years of marriage, John was away from Abigail more than half the time. Their enduring legacy of letters, so treasured by historians, is testimony to a life of farewells. Through it all, Abigail also kept her own journal, supplementing her husband's diary. In their reflections, a mutual sense of guilt mingles with pride and frustration. Traveling by horseback to expand his practice often involved John in Boston's increasingly volatile conflicts, little less when he journeyed to ever wider circuits. Success came at a price. "What a desultory Life," he complained in his daily journal, "a rambling, raving, vagrant, vagabond life"—while sending constant admonitions to his resilient but overburdened wife. Whatever the press of events, their offspring must be instructed "not only to do virtuously but to excell (sic)." Shades of his father.

Abigail had always sought a wider role for women "in the great theatre of life." With Johnny she had watched the flames from the Battle of Bunker Hill from a summit near their home. He was already marching as if in the militia. As war came she not only became her children's instructor of every basic subject, even teaching Latin to herself first, but also manager of the property, keeping it all afloat, guarding their welfare and safety, truly her husband's "dear partner in all the joys and sorrows of life."

Between 1774 and 1777 John was a prominent delegate to the Continental Congress in Philadelphia, including, in the words of Thomas Jefferson, becoming "the pillar of support" for the Declaration of Independence. Later, in 1777, Adams was sent to France to form an alliance against England now that the conflict had come. Somehow ten-year-old Johnny induced his father to take him along on the perilous voyage. He managed to study in France and Holland and gained an extraordinary opportunity assisting our minister to Russia before his eventual return to enroll at Harvard. For his father, assignments followed one after another.

As conditions in Braintree grew increasingly harsh, with all manner of shortages and a smallpox epidemic threatening, even Abigail gave way to momentary despair. "How lonely are my days?" she wrote to John, "How solitary my nights?" In 1785 his "heroine" wife finally got to rejoin him, in London. She was more impressed with such new friends as Jefferson than with the continental snobbery she encountered around European courts. With independence secured, in 1788 the Adamses happily returned home together, intent on restoring their homestead's productivity. Many had contributed their lives to the cause of American Independence. John Adams sacrificed his security. His fondest hope, at fifty-three, was to establish the legal firm of Adams and Adams with his son, and finally make some money.

However, the new nation had need of his talents and experience. In 1789 electors met and voted George Washington president. A distant second in the balloting, John Adams was named vice president. Although describing the office to Abigail as "the most insignificant . . . that ever the invention of man contrived," he could not responsibly decline it. Living in the temporary capital of Philadelphia was expensive, and his pay was so meager that it led to renewed separation. Abigail, too often ill, spent much of her time back in the bracing air of Quincy, as Braintree had been respectfully renamed.

Meanwhile, with his exceptional academic preparation, Johnny had graduated from Harvard in only two years, second in his class. He went on to study law by clerking with a distinguished attorney in Newburyport, north of Boston. It was surely what his parents desired, but what did *he* want? Introspective John Quincy had already developed a public demeanor even more somber than his father's. Physically, he had a much thinner face and frame. In Newburyport he had become engaged to a comely young lady named Mary Frazier, but his mother viewed any marriage as premature and he reluctantly broke it off. His father had not only contributed his legal library to Johnny but advanced him a hundred pounds a year, which he could ill afford. John Quincy Adams passed the bar in 1790 and set up a legal practice in Boston. He was all of twenty-three.

Having been stimulated by his European experiences, he was never happy with the limitations of a domestic legal practice. His devoted parents, so hopeful for their "exemplary son," had sustained him, but their pressures also became a source of his suffering. He developed a variety of ailments, real and imagined, even indulging in tranquilizing drugs. President Washington saved him, appointing Johnny at the age of twenty-six to be American "minister" to The Hague. (Ministers would later be called ambassadors.)

The family's separations were not yet at an end. Washington had determined to invest only one four-year term in the presidency and had to be induced in the interest of national unity to serve a second. Thirteen men received electoral votes to succeed him in 1796. This time John Adams came in first, winning the presidency by three electoral votes. Coming in second was his personal friend, Thomas Jefferson. However, with the rise of political parties, Adams as president and Jefferson as his vice president would present awkward problems of competing policies, leading to a bitter break that would take years to heal. Before the election, John Quincy had written in his own diary from the Netherlands, "I can only pray for the happiness and prosperity of my country."

It was neither a political career nor a political dynasty that John Adams had in mind. It was a progression. To Jefferson every generation stood on its own. To Adams each one built on the next, but in a most peculiar fashion. During his diplomatic mission to Paris he had mused about all this, concluding, "I must study politics and war so that my sons may have the liberty to study mathematics and philosophy. My sons ought to study mathematics and philosophy, geography, natural history, naval architecture, navigation, commerce, and agriculture in order to give their children a right to study paintings, poetry, music, architecture, tapestry, and porcelain." Perhaps he was simply affirming that the attainment of leisure is necessary for the appreciation of beauty. But none of his children or grandchildren was ever disposed to the contemplation of porcelain as a career.

Before he departed for Mount Vernon, Washington had one request to impart to his reluctant successor. Adams should "not withdraw merited promotion" for John Quincy, "the most valued public character we have abroad . . . because he is your son." Washington had planned to transfer him to Portugal. Adams changed the destination to the more prominent post of Prussia, and accusations of nepotism inevitably followed.

The great issue during Adams's term was our relationship with recklessly revolutionary France. Preserving peace turned out to be Adams's greatest triumph but also his downfall. In their perpetual conflict with England, the French had attacked American commerce and inflamed passions across the domestic political spectrum. Adams's building up of our armed forces, particularly our navy, met with popular approval. Through 1799, he had managed to become a most popular president, our potential war leader. By the election year of 1800, however, he was vilified as akin to a coward. He would not go to war with France.

From the first, he leaned on Abigail's counsel. Unelected and unelectable, she tried to keep as low a profile as possible, while urging her husband, among other suggestions, to "remember the ladies." Together or apart, they had a sort of telepathy. She did not merely echo his opinions but was his closest collaborator. Now he pleaded, "I never wanted your advice and assistance more in my life . . . I can do nothing without you." Although she insisted, "I want only to reign in the heart of my husband," her own nature argued against it.

She had always been opposed to the subjugation of anyone, whether slaves kidnapped from Africa, women denied opportunity, or the American colonies denied their rights by the mother country. She had urged John to come out for independence long before he had gradually reached the same conclusion. Now she supported his call for a strong national defense but a prudent foreign policy and the maintenance of internal order, particularly after such "vile libels" were leveled against her husband.

From his listening post in Prussia, John Quincy informed his father that he had learned the French were prepared to make a settlement. Putting his country's welfare ahead of the emotion of the moment, Adams agreed, realizing that in terms of 1800 he would be a candidate without a party. He may not have viewed himself as part of a political progression, but the fact is, in only one generation the Adams family had made the transition from governing a small town to governing an entire nation.

Toward the end of his one-term tenure, he and Abigail had moved into the unfinished executive mansion in the new capital city, marshy, muddy Washington. Abigail hung laundry in some of its rooms while preparing the premises for incoming President Jefferson, who had won by a surprisingly narrow margin. They did not wait for the new chief executive's inauguration but were happy to return to the comfortably familiar surroundings of Quincy, from which they were rarely to stray.

Back home, John had been able to purchase a larger house, which he hopefully named "Peacefield." Here, he craved repose, together with Abigail for the rest of their lives. Yet he still chafed over slights too recent to heal. He was convinced that his contributions to the nation's founding would be overshadowed by those of his more visible contemporaries. Now, however, he had the time to write his autobiography, continue his diary, and attend to a wide range of correspondence, almost all of which he saved for future generations.

Best of all, Johnny, finally tired of "foreign climes," was also coming home. He was not returning alone, however, but with a wife—lively, cosmopolitan Louisa Catherine Johnson. This time he'd had the sense not to consult his mother beforehand. In a joint letter, he assured both of his "Dear and honored" parents, "You will find her to prove such a daughter as you would wish for your son." They already had a five-month-old son, appropriately named George Washington Adams. That at least heartened an apprehensive Abigail, who voiced her approval, "By the love I bear my Country that the Syren is at least half blood."

As it turned out, it was Louisa who was intimidated by her diminutive but overwhelming mother-in-law. Abigail's joy in seeing them all did not prevent her from inquiring rather too quickly about just what Johnny planned to do in the future. Circumstances intervened. In 1802 John Quincy was elected as a Federalist to the state senate and the next year was selected to fill a vacancy in the United States Senate. There, he would prove as independent as his father, insisting on not adhering to any party line but considering every issue on its merits. The Federalist leadership decided that they might prefer regularity in his successor. The one constant was his father's counsel, no less reasoned when John was forty than when he had been fourteen, "My advice to you is steadily to pursue the path you are on . . . because I think it is the path of justice."

John Adams had also won over Louisa. Having heard him described as acerbic, she discovered instead a kindred spirit, warm and interested, who took an instant fancy to her. Her affection for the "old gentleman" would never wane. Abigail's advice to her son and daughter-in-law was far more specific than her husband's. With John Quincy, it was almost that of a political handler, covering everything from his clothes, his manners, his appearance, and his deportment in general to the delivery of his speeches—form more than content. Despite her husband's dismal experience in Washington, it appears that she had already surmised that her son might also aspire to the nation's highest office. A welcome reconciliation had been effected by mutual friend Benjamin Rush, who induced John Adams and Thomas Jefferson to start corresponding with each other again. Despite the recent past, Abigail soon joined in.

In everything affecting the future of John Quincy, she sought that Louisa should "unite" with her, and over time a close bond developed between these two very dissimilar women. When John Quincy was in Washington, Louisa and the children stayed behind in Quincy, just as Abigail had when John was vice president. The family was growing. Another John was born before John Quincy had gone to the Senate, a third son and daughter later. After his break with the Federalists, John Quincy supported Democratic-Republican James Madison for president. For a time, he returned to the practice of law and taught at Harvard. Then Madison appointed him to be his minister to Russia. Were the Adamses to always endure "a life of farewells"?

It was during the lonely years to come that Louisa's bond with Abigail strengthened, and the letters that took so many months to arrive were addressed to a "dear mother" from an "affectionate daughter." Her two oldest sons had been left in the care of their grandparents. Abigail's seemingly endless energy belied her always frail health. Louisa's own health had deteriorated in the harsh Russian climate, and her only daughter had died at one year old. Abigail, whose daughter Susanna had also lived for only a short time, could share in mourning such a loss and commiserate with her daughter-in-law's "solicitous" desire to return home. Both mother and daughter were cheered when in 1814 John Quincy was sent to Ghent as our senior representative to help negotiate an end to the War of 1812, but he traveled alone. It was only in 1815, his mission to Russia finally completed, that John Quincy sent for his wife and youngest son to join him in Paris. Delicate Louisa, negotiating the perils of that 2,000-mile journey, proved herself as resourceful as any Adams.

When John Quincy was named American minister to Great Britain and then finally called home to become President James Monroe's secretary of state, his professional path was becoming strikingly similar to his father's progression in the 1780s. The elder Adams, however, wrote him, "Your providence I know will be greater than mine ever was." His mother had written him in London, "The voice of the nation calls you home. The government calls you home—and your parents unite in the call." After eight years abroad their Johnny was returning to the United States to stay.

It cheered Abigail, now in her seventies, that at last her son and his family were close to the welcome warmth of Quincy, with a grand reunion in prospect. Abigail was so impressed with her son's lengthy explanation of the treaty that she laboriously copied out every word and then had it published and distributed as an anonymous communication "from one of the ministers to his friend." The ultimate campaign was underway.

John wrote John Quincy that he would be "overjoyed" to see how his mother had recovered "her former alacrity, spirit, wit" and that he took "great delight in riding out with her every fair day." But not every day was fair. Their adored daughter, also nicknamed Nabby, had died, as had their son Charles. Now only two sons remained from their original five children. Jefferson wrote empathetically, prescribing "time and silence" as "the only medicine for grief." More heartrending still, two grandchildren had already died. Of one of them John lamented, "Why was I preserved ¾ of a century and that rose cropped in the bud?"

Through it all, now limited physically to the reduced world of family and friends, Abigail's mind remained boundless. She knew she had little time left, but serenity was never her style. She thought deeply about religion. Having made the transition from the Congregational beliefs of her parents to the Episcopalian Church of her daughter-in-law, she now sought simplicity. Early in 1818 she wrote to Louisa, "True religion is from the Heart, between Man and his Creator." Abigail became a Unitarian, as would John Quincy.

To her grandchildren Abigail remained a font of advice, solicited or not, on everything from polished penmanship to feminine decorum. To her granddaughter Caroline, just before her marriage, Abigail stressed that American women should be content "with the show which nature bestows" rather than falling prey to blatantly licentious French influence. Ever the domestic traditionalist, she remained a political innovator, proposing such groups as a "council of the ladies," to be made up of the wives of government officials. Despite meddling in everyone's lives, she would always be "a mortal enemy of anything but a cheerful countenance and a merry heart." All in all, she reasoned, "This is a very good world," only capable of some improvement. Whatever the press of work in Washington, John Quincy came home as often as he could manage to see his parents. He knew his mother was weakening.

His apprehensive father would see him elected president. His mother would not. By the fall of 1817 she was suffering severe chills and a variety of other ailments. On October 28, 1818, she finally succumbed to typhoid fever, at the age of seventy-four. Always frail, she had simply wasted away. As Abigail was laid to rest beside her daughter, the minister celebrated "one who shone with no common splendor." Her last letter to Thomas Jefferson had been signed "Your old and steady friend." To a grief-stricken John Adams, Jefferson wrote with uncommon emotion of "mingling my tears with yours."

When he heard the news, John Quincy suffered something akin to an emotional collapse. Later he wrote, "The world feels to me like a solitude. . . . There is not a virtue that can abide in the human heart, but it was the ornament of hers." Whenever he had come home, "I felt as if the joys of childhood had returned to make me happy. All was kindness and affection." To Louisa, Abigail was "the guiding planet around which all revolved."

In her own life Abigail Smith Adams was obliged to fill many roles—wife, mother, grandmother, homemaker, writer, educator, farm manager, financial planner, patriot, and counselor to statesmen. Despite her self-confidence, she always considered her husband's and son's lives and careers to be far more significant than her own. Only in that singular sense was she a victim of her times. Yet much of what we know about them comes from her letters and journal. This most fitting memorial may have been more than Abigail herself would have wished, but it remains her gift to us all.

In time John Quincy concluded, "I cannot escape my destiny," a future most vigorously projected by his mother. More because of the controversial nature of his election over Andrew Jackson in 1824 and his own inflexibility, his promising presidency was doomed from the start. He had the drive of his mother without the saving grace of her wit and generosity. Every summer he would spend time with his father at Peacefield, adroitly managing his financial affairs. The old man's grief would never subside, but he affirmed, "I still live and enjoy life." The family legacy itself could be a burden. Of John Quincy's three sons, only the youngest, Charles Francis, achieved a career of distinction. Of the other two, one died of alcoholism; the other committed suicide.

There was a final, courageous chapter to John Quincy's own career, one that would have pleased both his parents. After his unhappy presidency, in a unique sequel, he ran for and won a seat in the House of Representatives. As "Old Man Eloquent," he would particularly rail against the extension of slavery and in favor of its ultimate abolition.

John and John Quincy Adams were both first sons, to whom much was given and from whom much was expected. It need not necessarily have been in politics. Their common goal, the first father and son to be elected to the presidency and the first two to fail to be reelected, was less the rewards of high office than its noblest ends.

John Adams's fondest hope was to live until July 4, 1826, the fiftieth anniversary of the Declaration of Independence. He just made it. Unable to attend festive celebrations of the sort he had predicted, when Adams was visited by a delegation and asked to propose a toast, his response was simply, "Independence forever!" Now, of the signers, only he and eighty-three-year-old Jefferson still drew breath. On the evening of July 4, at the age of ninety-one, Adams's life finally ebbed away. His last words were, "Thomas Jefferson lives." He was mistaken. The sage of Monticello had also died that day, some five hours earlier. To John Quincy and many others, such a coincidence was taken as "visible and palpable marks of Divine favor." John Adams was laid to rest in Quincy next to those he loved. His pastor read from the First Book of Chronicles, "He died in a good old age, full of days, riches, and honor, and Solomon, his son reigned in his stead."

John Quincy reflected, "For myself, all that I dare to ask is that I may live the remainder of my days in a manner worthy of him." Although it may seem "presumptuous," he also hoped, "May my last end be like his." It was not to be. Although John Quincy Adams also lived beyond his eightieth year, he did not die in bed but in harness, collapsing to the floor of the House of Representatives. Having suffered a cerebral hemorrhage, he died two days later, on February 21, 1848. Like his father and grandfather, he had also "served to great and useful purpose his nation, his age, and his God."

CHAPTER 4

Humble but Heroic—Elizabeth and Andrew Jackson Sr.

———— ⚬⚬⚬ ————

Even Thomas Jefferson, the most egalitarian of the founders, could not have foreseen a president in the mold of Andrew Jackson, the first first-generation American to be named to our highest office, a point of departure representing an enlarged electorate.

Jackson never knew the father for whom he had been named. He lost his mother when he was only fourteen, but he never ceased extolling the resourceful heroism of Elizabeth Hutchinson Jackson, who literally saved his life. Half a lifetime later, he still recalled her as "gentle as a dove, but brave as a lioness."

The senior Andrew Jackson was a restless, ambitious risk-taker as well as a man of prodigious energy. It was that ambition that brought him from the town of Carrickfergus in County Antrim in Ulster all the way to the Carolinas, and in the end it was that energy that did him in. His wife, Elizabeth, whom everyone called "Betty," came into their marriage with no more in the way of worldly goods than her husband. Described by Burke Davis as a "small, spirited woman," she and Andrew had two sons, Hugh and Robert, while still in the old country. Betty had her hands full tending to them by day and helping to earn a meager living weaving as a "linen draper" throughout the night.

Although his father, given the limitations of a small northern Irish town, had been relatively successful as both a skilled weaver and merchant, Andrew Sr. had no desire to clerk for him, convinced that occupation would lead nowhere. He longed for land of his own and something more than sustenance—an opportunity for his family to prosper. He couldn't see it in these surroundings. Betty shared his sentiments, buoyed by the knowledge that four of her married sisters were already settled across the Atlantic in an expansive place called "the Waxhaws," straddling what is now the border between North and South Carolina.

Before long, Jackson had persuaded twenty other local families to emigrate together to this new Eden, intending to farm on their own around a reconstituted Carrickfergus, with the Presbyterian church of their shared faith at its center. However, as the day of departure neared, the hardy band of potential pioneers had declined from twenty to only two. Second thoughts impacted their initial enthusiasm. Why leave a settled community, whatever its limitations, to venture into a savage wilderness?

When the two remaining families finally set sail in 1765, the Jacksons were still very much on board—Betty with two-year-old Hugh clinging tightly to her and five-month-old Robert at her breast. Upon reaching the port of Philadelphia, they still faced a long, taxing journey. The other remaining family had already begun to lose heart, and within two years they were back in Ireland. "But," Marquis James writes, Andrew "would not be dissuaded." When they finally arrived at their destination, Andrew and Betty were cheered to discover that, although still more a settlement than a real town, it was as populated with familiar folk as they had hoped. Even their accents were reassuring. With such congenial connections, the Jacksons set out to build a new life.

Unfortunately, Andrew's fortunes were to prove no better in the new world than they had in the old. In the words of Gerald Johnson, the family was "worse than poor, they were luckless." As Andrew set out to establish his farm, although it encompassed some 200 acres, all the land he could afford was far from town, at the forest's edge, near aptly named Twelve Mile Creek. Those with the means had purchased the best land, with clear titles within the already settled area closest to town.

Little deterred, and encouraged by his distant neighbors, the inexperienced farmer set to work. As Johnson writes, Andrew "attacked the forest resolutely and not without success, for the record testifies that he cleared his land, raised at least one crop and built his log house by the beginning of the year 1767." The Jacksons entered into the life of their extended community, and every Sunday they traveled twelve miles to church. After a little more than a year of unremitting toil, it appeared as if they might be on their way to self-sufficiency and the fulfilling new life Andrew had projected. However, despite all their efforts, the wilderness won out. Among the charred stumps of the hundreds of trees he had already felled, Andrew severely injured himself straining to lift a giant log. Within two days he was dead. Without clear title to their "public domain" land, his widow and sons would never again reside in the home he had labored so tirelessly to wrest from the forest in order to provide for their future. Elizabeth was pregnant with their third child.

Neighbors had gathered around Andrew's body in the manner of the old country, passing to each other a gourd of whisky to ward off the chill of the season and fortify their own spirits. The wake was followed the next morning by a solemn procession. In a crude farm wagon, Jackson's body was laboriously brought down to the Waxhaw churchyard for burial. The minister uttered his eulogy, and this energetic man from the north of Ireland who had been less than two years in the Carolina backwoods was laid to rest. No headstone marked the location of his grave.

A few days later, on March 15, 1767, in the nearby home of kindly relatives who took her in, Elizabeth Hutchinson Jackson gave birth to the last of her three sons. At least she could honor her late husband by giving the boy his name. Andrew Jackson Jr. would have liked his resolute father. Since they were never to meet, he could only admire him.

Penniless but determined to keep her family together, Betty ventured a few miles south to the home of her in-laws, the John Crawfords. Her sister Jane had become an invalid. In return for her brother-in-law's hospitality, Betty undertook to manage the entire household and to help nurse her sister. Elizabeth Jackson was small only in stature. A strong, energetic woman who could cook, clean, and sew was a valuable commodity on the American frontier. Still, Betty would never occupy a home of her own for the rest of her life. However, able to read and write a little, she was determined that all three of her sons be educated, not only the oldest—which was a great boon for young Andrew.

The local school was affiliated with the Presbyterian church, not surprising in an area where ministers were generally the most learned and esteemed members of the community. Although the loosely governed region was hardly a New England theocracy, a clergyman's views were often followed in temporal matters as well. When it became clear that her youngest was the most promising scholar of her three boys, Betty Jackson determined that ultimately he should become a man of the cloth.

Unfortunately, young Andrew was far more interested in riding, running, and fighting than in reading, writing, and orating. Still, by the age of eight, he could write in "a neat, legible hand," and by nine he was employed as a "public reader." Since most of the residents of the community were illiterate, they gathered regularly to have the news read to them by the equivalent of town criers. Andrew was proud of his ability to perform this task, generally accorded only to adults. In July 1776, he read in public the entire Declaration of Independence from a newspaper, his focus on the import of the words he uttered. Only a month earlier, his relative, Captain Robert Crawford, had led a local company of militia to help repel a British assault on Charleston. The War of Independence was all but under way.

At thirteen Andrew Jackson was a volatile combination of confidence, energy, and emotion. Davis writes, "Lean and graceful, with a thick shock of dark, reddish hair and bright blue eyes deeply set in a freckled face, he was already notorious for his temper." Protective of younger children, he was nonetheless feared by all. Any sign of ridicule could set him off. His mother had a Spartan side, insisting that her son never cry and always defend himself, whatever the odds. Although she was deeply religious, she felt that a Christian need not always be a pacifist.

The temper of the times did little to soften Andrew's belligerence. Neighbors were deeply divided by what became as much a civil as a revolutionary war. The Scots derived from the Highlands would stay largely loyal to the crown. Scotch-Irish like the Jacksons were more inclined to independence. As the regular armies came and went, the war in the Carolinas degenerated into ferocious blood feuds between bands of loyalist and insurgent bushwhackers. No one was spared, civilian or soldier.

Betty Jackson feared for her sons, but where was she to go? She was powerless to prevent her oldest, eighteen-year-old Hugh, from fighting for independence with the local militia. In 1779 he was killed at the Battle of Stono Ferry. With her two remaining sons she helped tend the wounded, their church turned into a makeshift hospital. Then she simply wandered about the countryside, hoping to keep her remaining family safe until hostilities receded. Instead, they heightened, as the feared troops of British Colonel Banastre Tarleton tore through the area surrounding the Waxhaws.

Pugnacious Andrew could no longer be restrained. Only thirteen years and four months old, he joined his sixteen-year-old brother Robert in the backwoods cavalry of Colonel William R. Davie. These hard-pressed volunteers weren't very particular about age. At first Davie tried to protect Andrew by limiting him to duty as a mounted messenger, but the youth was so skillful a rider and so knowledgeable about local terrain that he became a favorite of his commander, who gave him a handsome pistol with which to protect himself. Andrew had no intention of remaining a noncombatant, already possessing a valuable Irish rifle.

Unfortunately, he would see no action. A patrol of British dragoons surprised Jackson's band. It scattered, and Robert and Andrew took refuge in a relative's home. Betrayed by a Tory neighbor, the two boys were captured without firing a shot. When an imperious British officer ordered them to clean his muddy boots, Andrew insisted that they be treated like prisoners of war. The reply was a saber slash. Andrew thrust his hand up to ward it off. Blood gushed from wounds in both his scalp and hand. Robert was even less fortunate, knocked to the floor by the saber, opening a deeper wound, which soon became infected. After the house was plundered and burned, both were marched off to a foul prison camp in Camden, forty miles distant. A smallpox epidemic, the periodic and lethal affliction of the American colonies, made the condition of the captives even more perilous.

When word reached the boys' mother, she somehow kept her head. From a militia captain she secured the promise that thirteen British prisoners would be released in exchange for her two sons and several of their companions—if she could arrange it. Then she hastened by horseback to the prison camp, insisting that she see the local British commander, Lord Rawdon. As James writes, perhaps he simply admired the "pluck" of this "brisk, blue-eyed little Irishwoman whose country attire showed the stains of travel." The exchange was made and her sons were liberated, but they were more dead than alive. The ragged little group set off, all the way back to the Waxhaws. Betty had been able to obtain only two horses. On one, Robert was strapped in so that he could not fall off. She rode on the other. Andrew—barefoot, bareheaded, coatless, burning with fever, but still ambulatory—managed to walk with the other freed men. A drenching rain added to their miseries.

Within forty-eight hours of his arrival, Robert was dead, his wound and the effects of smallpox too severe to overcome. It was touch and go with Andrew. Having lost her husband and two of her three sons to the claims of wilderness and war, Elizabeth Jackson all but willed her last child to survive. After months of her ministrations, he was finally out of danger. But neighbors' sons lay ill with "ship fever" in fetid British prison ships in the harbor of Charleston. Elizabeth had to try to save them, just as she had saved Andrew and had hoped to save Robert. In the summer of 1781, confident of Andrew's uncommon ability to provide for himself, she set out with two other local women to travel the 160 miles to Charleston, hoping to find the prisoners and nurse them back to health. Both she and her son must have realized that her parting words to him were likely the last he would ever hear from her. "Andy," he recalled her saying, "never tell a lie, or take what is not yours. On your own you will need to make and keep friends. But, if ever in a dispute, don't sue for slander. Settle them cases yourself."

Inevitably, Betty contracted the fever herself, a form of cholera, and passed away in November 1781. Friends constructed a casket and buried her on a hillside outside of Charleston. It was not until 1949 that a statue of Elizabeth Hutchinson Jackson was erected next to the grave of her husband and sons in the local church cemetery. All Andrew had received by way of remembrance was a bundle of her spare clothes. At a tender age he had learned a great deal about poverty, war, and loss. He might have said, with greater justification than Jefferson, "I felt utterly alone."

Instead, he set about to justify his mother's confidence that he could make his way in the world. An unexpected bequest of several hundred pounds from his paternal grandfather in Ireland raised his sights. Ultimately, with all the Tory barristers gone, he saw his opportunity and took up the study of law in the office of a North Carolina attorney. In 1788 he moved to the new settlement of Nashville in what was then the western district of the state. In his twenties, he was already an established success. By thirty, he represented the new state of Tennessee in the U.S. House of Representatives.

Throughout his life, Andrew Jackson never forgot his mother's admonition to "settle them cases yourself." He proved adept at making friends but never forgave a slight. Leading his hastily assembled forces to victory in the Battle of New Orleans, even though the War of 1812 had already been officially settled, made him a national hero. Denied his election as president in 1824, he blamed Henry Clay and his followers and set about immediately to win in 1828, founding the Democratic Party in the process and serving two terms. When a technicality had delayed his wife, Rachel's, earlier divorce and his political opponents accused her of bigamy and worse, Jackson would have faced them in a duel to the death had it been possible.

A man of the people, Andy Jackson mixed with them openly, even as president. Attending an exposition, a potential assassin approached him and fired two pistols at point-blank range. Miraculously, they both mis-fired. Jackson calmly used his walking stick to subdue the man until help arrived. The assailant's grievance? He was convinced that somehow the president had prevented his rightful ascension as King of England. Whatever else, the incident proved once again that Elizabeth Jackson had not raised her son to be a weakling.

Although both she and Rachel were devout believers, Andrew did not join the little brick church he had built on the grounds of his hand-some home in Tennessee, the Hermitage, until eight years before he died at the age of seventy-eight on June 8, 1845. He is buried, next to Rachel, in the mansion's garden, under a handsome rotunda. Ever the realist, Andrew Jackson had declared, "Heaven would not be heaven" were he not to be reunited with his beloved wife and his saintly mother.

CHAPTER 5

Patriots and Pioneers—Van Burens to Buchanans

Maria and Abraham Van Buren

Old Kinderhook seemed frozen in time, a bit of Holland in the Hudson Valley. By the time Martin Van Buren was born, it had been a Dutch enclave for two centuries. Donald Cole refers to the area's "drowsy tranquility," a suitable setting for Washington Irving's "Rip Van Winkle," with gabled homes and imported tile interiors. Dutch was still spoken at the dinner table, virtually every family attended the Dutch Reformed Church, and for generations no one had married an outsider.

Abraham Van Buren's enterprising forebears had bequeathed him a tavern, ideally situated on the Post Road between Albany and New York, as well as substantial acreage of fertile farmland. He also served as town clerk and for a time as captain of militia, and he rented out his tavern for political meetings and as a polling place. He should have been prospering. The first of his family, Cornelius Maessen, had left the village of Buren in Holland to sail for America in 1681. He leased a plot of land from Kiliaen Van Rensselaer, a name that would later resonate in American finance, launching the Van Burens in their new country. As the tavern became Kinderhook's primary meeting place, Abraham seemed ideally suited as its proprietor. Because of his geniality and generosity, he became one of the most popular men in town.

In 1776, at the age of thirty-nine, he decided he should take a wife. Perhaps it was a compassionate heart that helped influence his proposal to Maria Hoes Van Alen, an attractive but hard-pressed widow with three children of her own. A decade younger than Abraham, she had known better times as the daughter of a respected family that had been among the original settlers of the town. As it turned out, she brought into his household the critical quality in which Abraham was most deficient—ambition.

Before Abraham went off to fight in the Revolutionary War, the couple had two girls, given the traditional Dutch names of Dirckie and Jannetje. After his return, they had a son, Martin Van Buren, born on December 5, 1782. In the years that followed, two more sons and another daughter joined the family. It is not surprising that Martin's earliest memories were of congestion. As John Niven writes, there was just enough space for a "modicum of respectability."

Like almost everyone else, Martin was very fond of his father, later characterizing him as an "unassuming man who was never known to have an enemy." All he lacked was "the spirit of accumulation." Abraham Van Buren defied ethnic stereotypes—an improvident Dutchman. It was Martin's well-organized mother who inspired his future success. When she passed away, the customary tributes, limited to "her long life was adorned by domestic virtues of the most useful kind," hardly do her justice.

Martin Van Buren was the first American president whose family was not descended from any part of the British Isles, the first from New York, and, most significantly, the first whose profession itself was politics. His earliest exposure to political discourse came from within his own home. By the end of the eighteenth century, Kinderhook was becoming more assimilated. If Martin wanted to hear heated political debate, all he had to do was come downstairs and listen.

Relishing the lively company his tavern afforded, his father was also a soft touch, rarely pressing anyone for repayment. As his children grew, the family's already modest circumstances were reduced to a state of penury.

In Cole's opinion, however, his overcrowded home was not without its benefits for Martin, as he grew into a bright, outgoing child. It taught him to accommodate to others. The constant stream of visitors, many very different from his homogeneous neighbors, vividly illustrated the variety of people inhabiting the great world beyond the environs of Kinderhook. All the children, treated equally, were given their tasks to perform on the farm or in the household, organized by their mother. It was soon clear that Martin possessed special talents. He even looked a bit different than the others. Niven writes, "A handsome child, small, rather delicate in appearance, his hair worn as was the custom, fell in fine reddish blond waves to his shoulders; bright blue deep-set eyes, a fair complexion, a merry disposition, and an infectious smile made him popular among his friends. Later he would grow more compact, but never very tall. As his hair receded, his forehead became more prominent."

Van Buren's poise and mental agility also impressed his elders. He was deferential without being obsequious. Even in homespun, he was always immaculately dressed by his mother. By the time he was twelve he could discuss adult subjects with clarity and a kind of natural ease. His mother managed to get him into Kinderhook Academy, where a dedicated schoolmaster worked with Martin almost like a personal tutor. When he was fifteen, Martin received Maria's most enduring contribution. She was able to obtain for him an opportunity to learn the law in the office of the town's leading attorney, Francis Silvester. In return for sweeping out his offices and working part-time in the store of the barrister's brother, Martin was given bed and board and the chance to clerk for Silvester. He made the most of it.

By the age of seventeen he was immersed in politics, the culmination of all those stimulating tavern discussions. Like most prominent citizens in the area, Silvester was a Federalist, but Van Buren could see that the patrician-based party was headed for extinction. Recognizing Jefferson's Democratic-Republicans as the emerging majority party, Van Buren managed to attend their 1800 district convention in Troy, New York, and adroitly helped his townsman and distant relative (as who was not in Kinderhook?) John P. Van Ness gain the nomination for Congress. Van Ness was so impressed with the youth's political acumen and energy that he paid for him to come to New York City to complete his legal education, master the complex New York legal code, and pass the bar there.

Van Buren went into private practice as soon as he could, becoming wealthy enough to increase his focus on politics. He was elected to his first state office by the age of thirty, already becoming an acknowledged power broker. Earning the nickname of "Little Magician," he worked with Andrew Jackson to found the truly national Democratic Party. In Van Buren's words, "Without strong political organizations, there would be nothing to moderate the prejudices between free and slaveholding states." Valuing victory over ideology, he became the pragmatic personification of the new politics—public life as a fulfilling profession in itself.

His own personal progress advanced from a variety of state offices to the U.S. Senate. He became governor of New York, then Andrew Jackson's secretary of state, and in the election of 1832, his vice president. In 1836 he reached the pinnacle as Jackson's chosen successor, elected eighth president of the United States.

His career should have concluded in triumph, but unfortunately success entails as much chance as calculation. In 1807 he had married his childhood sweetheart, Hannah Hoes, who blessed him with a daughter and five sons, four of whom survived. However, Hannah died of tuberculosis in 1819, leaving him to care for the boys, aged two to eleven. Martin remained a widower for more than half his life. His "amiable and loving" father had died in 1817, at the age of eighty; his devoted mother in 1818, at the age of seventy-one, and then his wife—three personal blows in succession.

Van Buren's presidency, limited to a single term, had been intended to follow in the footsteps of his illustrious predecessor—"Old Kinderhook" supplementing "Old Hickory." In his political campaigns Van Buren even originated the "OK" phrase we still use today in every context. Ironically, it may be that Jackson's own economic policies helped to bring about the catastrophic Panic of 1837, followed by an extended depression, bank failures, and record unemployment. All of Van Buren's plans were overshadowed by economic woes. His Whig opponents ridiculed him as "Martin Van Ruin." He died at the age of seventy-nine on

July 24, 1862, at home in, of course, Old Kinderhook. Throughout his career he had retained something of its small-town values, merging the energy of his mother with the amiability of his father, and always recalling both fondly.

Elizabeth and Benjamin Harrison V

There he was, stubborn William Henry Harrison, triumphant in the presidential election of 1840, coatless and hatless, dramatically riding his white charger through a driving rainstorm on the way to his inauguration, intent on uttering every word of the longest inaugural address in American history. Not even Daniel Webster could get him to reduce it to less than two hours. It included proposing a constitutional amendment limiting presidents to one term. His own was to last only one month. Within three weeks he caught pneumonia and died a week later, making his running mate, John Tyler, the nation's first accidental president.

Politics as a form of entertainment may have reached its pre-electronic zenith in 1840—with a proliferation of picnics, parades, and paraphernalia of all kinds. Using the catchy slogan "Tippecanoe and Tyler Too" merged Harrison's victory over the Indians with his running mate's talents. The patrician Harrison was portrayed as being derived from the humblest origins. His opponents, Van Buren's Democrats, share the blame. Their attempt to ridicule Harrison as fit only for bucolic retirement, contentedly sipping hard cider in his imaginary rustic cabin, was a gift to the Whigs. As for Van Buren, the only candidate personally acquainted with poverty, he was portrayed as the prissy embodiment of luxurious living, a "used up" tool of Eastern money interests, and it worked.

In the customary attempt to "balance" their ticket, the Whigs had paired one Virginia patrician with another, although Harrison had fortuitously moved to Ohio. Unfortunately, they completely disagreed with each other in terms of the most important issue facing the nation. William Henry Harrison was a fervent believer in nationalism. John

Tyler just as firmly espoused states' rights. But, of course, Tyler was never expected to become president. Here were the seeds of the Civil War, within a single slate, twenty years ahead of time. The Constitution implied that should a president die, his vice president would simply stand in until the next election. But that's not the way "Tyler too" saw it. He took the reins of office in their entirety, establishing the precedent that endures to this day.

The fathers of both men were former governors of Virginia. Fun-loving Benjamin Harrison V would have relished the election of 1840. Unfortunately, he had died almost a half-century before. Jeff Young describes the good-natured "portly patriot" as "six feet, four inches tall, and weighing 249 pounds," a lover of rich foods and lavish entertaining. The Harrisons, already prominent in England, had settled in Virginia in the mid-seventeenth century, prospering anew, their vast holdings anchored by a magnificent mansion called "Berkeley," overlooking the James River. There, on April 5, 1726, Benjamin Harrison V was born. (The youngest of his seven children, William Henry Harrison, was also born there, on February 9, 1773.) It is more likely that his father celebrated the event with a fine claret than with hard cider.

Like the families of the founders, the Harrisons enhanced their holdings with a series of fortuitous marriages. In 1748, Benjamin V married eighteen-year-old Elizabeth Bassett, who resided in the neighboring plantation. Celebrated for her beauty, piety, and benevolence, she was a niece of Martha Washington and seemed in her relative serenity an ideal contrast to the opulent lifestyle of the fifth (but not the last) of the Benjamin Harrisons.

Heading to Philadelphia as one of Virginia's seven delegates to the First Continental Congress, Harrison took his high spirits with him. For example, when John Hancock seemed hesitant to take the chair, Harrison simply picked him up bodily and placed him there. For the rest of his life Harrison would be in public service, evidencing a surprisingly serious side. Too old to fight in the Revolutionary War, he was fortunate enough to lose neither his life nor his lifestyle and ultimately was a significant signer of the Constitution. Unfortunately, his frequent absences denied

Benjamin's wife more of his cordial company, as it would deny slender young William the opportunity he craved to really get to know his father better.

As a younger son, William Henry Harrison contemplated inheriting relatively little land. While his father lived, he attended Hampden-Sydney College and later studied medicine in Philadelphia. However, after Benjamin Harrison V passed away at sixty-five, on April 24, 1791—probably (and not surprisingly) of gout—and his mother died the following year, William followed his own inclinations to pursue a military career.

Through the influence of "Light Horse" Harry Lee, Harrison, then only eighteen, received a commission in the First Regiment, United States Artillery, signed by President Washington himself. "How I wished my father were alive to be with me," William reflected. He went on to win a number of well-publicized military victories, such as at Tippecanoe, over Indian confederations denied much English aid. After he moved to Ohio, eventually becoming both a brigadier general and a senator, he was named ambassador to Colombia but shortly returned to manage his modest farm and take on a humble post as clerk of his county's court of common pleas. Managing to fall deeply into debt, it occurred to Harrison that perhaps his military renown might somehow translate into consideration for the presidency itself under the auspices of the emerging Whig Party. It was a conclusion shared by their leadership. Imagine, another war hero from the West. His strong showing in 1836 led to renomination in 1840. That time, the odds in his favor, he won handily but served only those thirty-one days after his inauguration.

Mary and John Tyler Sr.

All we really know about Mary Armistead Tyler is that, like Elizabeth Bassett Harrison, she was born to a prominent family and was reputed to be both beneficent and beautiful. At sixteen she married the third John Tyler, a widower far older than she. They had eight children, of whom young John was the sixth, and she died when the boy was only seven.

Accordingly, the elder Tyler was obliged to be both father and mother to his offspring. Young John Tyler had been born on March 29, 1790. The senior and junior John Tylers were inseparable. Many of the stories told of the one might well have been told of the other, such as playing the fiddle under a willow tree to entertain the local children. Unlike the Harrisons, the Tylers also looked very much alike. Robert Seagar writes of young John, "He was very slight in build; his long, thin, patrician face was dominated by the high cheekbones and prominent nose he would later joke about—'the Tyler nose' . . . His lips were thin and tight, his dark brown hair was silken. Physically, he was never robust."

If there was a difference, it was in personality. The senior Tyler's was more forceful. As Oliver Chitwood writes, "He was a man of strong convictions and prejudices, both of which he expressed with utter fearlessness." His son tried to demonstrate more tact, but it would help him little in terms of negotiating the first accidental presidency in American history.

The Tyler saga follows a now-familiar pattern—the old English gentry emigrating to Virginia and emerging as its new gentry, as their monarch lost his cause, his crown, and his head. There are as many Henrys and Johns among the Tylers as Benjamins among the Harrisons. In the middle of the seventeenth century, a Henry Tyler settled in the Virginia peninsula, between the James and York Rivers. Family tradition holds that the Tylers are descended from both an ancestor who came to England with William the Conqueror and from Wat Tyler, a humble blacksmith who led a revolt against King Richard II—merging royalty with revolution. By the time of the birth of the John Tyler who would father a president, on February 28, 1747, Tylers were firmly established among the celebrated First Families of Virginia. It is not surprising that, with so much to lose, the sentiments of successive generations would be so separated by the actual possibility of leaving the mother country and all it represented.

On a balmy spring day in 1764, two young law students from William and Mary College strode down the Duke of Gloucester Street in Williamsburg to head to the capitol building to witness a debate about the potential repeal of the resented Stamp Act. One was John Tyler, the other his roommate, Thomas Jefferson. They heard Patrick Henry threaten that, as things were going, George III might eventually go the way of prior tyrants. Tyler's positive reactions alarmed his staunchly Royalist father, Henry, just as a similar warning that he might lose his head had been issued to Benjamin Harrison V by his father.

When, nonetheless, separation did come a decade later, the senior John Tyler served in both the militia and legislature, once escaping just in time to avoid being hanged. After the conflict, "Judge Tyler" would be most noted for his service on the bench, his judicial career in both Virginia and Federal Courts lasting until his death. It was interrupted only for the three years he was governor and during his role in the Virginia Convention considering the adoption of the Constitution of the United States. Like Patrick Henry, he was opposed, fearing that the struggle for liberty might be compromised by yielding too much power to federal authority. No inheritance passed on to young John was of greater significance than his father's staunch support of states' rights.

John Tyler Jr. never ceased extolling the mother he hardly knew: "She who nurtured us in our infancy . . . taught us to raise our little hands in prayer . . . such a mother is of precious value." But he was with his father for decades. Although often described as "stern," the senior Tyler surely had a softer side. In addition to his own, he welcomed twenty-one additional children for whom he was guardian. Even with 1,900 acres to roam, surrounded by his seven siblings and all these others, young Tyler must have early developed some ability to compromise.

Although an excellent student, he found in his father his most notable teacher—imparting not only the lessons of his life but also a love of music, poetry, and the law. He was delighted to have young John serve as his aide during the three years he was governor in the new capital city of Richmond. For his son it was a priceless opportunity to meet some of his Revolutionary heroes in person.

His hopes for compromise could not contain his convictions. Nearing the end of what was to have been Harrison's term, Tyler was denounced in the North and misunderstood in the South. Always his own man, he opposed such Whig goals as a national bank, high tariffs, and internal improvements. Henry Clay called him a president without a party. Accordingly, before departing from the White House in 1845, Tyler and his wife Julia responded by giving one of the most lavish entertainments in the history of the executive mansion. His father would have immensely appreciated such a defiant gesture. Unfortunately, he had died at his home on January 6, 1813, at the age of sixty-five. The nation was once again at war with Great Britain, and his son was serving as a captain of militia. He predicted, with some despair, "The day is coming when an ounce of lead will be worth more than a pound of sense."

In a final irony, former President John Tyler was called back to Washington in 1861 by James Buchanan, who was desperate to avoid civil war. He presided over a last-ditch conference to bring both sides together. Of course, it was doomed to failure. His father, however, would not have disparaged such an effort. Above all, he was a patriot.

Jane and Samuel Polk

Once he made up his mind, you couldn't budge Samuel Polk. If many first fathers were restless, ambitious entrepreneurs, they came by it naturally. As Martha Morrell writes of Samuel's father Ezekial Polk, "The same venturesome spirit that had brought his great-grandfather to America more than a century earlier flowed through his veins with undiluted vigor." Those venturesome Polks had come from Scotland to Maryland and then settled in North Carolina, where Samuel was born in 1772. Three years later, an intrepid relative was one of those who assembled to proclaim the Mecklenburg Resolves, declaring British authority null and void a year before the Declaration of Independence in Philadelphia.

Ezekial's great opportunity came when, like so many others, he received a land grant as a result of his service in the War for American Independence. As a surveyor as well as a farmer, he energetically bought up additional grants from other veterans, expanding his holdings in North Carolina, and later moved on to explore even greater possibilities in Tennessee. In his seventy-six years he was married three times. His first wife bore him eight children, including Samuel, the father of James Knox Polk. His son and grandson inherited much of his energetic and independent outlook. Ezekial was a free-thinking deist, in the tradition of Franklin and Jefferson. He wrote his own engaging epitaph, a small portion of which reads, "His youthful days he spent in pleasure, his latter days in gath'ring treasure."

As young Samuel Polk eagerly awaited the return of his father from the war, another veteran was returning to the farm he had established in nearby Mecklenburg. Among those most anxious to greet Colonel James Knox was his daughter Jane, born in 1776, just before he had gone off to fight. That the Knox family was known for piety as well as industriousness is not a surprise. Jane Knox was the great-great-grandniece of John Knox, the founder of Scotch Presbyterianism, and it was a legacy she would not take lightly.

As Jane Knox and Samuel Polk grew to adulthood, and the boundaries of their region moved inexorably westward, the two farms expanded but remained within the same region. Even in this relative wilderness, opportunities for young people to meet socially were not lacking. Politics were avidly discussed around campfires, the outdoor equivalent of the Van Burens' tavern. Samuel Polk, the energetic son of an energetic father, viewed age as no barrier to his participation. The parents of both had taught them to read, write, and calculate—a rarity in their rural environment. It turned out that Jane Knox and Samuel Polk agreed on almost everything except religion. Both were devoted Jeffersonians, and their energetic temperaments were similar. That Samuel had inherited his father's free-thinking Deism can hardly have appealed to Jane, but perhaps she might convert him in time. The qualities they shared transcended any differences. Jane was hardly frivolous, but she didn't mind being called "Jenny." The attraction was mutual.

They were married on Christmas evening, 1794, in the Mecklenburg Presbyterian Church and settled on a large tract of land given to them by Samuel's father. Developing it was rigorous, but their future seemed bright. On November 4, 1795, the first of their ten children was born, a boy they named James Knox Polk. Trouble arrived with James's baptism. The minister insisted that the boy's father would first have to profess his own faith, which led to Samuel's angry departure from the premises. Jane was stunned, but at least she hadn't married a weakling.

Morrell describes young James as "frail" but "well formed," small but handsome. From very early he seemed ill-suited for the demanding rural routine that awaited him on his parents' farm. He was never to develop the physical strength to be much help in this regard. However, he came to enjoy riding, hunting, fishing, and the outdoors generally. As the family grew, his primary task was to be his mother's helper, assuming responsibility for the care and direction of his nine younger brothers and sisters. Both parents sought to impart their own rudimentary learning especially to their oldest son, and to share with him those campfire debates about politics, and memories of his grandfathers' war exploits. However, with the increasing demands of farming and in the absence of a local school or church, teaching became largely Jane's responsibility.

When James was nearly eleven, his family joined Ezekial's in Tennessee, described as a "bountiful land of promise," which had been admitted as a state in the year of James's birth. The roles of each of his parents became even more defined. By extraordinary effort Samuel prospered, not only as the proprietor of a larger farm, but as a surveyor, buying and selling the land of others, as well as such ventures as a bank, newspaper, and general store—turning a profit at everything. An established community leader, he determined to make only sound investments in the future.

Jane was the sole educator now, beyond administering her demanding household. Still as devout when it came to the temporal realm, all the children were encouraged to think for themselves. By now she was certain that James had the greatest potential, but she had to convince her husband that their eldest son's higher education would turn out to be a sound investment. Even Samuel realized that James was not cut out for farming or commerce.

Both parents were concerned with James's declining health. The nearest doctor was some 250 miles away in Kentucky, but Samuel set everything aside to undertake this journey with James, earning his son's enduring gratitude. The diagnosis was gallstones, but after James endured a painful, risky operation to remove them, his health markedly improved.

It was his mind he now longed to exercise. Meeting with James, Samuel Polk vowed, "Do well in your studies and I will send you to college. But mind, I will not waste my money if you waste your time." He need not have worried.

Buoyed by his mother's confidence, James was sent to a well-regarded academy in Murfreesboro, fifty miles away. Outworking everyone, he was a tireless if not brilliant student. The academy also opened wider vistas, enabling him to make friends outside his family circle. Some were young women. Polk would eventually marry the brightest of them, Sarah Childress. Polk's father then sent him to the University of North Carolina. Starting as a sophomore, James graduated with honors in 1818 and then went on to study law.

His mother, disappointed that he had not considered becoming a (baptized) Presbyterian minister, was nonetheless cheered when eventually James set up his legal partnership with a classmate. Looking up at their freshly painted shingle, she told her son, "It's a fine-looking sign. Never do anything to dishonor it." Samuel Polk died on November 5, 1827, at the age of fifty-five. Perhaps he had all but worked himself to death, but he surely never regretted the sound investment he had made in his eldest son.

The political rise of James Knox Polk demonstrated his tenacity. By twenty-seven he was elected to the state legislature, two years later to the same congressional seat that had been occupied by Andrew Jackson, an old acquaintance of his family. Jackson was such a hero to Polk that he cherished his new appellation as "Young Hickory." Eventually, he was elected governor of Tennessee, and in 1844 he emerged as a compromise candidate—the first "dark horse"—of the Democratic Party for the presidency itself. Running on an expansionist platform and supported by Jackson, he won a narrow victory over the more renowned Whig candidate, Henry Clay. In the White House, Polk centered as much power as possible into his own hands. The mystery is what influences had made him so suspicious of others. Like his father, once he made up his mind he couldn't be budged; and like his father, he just about worked himself to death—"a short man with a long program," the press called him—but surely there were similarly minded associates worthy of trust.

In any case, if we were to rank our presidents solely based on their success in office, Polk would come in first. Announcing at the outset that he would serve only one term, he had four major objectives and achieved them all. Most significant, he immensely increased the size of the nation by outmaneuvering the British to gain Oregon and precipitating a controversial war with Mexico to obtain California and the entire Southwest. He was so apprehensive that his two leading generals in that conflict, Winfield Scott and Zachary Taylor, devoid of any qualifications, might seek the presidency themselves, that he tried to play them off against each other. As a forceful chief executive, Polk had many admirers. It hardly seemed a source of concern that he didn't supplement them with close associates.

In 1849, his term concluded, James Knox Polk departed to his newly purchased mansion in Nashville, accompanied by his devoted wife, Sarah. She had served as his private secretary, a close confidant on policy, and also took no vacations. Nor was there any dancing or drinking in the White House during their tenure. They had no children. Polk was so worn out that he lived for only three and a half months into his retirement, dying on June 15, 1849, at the age of fifty-three, even younger than had his father. His mother would pass away two years later. His wife, who always wore a bit of mourning black, survived until 1891. Insisting that she belonged to the entire nation, she was highly esteemed throughout the Civil War in both the North and South, a personal regard beyond that accorded her hardworking husband.

Sarah and Richard Taylor

Zachary Taylor had never wanted to be anything but a soldier, emulating his father. Taylor's spare and premature autobiography, all of fifteen pages, dwells on Richard Taylor, that heroic patriot who had opposed "the Brittish (sic) at the commencement of the Revolution and remained in the service in the Continental Line at the close of the war & quit the Service as a Lt. Col." It concludes, "In the spring of 1808 I was appointed a first Lieutenant in the 7th Regiment United States Infantry." In fact, Zachary Taylor would invest ten times as much of his life in a military career as the father he so admired, emerging a major general, but these early exploits were his inspiration. Of Taylor's mother there is not one word in the autobiography. Yet without her instruction he could never have even written it.

The Taylors turn our ongoing story backwards. They were patrician-patriots who became pioneer-patriots. The problem was not lineage but land. By the end of the Revolution the Taylor family had been in Virginia for almost 150 years. The first American Taylors had come from England around 1640, when the entire colony had no more than ten thousand residents and its Tidewater region was only partially settled. Although established as a prominent family, the Taylors early demonstrated an inclination for exploration. In 1716 James Taylor was one of those celebrated Knights of the Golden Horseshoe who accompanied Governor Alexander Spotswood on his expedition over the Blue Ridge Mountains into the Shenandoah Valley. Taylor emerged with the acquisition of substantial holdings in the Piedmont on the Rapidan River. In 1721 his daughter, Frances, married Ambrose Madison, merging two families of future presidents. Through blood or marriage the Taylors would be related as well to Lees, Marshalls, and Monroes. Richard Taylor was born into this well-established Virginia family on April 3, 1744, one of the four children of a prior Zachary Taylor and Elizabeth Lee.

Richard's explorations took him farther than any of his forebears. Like many similarly situated young Virginians, Richard attended William and Mary College. Instead of opting for the comfortable serenity of plantation life, at twenty-five he demonstrated his own adventurous streak. With his brother and a friend, he journeyed down the Ohio and Mississippi Rivers, a year-long exploration not quite of Lewis and Clark dimensions but very ambitious for the time. Whatever its dangers, the trip convinced Taylor that there was a vast area of potential habitation beyond the Piedmont.

If he sought more immediate adventure, it came with the War for American Independence. In 1779 he somehow found the time to wed eighteen-year-old Sarah Dabney Strother, seventeen years his junior. Born to a prominent plantation family near Fredericksburg, charming "Sally" Strother had enjoyed all the advantages available to young women, including tutors imported from Europe to supplement local instruction. Her cultivated demeanor seemed a perfect complement to Richard's dashing persona. Richard Taylor was quite tall, blue-eyed, congenial, and strikingly handsome. Once he returned from the war, the children came quickly—in February 1781, their first son, named Hancock for both the brother who had accompanied Richard on his adventurous journey and an uncle who had been killed by Indians; in 1782, their second son, William Dabney Strother, named for Sally's brother who had been killed in the war.

As K. Jack Bauer points out, the first decade after American independence was a time of political uncertainty, social upheaval, and economic instability, to which even well-positioned families like the Taylors were not impervious. The lure of a fresh start appealed to young men whose wartime exploits had given them "a sense of their own strength and competence." Unable to pay returning veterans in cash for their services, hard-pressed states like Virginia offered them vast tracts of land in their western preserves.

Despite his substantial Hare Forest property, Richard Taylor couldn't resist an offer of some 7,000 acres in sparsely settled Kentucky, still a part of the "Old Dominion." He and Sally made the difficult decision to collect bag, baggage, and offspring and hasten west to claim their first thousand acres, outside the outpost village of Louisville. There was one complication. Sally was pregnant again. She completed her confinement only twelve miles into the journey, at Montebello, a plantation owned by a Taylor cousin. On March 4, 1784, Richard and Sarah Taylor had their third son, whom they named Zachary after his paternal grandfather. Then they ventured on together, endowing what would become the "Bluegrass State" with its claim to our twelfth president.

Eventually, the Taylors' new domain would transcend the scale of anything they had enjoyed in Virginia, but it would take years of toil. The move also denied Zachary the sort of education he would have enjoyed in settled Virginia. From time to time there were some sessions with itinerant schoolmasters, but there was no real local school on any continuing basis. With their father busy hacking their homestead out of the wilderness, it fell to Sally to instruct all her children. As Doris Faber points out, "Whatever learning [Zachary] had came from her, and one must doubt whether he would have been able to write even one page if she had not taught him his letters." Of course, he didn't write all that much.

Despite having no close neighbors, with eight brothers and sisters Zachary never wanted for playmates. Within a few years the Taylor domain would be graced by a handsome brick mansion named "Springfield." With Louisville's expansion, the Taylors would enjoy, in the words of Brainerd Dyer, all "the comforts, if not the luxuries of the older plantations of the east," and those would come later. However, upon the Taylors' arrival, the "dark and bloody ground" of Kentucky still came under frequent Indian attack. Richard fought in many such skirmishes and was wounded at least once. Young Zachary grew up not only hearing tales of the Revolutionary War but also witnessing and admiring actual evidence of his father's heroism. Long a prime hunting and fishing ground for many tribes, the land soon became the site of an unequal struggle for their survival.

By 1810, Richard also had thirty-seven slaves. Although a son of the slaveholding South, when the time came Zachary Taylor would be a fervent supporter of the preservation of the Union. After Kentucky had finally become a state, his father served on the commission that framed its constitution, in the state legislature, as a county magistrate, collector for the port of Louisville, and four times a presidential elector, granted the opportunity to vote for his own distant relations. His location on the Beargrass Creek, where goods could be docked and moved overland to Louisville, was key to his immense success. As the region prospered, he and Sally never had reason to regret their decision to relocate.

Despite professing to love the land, at the age of twenty-three, Zachary Taylor gained his commission in the infantry when President Jefferson tripled the size of the army. Although over the decades his military career had its ups and downs, his great opportunity came with President Polk's Mexican War. Despite Polk's efforts to minimize his impact, Taylor became a national hero. Renowned for his solicitude for the men who served under him, he earned popular favor as "Old Rough and Ready." The phrase also described his appealingly homely appearance and attire. Short and anything but dashing, Zachary Taylor looked nothing like the father he so admired. As Bauer writes, in later years he resembled either a prosperous farmer, with his lined and weathered countenance, or "a man who had spent most of his adult years in command of troops in the field or those manning frontier posts, the eyes are sharp, the mouth firm, the features lean."

Despite failing to credit his devoted mother for the modicum of education he had received, Zachary Taylor stressed the importance of maintaining schools for the children of those stationed at every post he commanded. He and his wife, Margaret Mackall Smith, whom he married in 1810, had only one son, Richard, who would study in Edinburgh and Paris before graduating from Yale. Two of their daughters died in an 1820 malaria epidemic in Louisiana, but at least three of their surviving children attended prominent schools in the East.

Neither of his parents would live to witness Zachary's tragically brief political career. Richard Taylor died at "Springfield" on January 19, 1829, at the age of eighty-four; Sarah Strother Taylor died just before her sixty-seventh birthday. Zachary's wife, now a semi-invalid, was as opposed to the popular appeal that had launched him to a possible presidential nomination as was former president Polk. Indeed, not much earlier Taylor had declared, "I have no aspirations for civic office of any kind."

The irony was that this soldiers' general might have been just what the nation needed at that pivotal time: a compassionate but strong, unifying president. He finally agreed to run, but his preference was to do so without any specific party designation. Technically a Whig, he presented himself as essentially unaffiliated, a truly "national candidate," and won in a close three-candidate race. He stressed not only the critical importance of preserving the Union at all costs but also such affiliated ideas as agricultural aid throughout the nation and building a transcontinental railroad. Polk to the contrary, Taylor must have done some thinking and reading between military engagements.

Only fifteen months after his narrow victory, sitting through an extremely warm Fourth of July celebration at the Washington Monument, Zachary Taylor suddenly fell ill. He died of typhoid fever five days later, on July 9, 1850, at the age of sixty-five. In a further irony, his well-educated son would serve as a Confederate general in the war to come, and one of his daughters would marry Jefferson Davis, although she lived only a short span thereafter.

Perhaps by 1850 no one could have preserved the Union as it was constituted. However, a man like Zachary Taylor, this steadfast son of pioneer parents, was certainly better suited to the task than any of his three well-intentioned successors would prove to be.

Phoebe and Nathaniel Fillmore

Dutiful Millard Fillmore, who ascended to the presidency upon the death of Taylor, was neither rough nor ready. He may not be viewed as among our most renowned presidents, but he has few rivals for most unlikely. His saga extends from almost Dickensian privation to a conclusion that would confound any cynic.

Fillmore was blessed with two loving parents. It was at his sensible mother's urging that his bungling but endlessly striving father Nathaniel finally found a way to give the ambitious youth his start. Little more than thirty years later, the two men stood proudly side by side at a White House reception given by the son to honor his father. Unfortunately, Millard Fillmore's mother, Phoebe, who had initiated it all, had died decades earlier, worn down by the years of struggle.

Things should have been a lot easier. Lieutenant Nathaniel Fillmore Sr., of old English stock, helped to settle Bennington, Vermont, and went on to defend it in the Revolutionary War. His son, also named Nathaniel, who had been born in 1771, inherited his father's love of the region but not of its impossibly stony soil. He wanted to farm where the yield might be as spectacular as the scenery. Young Nathaniel married well. Bright Phoebe Millard, the daughter of a prominent doctor in Pittsfield, Massachusetts, loved learning. At the age of sixteen, she also fell in love with strapping, blond, handsome, adventurous Nat Fillmore, who was all of twenty-five. He was intent on finding prosperity in the Wild West—that is to say, in the wilderness of Cayuga County, New York.

Just as other states lured veterans with offers of free land, New York opened a vast "military tract." Most of it wound up in the hands of speculators, and among the most gullible of their victims were Nathaniel Fillmore and his brother, Calvin. Anxious to get started, they bought a farm, sight unseen, within a deep forest, bringing their excited young brides with them. On it they built the requisite log cabin, in which both their families would live initially. The Fillmores were eventually to have nine children. Their second child and first son, born on January 7, 1800, was named Millard, his mother's maiden name. As their prospects dimmed, Phoebe Millard Fillmore would harbor her fondest hopes on this boy, early teaching him to read from the few books she had been able to bring with her.

After laboriously clearing much of the timber, as Robert Raybach writes, "Instead of fertile loam, the Fillmore brothers found unyielding clay. Instead of prosperity, they found poverty." To the "woes of poor crops, poor weather, and a crowded cabin was added a defective land title." They had been swindled and owned nothing.

When Millard was two, his family simply picked up and moved, set-tling some miles away and leasing 130 acres near a town called

Sempronius. Here, at least they could raise real crops like corn and wheat, but Nathaniel Fillmore would never again be an owner, only a tenant farmer on the land of others. As he grew, Millard worked alongside his father. As raw-boned and sturdy as an oak, he would recall, "Being large of my age and unusually strong, I learned to plow, to hoe, to chop, to log and clear land, to mow, to reap, and finally to do all kinds of work." Any schooling was a sometime thing. When Millard was about ten, one of those ubiquitous itinerant (was there any other kind?) New England schoolmasters made an appearance in the area. By then, however, he had been reading and spelling under the auspices of his mother for several years. As she had hoped, he also came to love learning.

His father had more immediate concerns—a growing family with no increase in income to help support it. Perhaps his daughters might manage to marry well, but his sons needed to learn some sort of productive trade. He sent Millard to apprentice at a cloth maker, but it turned out to be more like a workhouse than any sort of learning opportunity. Moving to a more reputable fabric-processing mill, frugal Millard was able to send home some money to help his destitute family. He also bought a dictionary and joined a circulating library, reading everything he could lay his hands on. In the process he began to develop a quiet confidence to supplement his physical strength, and he became interested in the law.

He also found time to fall in love. Abigail Powers, the bright daughter of a local minister, may have been socially superior to young Fillmore (as who was not?), but the two were more than compatible. Now Millard had even more incentive to make something of himself. He had saved enough from his meager earnings to finally pay off his employer, and he obtained a job as a schoolmaster. At least it was a start.

His father's perpetual dissatisfaction with his circumstances led him to move to a new tenancy in Montville, a dozen miles away. The proprietor of their new farm was the wealthiest person in the region, shrewd Quaker Judge Walter Wood, who also headed its largest law firm. Seeing her opportunity, Phoebe persuaded her husband to ask Judge Wood if he might give Millard a two-month trial as a law clerk. To his relief, the canny jurist agreed.

When Millard returned home for a visit and was told the news by his mother, he burst into tears. Whatever lay ahead, at last his future was in his own hands. The two months turned into two years. Judge Wood's suggestion that "I can get thee some employment" would eventually become a flourishing career with a major law firm in Buffalo, the political career that followed, and finally marriage to the patient Abigail Powers. Phoebe lived only long enough to witness the start. Her oldest son, who bore her family's name, having passed the bar in 1823, was elected to the New York State Assembly at the age of twenty-eight. His proud departure for Albany, a precursor of things to come, was satisfaction enough. Phoebe Millard Fillmore died on April 2, 1831, at the age of only fifty.

Eventually remarried, Nathaniel Fillmore would witness it all, from his son's prosperous legal practice to the U.S. House of Representatives, to election as New York's state controller, to becoming Zachary Taylor's running mate in 1848. It may seem peculiar that Millard's political career began with adherence to the Anti-Masonic Party and concluded with the embarrassment of representing the anti-immigrant Know-Nothing Party. But during Fillmore's lifetime the American political structure was rather traumatically emerging into more or less its present configuration. It was as a National Republican that Fillmore won his first race, and as a Whig that his career reached its zenith. After 1852, the Whigs disintegrated and the nation's two major parties had finally evolved into Republicans and Democrats. Unfortunately, there were more serious forms of separation ahead.

Although hardly as mismatched as Harrison and Tyler, Zachary Taylor and Millard Fillmore also represent the perils of ticket balancing. The magnanimous Fillmore was weak where Taylor would have been strong, a firmer advocate of preserving the Union at whatever cost. Fillmore hated slavery but invariably counseled moderation, agreeing to the Compromise of 1850, which Taylor had opposed. After Taylor's sudden death, a stunned Fillmore, thrust into leadership during a heightened climate of discord, managed only to delay the carnage for a decade. Perhaps his even-handed espousal of prosperity for all sections of the country might yet heal the breach. His presidency, like the man himself, was certainly well intentioned.

As his term wound down, he brought his father to a reception at the White House. There they stood, father and son, still both strikingly handsome six-footers. Asked how one raises a president, Nat Fillmore replied with a suitably colorful country allusion, "Cradle him in a sap trough." In they came to shake his hand, as if he, too, a life-long failure, deserved such a tribute.

Nathaniel Fillmore Jr. died on March 28, 1863, at the age of ninety-two, in the midst of the war his son had tried to avert. To the end of his days, he probably still couldn't quite grasp the heights reached by his son, a tribute to the tenacity of both, yet actually initiated by the timely intervention of Phoebe Millard Fillmore.

Anna and Benjamin Pierce

The face in his official portrait looks so familiar—a shock of gray hair, a prominent nose, a strong jaw, a penetrating gaze. No, it is not Andrew Jackson, but his great admirer, General Benjamin Pierce, governor of the "Granite State" of New Hampshire. Sometimes "The Age of Jackson" seems to have pervaded the entirety of the antebellum period. Pierce's regard for Jackson's person and politics were passed along to his son, Franklin, who in time would earn the campaign appellation of "Young Hickory of the Granite Hills." Frank Pierce also inherited his father's handsome countenance and robust health and benefitted from both the education and political contacts he provided. Because his upwardly mobile father had succeeded, young Pierce enjoyed a childhood as secure as Millard Fillmore's had been deprived. However, his life would not duplicate in its entirety our seemingly perpetual pattern of ambitious fathers and religious and literate mothers.

After the death of his mother, Anna Kendrick Pierce, Franklin wrote a rather equivocal tribute, "She was a most affectionate and tender mother, strong in many points and weak in some, but always weak on the side of tenderness and affection." What were these "weak" points? The most obvious is that Anna Pierce couldn't hold her liquor, and neither could he. Both drank excessively, but only Franklin tried periodically to overcome the addiction, not without inner turmoil. His mother's weakness for spirits, however, didn't prevent her from raising eight children, as well as the stepdaughter she acquired when she married widower Benjamin Pierce. Beyond her drinking, temperamentally they seemed an unlikely couple, the disciplined but ambitious military man and his fun-loving, unpredictable wife. Yet they lived together in apparent harmony for over half a century, dying within a year of each other.

Of English heritage from Shropshire, the Pierces had settled in the 1630s in the Massachusetts Bay Colony town of Chelmsford. Here, Benjamin was born on Christmas Day, 1757, the seventh of ten children. When he was six, his father died, leaving him no inheritance. Young Ben grew up poor but proud on the farm of his uncle, Robert Pierce. Fortunately, he managed to obtain at least some schooling. As Pierce put it in his succinct autobiography, he learned to read, write, and do sums "by attending school from the age of ten to sixteen years, three weeks in each year."

His future arrived quite suddenly when he was only seventeen, in 1775. The Redcoats were marching from Boston to Concord. In Pierce's words, "I was plowing in the field when the news first came that the British had fired upon the Americans at Lexington and killed eight men. I stepped between the cattle, dropped the chains from the plow, and without any further ceremony, shouldered my uncle's fowling piece, swung the bullet pouch and powder horn and hastened to the place where the first blood had been spilled." He was quite literally a minuteman.

Pierce would not soon return to his plow. He was gone for most of the next nine years, enlisting and reenlisting, fighting everywhere from Breed's Hill to Saratoga and spending a desolate winter at Valley Forge. Despite every privation, he recalled, "I enjoyed it much . . . Arms was my profession." Pierce ended the war as a captain. The title of "general" he would later bestow on himself as head of his own militia. After all, he had served in it for twenty-one years, an essential part of his self-made career.

He was much changed when he returned to Chelmsford in 1784, a grown man and a seasoned veteran. He had learned enough to do some surveying for a local landowner, Colonel Samson Stoddard, up north in New Hampshire. It struck him as a more promising place to settle, and in the town of Hillsborough (or Hillsboro, as he would spell it) he bought a small farm, reputedly for a dollar an acre, almost on the spur of the moment. The next year he took up residence, improving the small log hut that already existed on the property, and in the following year, 1787, he got married. Unfortunately, Elizabeth Andrews Pierce lived for only an additional eighteen months. She died in childbirth, a too-frequent occurrence in those times. Her grieving husband named his new daughter Elizabeth.

There was little time to mourn. Benjamin was already becoming more a public figure than a farmer. In 1789 he was elected to the state legislature, and he would be reelected sixteen times in succession. Later he would be named to the Governor's Council and a delegate to New Hampshire's constitutional convention as well as sheriff for the county of Hillsborough. Four times he would run for governor, winning twice. That these races were so closely contested is because Pierce remained a supporter of Jefferson and Jackson in an area still predominantly Federalist, a tribute to his political skills.

Meanwhile, his daughter needed a mother. When Pierce met pretty, plump, colorful, vivacious twenty-one-year-old Anna Kendrick, a new arrival in the area, it didn't take him long to propose. Nor did it take her long to accept this dashing suitor. Whether they toasted their nuptials with spirits is not a matter of record. That Anna Kendrick Pierce turned out to be a dutiful and productive mother and stepmother, in the words of Franklin, full of "kindness and affection," is beyond dispute. The sixth of her eight children, he was born on November 23, 1804. However, it was his mother's apparent excesses that shocked the prim, Puritan paragons of Hillsborough, which she didn't seem to mind in the least.

Vivacious and mercurial, Anna Pierce almost seemed to delight in the gossip about her imbibing, her outspokenness, and her colorfully provocative dress. Apparently, it became the major diversion of this modest community.

With his growing family and his growing responsibilities, Benjamin built a much larger home, almost a mansion, close to the village center. It was also adjacent to the turnpike that brought visitors and news to this still remote region by stagecoach, and it would serve as his political headquarters. Relishing his reputation as a good host, Ben Pierce converted part of his home into a tavern. Could he possibly be unaware of his wife's drinking problem, or did he simply ascribe it to her generally buoyant spirits?

As he grew, young Frank, genuinely fond of both his parents, managed to appreciate and even take advantage of their differing personalities. As Roy Franklin Nichols writes, "Between his father's strictness and his mother's easygoing ways there was sure to be a chance for the quick witted to escape many of the consequences of boyish disobedience." In what was still essentially a wilderness, Frank had ample opportunity to hunt, fish, skate, and swim, each in its own season.

Benjamin Pierce's focus was on education. Finding the local school somewhat lacking, he sent Frank at the age of twelve to board at the prestigious Hancock Academy in a nearby town. This first sustained separation was not easy on the boy, but he did well in his studies. After further preparation, he was entered in Maine's well-regarded Bowdoin College. One of Franklin Pierce's enduring memories, from the fall of 1820, symbolically wedged between his two contrasting parents in their chaise, was setting out together in a high state of excitement, bound for Bowdoin.

He blossomed there, in both academics and the kind of social life he had not previously experienced. There was drinking at Bowdoin, but apparently he did not indulge excessively there. As his friend and fellow student Nathaniel Hawthorne later observed, "At this early period of life he was distinguished by the same fascination of manner that has since proved so magical in winning him unbounded popularity." Pierce had also, however, become more introspective, impressed by the

Congregational sermons he had heard. He graduated third in his class, delivered an oration at commencement, and went on to study law. A decade later, he married the lovely but very delicate Jane Means Appleton, daughter of a former president of the college.

Admitted to the bar in 1827, only two years later he was elected to serve in the state legislature. During the same period his father was completing his second and final term as governor. It was a heady time. Helped by his father's influence Franklin moved steadily ahead, to the U.S. Congress in 1833 and then to the Senate, a combination of his father's convictions and his mother's undoubted charm. Pierce took a break from active politics, turning down additional opportunities, to open a legal practice in Concord, New Hampshire's state capital. Moreover, his wife never really liked living in Washington.

That he later volunteered to recruit a New England regiment to fight in the Mexican War, however, certainly enhanced his positive visibility. Two of his older brothers had fought in the War of 1812. Under the command of Winfield Scott, whom he would later face for the presidency (Polk was right again), Franklin saw little action but was elevated to the rank of brigadier general. At least one Pierce became a genuine general, returning to a hero's welcome in Concord.

His parents died within four months of each other—Anna Kendrick Pierce on December 7, 1838, at the age of seventy; Benjamin Pierce on April 1, 1839, at the age of eighty-one. Stalemated between four favorites, on their forty-ninth ballot the Democrats in 1852 finally settled on a compromise candidate, Franklin Pierce, a Northerner with Southern sympathies who boasted a spotless record of prior service. Letting others do the actual campaigning, and with Scott hampered by the defection of many former Whigs, Pierce won a substantial majority in the Electoral College.

His presidency would prove as frustrating as Fillmore's had been. Instead of the Compromise of 1850, Pierce's Waterloo was his approval of the even more divisive Kansas-Nebraska Act, leading to "Bleeding Kansas" and a virtual war zone in the Midwest. He had some solid achievements, such as opening Japan to American trade, but there is no possibility he could have been renominated in 1856, even if he had desired it.

Personal tragedy had intruded at the outset. The Pierces had only three children, all sons. One of them died in infancy, a second at the age of four. The third, eleven-year-old Benjamin, affectionately known as "Benny," was killed in a horrific railroad accident a few weeks before his father's inauguration. Jane Pierce went into a state of mourning from which she never entirely recovered. She died on December 2, 1863, in the midst of the Civil War. At his inauguration, which his wife did not attend, Pierce had said rather poignantly, "You have summoned me in my weakness. You must sustain me by your strength." He died in Concord, on October 8, 1869, at the age of sixty-four, and is interred next to his wife and two of his sons. Perhaps, despite all of his gifts and his temperate wife's pleas, he never entirely overcame the demon of drink.

Would it have mattered? Franklin Pierce, endowed with a unique combination of qualities by two seemingly mismatched parents, had such good fortune until the last tragic stage of his life. His parents were blessed not to have to witness it, or his inability to curb the coming conflict.

Elizabeth and James Buchanan Sr.

Did Anne Caroline Coleman take her own life, and if so, why? What we know is that in the summer of 1819, this belle of Lancaster, Pennsylvania, became engaged to a handsome, rising young local attorney named James Buchanan, but that only a few months later, after a quarrel, she broke off the engagement. During a subsequent visit to her sister in Philadelphia, she died mysteriously, and to this day the prevailing view is that it was a suicide. The last doctor to see her suggested that it might have been a unique case of "hysteria producing death" or an overdose of a form of opium.

Had she discovered that Buchanan was having an affair with another woman? Or did his sexual preference lay elsewhere? His uncommonly close relationship with William R. King, vice president under Franklin Pierce, and his intimate correspondence with other men have led many observers to the enduring conclusion that he was a homosexual. Or was it simply his fiancée's emotional fragility after their breakup? Whatever the cause, Anne's family was convinced that somehow James Buchanan was to blame for this tragedy, a view shared by many others. The Colemans would not even permit him to attend her funeral. The despair that had gripped Buchanan was undeniable. He wrote Anne's father, who had viewed him as simply a fortune hunter, a letter that was refused and returned unopened, in which he declared, "She, as well as I, have been much abused. God forgive the authors of it. . . . I feel that happiness has fled from me forever." That would not quite be true, but, for whatever reason, Buchanan never married.

The only place he could find solace that lonely Christmas was at his family hearth in nearby Mercersburg, surrounded by his sisters and his devoutly Presbyterian mother, Elizabeth Speer Buchanan. No other American president has written so extensively about his mother. Late in his life Buchanan concluded, "Under providence I attribute any little distinction which I may have acquired in this world to the blessing which he conferred on me by granting me such a mother."

As Philip Shriver Klein writes, "She had the kind of faith which assumed that whatever happened was an act of the deity intended especially for her instruction and benefit." James also marveled at his mother's curiosity, not only in terms of Scripture, but also imparting the poetry of Milton and Pope to her children. "What she read once, she remembered forever." Buchanan's parents may have also seemed mismatched, but they were more complementary than the Pierces. James's material ambition came from his hard-driving, detail-obsessed father. Any balanced joy in life was maternal.

In this ongoing chronicle of restless, relentless aspiration, few first fathers surpass James Buchanan Sr. His family had lived in Scotland and then County Donegal in Ireland for at least seven generations when Buchanan, in the wake of the American Revolution, glimpsed greater opportunities across the ocean. His uncle, Joshua Russell, had already settled near Gettysburg, Pennsylvania, and was the proprietor of a thriving tavern. James liked the look of this new land of opportunity almost as soon as he set foot in Philadelphia and was greeted by Russell. He liked it even more when he reached central Pennsylvania and encountered comely sixteen-year-old Elizabeth Speer. She kept house for her widower father and her four older brothers on a farm adjacent to Russell's tavern.

It didn't take long for James to discover economic opportunity. He found work some forty miles to the west at a trading post and warehouse at Cove Gap called "The Stony Batter," which sold provisions for wagons and packhorses headed off in all directions. Eventually, after Buchanan managed to purchase the entire operation, it became the mercantile keystone of his future success. Returning to visit Russell in Gettysburg, James rekindled his relationship with Elizabeth Speer. They were married in 1788, when she was twenty-one and he twenty-seven, and moved into the inevitable log cabin back at Stony Batter.

The following year, the couple had their first child, a girl they named Mary. On April 23, 1791, they had their first son, naming him James after his father. Little Mary died later that year, a tragedy sadly not uncommon in eighteenth-century America, but which severely tested Elizabeth's devout faith. However, Klein adds, "It would be an unusual mother who after this experience did not lavish more than the usual care on her surviving child. James Buchanan, from the very first year of his life, occupied a position of special importance in the household." The Buchanans would have eleven children in all, two of whom died in infancy and three more who died much too young, but there were no surviving boys for another fourteen years. Throughout his childhood young James was at the center of a circle of adoring females. He also became the focus of his ever-striving father's hopes for the future.

Supervising both a thriving business and a productive farm, James Buchanan Sr. was forging ahead. Bustling Stony Batter was hardly a healthy or even a safe place to bring up children, resounding, as Klein puts it, "with the turmoil of stamping horses, drunken drovers, and cursing wagoneers," but it was only a way station on his road to respectability. Putting his brother-in-law in charge, by 1794 Buchanan had prospered sufficiently to buy "Dunwoody Farm," a spacious three-hundred-acre estate. Two years later he built and moved his family into a handsome home in the settled town of Mercersburg, which would also serve as the headquarters for his expanding business interests.

A firm Federalist in politics, as were not only Eastern aristocrats but many who had risen through their own efforts, the senior Buchanan was scrupulously honest but hardly noted for idealism or compassion. He had little use for small talk or time for leisure, even if shared with his oldest son. When the two worked together, the father was particularly demanding, expecting more than he would of another's child. From his no-nonsense example, young James inherited not only ambition but an excessive passion for precision in all things, particularly in accounting for every penny. It would be evidenced in his successful legal career, when he announced, "I acknowledge no master but the law," but it would prove to be a fatal flaw in his presidency.

That influence is evident in the "Autobiographical Sketch" that would open Buchanan's self-justifying memoirs of 1866. Unlike with his free-flowing tribute to his mother, here one senses a stretching of objectivity. "My father," James Jr. wrote, "was a man of practical judgment and of great industry and perseverance. He had received a good English education, and had that knowledge of mankind which prevented him from ever being deceived in business. He was a man of great native force and character. He was not only respected, but beloved by everyone who approached him. . . . He was a kind father, a sincere friend, and an honest and religious man." Well, the senior Buchanan had certainly earned respect, but he was not quite "beloved" by everyone, particularly his competitors. His goal for his eldest son was characteristically specific. He would study the law, the ideal preparation to head any enterprise, particularly the flourishing business his father had labored so strenuously to assemble. Prosperity supplemented by prestige was the aim, not politics.

The move to Mercersburg had been a bit traumatic for young James, then only five. Among other things, it meant accepting the structure of a real school and sharing the spotlight with other children.

Nevertheless, at the Old Stone Academy, which would evolve into the renowned Mercersburg Academy, he made the transition rather smoothly, making friends while excelling in his studies. James's academic progress came to the attention of the family's learned Presbyterian minister, Dr. John King. At his suggestion, when James turned sixteen, his father enrolled him at Dickinson College, a well-regarded liberal arts school in nearby Carlisle.

Starting as a junior, James continued to do well, but in the company of forty-one other students he felt even more pressure to court popularity. As he would later recall, "Without much natural tendency to become dissipated . . . I engaged in every sort of extravagance and mischief." Worse, he showed off his intellectual prowess at the expense of some of his professors. They had him expelled for "disorderly conduct," even though he stood at the head of his class academically. It took all of Dr. King's influence, as head of the college's board of trustees, to have him readmitted for his senior year. Denied the coveted first honor at graduation, James was counseled by his father to take the disappointment like a man. "The more you know of mankind," he counseled, "the more you will distrust them. I hope you will have fortitude enough to surmount these things."

His mother was simply heartened by her son's accomplishments. To her, knowledge was its own reward. Throughout his career James would return from time to time simply to talk with her on virtually any subject, never ceasing to marvel at the breadth of her intellectual curiosity. He recalled, "I have often myself, during the vacations at school or college, sat down at the kitchen and whilst she was at the wash tub, entirely by choice, have spent hours pleasantly and instructively conversing with her." From her informal lyceum, she delighted in encouraging all her children's interests and entering "into all their joys and sorrows."

Disappointed but little deterred, James plowed straight ahead, studying law in Lancaster, and was admitted to the bar in 1812. He was already making a reputation for speaking out on public issues when he volunteered to help defend his country in a war he had opposed. During the next decade, Buchanan built a lucrative legal practice. He was elected district attorney for Lancaster County and then as a member of the Pennsylvania State Assembly. His father, although immensely proud of his son's success, would have preferred that he remain in private practice—more rewarding financially and, to his mind, more respectable than politics.

That young James Buchanan had developed a core of support, whatever his course, is evidenced by the effort of his friends in what amounted to almost an intervention, to supplement Buchanan's mother's efforts and bring him out of his melancholia after the death of Anne Coleman. By the following year, 1820, James was elected to the U.S. House of Representatives. He would be reelected five times, eventually changing his party registration from Federalist to Democrat.

His father was spared this defection. On June 11, 1821, he died at the age of sixty in a carriage accident. His son marveled at how his mother accepted the loss of her devoted husband as well as the subsequent deaths of her favorite daughter and two cherished sons, one of whom had been named for George Washington. "She was a woman of great firmness of character," he marveled, "and bore the afflictions of her life with Christian Philosophy." She had hoped he might devote his own talents to a higher purpose as a Presbyterian minister but always maintained an acute interest in his career, just as he never ceased to be inspired by an example he could only hope to emulate.

In 1831 she urged, without success, that her son decline an appointment by President Andrew Jackson to become minister to Russia. She was worldly enough to foresee greater domestic opportunities. Adding a poignant postscript to a letter to him, she asked, "At what time do you intend to pay us that visit, previous to the departure from the country that gave you birth, and I expect to me, the last visit. Do not disappoint me, but certainly come."

On May 14, 1833, at the age of sixty-six, Elizabeth Speer Buchanan died at the home of her son-in-law, appropriately a member of the clergy, in Greensburg, Pennsylvania. Her son, James, about to return from St. Petersburg, had written her, "You may rest assured that I shall . . . lose no time in paying you a visit, when I trust in Heaven that you will still be in the enjoyment of your usual health." She had already peacefully expired before the letter arrived, as James later observed, "in the calm but firm assurance that she was going home to her Father and her God."

Buchanan was later elected to the U.S. Senate, became chairman of its foreign relations committee, and chose to remain in that body rather than accept other positions. He did, however, accept President James K. Polk's offer to serve as his secretary of state, and later an appointment from President Franklin Pierce to become minister to Great Britain. It is interesting that Polk, conceding that Buchanan was undoubtedly able, added that he "sometimes acts like an old maid." The senior James would surely have agreed with a local judge's appraisal of his son: "He was cut out to be a great lawyer, and I think was spoiled by fortune when she made him a statesman."

Historian Paul Boller describes James Buchanan Jr. as "a gentleman of the old school. Distinguished-looking, faultlessly attired, and courtly, he looked, it was said, like a British nobleman of an earlier generation. An eye defect forced him to tilt his head slightly forward and sideways when engaged in conversation, which gave the impression of exceptional courteousness and sensitivity to others." His passion for precision throughout his legal, diplomatic, and political careers was the direct result of his father's early indoctrination. Both James Buchanans kept the most precise records, the younger becoming quite wealthy at least in part because of his thrift. His handsome mansion in Lancaster, called "Wheatland," bears testimony to that.

Buchanan won the presidential election of 1856 as a conservative Democrat on a "Save the Union" premise. He and his running mate, John C. Breckenridge of Kentucky, constituted an authentically balanced ticket. However, their earnest last-ditch effort proved no more successful than had their predecessors'. An ambitious program for national development was compromised by Buchanan's own emphasis on the limits of the law, his "only master." On the one hand, he viewed secession as illegal. On the other, he considered stopping it by the use of federal military force as equally illegal, making him seem a Southern sympathizer. Even after Edwin Stanton warned, "Mr. President, you are sitting on a volcano," Buchanan was unable to initiate any innovative new strategy to stem the upheaval. His reaction to the Fort Sumter crisis alienated both sides. With Lincoln's election, some seven states had already seceded. Buchanan told the somber incoming president on March 4, 1861, "If you are as happy entering the White House as I shall feel on returning to Wheatland, you are a happy man indeed."

It was not quite true. He had never stopped urging compromise, even through an eleventh-hour conference, and retrospectively blamed the war on the intransigence of Northern radicals. Shortly before his death, Buchanan predicted that "history will vindicate me." He had sought justification through his 1866 memoirs, *Mr. Buchanan's Administration on the Eve of the Rebellion*. Despite such efforts, he is still frequently rated in our excessive passion for evaluation, perhaps unfairly, as the worst president in American history.

Buchanan, the only president from Pennsylvania and the only one never to marry, in later years became guardian for many of his orphaned nephews and nieces. His favorite, the charming Harriet Lane, became his official hostess at the White House. To a visiting lady who in 1860 lamented that he had no wife, Buchanan replied, "That, madam, is my misfortune, not my fault." James Buchanan died at Wheatland of respiratory failure on June 1, 1868, at the age of seventy-seven. Of his severe trials as president his firm father would likely have counseled fortitude; his devout mother, in the necessity of ultimately trusting to a higher power.

CHAPTER 6

Elevated by Angels—Nancy, Sarah, and Thomas Lincoln

Nancy and Thomas Lincoln

When Abraham Lincoln proclaimed, "All that I am I owe to my angel mother," which mother was he referring to?—or did he mean both? Nancy, his birth mother, died before he turned ten. Sarah, his stepmother, would be with him until he set out on his own after he turned twenty-one, and they stayed in touch for the rest of his life. Indeed, she would outlive this "best boy I ever saw." Sarah Lincoln was likely the only person Abraham didn't mind addressing him as "Abe," a name he particularly disliked.

Since there have been more books written about Abraham Lincoln than all our other presidents combined, there are even theories about this. But does it really matter that he didn't refer instead to his "angel mothers"? In encouragement and loving care, one seems almost an extension of the other. "Larn (sic) all you can," Nancy Hanks Lincoln had urged her obviously bright son. "What I want to know is in books," he later confirmed to his stepmother, an opportunity enhanced when the widowed Sarah Bush Johnson Lincoln arrived, forming a bond that lasted a lifetime.

Despite the demands of working on his father's succession of farms, somehow Abraham gained a total of about one year's formal education, first at the limited "blab" schools of Kentucky and later at any nearby informal academy in rural Indiana. A quick learner, he managed to pick up rudimentary reading, writing, and math. However episodic, at least it was a foundation his mothers could build on, his light in an otherwise bleak childhood. Both mothers were devout Baptists, Nancy reputedly having said, "I would rather my son would be able to read the Bible than to own a farm."

Although he shared at least the faith of both his wives, Thomas Lincoln couldn't see the point of all this reading and reflecting that took his increasingly sturdy son from necessary farm chores. However, first Nancy and then Sarah were able to induce him to put up with it. It helped that each retained a mutually respectful relationship with Thomas who, after all, was the unquestioned head of their household.

In contrast to his comments about his mothers, there is no record anywhere of Abraham having said or written anything really favorable about his father. He didn't hate Thomas Lincoln. The opposite of love is more often indifference. By the time Abraham turned twenty-one, their lives were simply in separate orbits. Although he would miss his step-mother, Abraham ventured out on his own almost as soon as it was legally possible. He would provide for both of his parents in their later years. Perhaps he even came to appreciate that his father *must* have possessed some attractive personal qualities simply to have gained the affection of two such extraordinary women. When Lincoln mentioned his father at all, it was generally with such wry references as, "My father taught me to work, but he never taught me to love it." The closest he came to outright criticism was to observe that Thomas's brother Mordecai "ran away with all the talents in the family." In fairness, however, as a first son Mordecai also had all the luck. Later Lincoln was more objective, observing, "By the early death of a father, and the very narrow circumstance of his mother . . . [Thomas] was a wandering laboring boy and grew up literally without education. He never did more in the way of writing than bunglingly sign his own name."

In his own way, Thomas Lincoln is very much in the tradition of ambitious, restless first fathers. There was always a more bountiful farm somewhere just over the horizon, taking him from Virginia to Kentucky to Indiana to Illinois. Things had to be better somewhere else—a clearer land title, closer access to water, more fertile soil. In those endless Lincoln biographies, Thomas has been described as everything from improvident to industrious, harsh to humorous, indolent to energetic, "obtuse" to "sagacious." In truth he was all of these things. He was hardly the same man at twenty-eight, when he married Nancy Hanks in Kentucky and set out to expand his holdings, as he was at seventy, when Abraham had to pay to keep his father from losing his land in Illinois. Isn't it possible that Thomas Lincoln, like so many others, was eventually simply worn down by the wilderness?

When asked to supply material for campaign biographies, Abraham Lincoln invariably replied that there was little to write about. "It is a great piece of folly to attempt to make anything about my early life. It can all be condensed into a single sentence and that sentence you will find in Gray's Elegy, 'the short and simple annals of the poor.' That's my life and that's about all you or anyone else can make of it." Earlier Lincoln had said, "I was born on February 12, 1809, in Harlan County, Kentucky. My parents were both born in Virginia, of undistinguished families— second families perhaps I should say. My mother died in my tenth year, was of a family of the name of Hanks."

Such biographers as David Herbert Donald suggest that in Lincoln's mind, beyond the influence of his mother and stepmother, "He was a self-made man, who had little need to care about his family tree." Yet Lincoln did care about it, although only tracing it back to his grandfather, an earlier Abraham. Had he delved further he might have been surprised to find evidence of authentic achievement.

The first Lincoln to emigrate from England was a weaver's apprentice who arrived in the Massachusetts Bay Colony in 1637, settled in Hingham, and ultimately became a prosperous trader and businessman. Later Lincolns improved their circumstances, maintaining flourishing farms in Pennsylvania and Virginia. One particularly wealthy Lincoln was an ironmaster. Most were engaged in public service. A Lincoln in Virginia married the niece of the royal governor. An earlier biographer, Benjamin Thomas, writes, "Without exception Lincoln's forebears proved to be self-reliant, upright men of even comfortable means, who earned the respect of their neighbors. Some Lincolns in collateral lines even earned distinction. . . . In the father, Thomas, there seemed to be a falling off in the general level of Abraham's ancestry."

Donald is more generous to Lincoln's father: "In sum, Abraham Lincoln, instead of being the unique blossom of an otherwise barren family tree, belonged to the seventh American generation of a family with competent means, a reputation for integrity, and a modest record of public service. . . . A closer study of the historical records would have given Abraham Lincoln a different and probably a kinder view of his father Thomas." It also would have confirmed that in his earlier years Thomas had farmed more successfully, owned horses, was in addition a skilled cabinetmaker and carpenter, and enjoyed the esteem of his neighbors to the extent that he served on juries and in his local militia. He was a church member, sober, and not given to crude language—qualities that helped win him both his wives.

Thomas and Abraham Lincoln looked very little alike. The skin of both was rough, the result of so many years in the outdoors. Both had a shock of black hair, although Thomas's was straight, and Abraham's unruly. Abraham, however, was tall and slender, already six-feet-two by the time he was sixteen (eventually he grew to six-feet-four), lanky, raw-boned, with the familiar long face, beardless in youth, but already full of melancholia, and with deep-set eyes. Thomas was short and stocky, round-faced, with a weak chin, a long mouth, and a prominent nose. They also shared some traits, however: both men loved to tell stories, both were given to bouts of depression, and both were immensely strong physically. Had the son been as immersed in farming as the father, they would have worked well together, whatever the outcome. However, as Michael Burlingame puts it, Abraham eventually distanced himself from Thomas Lincoln "physically, socially, culturally, and politically." Abraham insisted that "love is the chain whereby to bind a child to his parents." When Abraham ultimately had his own sons, he was noted as an uncommonly indulgent and involved parent, surely in part a reaction to his own father's perceived shortcomings. Not until his fourth and last son was born did Lincoln name one for his father, but he always called the boy "Tad" rather than "Tom" or "Thomas."

Thomas Herring Lincoln Sr. was born in Virginia on January 6, 1778, the youngest of the three sons of that prior Abraham Lincoln. Their family moved to Kentucky in 1782 after a distant relative, Daniel Boone (who seems to have had a lot of distant relatives), had returned with visions of a "second paradise" of bountiful acreage over the mountains. This elder Abraham Lincoln, like his family before him, had long worked the rich soil of Rockingham County without benefit of slaves. His new holdings near Louisville grew to over 5,500 acres. Of course, there were perils on the frontier. Indians long in the vicinity questioned the legitimacy of any of these land claims, using the only means at their disposal.

In 1786, while Abraham and his sons—Mordecai, Josiah, and Thomas—were planting corn near the adjoining woods, they were ambushed, and Abraham was killed instantly. Mordecai, the oldest son, although only fifteen, kept his head. Sending Josiah to seek help from the settlement a half-mile away, he raced to their cabin and picked up his rifle. An Indian coming out of the forest approached eight-year-old Thomas, who was sitting next to the body of his father. Before he could pick the child up, Mordecai shot the intruder. Young Abraham Lincoln would hear this story repeated so frequently by his father, the surviving Thomas, that it became "the legend more strongly than any others imprinted on my mind and memory."

This violent incident had economic consequences. As soon as he came of age, the one-time hero Mordecai "ran away" with his father's entire estate, leaving his brothers to fend for themselves. Starting as a manual laborer, Tom, that "wandering boy," learned carpentry and cabinetmaking from Joseph Hanks, who had a niece named Nancy. Eventually, demonstrating a high degree of tenacity, Thomas Lincoln earned enough to settle in one spot and bought his first farm, some 238 acres in Hardin County, Kentucky. These were likely his most industrious and least isolated years, when he served on juries and in the militia and was high in the regard of a real community. Donald quotes a typical neighbor who remembered unpretentious, plain Tom Lincoln as conscientious, peaceable, respectable, "quiet and good natured." He was most often described as "honest," a precursor of "Honest Abe."

By his late twenties, Thomas felt secure enough to seek a bride. He was enamored of Sarah Bush, daughter of the local jailer, and ventured into Elizabethtown to seek her hand. When it became clear that she preferred another, Thomas turned his attentions to bright, diligent Nancy Hanks, whom he had also met before. Nancy Hanks was born on February 5, 1784, in Hampshire County, Virginia, part of what is now West Virginia. The consensus of Lincoln's earliest biographers is that she was slender, dark, quiet, and rather pretty. Philip B. Kunhardt describes Nancy as "mild, tender, and intellectually inclined," both cheerful and melancholy, endowing Abraham with something of her own demeanor.

The moment the martyred Abraham Lincoln died and was consigned to "the ages," his deification began, followed almost immediately by worshipful biographies. One of the first of Lincoln's friends to take exception to this excess was his law partner, William Herndon. Not that he sought to denigrate the "most generous, forbearing, and most charitable man I ever knew," but Herndon wanted to portray Lincoln as a believable, flesh-and-blood human being, no less great or humane for the imperfections that are everyone's lot in life. Lincoln's ambition, for example, was "a little engine that knew no rest." Because he imbibed with some frequency and also required considerable assistance in constructing an actual book, *Herndon's Life of Lincoln: The True Story of a Great Life* didn't appear for another twenty-four years.

Lincoln may have been more concerned with his future than with his past, but as Herndon relates it, he was convinced that his mother, Nancy Hanks Lincoln, was illegitimate. Whatever his sources, Lincoln believed she had been born of a union between Nancy's mother, Lucy Hanks, and an unnamed aristocratic Virginia planter. The resulting blood he carried in his veins accounted for qualities that, however outgoing his nature, elevated Lincoln above his backwoods playmates. Such an emphasis on antecedents doesn't sound very much like Lincoln, but in the limitless lore of Lincolniana, little is ever fully resolved. However, we're reasonably certain that Lincoln didn't slay vampires. Starting with his presidential nomination in 1860, at least sixteen notables suggested that Lincoln himself was illegitimate; all such notions were later discounted.

When Thomas Lincoln sought her out, Nancy Hanks was living with one of her sisters, who was married to a man named Sparrow. Trained as a seamstress, Nancy possessed skills any potential husband might find appealing. Unlike most of her neighbors, Nancy could read, although she never learned to write. Carl Sandburg speculates, "Tom Lincoln had seen this particular Nancy Hanks . . . and noticed that she was shrewd, dry, and lonesome." Sandburg concurs that she was reputed to be "intelligent, deeply religious, kindly, and affectionate."

It is not surprising that she accepted Tom Lincoln's proposal. He might not be well educated and was surely more robust than handsome, but she admired his regular habits and his respectful manner. Unlike most of the men she met, he neither cursed nor drank, no small matter in their compact community. Moreover, she probably longed for a home of her own. After Nancy Hanks, twenty-three, and Thomas Lincoln, twenty-eight, were married at the home of a friend, Tom bought a larger farm called "Sinking Spring" and constructed a sturdy little log cabin for his bride. Their first child, Sarah, whom everyone would call "Sally," was born on February 10, 1807.

Two years later, on February 12, 1809, Nancy and Tom had a son. They named him Abraham after his deceased grandfather. The boy would have no memory of Sinking Spring. By the time he was two, the family's exodus had begun. Deciding that these springs might actually be sinking, Thomas moved his family some ten miles away to Knob Creek. Although only a portion of this hilly acreage proved to be tillable, it was more fertile than Sinking Spring, the main crop being corn.

During the five years his family lived there, Tom's spirit had its trials. A third child, a son they named Thomas Herring Lincoln Jr. after his father, died in infancy. Albert Beveridge describes Tom at this stage of his life in the familiar puzzling pattern: "He was improvident, yet in a slow and plodding way industrious. He was good-natured, inoffensive, law abiding, notably honest." Opportunity for Thomas Lincoln was still limited to that idealized truly productive farm, still out there somewhere over the horizon.

His wife, however, even if seemingly silent and sad, encouraged young Abraham to see the limitless opportunities learning could initiate. She read to him not only her Bible but also any other stories she could find. Abraham's only memory of the War of 1812 was of his mother's gentle care of injured soldiers. His earliest memory of his father reflected ominously on Thomas's future problems. Abraham recalled dropping pumpkin seeds behind his father and using a hoe to plant them in the bottomland, only to see all their work washed away by a thunderstorm. Yet records reveal that Thomas was still a relatively successful farmer, celebrated for his good nature and his ability to tell stories—one quality his son did inherit.

Tom's next move, from Kentucky across the Ohio River to Indiana, was based on solid reasoning. Lincoln hated slavery on both moral and practical grounds. In his late thirties, for perhaps the final time he asserted all of his physical strength and residual energy. He and his wife were both "separate Baptists," sharing the joy of their faith but affirming a strict moral code opposed to intoxicants, profanity, gambling, dancing, gossip, and the ultimate immorality of slavery. How could small family farmers like the Lincolns long compete economically with the slave labor of large Kentucky plantations? Adding to this somber prognosis is that Lincoln had experienced difficulty obtaining clear land titles to all three of his Kentucky farms, a familiar theme on the emerging frontier. In the Indiana Territory, from which slavery had been excluded by the Northwest Ordinance, fully surveyed land with guaranteed titles could be purchased directly from the U.S. government.

First, Thomas had to see it for himself. It was quite a trip. The flatboat he had constructed capsized in the Ohio River. Starting over, he finally found the sort of site he sought, "a more inviting lodgment" some sixteen miles from the river, and made his way back to Kentucky to fetch his family. Abraham was then seven. By the end of 1816, the Lincolns were in residence near Little Pigeon Creek in Indiana; and for a time, even in this wilderness, Thomas Lincoln again became a resolute path-finder and farmer. Clearing the land was his first priority, then hacking a rough trail to his property, at first only a rude "half-faced" three-sided shelter of timber and brush, without a finished floor, about fifteen feet square. It was not until the following year that Thomas had time to build the customary log cabin, its logs chinked together by mud. In the winter chill, with at least some heat by the fire and a full enclosure, it must have seemed comparatively comfortable. By spring he had planted corn, wheat, and oats and had acquired some sheep, hogs, and cattle.

Abraham was now old enough to help. He went hunting with his father—the abundant local game was now his family's primary source of sustenance—but he never really enjoyed it. From the age of eight he had his own axe and knew how to use it. He also planted crops, tended live-stock, and generally did whatever he could to help his parents. But even this early in his life he was determined never to be a farmer or simply a splitter of logs when he grew to manhood. Any book in the vicinity was soon in his possession. He was a lively, outwardly friendly child, gan-gling as he outgrew his crude homespun clothing, but he also developed a less obvious remoteness that he would retain all his life. He enjoyed wrestling, telling jokes, and swapping stories with his companions, but somehow he was different from them, and he knew it.

The first of these friends, although ten years older than Abraham, was Dennis Hanks, the nephew of Nancy's aunt and uncle, Elizabeth and Thomas Sparrow, who had come to join the Lincolns in their new home. The two families built a second cabin. Things were improving, and Thomas traveled sixty miles to Vincennes to make payments for adjoining tracts of land. Yet despite everyone's efforts, this venturesome move to Indiana not only finally resulted in failure, it also proved fatal.

In the summer of 1818 a mysterious disease swept through south-western Indiana. It was called "milk sickness," or simply "milk sick," because it was apparently caused by drinking the milk of local cows. The lethal element turned out to be poisonous roots that free-roaming cattle had consumed. There was no cure; and for that matter, the nearest doctor was some thirty-five miles away. First, both of the Sparrows died. Then Nancy Hanks Lincoln contracted the illness. Seven days later, on October 5, 1818, she, too, passed away at the age of thirty-four—a "pioneer sacrifice," as Carl Sandburg put it. Near the end she had called her children to her bedside, telling them to be "good and kind to their father, and to one another, and to all the world." Nine-year-old Abraham helped his father construct a casket, and the grief-stricken children watched him bury their mother next to the Sparrows. A few months later, a visiting preacher said a few words over their graves.

Donald believes that the loss of his mother gave Abraham Lincoln "a sense of isolation" he never entirely overcame. Lincoln was so moved by a return to her gravesite in 1844 that he could only express himself in poetry. It fell to twelve-year-old Sally to try to cook, mend, and clean for the men now in her care, but inevitably their domicile sank into squalor.

Sarah and Thomas Lincoln

In less than a year Tom felt impelled to go back to Kentucky, to Elizabethtown, to seek another wife. His thoughts turned back to Sarah Bush. He understood that she had married a man named Johnson, borne three children, and then been widowed. There may well have been residual affection, but Thomas's proposal was more practical than romantic. They had need of each other. Tom sought a really competent woman to take charge of his household. Sarah needed someone to pay off the debts with which Daniel Johnson had left her, although she was reluctant to bring the subject up. She and Thomas Lincoln were soon married, and they set off for Pigeon Creek with her three young children in tow in an overloaded, borrowed wagon.

Despite her circumstances, Sarah had accumulated possessions that to the Lincolns would seem like the luxuries of a potentate—a solid table and chairs, a walnut bureau, a spinning wheel, feather beds, and matched sets of real cutlery. Most relevant to Abraham was that although Sarah couldn't read, she brought books: a handsome family Bible, *Pilgrim's Progress*, *Robinson Crusoe*, *Sinbad the Sailor*, *Aesop's Fables*, Weems's *Life of Washington*, Grimshaw's *History of the United States*, and such practical guides as *Lessons of Elocution*. When they finally arrived and his father announced, "Here's your new mammy," Abraham simply fell in love with her. Reportedly, he was so starved for affection that he called her "Mama" from the start and hid himself in her ample skirts, hoping it would not be taken as disrespect for her predecessor.

Benjamin Thomas describes Sarah Bush Lincoln as "tall and attractive." Sandburg reconstructs her as "a strong, large-boned, rosy woman with a kindly face and eyes, with a steady voice, steady ways." A granddaughter recalled her as "a very tall woman, straight as an Indian, fair complexion, and when I first remember her, very handsome, sprightly talking, and proud. Wore her hair curled till gray . . . kind hearted and very charitable and also very industrious." If Sarah did not quite save Abraham's life, it is not too much to say that she made it possible. His already evident determination to make something of himself, encouraged by his mother, was even more motivated by the extended tenure of his stepmother. In the words of Ida Tarbell, "These two women, both of unusual earnestness and sweetness of spirit were one or the other at his side throughout his youth and young manhood."

Sarah's first task was simply to clean the place up. The change in living conditions was so pronounced that some thirty-five years later Lincoln still marveled at it. Somehow Sarah accommodated eight people in a rough-hewn cabin that had already been cramped with four. All the children were assigned tasks in cleaning and reconfiguring before they were permitted to go outdoors to help their father. As Benjamin Thomas writes, "despite the overcrowding, the conditions of the Lincolns became better as the kindly, hardworking stepmother brought order out of chaos and took the motherless children to her heart."

Abraham profited most of all. In only his few months of informal schooling, he had learned to read well enough that as the community expanded, he composed all the letters for his illiterate neighbors and read to them any that they received. Reversing his relationship with Nancy, now it was he who read to a receptive Sarah from all the books she had brought. He also learned to cipher, and until his stepmother could find paper or slate, did it on boards she obtained. Abraham was becoming as renowned locally for his learning as for his storytelling and athletic feats. Although he did not attend the local Baptist church with his parents, he was thoroughly acquainted with both the Old and New Testaments.

However, the better living conditions Sarah had made possible had somehow to be sustained. With four more additional mouths to feed and no improvement in his own financial resources, Thomas Lincoln needed more help than ever. His demonstrably strong son was becoming more reluctant to provide it. At times during the 1820s, Thomas insisted that Abraham put his books aside and work from sunup to sundown on the farm. He would also rent him out to neighboring farmers. Until he was twenty-one, Abraham was obliged to turn every penny he made over to his father.

Although Abraham worked many odd jobs during his teens— woodcutting and rail-splitting as well as planting and harvesting—he learned far more of the wider world as a deckhand working on a ferry-boat on the Ohio River and particularly as a crewmember on two adventurous trips on flatboats all the way down the Mississippi to New Orleans, taking provisions from a local merchant to the Crescent City. The first trip was a revelation. At his destination Lincoln saw for the first time the brutal reality of slavery, a vivid memory he would carry with him into his public life. The death of his sister, Sally, in childbirth only deepened his melancholy and separation from his roots.

In 1830, having moved three times since his first marriage and still no better off financially than he had been at the outset, Thomas Lincoln, this "roving, melancholy spirit," set out for the brighter prospects of Illinois. He sold most of what he and Sarah possessed and moved to an area near Decatur. In the last twenty years of his life Thomas would move three more times within the state, finally settling on a modest homestead in Coles County called "Goosenest Prairie." His family and goods were transported on ox-drawn wagons. Perhaps symbolically, Thomas gave Abraham the ox whip and told him to lead the procession. It was too late. By then, having passed his twenty-first birthday, he would stay with them less than a year. After taking that second trip to New Orleans, his wages now his own, he set out to his new life in New Salem, Illinois, working a variety of jobs before settling into his legal and political careers. As he ultimately prospered, he left instructions with his stepbrother John Johnson that neither parent should ever be in want. In miles, New Salem and then Springfield were not all that far from Coles County, but in independence they were a world apart.

The familiar saga of Abraham Lincoln's subsequent decades of tragedy and triumph unfolded: an amiable but unsuccessful shopkeeper; his love for Ann Rutledge and almost suicidal depression after her death; his success as a lawyer; his tumultuous marriage to the ambitious Mary Todd, whom he had first left at the altar; only one of their four sons surviving to manhood; the ultimate political career from Whig to Republican, culminating in a narrow victory in the four-sided presidential election of 1860 amidst unprecedented crisis. All have been documented beyond any other career in American history. Looking at the later photographs of Lincoln, it is hard to believe that he was only fifty-six when he died of an assassin's bullet on April 15, 1865.

During his wide legal circuits of the state, Lincoln visited his parents whenever he could. His greatest concern was that his largesse was being administered by his unreliable stepbrother, John Johnson. As the years went by, his entreaties to Abraham for more assistance became increasingly urgent, particularly stressing Thomas Lincoln's declining health. Now settled in Springfield and increasingly busy with his flourishing law practice and his own family, Abraham responded with more than money. It was a three-day trip each way to his parents' home. After a typical letter from Johnson in the spring of 1849, insisting that Thomas was sinking fast, and "He Craves to See you all the Time," Lincoln delayed an important trip to Washington and made a special visit to Coles County. His father was indeed ill, but he soon recovered. When similar letters continued throughout 1850, Lincoln replied in writing to his stepbrother, "I sincerely hope that Father may yet recover his health; but at all events tell him to call upon and confide in our great, and good, and merciful Maker."

He never saw his father again. Thomas Herring Lincoln Sr. died on January 17, 1851, at the age of seventy-three. Nine years later two railroad ties were presented at the Republican National Convention that nominated his son for president, purportedly "made by Thomas Hanks and Abraham Lincoln, whose father was the first pioneer of Macon County." Shortly before his own death in 1865, Lincoln expressed the desire to place a marker on his father's gravesite. It was finally done in 1880 by Robert Todd Lincoln, Abraham's only surviving son.

Particularly after the death of his father, Lincoln became even more solicitous of his stepmother's welfare. Lincoln finally told John Johnson plainly that "Work is the only cure for your case." One way or another, Abraham made certain that his stepmother was provided for. She never experienced the want, real or imagined, of Mary Ball Washington.

Shortly before embarking by train for Washington in 1860, under Pinkerton protection, Abraham Lincoln paid a long and emotional visit to his seventy-three-year-old stepmother. It would be his last. She was convinced that something terrible would happen to him. Even though he had campaigned in a spirit of moderation and conciliation, secession of the Southern states was now certain, and threats were already being voiced to his personal peril. Abraham replied, in terms of her own faith, that if she continued to trust in the Lord, somehow all would be well. Then, for the final time, he embraced this woman who had almost seamlessly supplanted his mother as first in his affections.

The nature of Lincoln's own religious faith, like so much else in his life, remains a subject of speculation. Although he never joined a church, Biblical exhortations formed the foundation of his most enduring public utterances, virtually sermons to the nation. "I know there is a God," he declared on the eve of the coming conflict, "If He has a plan for me . . . I believe I am ready. I am nothing, but truth is everything." Allen C. Guelzo considers, however, that this "redeemer president" fell short of coming the whole way to such absolute belief, sometimes wishing in his fatalism that he could be more personally devout. He must nonetheless have been sustained by his stepmother's framework of faith to endure the nation's greatest trial.

Sarah Bush Johnson Lincoln died on April 12, 1869, at the age of eighty, four years after Abraham's tragic end had fulfilled her fears. She had reflected with an appealing candor on her relationship with "Abe," her favored stepson, telling a writer, "Abe was a dutiful son to me always, and we took particular care not to disturb him. . . . Abe was a good boy and I can say what scarcely one woman—a mother—can say in a thousand: Abe never gave me a cross word in all my life. His mind and mine—what little I had—seemed to run together. He was here after he was elected president. . . . I think he loved me truly. . . . I had a son, John, who was raised with Abe. Both were good boys, but I must say, both now being dead, that Abe was the best boy I ever saw, or hope to see."

CHAPTER 7

Ambition's Sterner Stuff—Johnsons to Arthurs

Mary and Jacob Johnson

Was there ever a less likely hero than Jacob Johnson? He saved two men from drowning. Because one of them was the publisher of the local newspaper, Jacob's posthumous reward was an obituary of uncommon length for one of his humble station in life. Jacob was praised for his "honesty, sobriety, industry, and his humane, friendly disposition." His hard-pressed widow, Polly, had little time to dwell on such qualities— she couldn't read, in any case—or even the luxury to mourn. She had two sons to care for and a paucity of resources.

Energy and ambition are not necessarily synonymous. It is not difficult to determine which American presidents came from backgrounds of affluence. However, with so many real and reconstructed log cabins dotting the electoral landscape, which chief executive came from a background of the direst deprivation? Andrew Johnson was surely the most self-made man who ever rose to the presidency. When he was selected to run with Abraham Lincoln on a ticket of national unity in the extraordinary wartime election of 1864, much was made of the similarity of their humble origins—"the railsplitter and the tailor." Born six weeks apart, both overcame hardships in their rise to prominence. In all, Lincoln had perhaps one year of formal schooling, but, as Lately Thomas points out, "Johnson did not attend school a single day in his life." Of his extraordinary career, a childhood friend remarked, "I reckon he started underground."

Andrew Johnson was the son of a porter and a chambermaid. However, Andrew's father, Jacob Johnson, never lacked for energy. He had emigrated from England around the end of the eighteenth century with no particular goal in mind. Wandering around the countryside, doing all sorts of odd jobs to support himself, Jacob finally came to Raleigh, North Carolina, and found it to his liking. The capital of a state only recently admitted to the Union, Raleigh was bustling with lawyers and legislators. There was already an acquisitive new aristocracy of sorts in place, with the means to employ anyone willing to work. That suited Jacob, who would try almost anything. He quickly established a reputation for availability, reliability, and honesty, serving as everything from county constable and sexton to porter of the state bank. He even tolled the town bell, announcing major events in the community. Much of his time was spent helping out at Cassio's, the lively new inn and tavern that had opened opposite the bank.

There he met and fell in love with an attractive eighteen-year-old chambermaid named Mary McDonough, known to all as "Polly." As industrious as Jacob Johnson, Polly was also a skilled seamstress. In 1801 they wed, signified by making their marks in the town registry. The couple then moved into a small log house adjacent to the inn, where Polly took in washing and mending to supplement her husband's modest income. Their first child, a girl, died in infancy. Their second survived, a sturdy fair-haired boy born in 1803, whom they called William.

It would be six years before the arrival of their next child, fated to be their last. Polly Johnson gave birth on December 29, 1808, to another boy. Sounds of fiddles accompanied the child's first cries. Thomas writes, "This boy was as dark as the other was light, and he too gave promise of being strong and hearty." News of the birth spread to the revelers in the adjacent tavern, some of whom were from Tennessee. Invading the Johnson cabin, they reportedly insisted that the boy be named for Andrew Jackson.

On one of the coldest days of December 1811, three prominent local citizens planned a fishing outing and hired Jacob to accompany them, probably to clean their catch and bring along food and drink. Some of these spirits must have been consumed prematurely, because one of the men, Colonel Thomas Henderson, owner of the *Raleigh Star*, engaged in a bit of horseplay, rocking the fishing skiff he had boarded with his two friends. All three fell overboard. One made it back to the shore. A second, who could not swim, frantically clung to Henderson, taking them both down to the icy depths. Jacob promptly dived in, and with immense effort managed to pull both men back to safety. He contracted pneumonia but subsequently appeared to be making a recovery. However, when he was at his post two months later, on February 4, 1812, ringing the town bell for another's funeral, Jacob Johnson collapsed and died. He was only thirty-three. There would be no marker on the grave of this "humane, friendly" man for fifty-five years, until the unlikely presidency of his younger son.

Polly's friends contributed whatever aid they could, but it hardly relieved the financial burdens of even so energetic a widow. The adult Andrew Johnson recalled grappling "with the gaunt and haggard monster called hunger." Polly finally settled for the only solution really available to one in her circumstances—she married again. Had it been to someone like Jacob there might at least have been some hope of educating her sons. Instead, she had the misfortune to wed shiftless Turner Dougherty (or Doughtry), who apparently possessed neither skills nor the inclination to use them.

To relieve some of the pressure, both sons were apprenticed to a Raleigh tailor to learn a trade. When Andrew Johnson finally established his own tailoring shop in Tennessee, he still wasn't quite on his own. His mother and stepfather were by then in such dire financial straits that at the age of seventeen he was their sole means of support. His older brother, William, had vanished to Texas. He cared for his mother and stepfather for the rest of their lives, eventually settling them on a farm.

Yet Johnson went on to one of the most improbable and controversial careers in American history. Of course, his mother would have liked to help. Unfortunately, her first husband was a good man who died too soon; her second, from all accounts, a wastrel who lingered too long. At least she was able to witness a measure of Andrew's remarkable political success, his election to Congress and as governor of Tennessee, before she passed away on February 13, 1856, at the age of seventy-two. Somehow Andrew had learned to read such basic texts as the Bible but was essentially taught to both read and write by the remarkable woman he met and wed in Tennessee, Eliza McCardle Johnson, with whom he would have five children.

Johnson's mother was still alive when, during an especially bitter reelection campaign for Congress, he was opposed by William "Parson" Brownlow, whose rhetorical restraint little reflected his nickname. How was it possible, Brownlow queried, for someone of such undeniable consequence as Andrew Johnson to have been the son of an "illiterate loafer" like Jacob Johnson? His birth must have been illegitimate. Overcoming his ire, Johnson gathered the legal affidavits regarding his birth and detailed them in an open letter to the voters, characterizing Brownlow as a "hyena," "vandal," "devil," "coward," and other less moderate epithets. Johnson won. His combative temperament did little to diminish controversy during his tumultuous political career, although the issues he faced after the Civil War would have tried the talents of a Lincoln.

Yet a decade after being thrust into his sole presidential term, dominated by Reconstruction and his impeachment trial, Johnson made an impressive political comeback. He was reelected to the Senate from Tennessee, although he served for only one session. To Johnson, reuniting the nation through reintegrating its Southern states transcended any other considerations. Claude Bowers reflects that Andrew Johnson's "was a complex nature . . . honest, inflexible, tender, able, forceful, and tactless. . . . It was fortunate for the Republic that he had two passions—the Constitution and the Union."

Immaculately attired in clothes of his own cut, Johnson was anything but embarrassed by his origins. Once, on the floor of the Senate, he reminded a colleague, "Sir, I do not forget that I am a mechanic, neither do I forget that Adam was a tailor . . . or that our Savior was the son of a carpenter." Johnson himself was the son of a man of many humble vocations, more energetic than ambitious but in the end also a hero.

Andrew Johnson died at the home of one of his daughters on July 31, 1875, at the age of sixty-six. At his request, his body was wrapped in an American flag and a copy of the Constitution placed under his head.

Hannah and Jesse Grant

Young Ulysses Grant couldn't bear to see bloodshed. He had a more natural affinity with animals, particularly horses, than with people. The notable exception was his equally understated mother, Hannah Simpson Grant, with whom he had a sort of silent communion, a relationship too deep for words. He particularly hated being around his father's tannery. All this mystified garrulous Jesse Root Grant. How could his oldest son, "my Ulyss," the favorite of his six children, be so utterly unlike him? And so Jesse made the decision that would change everything. Without it there would never have been a general, let alone a president, named Ulysses S. Grant.

At the outset of his memoirs, Grant observed, "My family is American, and has been for generations, in all its branches, direct and collateral." Matthew and Priscilla Grant, from Dorsetshire in England, arrived in Plymouth, in the Massachusetts Bay Colony, on the *John and Mary* in 1630, only ten years after the *Mayflower*. By the time of the Revolution, the Grants were established as a prosperous farm family throughout Connecticut, active in community affairs.

Something went wrong with the advent of "Captain" Noah Grant, Jesse's father, who was born in 1748. His first wife bore him two sons before she died. A cobbler and a land speculator as well as a farmer, but addicted to strong spirits, Noah managed to lose all of his inheritance and set out on foot to find a fresh start to the west, in Pennsylvania. He began to trade in animal skins, a much-needed frontier commodity, and married a young widow named Rachel Kelley, who bore him seven children. The fourth, Jesse Root Grant, was born on January 23, 1794. After Rachel's death in 1804, restless Noah Grant dispersed his family. Jesse, only ten, had the good fortune to be sent to work on the farm of Ohio Supreme Court Judge George Tod. Taking a liking to the boy, Tod taught Jesse to read and sent him to the local school. At the Tod residence, Jesse glimpsed the components of a new life, laid out for him not only in its comparative opulence, with china, silverware, fine furniture, and all the books in Tod's library, but also in a close-knit family. Encouraged by Tod, Jesse, at sixteen, devised a plan for his own life, the foundation of which was to be as unlike the father who had abandoned him as possible.

But what calling should he pursue? He only knew about farming and selling animal skins. There was nothing particularly appealing about this bloody business of working with hides, but leather in all its forms was absolutely essential to western expansion. It had about it the odor of wealth—and on the frontier, wealth, whatever its source, led to social acceptance. Managing to avoid service in the War of 1812, Jesse thoroughly learned the business until he finally opened his own tanning yard in Point Pleasant, Ohio.

The plan for his life was set: to be financially secure by twenty-five, to marry well and build a fine home, to improve his education and become a community leader, to raise a loving family in comfortable circumstances, and then to retire by sixty. Only an attack of malaria set him back a year. And so he was twenty-six when he met Hannah Simpson.

On a business trip nearby, brash young Grant swept into a household that seemed ideally suited to hasten his ambitions. It harbored a daughter nearing twenty-three, on the verge of spinsterhood, named Hannah Simpson. An unpretentious country girl, Hannah was described in later years by Dwight and Nancy Anderson as a "well-groomed, smallish woman with an open face and smooth, dark hair" and by Jean Edward Smith as "slim, above medium height, handsome . . . serious, steadfast, and supremely reserved." Jesse could find little fault with neat Hannah's seeming reticence. He could talk enough for both of them.

Jesse was also impressed by the attractive stability he saw in her family. Jesse Grant was hardly handsome himself, with a long face and his sandy brown hair slicked to one side. Later he would grow chin-whiskers and sideburns, in the fashion of the Pennsylvania Dutch, and read with the small, wire-rimmed spectacles Hannah also favored. But he had a keen look in his blue eyes, a healthy glow, an energetic manner, and a sturdy frame almost six feet in height. Jesse's aggressiveness failed to put off Hannah's father, John Simpson. He saw instead the young man's yearning for knowledge and his obvious ambition.

The Simpsons, devout Scotch Presbyterians, had come to Philadelphia in 1762, established a fertile farm in Berks County, fought in the Revolutionary War, and like so many others moved further west after the War of 1812, where they prospered. They were a loving, close-knit family. Hannah's mother had died when she was three, but her stepmother, Rebecca, utterly devoted to her, insisted she attend the local school while they were still in Pennsylvania. After moving to Ohio, the Simpsons had retained their propriety, piety, and love of learning.

On July 24, 1821, Hannah and Jesse were married, and they moved to the small frame house he had built at Point Pleasant. It represented only a way station on his road to respectability. Here, ten months later, on April 22, 1822, their first child was born, a large, healthy son weighing almost eleven pounds. For six weeks he had no name. To Jesse, his first son merited something special. Hannah's pious father was partial to Hiram, the Phoenician king from the Old Testament who helped King Solomon build his temple. Hannah's mother admired the ancient Greek hero Ulysses. That was fine with Jesse Grant, affirming that he was also acquainted with both religious history and mythology. So the rather unique name Hiram Ulysses Grant was settled on. His strong son, "my Ulyss," Jesse would boast, "is a most beautiful child." Geoffrey Perret writes, "With his russet hair, blue eyes, and pink complexion, Ulysses Grant looked in childhood like a glowing miniature of his robust energetic father."

By the time the boy was eighteen months old, Jesse moved his family to a larger brick home, a tangible symbol of his status, in Georgetown, Ohio, the new county seat, on the White Oak River. The town was surrounded by a hardwood forest of oak trees, the prime source of tanbark. As McFeely writes, "In one way or another, Jesse Grant was always struggling to establish himself." He wrote letters to newspapers on every conceivable subject, particularly in favor of abolition. His own treasured library grew. He became master of the local Masonic lodge and for one term was even elected mayor of Georgetown.

He and Hannah had two more boys and three girls, each blessed with a more normal name: Simpson, Clara, Jennie, Orvil, and Mary. But to Jesse, his first-born son remained special. Only, as he grew, Ulysses didn't feel all that heroic. Despite her unpretentiousness, Hannah dressed him in rather a fastidious fashion, very different from other boys in what was still the American frontier. Nor did he look very robust. Ulysses was undersized for his age, given to colds and other ailments, and as a teenager he stood only five-foot-one and weighed only 115 pounds. He would grow sturdier and stronger but would never rise to the height of his father. Yet apparently other children never made him the object of ridicule. Jesse later remarked, "He never had a personal controversy with man or boy in his life."

Something about young Ulysses seemed almost intimidating. He said little but appeared to be taking everything in, his steady gaze much like his mother's. Jesse tried to make sense of it all, noting that Ulysses "rarely ever laughs, never sheds a tear or becomes excited . . . never says a profane word or indulges in jokes." Similarly, the Andersons write that Hannah "seldom smiled and spoke only when she had to. . . . No one played cards in Hannah Grant's house and no one danced or played music there either." If the somber setting depressed Jesse, there is no record of it. After all, hadn't he longed for a home life of serenity and security? Indeed, Jesse wrote of Hannah, "Her steadfastness, firmness, and strength of character have been the stay of the family through life."

Hannah's form of child-rearing, however, was the talk of Georgetown. Even when Ulysses was an infant, she let him crawl without supervision between the feet of horses tethered outside the tannery. God will provide. Despite the lack of parental direction, all the children were well behaved, and after school each of them worked hard to help their parents. Ulysses did everything for his father's business that involved horses and avoided everything else. Eventually, his sisters made good marriages and his brothers each entered the business with their father, never an option for Ulysses.

Although seeming to prefer the company of adults and solitary pursuits, Ulysses entered into games with his classmates and enjoying fishing but never hunting. His parents provided him with the best education possible in the region, including Marysville Academy in Kentucky. He proved to be a dutiful if not exceptional student, although he dreaded speaking in public. What he most enjoyed was to drive his neighbors on their trips out of town, in a coach with his own horses. Precisely where, his perplexed father wondered, was Ulysses himself heading?

That Ulysses was scrupulously honest and truthful reflected the way he'd been raised. But how, Jesse pondered, had this favored son inherited so little of his father's instinctive shrewdness? In one notable instance, Jesse had sent Ulysses to buy a colt, instructing him to offer twenty-two and a half dollars but adding that if necessary he could go as high as twenty-five. Ulysses instead revealed everything to the seller at the outset and of course paid the higher price. By now his father knew there was no possibility that Ulysses would join him in expanding the tannery. How suitable would he be for any potential business?

Jesse Grant made the decision that would resonate for a lifetime. He approached his local congressman, with whom he had become acquainted, and sought an appointment for his son to enter the United States Military Academy at West Point. His goal was not so much a military career for Ulysses as to direct his unfocused son toward a productive future of some sort. When Jesse told his startled son, the boy blurted out, "But I won't go!" In a tone of unusual assertiveness, his father replied, "I think you will go," and then calmly outlined all the potential advantages, most of all the opportunity to make something of himself.

McFeely observes how this represented the growing ambivalence between the two. He writes, "Ulysses spent his life alternately repudiating Jesse Grant's bleak world and trying to prove himself worthy of it." His father's attitude would prove equally cyclical, excessive praise alternating with perplexed disappointment. The matter settled, Ulysses's uncertainty mingled with undeniable excitement. For one thing, he had never traveled so far from home. In his haste, the local congressman had submitted his appointment in the name of "Ulysses S. Grant," assuming that his middle name must be Simpson, for his mother's family. So it would remain. The neighbors gave Ulysses a tearful sendoff, but the farewells at home were predictably less emotional. "They don't cry at our house," Ulysses explained.

He did better than anyone expected at the academy, including himself. Moreover, he grew physically, both taller (to five-foot-eight) and broader, as well as in self-confidence. Yet his first visit home elicited little more overt excitement from his parents than had his departure. His father, perhaps finally conditioned to domestic restraint, initially simply asked, "How are you, son?" His mother noted that he seemed to be standing much straighter.

Yet Ulysses's letters home from West Point to his mother are surprisingly tender, the only tangible evidence of the depth of his feelings for her. "I seem alone in the world without my mother. . . . I cannot tell you how much I miss you. I was so often alone with you, and you so frequently spoke to me in private, that the solitude of my situation here . . . is all the more striking. It reminds me the more forcibly of home, and most of all, dear Mother, of you. . . . Your kindly instructions and admonitions are ever present with me."

His close friendship with his senior class roommate, Frederick Dent of St. Louis, was one of a number he formed with classmates. Grant was commissioned a second lieutenant in the infantry, not quite the glamorous cavalry appointment he had coveted, but his first posting, and Dent's, at Jefferson Barracks in Missouri, carried an unexpected bonus. Grant met Dent's sister, Julia, and fell in love.

Seventeen-year-old Julia Boggs Dent was reputedly rather plain, suffering in comparison with her graceful, aristocratic mother, but Julia had two qualities that were immediately appealing to Ulysses S. Grant. She, too, loved to ride, and her sociable nature brought the lonely, still rather shy young lieutenant out of his shell. The Dents lived in a Missouri imitation of a Southern plantation. Its proprietor, self-styled "Colonel" Frederick Dent the elder, was a boorish, slave-owning businessman turned country squire, whose fortunes fluctuated more than his limited energies. He was as opinionated as Jesse Grant—but of entirely different convictions. It had little impact on Ulysses or Julia. She had sensed a kind of inner resolve in her sandy-haired suitor and even extravagantly praised her future mother-in-law as "like a rose in the sun."

However, Julia and Ulysses did not marry until August 1848, over five years after they had met. Grant's regiment was sent to Louisiana, as tensions with Mexico escalated, and then to Texas. Grant opposed the Mexican War, but, as he later put it, "With a soldier the flag is paramount." Lieutenant Grant's regiment was awarded ten battle honors, and his personal heroism and cool leadership were much praised. When he and Julia were finally able to wed, all his groomsmen would serve as future officers of the Confederacy, a position also urged on him by his father-in-law.

Despite the vast new territory to be defended, the size of the army was reduced, and Grant's new postings were disappointing. He was sent to Detroit; to Sackets Harbor, New York; and then back to Michigan to be, of all things, a quartermaster. Julia loyally accompanied him, but in the fall of 1849 she became pregnant and returned home to have the first of their four children. A boy, he was named Frederick Dent Grant, after Julia's father. One can imagine Jesse's reaction. It was at about this time that, bored and lonely, Ulysses turned to the solace of alcohol. His drinking became so excessive that he joined the Sons of Temperance to try to overcome a potential addiction.

Pregnant with a second son, who would be named Ulysses Jr., Julia couldn't accompany her husband as he moved from one dismal assignment to another. By then, under a commander he particularly disliked, Grant wrote Julia, "How forsaken I feel here." He simply hadn't the means to bring his family to be with him. In 1854 he was finally commissioned a permanent captain. After sending in his acceptance, assured of the rank, Ulysses dispatched a second letter, resigning from the United States Army.

In Covington, Kentucky, where he had moved, Jesse Grant was thunderstruck. True, West Point had not been intended solely to lead to a permanent military career, but it seemed to suit his son. Jesse wrote to his local congressman to intervene, and then, with an irony that could only be appreciated in future years, wrote directly to the secretary of war, Jefferson Davis himself. In Jesse's view, Ulysses, after "spending so many years in the servic (sic) . . . would be poorly equipped for the pursuit of private life." Davis replied that a resignation, once tendered, could not be reconsidered. Ulysses arrived home, dejected and penniless but anxious to make a fresh start with his family. The month he returned, Julia became pregnant with their third child, Nellie, their only girl.

In 1854 Jesse Root Grant turned sixty, the age he had settled on for his retirement so many years earlier. By any measure he was wealthy, and his children were well settled—all but Ulysses. In an awkward meeting with his oldest son, Jesse offered him a job in his store in Galena, Illinois, initially without his family. Ulysses indignantly refused, and instead he decided to go into farming. Julia's father had given her a modest farm as a wedding gift. To Jesse's credit, he put up most of the money needed to buy stock and build a house. At first the farm, which Ulysses called "Hardscrabble," seemed to prosper. Ulysses wrote his father around the end of 1856, "Every day I like farming better." Only a few months later, however, the Depression of 1857 demolished his dreams. In 1858 the couple's fourth and last child was born, finally (and thankfully) another Jesse. By the end of the year, dispirited and ailing, Ulysses gave up farming for good.

Perhaps Julia's helpful performance in the ill-fated enterprise had impressed Jesse. He renewed his offer to employ Ulysses at Galena, this time with his entire family in residence. It was the summer of 1860. Ulysses was not only to be a clerk at the store but also a buyer of hides, which must have struck him as a supreme irony, and would eventually become a partner in the business. Ulysses made an honest effort, but his heart was never in it.

In the presidential election of 1860 he voted for Stephen A. Douglas, one of the two Democratic candidates. The party's suicidal divisiveness helped assure the election of Republican Abraham Lincoln, the enthusiastic choice of Jesse Grant. His son understood what it meant. "The South will fight," he calmly predicted, and wrote his father, suggesting he had best leave the slaveholding state of Kentucky. When Ulysses's prediction came true, as the only man in Galena who had actually commanded troops, he declined an offer to lead a regiment of local militia—although he trained them—and then sought a command in the regular army. His feelings conflicted, he might now validate his worth, but he had little enthusiasm for the carnage he knew was coming. Grant finally obtained command of a notoriously undisciplined regiment of volunteers from Ohio and was named a colonel.

His father no longer controlled his future but never gave up trying. For the last twelve years of Jesse's life, the positions of father and son were reversed. Now it would not be Jesse urging Ulysses to become more ambitious but Ulysses remonstrating with his father to please exercise some restraint in his unsolicited outbursts. One acquaintance remarked that Grant "could remain silent in several languages." His father couldn't remain silent in any.

As Grant's role in the Union army escalated, rumors circulated that perhaps a military leader should oppose embattled Abraham Lincoln in the presidential election of 1864. Grant denied any such ambition, writing his father, "Nothing personal could ever induce me to accept a political office." His victories, however, helped assure Lincoln's triumph over politically minded General George B. McClellan. Now a commanding general himself, Grant accepted Robert E. Lee's surrender at Appomattox Court House.

Just as victory was finally at hand, an assassin's bullet denied the nation Lincoln's leadership. Named Secretary of War in the transitional administration of Andrew Johnson, Grant tried to stay above the partisan turmoil. Despite the fearsome toll of casualties under his command, Grant had been anointed the foremost of national heroes. Having become a nominal Republican during the war, he seemed to many Americans a logical candidate for president in 1868, the personification of restored national unity. A steady stream of prominent visitors asked him to permit his name to be placed in nomination at the Republican national convention in Chicago. He repeated to Julia that he harbored no such ambition, but were he nominated under these circumstances, he could hardly refuse. Grant's personal platform was no more specific than "Let us have peace."

His father, devoid of doubt, was already campaigning. He tirelessly planted "inside accounts" in major newspapers, bearing such titles as "The Early Life of General Grant by His Father." When the patriotic procession opening the Republican convention was led in by one-legged General Dan Sickles, there was Jesse Root Grant, seated prominently among the dignitaries on the stage waiting to welcome the delegates. Grant was nominated on the first ballot. The election, against Democrat Horatio Seymour, was surprisingly close, at least in the popular vote. Grant's reelection in 1872 was by a wider margin.

Despite his good intentions, Grant was not among the more successful of American presidents. The scandals that plagued his two terms, however, failed to diminish his personal popularity. A subsequent tour around the world was a triumph. But the failure of Grant and Ward, a New York brokerage firm to which he lent his name but paid too little heed, ruined thousands, including the demolition of Grant's own savings. Perhaps those earlier conclusions of Jesse Grant that his son simply had no head for business and too trusting a nature had been on the mark after all.

Jesse had attended both of his son's presidential inaugurations and came, invited or not, for extended stays several times a year at the White House, always avoiding Colonel Dent, who had virtually taken up residence there. As McFeely writes, publicity-minded Jesse could always be counted on "to the delight of reporters" and the embarrassment of his son "for outlandish comments" about personalities and policies. He even managed to be appointed to his own public office, postmaster of Covington.

At the inauguration of 1873, Jesse Root Grant slipped on some ice and fell. He died in Covington three months later, on June 29, 1873, at the age of seventy-nine. The fall had only weakened the tough old tanner. The real cause of death was cancer. When he heard the news, Ulysses was inconsolable. Perret writes that Grant "was so prostrated by grief he couldn't utter a word in reply" to other mourners who tried to comfort him. Exploring a more complex web of emotions, McFeely notes, "We can only speculate about the sense of relief, mingled with guilt that Grant must have felt at being at last not beholden to such a father." When Ulysses became a major general, the ambivalence was still evident. He asked of his wife, "Is father yet afraid that I will not be able to sustain myself?"

By contrast, there was only undiluted grief when Hannah Simpson Grant died a decade later, on May 11, 1883, at the age of eighty-four, at a daughter's home in Mt. Vernon, New York. She never visited the White House or attended either of her son's presidential inaugurations. President Grant would surely have welcomed her warmly, but she may have felt a visit would have only added an unnecessary burden to those he already carried. She knew her place in his heart. In her stoical way, she had supplied the inner strength that enabled her oldest son to transcend the triumphs and tragedies of this world. It was from personal experience that General Grant had concluded, "How much American soldiers are indebted to good American mothers! When they go to the front, what prayers go with them!"

Two years later, as he was dying of inoperable throat cancer, Ulysses S. Grant's final act of quiet heroism was a race against time. At the urging of Mark Twain, he completed his memoirs, two volumes still viewed as among the most informative ever written. As he sat bundled up on his front porch, working away, occasionally groups of veterans would march past in silent tribute. They viewed the investment debacle as his misfortune, due to the deviousness of others. Hiram Ulysses Grant died on July 23, 1885, at the age of sixty-three, four days after completing his manuscript. His memoirs would sell over 300,000 copies, rescuing his wife and family from financial ruin.

As he grew older, Grant reflected fondly on his years at West Point. "If a man graduates from here," he wrote a cousin, "he is set for life." Of course, that was not always the case. His father's decision, however, surely set up his own life and the one triumph they both could share.

Sophia and Rutherford Hayes Jr.

"Rud" Hayes could describe his father vividly. He was "of medium height—about five feet, nine inches, straight, slender, healthy, and active," ambitious, always busy, yet a loving husband, a devoted father, and a community leader. Such a description was all the more remarkable in that the younger Hayes had never set eyes on his father. "Ruddy" Hayes had died ten weeks before his son was born. The boy's mother, Sophia, had supplied all of the details. She would mourn Rutherford Hayes Jr. for the rest of her life and was intent that her son live up to his legacy.

Sophia Birchard Hayes is reminiscent of many other strong-willed presidential mothers—pious, protective, and resolute. That she carried such qualities to extremes is little wonder. She had lost so many loved ones that she virtually willed her sole remaining son to survive. To Sophia, any good news was a precursor of calamity. Yet even as she strived to protect young Rud from potential peril, she urged him to emulate his father's example in every way possible.

Certainly Rutherford Hayes Jr., known to everyone as Ruddy, was among the most attractive, most admired men who fathered future American presidents. Ruddy's father, Rutherford Hayes Sr., followed the tradition of multiple careers common in the American colonies. He was a blacksmith, a farmer, and eventually an innkeeper. From a Scottish family originally named Haie, renowned for their valor, Hayes didn't exactly duplicate his highland heritage. His earliest American ancestor had come to Connecticut in 1625, and others in the family later fought for independence. Hayes avoided such involvement by moving to Vermont, where there was no conscription, and was one of the signers of the subsequent "Plea of Conciliation" between Vermont and New York. He simply wanted to live in peace. His popular Brattleboro Tavern was really run by his more practical wife, Chloe.

Their fourth child and second son, Rutherford Hayes Jr., dubbed Ruddy, was born on January 4, 1787. He was frail as a child and would always be slender, but by his teens he was strong-bodied. What struck everyone about Ruddy, beyond his flaming red hair, was an unusual combination of energy and amiability, an amalgam of both his parents. Named for his father, Ruddy was sent across the river to New Hampshire to attend the select school at Atkinson and did well, winning academic awards. His parents might have sent him on to Dartmouth, but he preferred to get started in business. Ruddy went into retailing as a clerk for the growing firm of Noyes and Mann. John Noyes had married Ruddy's sister, Polly.

Noyes and his partner, John Mann, had decided to expand their business. First, they went to Putney and then opened a general store in Wilmington, sending young Ruddy to manage it. He made his customary favorable impression, on no one more than an early customer named Sophia Birchard. Harry Barnard describes her as "attractive in a clean and chaste way," with a trim figure. She had rather a long "Yankee face," tightly combed brown hair, and blue eyes. Her other memorable feature was her extremely rosy cheeks, which caused her no end of embarrassment, implying artificial embellishment. Despite her aversion to crimson, when Sophia glimpsed Ruddy behind the counter, the sparks were instantaneous. Later Ruddy would write her, in the florid fashion of the time, that "the lass with the roseate cheeks shall not be long forgotten by the lad with the rubicund hair."

The first American Birchard brought his family to Roxbury in the Massachusetts Bay Colony in 1635. There were Birchards at Bunker Hill, and Sophia's maternal grandfather, "Old Captain" Daniel Austin, lived long enough to regale her with stories of the Revolution. Sophia was born in Wilmington, Vermont, on April 15, 1792. Her father, a farmer and merchant, died when she was only thirteen. Her mother remarried and then divorced, a scandalous occurrence in nineteenth-century Vermont. She died of spotted fever when Sophia was eighteen, an epidemic that also cost her a younger brother and sister and a number of other relatives. Her acquaintance with grief came early. From her formative years Sophia was devoutly religious and read endlessly by candlelight—not frivolous books, but such weighty works as *Pilgrim's Progress*. Like Ruddy Hayes, she had excelled at the district school, but each undertook early responsibilities.

As Ruddy was transferred to another location, they carried on an affectionate correspondence, and on September 13, 1813, twenty-one-year-old Sophia married twenty-six-year-old Ruddy. They moved to the bustling Vermont town of Dummerston. Two of the brothers Sophia had been caring for moved in with relatives, and a third, twelve-year-old Sardis, came to live with them. In August 1814, their first child was born, but he lived for only a matter of minutes. For the first time, Sophia witnessed a terrible melancholy in her normally lighthearted husband. Of course, she was already no stranger to tragedy, but stemming her own tears, she pulled them through. Many years later her daughter Fanny defined it as Sophia's "singular trait." She was disposed to "look on the dark side when others are joyous, and rising when others are depressed . . . thus preserving the equilibrium of our family."

The next year should have been a time for joy. In 1815 Sophia gave birth to another son. Thankfully, this one was healthy, his hair as bright red as his father's. They named him Lorenzo. It was a different sort of depression that determined Ruddy to take his family west. In 1814, John Noyes was elected to Congress, and Jonas Mann withdrew from the partnership. The end of the War of 1812 had brought not only rejoicing but also a severe economic depression, extending to the Panic of 1819. In New England, retailing was as hard hit as manufacturing and farming.

Ruddy had heard of "golden opportunities" in Ohio. Although many of their friends and relatives had already caught the western fever, Sophia was particularly reluctant to abandon the surroundings she had always known. Nor was Ruddy anxious to leave, but he had to see these new lands for himself. And Sophia was pregnant again. Ruddy set out on horseback, ultimately riding throughout Ohio. Following a new stagecoach route, he found a large tract of land to his liking near the settled town of Delaware. It already had some four hundred residents, many of them fellow Vermonters. She had already given birth to a daughter, whom they named Sarah Sophia, and agreed to the move.

In 1817 the firm of Noyes & Hayes was dissolved and its assets sold. That fall, Sophia, Ruddy, and their two children set out for what Ruddy's mother called "a distant land," a trip that would take forty days, their belongings in three wagons. They stopped first to visit Ruddy's parents in Brattleboro. On the day of their departure, Chloe Hayes wrote in her diary, "Sept. 10, 1817. With tender emotions and feelings which cannot be erased from my mind I will reckon the transactions of this day. . . . I hope a kind Providence will protect them thru all the dangers they may have to pass." Chloe Hayes was convinced she would never again see her son, the "glory and pride" of her family.

From the day he arrived in Delaware, as Sophia recounts, Ruddy was "always busy." After some five rigorous years in Ohio, Sophia had reason to feel a sense of satisfaction in a handsome home, abundant fruit orchards, congenial company, fulfilling work in community activities, a loving husband, and a growing family. She had given birth to a second daughter, Fanny, a delightful child, and was pregnant yet again. It must be time for things to go bad. This time the epidemic was typhoid fever. In the summer of 1822, a pervasive strain of the contagious disease swept through Ohio. First, little Sarah Sophia died. In only three days, her father, too, was gone. He was only thirty-five. Although virtually everyone else in the household and throughout the community was sick, Ruddy was mourned by the largest assemblage of residents who had ever attended a local funeral. Sophia would mourn him the rest of her life.

On October 4, 1822, still feverish, she gave birth to a frail baby boy. With undaunted faith, she named him Rutherford Birchard Hayes for the father and older brother he would never know. However, Sophia's succession of personal tragedies was not yet at an end. Only three years later, while skating, Lorenzo fell through the ice and drowned. At home, young Rud would have only his surviving sister, Fanny, to be his childhood companion. Is it any wonder his mother cherished and protected him against every peril, real or imagined?

Sophia's bachelor brother, Sardis, whom Ruddy had generously adopted, became a supportive surrogate father figure. However, it was essentially a little world of women, particularly after Sophia's spinster aunt, Arcena Smith, came to reside with them. Characteristically, Sophia wrote to relatives, "My dear children are perfectly well, but I am filled with fear for them." It would never leave her.

As Harry Barnard observes, Rud's much-loved sister Fanny was so superior at sports that she became the equivalent of a stronger, more secure older brother. He writes, "It was no wonder that neighbors considered him 'timid as a girl' . . . and not even forty years later could his mother see him as other than a boy in need of sheltering." Rutherford was not really separated from his mother until he was nearly fourteen. She had been his primary instructor in almost every subject. Sardis had recommended an excellent boys' boarding school—Norwalk Academy—and Sophia was obliged to agree that it was time for some institutional education. Rud found that he loved the school, and despite his sheltered childhood, it was remarkable how readily he adapted to the male world outside his home. Now Sophia's concerns were reduced to whether his manners might be less polished away from her influence. At sixteen he went on to Kenyon College, graduating in 1842 as valedictorian, the acknowledged leader of his class. For once, his mother's joy was unalloyed, proudly witnessing his commencement oration. How much like his father he seemed now, self-confident and assertive, the solace for so much suffering.

What path would he follow? Fanny, now married, welcomed her brother to her new home in Columbus, where he had decided to read law. Surprisingly, Sophia was pleased. Law was a respectable profession, so long as it didn't lead to politics. All being elected to Congress had done for her husband's brother-in-law was turn him into an alcoholic. When a now-affluent Sardis paid Rud's tuition at Harvard Law School, Sophia was hardly upset, only saddened by another separation. Her correspondence never ceased. To Rud, now financially secure and fully his own man, his mother remained a perceptive observer. With respect to President Polk's expansionist agenda, she wrote Rud this timeless admonition, "If the time wasted talking about Oregon had been spent in educating the ignorant or in improving the moral condition of the young of this land, instead of inflaming their minds about 'war and honor,' it would be better."

Rutherford's choice of a bride, unlike his transition to politics, met with Sophia's unqualified approval. In 1852 he wed Lucy Ware Webb, a college-educated young woman so devout and morally attuned that she might have been related to Sophia. They were to have eight children, although three of their sons died in infancy. Nor were Sophia's personal blows yet at an end. Her daughter, Fanny, so loved by both her mother and brother, lived only to be thirty-five, the same age at which her father had died. Rud was now Sophia's sole surviving child.

The Civil War came like a specter from the past. Sophia's mind filled with new premonitions of death. She hated the war but viewed secession and slavery as "more wicked," writing Rud, "If I had ten sons, I would rather they were with you." This time there was no looking at the bright side of disaster. With her daughter-in-law, Lucy, she could only pray and share the ordeal. When Ohio Republican leaders suggested he take a furlough to campaign for a seat in the U.S. House of Representatives, Hayes replied, "An officer fit for duty, who at this crisis would abandon his post to electioneer for a seat in Congress, ought to be scalped." Somehow he survived, despite being wounded four times. He ended the war as a brigadier general and a genuine hero. Sophia felt pride, relief, and probably puzzlement. How was it possible he had not been taken from her?

Sophia Birchard Hayes died on October 30, 1866, at the age of seventy-four. A decade later, her son became president of the United States in the most controversial election since that of John Quincy Adams. A congressional commission, by a vote of eight to seven, awarded the election to an incredulous Hayes over Samuel Tilden. One pivotal condition was that he, although a Republican, oversee the final end of Reconstruction in the South.

It is ironic that such a deal dominated the tenure of so well-intentioned a man as Hayes, overshadowing his espousal of broad-based reform and sound money. Perhaps his occupancy in the White House is popularly most remembered for the decision of his wife, "Lemonade Lucy," to ban alcoholic beverages—even wine—from the premises, going Sarah Polk one better. Well, Rud's mother had warned him of "the vice and frivolous company" that infested Washington.

Rutherford Birchard Hayes died of the results of a heart attack in Fremont, Ohio, on January 17, 1893. He was seventy. Even though Hayes had never joined his mother's church, Barnard concludes that, "from his tender attentions" to her, his "clean look," the contentment with his wife and family, and "the absence of any scandal in his affairs," even Sophia would have concluded that he had not been corrupted by his chosen career path. Most of all, after so much loss in her life, this favored child she had sheltered had somehow managed to survive to a career worthy of his father's honored name.

Eliza and Abram Garfield

Just as Rud Hayes carried with him a vivid depiction of the father he had never known, so did James Abram Garfield. However, Garfield's father had been dead for three decades when, in her sixties, his widow Eliza felt she finally must take the time to compose a "brief sketch of my early life for the Gratification of my Children after I am laid in the Grave." Her "early life" included an understandably excessive appraisal of her husband.

"Your father," she wrote, "was five feet and eleven inches high, large head, broad shoulders and chest, high forehead, brown hair, blue eyes, light complexion, as beautiful a set of teeth as any man ever had . . . cheeks very red, lips tolerably full but to me very handsome. . . . His bearing noble and brave, his benevolence was finely developed, fond of his friends, everybody liked him, his judgment was very good." In short, another Ruddy Hayes. Unfortunately, Garfield left his wife with so much less than Hayes did that it rendered Eliza Garfield's subsequent struggles virtually a matter of survival.

In particular, she sought to inspire the youngest, brightest, and most rambunctious of her sons to a more positive purpose. It was to his mother that the twenty-one-year-old James Garfield expressed his gratitude, reflecting, "In reviewing the varied scenes of my short yet eventful life, I can see the golden thread running through the whole—my mother's influence on me." Of course, to an appreciative Eliza Garfield, it was also an inheritance from his father. In the thirteen years of their marriage they had given so much to each other that any reflection of it to their children must be from both parents. Although Eliza had been left with a small farm, her husband had died as suddenly as had Jacob Johnson, leaving her with four children to support. For sheer fortitude in the face of adversity, Eliza Ballou Garfield has few if any equals in the mothers of American presidents.

Her family and her husband's, so seemingly different, had kept running into each other across the expansive American frontier, from New York State to the Western Reserve of Ohio. The Garfields, as Theodore Smith writes, were "typical New England stock" of Norman-English extraction, arriving in 1630 among the earliest settlers of the Massachusetts Bay Colony. They tended to be tall and sturdy, given to action and evincing little in the way of intellectual curiosity.

Following the Revolutionary War, in which Garfields had fought, Abram's grandfather left New England for Worcester, in central New York. Abram was born there on December 28, 1799. He was christened Abraham but always went by Abram. Shortly thereafter his father, Thomas, died, and his mother married a similarly solid man named Caleb Boynton. As a youth, Abram, described by Margaret Leech and Harry Brown, was a "warm, open-hearted boy, stamped with the Garfield pattern of exceptional muscular strength," as typical a representation of his family as Eliza Ballou was of hers.

The Ballous were of French Huguenot extraction, noted for their diminutive size and quick wit. They settled in Rhode Island around the end of the seventeenth century and then moved throughout New England. Many were creative and intellectual. Hosea Ballou founded Universalism, forerunner of the Unitarian Church. Eliza's father died in 1808, when she was only six, leaving his widow in dire straits. However, she was a skilled weaver and put her talents to use, taking her five children to New York State, where she had relatives near the town of Worcester. There Eliza first ran into Abram Garfield. He was fourteen; she was twelve. Initially, she didn't like this "green boy" very much, who had so little use for learning. However, because of the increased mobility after the War of 1812, they would meet again.

Eliza, a true Ballou, was as much the physical embodiment of her family as Abram was of his. In her late teens she is described by Allen Peskin as having "features perhaps already sharp and set" and also as having inherited her mother's bright coloring as well as her clever hands. "Her fine singing voice made her welcome in any gathering. . . . She was small and quick . . . fond of company and chatter." Hendrick Booraem adds that Eliza was short in stature but noted for her "saucy" wit and energy by her many friends. Abram Garfield sought to be numbered among them. His stepfather, Caleb Boynton, had brought his vast brood of Garfields and Boyntons to Ohio in 1814, seeking land and opportunity in an area only recently wrested from Chief Tecumseh and his Indian allies. After the Ballous had also moved to Ohio, Abram set out to renew his acquaintance with them. Something in his more confident demeanor finally won Eliza over. She surely shared his sense of adventure. Eliza and Abram were married on February 3, 1820. He was twenty, she eighteen.

Joining thousands of like-minded pioneers, they set out with high spirits to seek their fortune in the Western Reserve, Ohio's northwest frontier. The newlyweds settled on forty acres of land, but before Abram could even use his woodworking skills to build them a snug log home, both he and Eliza fell ill. It was that common frontier ailment called "ague," probably a form of malaria. For portions of their first four years together, even hearty Abram was terribly weak. Fortunately, a number of Boyntons who lived nearby provided a ready refuge. Despite everything, Eliza gave birth to four children, two boys and two girls.

When Abram, anxious to improve their circumstances, was finally up to working, he used his Garfield charm to talk twenty other men into joining him in taking on a contract to construct part of the new Erie Canal. Unfortunately, a second, larger contract was compromised by rising costs and wiped out all his profits from the first. After eight years of marriage, initiated with such high hopes, he was back where he started, but now with a family to support. His strength and his wife's undiminished confidence remained his only assets. Eliza helped out by weaving for others.

Assistance, emotional and physical, came from the Boyntons. Before long, they helped Abram raise the roof of a substantial log house. Just constructing it buoyed his spirits. Abram cleared new acres and planted wheat and other crops. Things seemed to be looking up. It remained in Eliza's memory as "a golden time." Abram's energy supplemented Eliza's spirit, and they were soon living as well as their neighbors.

Then tragedy struck without warning, as it so often did on the frontier, breaking their family circle. Their two-year-old son, Jimmy, died of an undisclosed ailment in his mother's arms. Soon, Eliza gave birth again. Her final child, another boy, was born in their log cabin in Orange, Ohio, on November 19, 1831. Named for both his father and a departed brother, a not uncommon practice in those times, James Abram Garfield was, in his mother's words, "the largest Babe I ever had." He "looked like a red Irishman, a very large head and shoulders. . . . He was a very good natured child." James, even in infancy, seemed so like his father, with dimensions appropriate to a Garfield. Unlike so many presidential parents who favored their oldest sons, the Garfields saw something special in their youngest.

James would know neither of those for whom he had been named. In the dry, dangerous spring months of 1833, a fire broke out in the woods surrounding the Garfield home and the acres Abram had cleared. To keep it from spreading, he fought the blaze all day. Coming home drenched and exhausted, Abram caught a violent cold, probably pneumonia. Two days later, on May 3, 1833, he was gone, dying at the age of only thirty-three. Reputedly, realizing that the end was near, Abram said to his wife, "Eliza, I have brought you four young saplings into these woods. Take care of them." That she did. James was eighteen months old.

Many years later, in a campaign biography, James Garfield recalled what he had learned of his mother's reaction: "She lost no time in irresolution, but plunged at once into the roughest sort of men's labor. The wheat field was only half-fenced, the precious harvest still ungathered." A slight woman of thirty-two, with her four children to provide for, Eliza had little time for the luxury of grief. Her neighbors would help her bring in the spring crop. But what then? She and her son Tom, who grew up quickly under the circumstances, split rails, truly "man's labor," from timber Abram had cut for that purpose. Together they completed the fence enclosing their fields, protecting the ripening wheat from roaming cattle that had been let loose during the forest fire. If the family were to remain intact, it must be self-sustaining. The only Garfield exempted from farm chores, of necessity, was baby James.

A skilled seamstress, the vocation of so many first mothers, Eliza bartered her handiwork with the local cobbler for shoes. Wheat was traded for corn. From their few sheep Eliza made all the family's garments. Eliza insisted to her children that they were not a poor family. Perhaps sustenance was not abundance, but the family and a loving God would provide. Eliza led daily Bible readings, and the family walked together, as James grew, to the Christian meetinghouse every Sunday. Upon their return they reflected on everything they had heard.

None of this was done, however, in a sanctimonious spirit. The young widow would be recalled by her children as joyful, cheerful, and affectionate, as well as vigorous. After all, she was a Ballou as well as a Garfield. With her beautiful singing voice she led them not only in hymns but also in sea chanteys, ballads of the day, and patriotic songs from the War of 1812. She held them all spellbound with stories and song. Certainly, Eliza loved all four of her children, but as Margaret Leech and Harry Brown suggest, "She could see her handsome husband in the fair, square-shouldered little man who frolicked at her knee." Even when he grew old enough to help out, picking berries, herding their few livestock, and the like, James was always encouraged by his mother to take time to read. Not entirely because of age—he was the chosen one. Perhaps, despite the best of intentions, too much so.

If James owed his intellectual interests to his mother, he continued to physically resemble his father. The "red Irishman" at ten or twelve towered over other children, was immensely powerful, and had a great, unruly shock of brown hair. In practical skills and temperament, however, he was growing up to be little like his father. James had no more love for farming than had Abraham Lincoln. Wielding an axe, he was a danger to himself and anyone else in the vicinity. It is a wonder he could hunt without accident. Already a restless bundle of contradictions, into his teens he was becoming mercurial, clumsy yet hyperactive, with a temper little like his father's. Yet, as soon as his love for reading became apparent, Eliza brought him every book she could find—history, the classics, adventure. An early indication of his restlessness was that he particularly loved stories of the sea. Clearly, James had the potential Eliza had foreseen, but how was it to be harnessed? Fortunately, as the Western Reserve developed, Eliza was not alone in her love of learning. When the township of Orange looked about to establish its own schoolhouse, Eliza was happy to oblige, offering a corner of her farm for the school's location.

His sisters married and his brother Tom departed to his own farm, finally James and his mother were living alone, the glow of their hearth undiminished, their modest domain at least stabilized. Most of their neighbors enjoyed a relative prosperity in which even the thrifty Eliza Garfield was still unable to share. Despite his disdain for farming, James had helped her diversify the property, raising corn and potatoes as well as wheat. He took on odd jobs, even farming for neighbors, but his restlessness increased. All those books he had read about nautical adventures only fueled his wanderlust.

At sixteen, James announced to his incredulous mother that he, too, was leaving home to seek his fortune—if not on the seven seas, at least on a vessel plying the Great Lakes. She did not protest excessively. After all, it was her own sense of adventure, joined with Abram's, that had brought them to the Western Reserve. Rebuffed in his attempt on the Cleveland waterfront to be hired on a large vessel, James settled for a berth on a humble canal boat, following the route his father had helped construct. The next few months were the most harrowing of his life. He nearly drowned on three occasions. At about the same time, in 1848, he started writing a personal journal. When he returned home, still intent on going back to the canal boat for a second tour, his mother welcomed him without a word of reproach. James promptly fell terribly ill. While his mother nursed his now "haggard and forbidding" frame back to health, she also adroitly suggested at least a "short-term" alternative. Why not consider going back to school until he had fully recovered his strength? Even sailors could use some education. Eliza brought over a gifted young teacher named Samuel Bates, who instructed students in advanced mathematics at Geauga Academy in nearby Chester. The two men got on very well, as Eliza had hoped.

Garfield later wrote of this time, "My mother captured me. . . . She simply went about her duties quietly and permitted things to work themselves out." Of course, it wasn't quite that simple. She had been convinced from the first that this special son was her "child of high destiny, born to be good and great." Channeling him from the canal to the classroom had to be done gradually. Eliza suggested that if James would commit to taking only two semesters at Geauga, she would talk several of his old friends into accompanying him there. After she had somehow managed to do this, and he finally agreed to go, she also scraped together the seventeen dollars for his first year's board and tuition.

On the day her son departed, she was already certain her prayers had been answered. "Her plans for James were unfolding just as she had hoped," Booraem writes. As James progressed at Geauga, memories of his free life as a sailor receded, and his future spread out before him. He became "very industrious in his studies. . . . He was willing to work long hours just to get back" to school. He even labored as a custodian to earn the second year's tuition.

His path led all the way to Williams College in Massachusetts, to heading a school in Ohio that became Hiram College, to becoming a lay preacher for the Disciples of Christ, to studying law, and to heroic service in the Civil War, where he would end up a major general. His political career led from the Ohio Senate to eighteen years in the U.S. Congress to nomination and election, however closely contested, as the twentieth president of the United States.

In 1853 Eliza finally sold the farm she had struggled so tenaciously to maintain. Her children returned for a last meal together at the old homestead, when Eliza insisted on serving them personally. In later years, James was able to take her back to her childhood home in New Hampshire, gaining pleasure in sharing her enjoyment at being "a girl once more" and evoking such memories of Abram, whom she had viewed initially as a "green boy."

It was only a little more than a decade after going off to Geauga that Garfield was leading Union troops into battle. His mother truly believed in the "Era of Universal Peace" her son had spoken of, but she hated slavery more. "By now," as Doris Faber writes, "James was married to a sweet and steadfast former teacher who might have been Eliza's own daughter, and together the two women trembled for him when he was away." They also prayed, and their prayers were answered. James and Lucretia Rudolph Garfield of Hiram, Ohio, whom everyone called "Crete," had been wed in 1858. They had five sons and two daughters, but two of their children died in infancy.

Although not the first presidential mother to experience the election of her son, Eliza was the first to attend his inauguration. "From the tow path to the White House," Garfield's campaign literature had trumpeted, but it was really more from the schoolhouse to the White House. Nearing her eightieth year, Eliza was "proud and happy" but perhaps not all that surprised to see her son take the oath of office. As Peskin recounts, wearing the relative finery of "black silk, under her demure bonnet, her bright eyes . . . taking in everything," Eliza was a small but striking figure at the ceremonies. If, as Peskin adds, James Garfield "would be more remembered for what he was than what he did," that only enhances the role his mother played in his life.

Only a few months later, while awaiting a train that was to take him to deliver the commencement address at Williams, Garfield was shot by a deranged, disappointed office seeker. One bullet lodged near his spine, a second grazed his arm. Garfield was rushed back to the White House, where he remained for two months while doctors probed unsuccessfully for the bullet in his back. He then asked to be moved to his shore-side cottage in Elberon, New Jersey, in hope that the sea air might prove beneficial. At first the news of his condition had been kept from his increasingly frail mother, who had returned to Ohio. As James's life ebbed away, one of his final letters assured her that he was on the way to recovery. James Abram Garfield died on September 19, 1881, two months short of his fiftieth birthday. The nation's outpouring of grief rivaled that accorded to Lincoln.

Eliza's physical and emotional strength as a slight young widow had astonished her neighbors and sustained her children. Now even tinier and enfeebled by age, her only desire was to join the youngest of them. Instead, she endured more than another six years of sorrow. Her final prayer was answered on January 21, 1888, at the age of eighty-six. James Garfield had matured through the ceaseless efforts of a mother he knew, but also through the reflection of a father he knew only through her. Their dedication transcended their time together.

Malvina and William Arthur

As Vice President Chester Alan Arthur anxiously awaited news of Garfield's condition, there were still rumors that Arthur had been born in Canada, making him ineligible to ascend to the presidency. American political history is replete with such colorful complications. The Republicans of that era, split between "Stalwarts" and "Half-Breeds," offered some lucrative opportunities. In 1871 President Grant named Arthur to one of the most coveted posts, collector of the port of New York. In 1878, President Hayes fired him as part of his campaign against the "spoils system." Then his fortunes took another turn. Although Arthur had never held elective office, he accepted running with Garfield in 1880 to balance the ticket, and they narrowly defeated the Democrats.

Chester was one of the nine children of Malvina and William Arthur. In effect, William was born twice—first in Ulster in 1796, and then "born again," as it is put today, in Vermont in 1827, called to preach the gospel. The first of the three first fathers who became ministers, he had turned to religion in his thirties, after pursuing very different careers.

Born a Presbyterian, he was also a lay reader in the Episcopal Church, and he married a Methodist, but it was as a Baptist that he preached to parishioners in a succession of pulpits. He and his equally devout wife, Malvina, sought to impart the certainty of their faith to their children, particularly as their increasingly worldly son Chester matured. Even more significant was their fundamental honesty.

The Arthurs were from Scotland, tracing their lineage as far back as the MacArthurs in the fifteenth century and then to the Campbell clan. Like many Scots, they ultimately found their way to the north of Ireland. William Arthur was born to a farming family in 1796, located, in the mellifluous words of Thomas Reeves, "in the townland of Dreen, across the bridge from the village of Cullybackey in County Antrim." At eighteen he graduated from Belfast College. In 1818 or 1819, with prosperity receding in Ulster, he emigrated to Canada.

To get started, he worked at a series of jobs in Quebec, notably teaching in Dunham, fifteen miles north of the Vermont border. He also discovered eighteen-year-old Malvina Stone, whose English forebears had settled in northern New Hampshire in the mid-1700s and then moved throughout New England. Her grandfather, a veteran of the French and Indian War, lived an eventful life. He ran a ferry over the Connecticut River, developed a prosperous farm, and sired twelve children. One of them, George Washington Stone, Malvina's father, decided to move his family north, over the border, and settled in Dunham, Quebec, where he lived for the rest of his life. Accordingly, Malvina enjoyed the heritage of two countries, although her own birth in Vermont is a matter of record. She had met William Arthur in Quebec. They fell in love, eloped in 1821, and had a daughter, the first of four. Torn between teaching and the law, William decided that the latter would constitute a more productive vocation and moved his family south to Burlington, Vermont, where he could pursue his legal studies.

In Burlington, William readily found a clerkship in a lawyer's office, taught school to help support his family, and looked forward to an eventually prosperous career. Instead, he had an epiphany. Always interested in religion, he happened to attend a Baptist revival meeting in nearby Waterville and felt the call, as had Malvina's Uncle John, to personally preach the gospel. The emotional preacher at the meeting seemed to be talking directly to him. William decided on the spot that *his* life, too, must be devoted to saving souls for the Lord. He went on to be licensed as a "Free Will" Baptist preacher in 1827 and, after a rigorous clerical examination, was ordained in the regular Baptist clergy in 1828. William brought eloquence and energy to his new calling, but his spellbinding sermons were to bring him more converts than comfort, and his uncompromising nature led him during the next three decades to eleven different congregations.

The first of them was in the small farming community of Fairfield, Vermont. Already in his thirties, William and his perpetually supportive wife now had those four daughters to support. With an annual salary of only $250, to come even reasonably close to making ends meet, William was obliged to also teach school, fulfill his pastoral duties in Fairfield, and serve as a visiting preacher at other small congregations on both sides of the Canadian border.

On the night of October 5, 1830, the Arthurs finally gave birth to a son, a healthy nine-pound boy they named Chester Alan Arthur. Reportedly, his father, hard-pressed or not, was so carried away that he literally danced for joy, naming his son for the doctor who had delivered him. William Arthur didn't view the new arrival as an extra mouth to feed but rather as the heir of a legacy of faith more precious than riches. Eventually, the Arthurs had nine children, although a later son died at two and a favorite daughter at eighteen. Of Chester's upbringing, William Judson Hampton writes, "In youth there had been the training and influence of the Christian home; the start of life with no other endowments than health, character, courage, and honorable ambition." Financial problems would dog Malvina and William Arthur throughout their life together.

Moving from parish to parish in Vermont and New York may have given him the aspect of an itinerant preacher, but William possessed a formidable intellect. During his uncommonly lengthy five-year tenure in Greenwich, New York, William was so renowned for scholarship that he was awarded an honorary master of arts degree from Union College. In Schenectady he edited for four years a magazine of "popular knowledge" called the *Antiquarian and General Review*. He spoke Greek, Latin, and Hebrew. As time allowed, he took in students to tutor and prepare for college, augmenting his always meager income.

Reeves describes William as "of medium size," clean-shaven, with a thatch of dark hair, and "a keen, penetrating eye." He was a man who left a strong impression—articulate, witty, passionate—but whose sarcasm could be cutting. He never lost his thick Irish accent. Although a man of the cloth, he had a rather unclerical temper and argumentative spirit. Sometimes it seemed almost as if he enjoyed shocking his parishioners with hard truths about what leading a Christian life really entailed. His uncompromising attitude led to frequent disputes with the deacons and trustees of his churches. It is little wonder that he was obliged to move so frequently.

To someone of William's convictions, one had not only to espouse the literal lessons of the Bible but, whether comfortable or not, to live them without compromise. He viewed slavery as an abomination no Christian could possibly sanction, and he didn't mind saying so in his sermons. He is believed to have cofounded the New York Anti-Slavery Society in 1835, before such abolitionist views were widely shared, even in the North.

He and Malvina suffered many sorrows, but whatever problems dogged the devout couple, they helped their remaining children in every way possible, none more than Chester. Always an amiable child, "Chet," as he was called, started school at the Union Village Academy, went on to the local lyceum, where he edited the student newspaper, and finally entered renowned Union College as a sophomore. He pursued a demanding classical education. Although seemingly more sociable than scholarly, he graduated in 1848 Phi Beta Kappa, near the top of his class. A paper he wrote denouncing the practice of slavery anywhere as "disgraceful" particularly pleased his father.

They had some physical similarities, although the mature Chester Alan Arthur featured sideburns and a mustache. He stood six-foot-two, taller than his father, was slender but quite strong physically, and is often described as "strikingly handsome." An early teacher referred to Chester's "dark and brilliant eyes," much like his father's, but also noted the already profound difference in their temperaments. Chester was "frank and open in his manners and genial in his disposition." William may have been similarly frank and open, but he was only genial if you agreed with him. It was on the basis of that geniality, and his adaptability, that Chet Arthur launched his political career.

There was only one problem. Was he an American? Unfortunately, most of Arthur's private papers had been destroyed in a fire. Had his birth really taken place in Fairfield or Waterville, Vermont, in 1830? As his political star ascended, some of his opponents found his family's Canadian connections too tempting to ignore. Finally a thorough investigative reporter for the *New York Sun* put all the rumors to relative rest, and it was good enough for the U.S. government. When James Garfield expired after those traumatic 199 days, Arthur was duly sworn in as president, after which he would surprise everyone.

The 1850s had seemed a promising decade even for Parson William Arthur. While his son taught for a time in Vermont, went on to study law, and was admitted to the bar with bright prospects in 1854, William contemplated his own future. Need piety always be accompanied by privation? Contemplating retirement from the final location of his peripatetic ministry at the Calvary Baptist Church in Albany, William settled his family in nearby Newtonville, New York. It looked as if he might be able to expand his well-regarded boarding school for college-bound students to a level of profitability, but, of course, something intervened—the Civil War.

As Chester went off to serve, although his cushy assignment would be no more dangerous than as inspector general and quartermaster general in New York (ever after, he still liked to be called "General"), his father's advice followed him. "Pray daily," William exhorted, "for you know not, when called to meet the enemy, you may fall in Battle." By then, Chester had become increasingly sophisticated in his urban environment and far removed from the literal Christianity epitomized by what seemed the simple country faith of his parents. However, it never diminished his appreciation of how much they had sacrificed for him. Amiable Chester Arthur's legal and evolving political career, in apparent alliance with some thoroughly venal New York Republican political factions, could be characterized by the titles of his two major biographies: *A Quarter Century of Machine Politics* and *Gentleman Boss*.

He became renowned for his opulent, luxurious lifestyle—attired elegantly and residing in a handsome brownstone. Yet all those warm memories of his childhood must have returned whenever Arthur visited his parents, which he did as often as he could. Neither lived to see him in the White House. William Arthur died of stomach cancer on October 27, 1875, at the age of seventy-nine. Malvina had passed away on January 16, 1869, at the age of sixty-seven. Late in her life, she too had appealed in a letter to both her remaining sons, "Oh that God would answer my prayer, that before I am taken from life, you . . . may come out publicly and confess Christ. . . . I know He will lead you to everlasting life and glory, if you are willing." Although their most prominent son never went that far, his support had helped to ease his parents' final years, and he had never quite forsaken their values. As Howe testifies, habits of generosity and kindness "were included throughout his boyhood" and guided him throughout his life.

When he became president, Arthur surprised both his friends and his critics. As he explained when refusing to grant political favors to an incredulous visitor, "Since I came here I have learned that Chester A. Arthur is one man and the president of the United States is another." Among other reforms, he backed the investigation of post-office scandals, supported the civil service, and reduced the national debt. His wife having died before him, a sister had served as White House hostess. Chester Alan Arthur died of Bright's disease in New York City on November 18, 1886, at the age of fifty-seven. A son and daughter survived him. He had served a creditable tenure in fulfilling Garfield's term. When granted for a time the greatest power he would ever possess, President Chester Alan Arthur came to represent the most important quality he had inherited from his parents—an honesty transcending the pragmatism of politics.

CHAPTER 8

An Inheritance of Values— Clevelands, Harrisons, and McKinleys

Ann and Richard Cleveland

There was little doubt that Richard Falley Cleveland would be a clergyman. Generations of Clevelands (and Cleavelands) had committed sons to the Protestant clergy, on both sides of the Atlantic, emigrating to the Massachusetts Bay Colony in 1635 from the rocky "cleves" of their native England. The Clevelands produced prominent intellectuals as well as clergymen, and Richard's aspirations encompassed both. Born on June 18, 1804, he graduated from Yale in 1824 and then began studying for the ministry in Baltimore, prior to going on to Princeton Theological Seminary. To support himself, he also worked as a tutor in a private academy.

Somehow he met lively, fun-loving, socially prominent Ann Neal, whose preoccupation was more with possessions than piety. Ann loved luxury almost to the point of ostentation, yet she fell in love with this seemingly somber Yankee divinity student. H. Paul Jeffers does note that Cleveland was rather handsome and even sociable in his rather earnest way. His "genial blue eyes," prominent Roman nose, and firm mouth gave him an aspect both aristocratic and kindly. Was Ann Neal simply seeking someone of substance? Whatever Richard's attraction, it did not recede with time. After completing his studies in 1828, Cleveland accepted a pastorate at the First Congregational Church in Windham,

Connecticut. To the incredulity of her family and friends, Ann Neal became Mrs. Richard Falley Cleveland in 1829. He was twenty-five, she twenty-three.

Perhaps in his own blissful state Richard had overlooked the abundance of trunks full of clothes and adornments or Ann's black personal maid, who was to accompany them by coach and canal up to Connecticut. Predictably, once the couple had arrived, the Reverend Cleveland's new parishioners were appalled at having a slave in their midst, let alone one who was the servant of their new parson's wife. They were equally aghast when they witnessed the costly and colorful embellishments of Mrs. Cleveland's person. She seemed to be a pleasant enough young woman, but had she no knowledge of the scriptural admonitions against vanity and display? Quickly, the maid was dispatched back to Baltimore. Ann Neal Cleveland in the first month of her marriage determined to be more Puritan than the Puritans, at least in terms of appearance.

She would need to be. Despite his earnest efforts and undeniable talents, Richard never quite fulfilled his potential in the pulpit. Perhaps his true calling was in academia—a better teacher than preacher. Yet his churches prospered, even if the Clevelands did not. Alyn Brodsky writes that Richard and Ann were "poor only in goods. They had culture, congeniality, and spiritual wealth." Soon, however, they would also have children to nurture and support, four during the first five years of their marriage.

There is no doubt that in time Ann's faith evolved to firmly based convictions. It gave her the strength to bolster her growing family through one disappointment after another as the Reverend Cleveland moved from one posting to another. Perhaps Jeffers puts his finger on why Cleveland failed to rise higher in the church hierarchy: he had no single outstanding quality. "His flocks found him kindly, expansive and somewhat of a charmer who was serious but not brilliant." The quality Richard most lacked was the ability to stand out, to fire a congregation with the power of his sermons. He was almost the complete opposite of William Arthur.

The Clevelands had nine children. In the Caldwell manse Ann gave birth on March 18, 1837, to her fifth child and third son, a healthy boy they named Stephen Grover Cleveland in honor of his father's predecessor, the Reverend Stephen Grover. As soon as he came of age, Grover discarded his first name. However, he had been called "Big Steve" as well as "Uncle Jimbo" by his playmates. From almost the very beginning, Ann Cleveland sensed something special in her third son. As he grew, that conviction became stronger. Certainly, she loved all her children, but Grover indeed turned out to be the most promising, even if not the most intellectual. As the years passed, with little improvement in their circumstances, he became her new focus, replacing his father not in affection but in expectations.

At Fayetteville, New York, Reverend Cleveland enjoyed his longest tenure, nine years. It was "this pretty village" that Grover would always view as his childhood home, even if the pleasures it offered were within a framework of piety and poverty, worship, and work. As he grew, Grover supplemented the family income by such muscle-building jobs as hauling rock lime and directing barges on the Erie Canal to where they could be loaded. His education started with Bible study at home, at the local schoolhouse, and then at Fayetteville Academy. After the obligations of each day were completed, family games involved everyone. Grover particularly enjoyed fishing, swimming, and taking long hikes. His sister Susan recalled "a little round-faced, blue-eyed boy . . . chuck full of fun."

When Grover was thirteen, in 1850, his father faced the harsh reality that, however much they all scrimped and saved, he simply could not support a family of eleven on a small-church parson's scant stipend. He accepted a position as district secretary of the American Home Missionary Society, which meant traveling through the central part of the state but paid the munificent sum of $1,000 a year. The family moved to the handsome town of Clinton, New York, which had a particular attraction for Grover, because it was the home of Hamilton College, which he hoped to attend.

But time was running out for even this remote expectation. All the travel, over rudimentary roads and in all sorts of weather, took a terrible toll on his father. With great reluctance Richard finally resigned and took a position at half the salary as minister of the Presbyterian church at Holland Patent, a quiet village ten miles from Utica on the Black River. His first sermon there, in September 1853, would be his last. He had been diagnosed with gastric ulcers, and the affliction left him too weak to even get out of bed. Richard Falley Cleveland died on October 1, 1853, at forty-nine. Although Grover's dream of going to college was buried with his father, he never blamed him or ceased extolling his virtues. Only months before his own death, Grover Cleveland reflected, "Looking back over my life, nothing seems to me to have more of pathos and interest than the spectacle of my father, a hard-working clergyman, bringing up acceptably a family of nine children . . . upon a salary which at no time exceeded a thousand dollars a year. It would be impossible to exaggerate the strength of character thus revealed."

In their maturity, father and son had many similarities. Physically, Richard's frame had thickened over the years. Brodsky writes, "In the son we see the father's generous height and portly figure, blue eyes, balding brow, and their most distinctive shared trait, the prominent Roman nose." Grover would add an equally prominent mustache. In addition, both had a "charming manner and a studiousness that stopped short of brilliant." Always enthused about education, following his presidency Cleveland accepted an invitation to join Princeton University's board of trustees in 1901, eventually becoming its chairman, but even his cherished Sigma Chi badge was honorary.

The only man to serve two nonconsecutive terms in the presidency, Grover Cleveland was technically our twenty-second and twenty-fourth president. At his second inauguration, in 1893, Cleveland inserted a bookmark at verse twelve of the Twenty-First Psalm, "They shall bear these up in their hand . . ." To be borne up by the prayers of Ann Neal would have seemed beyond improbable to those who had known her as a frivolous Baltimore belle.

Cleveland's marriage in the White House surely raised some eyebrows. The twenty-one-year-old bride, Francis Folsom, was twenty-eight years younger than Cleveland. She was the daughter of his late law partner, and Cleveland had been her legal guardian since she was six. She would become a most popular first lady, and the couple had five children. However, it was a prior event that caused the major stir. It is ironic that such a scrupulously honest man as Cleveland is so vividly remembered for an indiscretion. He had taken the responsibility for fathering an illegitimate child, whom he continued to support. Apparently, all the promiscuous mother's other lovers were married. To his anxious campaign staff in 1884 who asked how they should handle the situation, he issued a simple directive, "Tell the truth," and went on to win his first presidential term, inspiring the famous cartoon and doggerel, "Ma! Ma! Where's my Pa? Gone to the White House, Ha! Ha! Ha!"

Cleveland was a prudent reformer in office. As even the acerbic H. L. Mencken was moved to write, "We have had more brilliant presidents than Cleveland, but we have never had one, at least since Washington, whose fundamental character was solider and more admirable."

Grover Cleveland's eventful life, including serving as the chairman of Princeton University's Board of Trustees, ended on June 24, 1908, at the age of seventy-one. His mother had lived long enough to know that her favored son was well on his way. She passed away in Holland Patent on July 13, 1883, in her seventy-sixth year, shortly after Grover had been elected mayor of Buffalo. All her surviving children kept watch at her bedside until she was gone. The mother they had known had been the supporting foundation of their own faith. A grieving Grover Cleveland lamented "the desolation of a life without a mother's prayers." Proposing that "Her Children Arise and Call Her Blessed" be on her headstone, his mind must have also reflected on that hard-working country clergyman who had initiated it all.

Elizabeth and John Scott Harrison

John Scott Harrison was a man in the middle. Both the son and the father of American presidents, a unique distinction, Harrison really only wanted to be left alone. He loved farming and also sought to be a good husband and father, but staying out of the limelight was not so simple. Grandson of the colorful signer of the Declaration of Independence,

Benjamin Harrison V, and third son of doughty President William Henry Harrison, John was born on October 4, 1804, in Vincennes, Indiana. His ambitious father, then governor of the territory of Indiana and later to be renowned as "the hero of Tippecanoe," had some difficulty supporting his ten children after resigning his army commission in 1814. Somehow he managed to be elected president, serving only a full month.

Harrison graduated at the top of his class at Cincinnati College and went on to study law, but he always preferred the lure of the land. When his father was named minister to Colombia in 1828, John was left in charge of the Harrison's 600-acre farm near North Bend, Ohio, called "The Point." In good times and bad it was John's home for the rest of his life. More than John's acreage was fertile. He had three children by his first wife, Lucretia, before she died in 1830, and ten more (four of whom died in infancy) by his second wife, Elizabeth Irwin Harrison, whom he married in 1831, when she was twenty-one.

Of Scottish ancestry, Elizabeth Irwin was born in the lovely town of Mercersburg, Pennsylvania, home also of the Buchanan family, where her grandfather had established a prosperous flour mill. In the customary pattern after the War of 1812, her father, Captain Archibald Irwin, moved his family west to Ohio, where Elizabeth met and married widower John Scott Harrison. Their second child and second son, Benjamin, was born at The Point on August 20, 1833. Technically, he was Benjamin Harrison VI, or even VII, but he went simply by Benjamin.

Although John Harrison never achieved consistent prosperity, Benjamin was able to attend Miami University of Ohio, which he entered as a junior. After urging on him piety and duty, a typical letter from his mother goes on, "I hope you will be prudent in your Diet . . . and abstain from cucumbers." How sad that so little of such colorful correspondence remains. Elizabeth Myers notes that both parents talked with their children in an admirably honest way, treating them almost as adults. Elizabeth Irwin Harrison died giving birth to her last child on August 15, 1850, at the age of forty, when Benjamin was not yet seventeen. John Scott Harrison had become a widower again, this time for the remainder of his life.

At Miami University, Benjamin made two major discoveries. He met and fell in love with Caroline Livinia Scott, the daughter of a professor, and decided he wanted to become a lawyer. After he returned home, having graduated with honors in 1852, he informed his father of his professional plans. John obtained a clerkship for Ben in a prominent Cincinnati law firm, an alternative to law school. The next year Ben married Carrie Scott, and in 1854 he established his own legal practice. Prior to this, he filled in for his father, living for a time at The Point, despite his aversion to farming, and looked after the young children still at home. It was a boon for his father, enabling John Scott Harrison to run for Congress.

The Harrison name still stood for something. When John's neighbors asked him to run, he felt obliged to accept. Very likely, it was the prospect of even a modest regular salary that was particularly enticing. Characteristically, after his election John Harrison said little, meditated much, and voted his conscience—all but guaranteeing a short tenure. His lasted two terms.

Although keenly interested in politics, John had never viewed it as a career for himself. As he had written to his son, "My thoughts are continually wandering from the hall of legislation to my children and my home."

After returning home, Harrison was obliged to sell off piece after piece of the land he had inherited, until only a few precious acres were left. Eventually, he was bankrupted, enabled to continue living in his lifelong home only through the charity of his sons. As his father's short-lived political career waned, Benjamin's took off. When introduced to the 1856 Republican National Convention as "Young Tippecanoe," Ben stated, in the spirit of his father, "I do not wish to be acclaimed as the grandson of anyone. I think every man should stand on his own merits."

However they may have differed—John, a democrat, and Benjamin, affiliated with the new Republican Party—John was extremely proud of his son. Ben's heroic services in the Civil War, from which he emerged as a brigadier general, cemented his father's admiration. As Stephen

Hess points out, within one month Benjamin Harrison fought in more battles than had William Henry Harrison or Andrew Jackson in their entire lives.

"Little Ben," barely five-and-a-half-feet tall, was neither a typical politician nor a typical Harrison. He came, as Hess writes, "from a tribe of giants and congenial hail fellows." Although hardly the latter, tall John Scott Harrison, with his lean, long face, at least bore some resemblance to his father and prior Harrisons. Even though Ben was viewed as being rather shy and unassertive, his oratory could sway an audience. He took to wearing a silk hat everywhere, perhaps to look more imposing, although it became a rather patrician trademark.

Whether he liked it or not, when he finally ran for president, Harrison was nominated at the 1888 Republican convention as the bearer of a "name woven into the very fabric of American history." Democrats proclaimed, "Grandpa's pants won't fit Benny." Republicans replied, "Yes, but grandfather's hat fits Ben!" In that unique series of elections, Harrison managed in 1888 to narrowly defeat the incumbent, Grover Cleveland, in the Electoral College, although Cleveland won the popular vote. The clan could still claim, "'Old Tippecanoe' and Benjamin, too!" Later, however, in 1892, Cleveland reclaimed the office from Harrison.

Caroline Scott Harrison died in the White House on October 25, 1892. The couple had two children. Four years later, Benjamin Harrison married a niece of his first wife. They had a daughter when he was sixty-three and subsequently toured Europe. Harrison's postpresidential career had been quite productive, but he would not permit his name to be placed in nomination again. He died on March 13, 1901, at the age of sixty-seven.

John Harrison had been most impressed by his son's skill as a lawyer. Although he didn't live long enough to witness Ben's campaigns for the presidency, he would have much preferred that his son avoid the "demagoguery" of politics. It was, of course, too late. By the 1870s, time was running out for John Harrison. The white-bearded patriarch still resided in the North Bend home that his son's contributions had secured for his old age. To help support himself, the elder Harrison had turned to a most surprising avocation. He became, of all things, an inspirational public speaker. His most popular talk was on "The World's Race for Wealth." He was against it.

On the evening of May 25, 1878, John Scott Harrison quietly passed away at the age of seventy-three. The last son of President William Henry Harrison and the father of future President Benjamin Harrison was laid to rest on May 29. At the small Presbyterian church known as "The Little Church on the Hill," the services, modest as the man, were simple and brief. One of two eulogies aptly extolled Harrison not as a farmer or political figure but as a "consistent Christian, a faithful husband and a kind and just father."

John Scott Harrison, a man in the middle, uncomfortable with the famous name he bore and its implications for his life, was successful, as we measure success, only as a husband and father. In that alone, however, despite the tragic loss of two supportive wives and too many of his children, and his ultimate failure as a farmer, he had the satisfaction of living life on his own terms.

Nancy and William McKinley Sr.

With "Mother McKinley" we reach the peak of piety. For so many mothers of prior presidents, the hope was evident that their favored sons might find fulfillment in the ministry. With Nancy Campbell Allison McKinley, it became a specific objective. She hoped her son would one day rise to be a bishop in her Methodist Episcopal Church. Yet even though William McKinley never ascended to the elevated ecclesiastical post she had hoped for, but had been elected to the presidency instead, she still prayed, "Oh, God, keep him humble." By then, long before the advent of mass media, she had become virtually the nation's mother— the personification of small-town American values at a time when everything seemed to be undergoing such rapid change.

Stories abound about her endearing Midwestern unpretentiousness, undiminished even as her son became so prominent. Visiting him by train when he was governor of Ohio, she was asked by a fellow passenger if she had any relatives in Columbus. All Mother McKinley replied was, "Yes, I have a son there." Traveling to his presidential inauguration, she gathered a bouquet of roses from the train's dining car. Pomp was foreign to her person.

Of course, after William chose to pursue a political career, she would not deny him her support. In his celebrated "front porch" campaign of 1896, his mother made a notable contribution simply by showing up. There she was, rocking away benignly, a comfortably symbolic substitute for his often ailing wife, as William personally greeted the multitudes who came to his home in Canton, Ohio, to see him. With surrogates doing the extensive campaigning, McKinley won handily. When he ran for reelection in 1900, his vice president having died, the unpredictable Theodore Roosevelt was nominated to be his new running mate. Apprehensive Republican boss Mark Hanna insisted to McKinley, "Your duty to the country is to live for four years from next March."

William McKinley Sr. had died when his son was still governor of Ohio. As H. Wayne Morgan puts it, the elder McKinley may not have been extraordinary "except in the force of his character," but that quality in itself was profoundly admired by his son. The senior McKinley so valued education he would sacrifice anything so that his children might have the best available. He always carried three books with him, even as he tended the blast furnaces that had become his vocation—a well-worn Bible and works by Dante and Shakespeare.

When in 1743 the first McKinley came to America, his heritage from Scotland and Ireland not only encompassed strength, hard work, high spirits, and independence but also a profound regard for learning. He was called "David the Weaver," although the primitive nature of his new land required that he undertake multiple tasks—not only weaving but also farming and, most significant for the future of his family, working with iron. Notably industrious, David set the tone for the future of his family.

In America, the McKinleys became increasingly immersed in mining and manufacturing pig iron. Some of them only left the line of battle in the American Revolution to cast lead bullets and cannon, a task even more critical to the Continental Army's success than leveling a musket at the enemy. After the War of 1812, in which the family also participated, David's son, James, joined the western migration, moving with his wife, Rose, to New Lisbon, Ohio, in search of more extensive opportunities. The iron foundry business, in which Rose's family also had deep roots, moved with him. Just as Jesse Grant grasped the need for leather goods on the frontier, James McKinley knew that everything the westward wagons contained moved on wheels of iron.

His son, William, born on November 15, 1807, in New Lisbon, was strong of physique and, like other McKinleys, taciturn, hardworking yet fun loving, conditioned to rising and retiring early, and adaptable to many tasks. In his teens he already had the firm jaw and "keen eyes" that reflected his determination to succeed in the harsh environment of the American frontier. Despite an education limited to the local grammar school and enhanced by his reading, he loved books—another McKinley trait—and had shown some talent for figuring.

Morgan notes that "on both sides of President McKinley's family were ironworkers and tinkers." Nancy Allison's ancestors were English Puritans who eventually fled to Holland and then accompanied William Penn to Pennsylvania. Some were Quakers, but Nancy's branch of the family became staunch Methodists. The Allisons were inclined more to farming, the McKinleys more to tinkering, but the men of both families were obliged to continue to undertake multiple tasks. Their wives worked just as hard, rearing large families and dealing with the heartbreak of inevitable loss but providing for the welfare of all.

By the time William was sixteen, he was already operating three coal furnaces of his own. It was either in the local schoolhouse or the Methodist church that he met bright, strong-minded, capable Nancy Allison. She attended both regularly, committed to learning and so religious that had she been a man, the ministry would almost surely have been her calling. She had been born in 1809, two years later than William, in a humble abode just over the Ohio line from Pennsylvania. In this instance it was the mother of a future president who was reared in a log cabin.

The attraction was mutual. In 1829 Nancy wed this strong, kindly, and industrious young man in a ceremony in which they symbolically pledged their troth by venturing to a spring where they shared a gourdful of icy water. They settled in the small Ohio town of Niles. Despite his energetic efforts, William never quite found the success he sought, and he was constantly on the road seeking business for his foundry. That left Nancy largely in charge of the household, but there was rarely any discord.

Family and faith were essential to Nancy's life. With her sister, she all but kept the Niles Methodist Church functioning. Eventually, Nancy McKinley became a sort of one-woman self-help agency as well, tying the small town together. As Morgan relates, "She tended sick friends, helped with welfare cases, bore her share of community problems . . . boarded visiting ministers and teachers . . ."

Nancy and William were of one mind in terms of how their children should be reared. There would be nine in all, the same number as Nancy's mother had had, four boys and five girls. Remarkably for those times, only one child, a girl who would have been her tenth offspring, died in infancy. Yet it was their seventh child, not the firstborn male, who was named for his father. Until the day of the senior William McKinley's death, his son would sign his name "William A. McKinley Jr." He was born on January 29, 1843, in the long, low clapboard house that was attached to a general store. From a young age William seemed to measure things in a rather adult, reflective way.

As Eva Higgins details, there was no card playing, drinking, or very much levity in the McKinley household, but this did not prevent young William from enjoying a normal, happy childhood he would always remember fondly. He was much like other boys, only more serious, and he actually looked forward to school. His first formal instruction, with his siblings, was in the well-worn frame schoolhouse in Niles. However, he had already been attending Sunday school, a priority of his mother. As she said, "He was just like other boys, except that he was of a more serious turn of mind." He actually looked forward to both school and church, professing his faith at the age of fourteen. Might he not one day become the learned minister his mother envisioned?

William's parents had already agreed on a significant decision expressing their preoccupation with education. Niles was a pleasant but rather isolated community. In the larger nearby town of Poland there was a more advanced academy, Union Seminary, founded by New England Presbyterians but now administered by Methodists. The three older children were all but ready to make their way in the world. Nancy and the six remaining children went to live in Poland. It was to benefit all of them, but particularly William. At the same time, it represented a substantial sacrifice for their father, whose business kept him in Niles, but one he fully agreed was necessary. He saw his children only on weekends.

Years later, President McKinley recalled Poland with great nostalgia, "the trim neat little village on the yellow creek, with its . . . white frame dwellings, its dear old academy, and the village store from which we got our political inspiration." Poland was also a way station on the Underground Railroad. The McKinleys hated slavery. With teen-aged William's keen interest in the church, Mother McKinley must have viewed the future with promise. Gradually, her dreams for young William escalated to a bishopric, although Nancy admonished herself for such unseemly ambition. By the time William graduated from Poland's Union Seminary in 1859, at the age of seventeen, Morgan describes him as "a handsome boy, with ample dark hair, a somewhat slight but muscular build, and penetrating eyes. His courtesy and kindness enhanced his physical attractiveness." Despite the financial panic of 1857, William managed to enroll at Allegheny College in Meadville, Pennsylvania, but he was able to stay for only a year.

For a time he taught school and worked in the post office, but a more serious crisis was coming. In its own way it led to the demise of all of Nancy McKinley's ecclesiastical plans for her favored son. With the advent of the Civil War in 1861, William enlisted as a private in the 23rd Ohio Volunteer Regiment, under the command of Rutherford B. Hayes. By the end of the war he emerged as a twenty-two-year-old major who had been decorated for bravery in several engagements. In 1864 he had cast his first vote, for Abraham Lincoln. He, too, would be a Republican.

Encouraged by Hayes, whose own future would lead to the White House, McKinley turned to the study of law. He had already completed law school in Canton, Ohio, when his parents in 1867 chose to settle there, uniting all of their family who remained in the area. In 1871 McKinley married Ida Saxton, daughter of a prominent Ohio banker. Although she was afflicted with epilepsy and phlebitis for most of her adult life, the couple had two daughters. Unfortunately, neither lived beyond the age of four. As his career prospered, McKinley had no small acquaintance with grief. From 1871 to 1876 he practiced law in Canton and, in the year Hayes ascended to the presidency, won election to the U.S. House of Representatives. A bit thicker around the waist, his hair receding, he was still strikingly handsome. After seven terms, he was elected governor of Ohio.

His mother's reaction was understandably mixed. More than anyone else, she had inspired her son to high achievement; but even if he had become no more than a dedicated country parson, she still would have felt a measure of satisfaction. Yet McKinley's chosen vocation suited him, and she would see him elected to the presidency itself. His proud father lived to witness William Jr. serve as governor. William McKinley Sr. passed away on November 24, 1892, at the age of eighty-five. Perhaps only his character was "extraordinary," but it had never failed to inspire the son who bore his name and was still by his side on the day he died.

On the evening of McKinley's election to the presidency, excited supporters discovered him and his wife kneeling beside his mother while they prayed together. At the inauguration, another son suggested to Nancy McKinley, "Mother, this is better than a bishopric." There is no record of a response. As Morgan relates, "the photographers, the smiling crowds to whom she waved, never turned her head. The spectacle and pageantry of power meant little to her. William was her dearest, but she cherished another dream for him that died hard." When asked if she were not proud of William, she replied, "No, I am thankful to the Great Giver that he has bestowed upon me such a blessing."

McKinley had not chosen the path that led to the ministry, but his strong religious convictions lasted to the end of his life. As he told a committee of clergymen who visited the White House in 1899, "I am a Methodist, and nothing but a Methodist—a Christian, and nothing but a Christian. By the blessings of Heaven I mean to live and die, please God, in the faith of my mother." Even in the summer of his first year as president, McKinley went back to Canton to see his now very frail mother, taking her to Sunday services one final time.

Nancy Campbell Allison McKinley died on December 12, 1897, in her eighty-eighth year. It was the only time the president's associates saw him break down in tears. He would die at an assassin's hand only four years later. McKinley had won reelection in 1900 by a wider margin than in 1896, only this time with the running mate who made Mark Hanna so uneasy. Six months after his second inauguration, greeting thousands of visitors who stood in line to meet him at the Pan-American Exposition in Buffalo, McKinley was shot twice by an anarchist named Leon Czolgosz. For a time, as with President Garfield, it looked as if he might recover, but after a week gangrene set in. William McKinley Jr. died on the morning of September 14, 1901. He was fifty-eight.

Unlike Garfield's mother and Lincoln's stepmother, Nancy McKinley was spared the burden of outliving her son. Her homely comments upon his election to the presidency, however, are reminiscent of those of Sarah Lincoln after Abraham had died. Mother McKinley said, "William has always been a good boy. He never gave me a cross word, and I do not believe he ever told me a lie. I am glad that he is president for his sake." To his own pastor, McKinley frequently reflected on the sheer goodness of his mother and, with no disparagement of his supportive father, how much he owed to her inspiration.

CHAPTER 9

Parents as Best Friends—Martha and Theodore Roosevelt Sr.

———— ∞∞∞ ————

Flags throughout the city were at half-staff. Over two thousand people packed the Fifth Avenue Presbyterian Church for the funeral service. Hundreds had kept a vigil at the home of the stricken man. Few pulpits that Sunday did not extol the virtues of the deceased. Every newspaper in New York and many elsewhere detailed his life not only in obituaries but also in their editorials and even on their front pages. Perhaps the *New York World* put it best, celebrating one "who was eyes to the blind, feet to the lame, good to all." The deceased was not a head of state or even his municipality. He never held or sought to hold public office. Yet, although he had always avoided publicity, he was esteemed when he died at the age of only forty-six, just before midnight on February 9, 1878, as the first citizen of New York. His name was Theodore Roosevelt. Only many years later would he be remembered as Theodore Roosevelt Sr.

His son, the younger Theodore, a sophomore at Harvard, had received an urgent summons to come home on the next train, but he arrived too late. His father had characteristically cautioned him, upon his departure for college, to "take care of your morals first, your health next, and finally your studies." The son had written home early in his freshman year, "Not another boy in college has a family who loves him as you all do me, and I am *sure* there is no one who has a Father who is also his best and most intimate friend, as you are mine."

Three days after his father's death, young Theodore Roosevelt reflected in his diary, "He was everything to me, the one I loved dearest on earth." When he had finally recovered from "the first sharpness of grief," he wrote his mother on March 24, 1878, "Darling little Motherling, I have just been looking over a letter of my dear Father's. I do not think I *could* do anything wrong while I have his letters." And reflecting still later, "My father . . . was the best man I ever knew. He combined strength and courage with gentleness, tenderness, and great unselfishness."

What had made the elder Theodore Roosevelt such a beloved figure to so many? The progression of seven previous generations of Roosevelts in America had achieved distinction and wealth, but no previous Roosevelt had ever exhibited anything remotely approaching Theodore's relentless commitment to helping others.

That Claes (or Klaes) Martenszen van Rosenvelt had chosen in 1649 to make the arduous journey to the New World is evidence of his ambition. There were abundant opportunities at home, but overseas trade was essential to a world power. With eminent practicality, the Dutch settled only one colony in North America, crowned by the finest natural harbor they could find. They called it New Netherlands, and the city that would develop around its harbor, New Amsterdam. In less than forty years it would be New York, but politics was not the first priority to those already established in commerce.

Claes was both a farmer and a merchant. His sons, their family name now anglicized to Roosevelt, developed two notable branches as they expanded, essentially city and country Roosevelts. The most prominent of what became the Hyde Park lineup along the Hudson River was the first Isaac Roosevelt, a sugar planter and American patriot who helped secure the adoption of the Constitution. The most prominent of the Manhattan line was the formidable Cornelius Van Schaak Roosevelt, who turned what had been essentially a hardware business in other directions—importing glass, selling real estate, and eventually establishing a private bank. Known as "C. V. S.," he became the family's first millionaire and was the father of the elder Theodore Roosevelt, called "Thee" by the family.

Thee was the youngest of the five sons of C. V. S. He was born on September 22, 1831, into a lively household ensconced in a sizeable red brick mansion on bustling Fourteenth Street. Allen Churchill notes that even as a child Theodore exhibited a balanced, cheerful personality. Perhaps because he was the youngest of their boys, both parents doted on him. His mother was not of Dutch origin—Margaret Barnhill Roosevelt's Quaker forebears had come over with William Penn. Thee enjoyed the influence of more than one tradition.

He loved animals of all kinds, especially horses. As he grew, he delighted in riding his favorite mount or driving his four-in-hand carriage through the still-rural environs of upper Manhattan. Edmund Morris refers to Thee's "leonine features and big sloping shoulders." David McCullough describes Thee, who would later grow a neat beard and mustache, as "a fine figure" of a man, "physically imposing, athletic, with china blue eyes, chestnut hair . . . and a good, square Dutch jaw."

Education in the practical Roosevelt household was still largely conducted by tutors. Only one son went to college, his Columbia degree a specific preparation for the law. Yet when Theodore was nineteen, his parents decided it would be beneficial to send him on a grand tour of Europe. He made the customary rounds of castles and cathedrals, but his letters dwelt more on observations that reveal an emerging social conscience. He was struck by the extremes of public squalor and private splendor. Still, upon returning home he joined the family business, now Roosevelt and Sons. His income was enhanced by a hefty inheritance after his father died. But try as he might, it would never be his true calling. It simply didn't challenge him as it did his brothers. He had loftier pursuits.

And, more immediately, the pursuit of the most captivating girl in the world, "Mittie" Bulloch. He had met her in Roswell, Georgia, in 1850 on his first trip south, to join a wedding party. The bride's fifteen-year-old sister, diminutive Martha Bulloch, called "Missie" throughout the region but "Mittie" by her friends, is described by Doris Faber as altogether exquisite and bewitching. Reportedly, "she had the sort of silky black hair that takes a russet tinge under the glow of candles. . . . Her skin was the purest white, with a coral rather than a rose tint in her cheeks." Mittie embodied the less languid variety of Southern belle. During the same day she might read poetry under the wisteria but then later tear about the expansive acreage of her father's estate on her spirited mount as recklessly as Theodore Roosevelt in upper Manhattan. The Bullochs were a colorful clan with Scottish roots. A Bulloch had served as governor of Georgia, and unlike the Roosevelts they had fought in both the Revolution and the War of 1812. Mittie's father, Major James Stephens Bulloch, had rather a rakish reputation, although he died of a stroke while teaching Sunday school.

Beyond attractiveness and affluence, Mittie and Thee seemed initially to have little in common. Mittie was slight, creative, emotional, and very Southern; Thee was large, serious, motivated, self-contained, and very Northern. And yet they fell almost immediately and mutually in love. Their youthful affection, so quickly kindled, never waned, an example of lifelong constancy that would never cease to inspire their children. Although they would not marry for nearly three years, they were secretly engaged before Theodore's departure for home.

Their letters reveal great tenderness. In a typical exchange, Mittie wrote, "I feel dear Thee—as though you were part of my existence, and that I can only live in your being." When he received this letter, Thee, "feeling the blood rush to my temple," responded, "Oh, Mittie, how deeply, how devotedly I love you!" The delay in their nuptials was likely influenced by concerns about Mittie's age and the suddenness of her sentiments. Since her mother, also named Martha, was already favorably disposed to Roosevelt, she finally gave her consent. The wedding at Bulloch Hall in Roswell on December 22, 1853, was followed by a week of festivities. After a brief honeymoon, the couple arrived at their new home in New York City—a substantial four-story brownstone on Twentieth Street.

The transition from Southern plantation to Northern townhouse could not be measured merely in miles. However smitten, Mittie understood that New York represented as much a new world as a new state. At eighteen, she had never been obliged to run anything, let alone such a house in a great city she found "bewildering." And here was a seeming regiment of retainers waiting to do her bidding, whatever that might be. Certainly, she brought light and laughter to such a somber setting, and her devotion to Thee was never in doubt, but it took a period of adjustment to feel fully in charge.

Within a year she was pregnant. Her first child was a girl they named Anna after Mittie's favorite sister, and nicknamed "Bamie," after the Italian "bambina." She was a joy to both her parents but also a challenge, and a precursor of problems to come. Anna was born with curvature of the spine. She was patiently nursed and exercised by her parents, only strengthening the bond between them. The seemingly fragile Martha Bulloch Roosevelt had surprising stamina. Thee resolved to do something for others similarly afflicted, and he helped to found and fund the New York Orthopedic Dispensary and Hospital, turning ever more to the concerns that would consume him.

In 1856 Mittie's widowed mother sold their Georgia plantation and with her daughter Anna moved to the Roosevelt domicile in New York. Mittie was bolstered by their arrival, enabling her to become a more confident mistress of this bustling household. Her mother was by her side when she endured the very difficult delivery of her second child, on October 27, 1858, her first son. They called the eight-pound boy Theodore, for his father, and he was promptly dubbed "Teedie" to differentiate them (he would always hate "Teddy"). Mittie thought him the homeliest baby she had ever laid eyes on—and loved him all the more. Theodore Roosevelt Jr. was the first American president to be born in a great city.

The Roosevelts had two more children—Elliott, called "Ellie," in 1860, and Corinne, called "Conie," in 1861. None of the four was entirely healthy. Bamie might have been crippled for life, but for young Teedie it would be a question of life itself. Almost from birth, he had difficulty breathing. His asthma became so severe that he could sleep only when propped up in bed or wrapped in blankets in a chair. Both parents attended to him around the clock. And he seemed to be developing additional ailments.

"My really great father," young Theodore recalled, "saved my life. . . . I remember . . . him carrying me in my battles for breath, up and down a room all night. . . . I could breathe, I could sleep when he had me in his arms. . . . He got me breath, he got me lungs, strength, life." Even on blustery winter nights, Thee would have the carriage brought around and bundle his son in rugs, holding him tight, while they raced through the silent streets to catch the air. At home, his mother comforted him. As Doris Faber writes, "Night after night she sat up with him, cradling his dear funny old man's face in her lap while she soothed his asthmatic gasping with comic stories" from her Southern childhood. It is little wonder that he would see both his parents in mythic terms.

Still, they must both at times have wondered, however deep their devotion, what perverse fate had brought so beautiful a mother as Mittie such homely children, and so vigorous a father as Thee such debilitating sickness in his offspring. Perhaps this helped encourage Thee's inclinations to philanthropy, although he was already on his way to a lifelong commitment, his true vocation. Thee restlessly roamed the city. Seeing shivering newsboys on street corners, he founded a Newsboys Lodging House. He spent every Sunday evening there, serving them dinner, encouraging the homeless boys with no trace of condescension. As his children grew, he would take each of them along, in turn, to join him. Young Theodore Roosevelt may have grown up in affluence, but he had an acquaintance with the reality of most people's lives that was denied to his Hyde Park cousins.

Thee set aside Monday nights for visiting families in New York's rapidly expanding slums. He often picked up stray kittens on his rounds. Naturally, he helped to found the Society for the Prevention of Cruelty to Animals, as he had the Young Men's Christian Association. Seeing so many homeless children on the city's streets, he initiated the Children's Aid Society. He served on every charitable board he could induce the city and state of New York to set up, never taking a salary and avoiding publicity. He nurtured institutions that aided the blind and deaf as well as schools for immigrant children. He helped to found the Metropolitan Museum of Art and the American Museum of Natural History. Virtually every charity, every hospital, every cultural institution bore his imprint. He was obtrusive only when soliciting help from others. Beyond contributing his own time and money, he ceaselessly sought the support of his many wealthy friends. Others, watching him approach with his great strides, the glint in his eyes, would simply ask, "How much this time, Theodore?"

At a time of rampant political corruption throughout New York, Thee's politics were largely an amalgam of well-intentioned reforms. Originally a Democrat, Thee would become, to his wife's consternation, a Lincoln Republican. His hope, as McCullough points out, was for what New York might become—an authentic melting-pot symbol for the nation, as the nation should be for the world. In his view, "No other city offered such opportunities for those wishing to do something for the good of mankind."

Martha Roosevelt lavished unconditional love on all four of her children in a fashion so public it would have offended many another society matron's sense of propriety. More given to affection than advice, Martha called her family's hugging sessions "melts." But she, too, could be serious, just as Thee could be fun loving. Put simply, they were better together. Each day started with family prayers. Afterwards, Thee would send Teedie out to buy fresh strawberries from a nearby market for breakfast. The sights, sounds, and smells of the great city were never foreign to him. As Teedie grew, in the words of Churchill, "into a wan wistful child, with a wide mouth, large teeth, unruly hair, and spindly legs," physicians believed that if he exerted himself as little as possible he might somehow outgrow the asthma. His father suspected otherwise. Might not a stronger, more active body provide the best antidote to any ailment? Teedie loved the natural world, just as his father did—from birds to botany.

Not even the War between the States could sever the ties between Mittie and Thee. In 1861 Thee made an agonizing decision, one he regretted for the rest of his life. There could be no doubt of his Union loyalties. Yet he simply could not bring himself to fight against his wife's kin, and so he hired a substitute. Instead, he pursued other means of selfless service, helping to form an Allotment Commission to convince Union soldiers to send a portion of their paychecks home to their families, and supporting the Sanitary Commission, predecessor of the Red Cross, and the Freedmen's Bureau. Mittie's brothers' service in the Confederacy was so conspicuous that they were excluded from the general amnesty after the war, and they moved to England.

Despite Teedie's many activities and interests, by the time he was ten his parents continued to be alarmed by his pallor and the lack of development in his frail physique. He had started to keep a diary of his observations, yet his eyes remained as weak as his legs. He read any book he could find, and books were abundant in his home. His tutors were more than impressed. If only Teedie were strong enough, Thee vowed, the boy must go to college. He early settled on Harvard.

Concerned not only with Teedie's lack of development but also the generally poor health of her other children, Mittie suggested a bracing tour of Europe. Thee worked out an itinerary. The children were not particularly excited about it, preferring the more leisurely summers they had enjoyed, most recently in Oyster Bay, Long Island, their enduring summer home, an "enchanting" place of "special delights," as Conie Roosevelt recalled it. Nevertheless, in 1869 the full Roosevelt family embarked on their grand tour. Tirelessly visiting museums, Teedie protested, "If only Raphael had painted landscapes instead of church things." A highlight was the festive celebration of his eleventh birthday in Cologne, which his parents attended in full dinner dress. Having seen them dance with such effortless ease only heightened Teedie's resolve to join "the fellowship of the doers." He yearned to become stronger, concurring with his father's conviction that the doctors had been totally wrong in recommending rest as the cure for Teedie's ailments.

After they returned home, Thee took his son aside and gave him the advice that would shape his life. "You have the mind," Thee said, "but not the body. Without the help of the body the mind cannot go as far as it should. You must *make* your body. It is hard drudgery, but I know you will do it." Thee transformed the second-floor piazza of their home into a fully furnished gym. Intended for all his children, it became Teedie's haunt. Hour after hour, he lifted dumbbells, worked with horizontal bars, and punched a large bag. The gym was not drudgery to Teedie, it was salvation. He gloried in any modestly measurable improvement in his body. By the time Teedie returned from a second family trip to Europe, this one extending to the Middle East and Africa, he was all but physically transformed.

Thee returned home several months before the rest of his family. Some projects couldn't wait. When they finally arrived back in October 1873, he had a staggering surprise waiting for them. He had secretly supervised the construction of an immense new home, literally a mansion, on West Fifty-Seventh Street, near the green expanse of Central Park. Thee told Mittie, "We have now probably one abiding resting place for the rest of our days."

With the aid of an excellent tutor, Teedie was accepted at Harvard in the class of 1880. In October of his freshman year he wrote his father, "I have kept the first letter you wrote me and shall do my best to deserve your trust." By the fall of his sophomore year, Teedie knew that his father had fallen sick with an undetermined ailment. He tried to cheer him up by writing home on December 8, 1877, "I am anticipating the most glorious fun during the holidays."

Thee seemed better upon Teedie's arrival. Perhaps it had served as a tonic. Teedie proudly wrote in his diary his father's pronouncement that "after all I was the dearest of his children to him." Now, even more, he must prove worthy of "the best and most loving of men." After Teedie returned to Cambridge, his family finally learned the truth about Thee's illness. There had been only a brief period of remission. What had been initially diagnosed as "peritonitis" was in fact inoperable cancer of the bowel. When that urgent telegram went to young Theodore to return home as quickly as possible, the news had already spread throughout the community. Mittie took the terrible loss bravely, as least publicly, feeling that her task, as in the past, was somehow to try to cheer everyone up. What a heritage they had to live up to! She would never regain the buoyancy of her youth, but as Thee had stressed, "One must live for the living."

Young Theodore stayed at Harvard, graduated Phi Beta Kappa in 1880, abandoned natural science for politics, and married a lovely young lady named Alice Lee, who reminded him of his mother. "You must not feel melancholy, sweet Motherling," he wrote her, "I shall only love you all the more." She had no doubt of that, nor of her son's bright future. Four years later, with Theodore already in the New York State Assembly, his wife gave birth to a girl they also named Alice. In less than forty-eight hours, at the age of only twenty-two, Alice Lee Roosevelt was dead. Her Bright's disease had not been diagnosed. On the same day, February 14, 1884, in the same house, now viewed as "cursed" by Theodore's brother Elliott, their mother, Martha Bulloch Roosevelt, died of typhoid fever at the age of forty-eight. It was six years since her husband had passed away. Neither lived to the age of fifty. The joint funeral of wife and mother was so poignant that even the minister was too moved to muster many words of solace.

Theodore Roosevelt Jr. went on to marry a second supportive wife, Edith Kermit Carow, with whom he would have five more children and rebuild his life, while retaining every cherished memory of a childhood marred only by sickness. Edith would outlive him by nearly thirty years.

In the autobiography Roosevelt wrote six years before his own death, he recalled his mother as "a sweet, gracious, beautiful Southern woman, a delightful companion, and beloved by everybody." Perhaps Theodore Roosevelt's confidence came more from his father and his ebullience more from his mother, but he viewed both as little short of perfection. Together they had breathed the very gift of life into their first son.

As it turned out, Roosevelt's tumultuous tenure as president began upon McKinley's death in 1901, on his father's birthday, September 14. His sisters happened to be visiting. "It is a good omen," he told them. "I feel as if my father's hand were on my shoulder and as if there were a special blessing on the life I should lead here."

CHAPTER 10

The Weight of Expectations—Louisa and Alphonso Taft

———∞∞∞———

"I do not believe we can love our children too much." While this echoes the sentiments of Mittie Roosevelt, it was in fact contained in a letter the equally devoted Louisa Torrey Taft wrote to her mother in 1858. The child she referred to specifically was her already plump and pleasant one-year-old, William Howard Taft, born at home in Cincinnati on September 15, 1857. He would spend a good deal of his life trying to justify the expectations of others, particularly his parents and his close friend, Theodore Roosevelt, who insisted that Taft run for the presidency in 1908 as his chosen successor. Both of Taft's parents were accomplished, kindly, dedicated, and involved—unfortunately so involved that the pressures placed on Will could be unreasonably excessive. Perhaps the prior loss of her first-born, "Sammie," made William all the more precious to Louisa. She would have three more children, two boys and a girl, as well as two stepsons, but there would always be a special attachment to her first surviving son. As she wrote her older sister, Delia, "I feel as if my hands and feet were tied to this baby."

Louisa's marriage itself represented the severest shock of Delia's life. This was not the future either of them had envisioned. Born in

Massachusetts on September 11, 1827, as Louisa Marie Torrey but known to her family and friends as "Louise," she and her sister were raised in an enlightened environment. They had agreed to find fulfillment together to enjoy independent lives of high adventure and travel. Indeed, they had already embarked on their joint venture, although sustaining it financially had proved challenging. Marriage didn't enter into their plans. As Louise put it, "I feel like asserting myself as having been *somebody* by my own account."

At least the Torrey sisters, unlike Abigail Adams, had the opportunity for a measure of formal education. On both sides, the Torreys had been in Massachusetts since the mid-1600s. Samuel Davenport Torrey did so well as a Boston importer that he decided to retire to the more salubrious environment of the small town of Millbury, some forty miles away, when he was only forty-two. Always concerned about his health—as it turned out, unnecessarily—his major avocations for the next forty-six years were taking care of himself and expressing his progressive views without inhibition. These encompassed women's suffrage and full legal rights, also espoused by his wife, Susan.

Their two oldest daughters, Delia and Louisa, divided by a decade from their other sisters, were particularly amenable. Already enlightened by visits to their home by every distinguished scholar who found his way to Millbury, Delia, at eighteen, and Louisa, at sixteen, were dispatched to the new Mount Holyoke Female Seminary. Although Louise hoped to ultimately earn her living by writing, it was clear that the independent lifestyle so enticing to Delia meant that both sisters might be obliged to undertake at least a modicum of teaching. Even in the 1840s this profession required some form of certification.

Delia and Louise were then sent to New Haven to board with their mother's sister, Harriet Dutton. They would not only take lessons from an experienced teacher, a relative of Harriet's—rather like "reading" law in an office—but be permitted to round off their education by attending courses in natural science and philosophy at all-male Yale. Aunt Harriet had observed that, although Delia might be the brighter of the two sisters, Louise, "partly to her confidence in herself and partly to her musical gifts and also to her fine figure and manners" was more attractive to members of the opposite sex. As Doris Faber writes, "Louise was taller and handsomer . . . her glossy dark hair parted in the middle and drawn back into a quite elegant chignon." She was also not averse to flirting, but none of her male acquaintances seemed to suit her.

For several years she and Delia pursued their dream, teaching a semester or two at private academies and then venturing off to New York or Quebec. However, too often they had to write home, chagrined, for money from their parents. It was never refused, but Louise eventually confided to Delia, "If Father finds us too expensive, I'm afraid we shall have to get married." Their younger sisters both married, but Delia never would.

Louise's conclusions coincided with a return visit to her Aunt Harriet in New Haven. There was another visitor, a Yale classmate of her Uncle Samuel's, named Alphonso Taft. He was an imposing six-footer, well over two hundred pounds, whose family had roots in New England as deep as the Torreys'. Born on November 5, 1810, at his family's farm near Townshend in the Vermont uplands, Alphonso Taft was the fifth generation of his family to reside in New England. His father, Peter Rawson Taft, a good-natured but unsuccessful farmer, was also a self-educated lawyer who became a judge. He managed well enough to send Alphonso to college, first to Amherst and then to Yale. Both frugal and energetic, he is reputed to have walked all the way to New Haven.

By the time he was twenty, Alphonso presented quite a striking figure—clean-shaven, with a thatch of dark hair, penetrating eyes, a firm mouth, and a rather prominent nose. In every photograph of him that survives, his gaze is set and serious. After graduating Phi Beta Kappa in 1833, he taught school for a time in Connecticut and then went back to Yale to earn his law degree in 1838. Alphonso may have enjoyed his childhood, but as a place to prosper, he viewed Vermont much as a contemporary had characterized New Hampshire: "It is a noble state to emigrate from."

He looked to establish his practice in a major city. Traveling as far west as Ohio by canal boat, stage, and railroad, he was impressed by

Cincinnati. The "Queen City" was growing rapidly, with over forty thousand inhabitants. There was a good deal of legal business and, as he wrote his parents, "very few men of the Bar of much talent." He settled there and never had cause to regret it. He then set about renewing his acquaintance with pretty Fanny Phelps, daughter of a Vermont judge. Fanny and Alphonso were married on August 29, 1841. She was only eighteen; he was thirty.

Alphonso prospered in Cincinnati. His careful preparation of cases and dignified courtroom bearing belied his age. He became active in politics, later helping to found the Republican Party. In Fanny he found an ideal helpmate. Immersed in charitable and church activities, she considered their life together an "unbroken sea of happiness." Unfortunately, it lasted only eleven years. Fanny was very delicate, and she died of what was probably tuberculosis in 1852 at the age of twenty-nine. She left Alphonso with two young sons, Charles Phelps and Peter Rawson Taft.

On a trip back to New England, Alphonso was completely capti-vated by Louise Torrey, "a splendid woman—one of whom a man might be proud." However robust and handsome, Alphonso was forty-three, Louise only twenty-six. Alphonso's excessively serious demeanor made him seem even older. Still, she was intrigued. The persistent Alphonso managed to capture her heart, in part by winning over her head, con-vincing her their marriage would be a merger of equals. Despite his seeming stolidity, Alphonso was genuinely sympathetic to Louise's wide interests. He would respect what today is called her "space," and there was no doubt about the depth of his affection for her. The engagement was brief, and Louise and Alphonso were married at the home of her parents on December 26, 1853. Susan Torrey was delighted to have such an imposing, enlightened son-in-law; Samuel Torrey was relieved to finally have Louise married. Only Delia was distraught, although she must have recognized that her sister might have done a lot worse.

When Louise and Alphonso's first son together, Sammie, died of whooping cough after his first birthday, perhaps it made William Howard Taft even more special to his parents. Moreover, he was such a pleasant child. Louise would love his three subsequent siblings and their two half-brothers no less, but there always seemed to be something special about this boy they initially called "Willie" (a name he would dislike as much as Lincoln disdained "Abe" and Roosevelt "Teddy"). It would ultimately be "Will." Early on, his mother gushed in letters, "He is very large for his age and grows fat every day. . . . He has such a large waist that he cannot wear any of the dresses made with belts." That was surely prophetic. When Will was only seven weeks old, Louise observed, "He spreads his hands to anyone who will take him and his face is wreathed in smiles at the slightest provocation." His father also discerned special qualities in Will. Henry Pringle observes, "The austerity of Alphonso Taft masked a gentleness and sweetness far more familiar to the children than the austerity itself." However, for whatever reasons, both parents decided that Will was "foremost" among their children. Perhaps temperament implied talent. So friendly and outgoing a child must have potential abilities that would come to fruition as an adult. His parents' expectations would evolve into pressure.

Given his congenial nature, is it any wonder that throughout his life William Howard Taft would strive to please others, to satisfy their expectations of him? First it was his parents, then his wife, then Theodore Roosevelt, and, finally, the Republican Party and the nation. Even as president, as Pringle writes, Taft was "a large, good-natured body, entirely surrounded by people who know exactly what they want."

While his father pursued his judicial career, young Will was indeed working suitably hard. Even in grammar school his efforts exceeded those of his classmates, so eager was he to gratify his parents. He *was* bright. Louise and Alphonso were right about that. But he was hardly brilliant—a plodder, not a plunger. Perhaps through all the good cheer, his anxiety induced overeating, resulting in a girth that would reach 330 pounds. He loved sports and was an excellent hitter in baseball, but—not surprisingly—he couldn't run very fast. In later life, despite his size, he would enjoy horseback riding and golf. By the time he entered high school, Will was certain he wanted to be a lawyer—and, hopefully, one day a judge, like his father. Graduating second in his class at Woodward

High School in 1874 at the age of sixteen, at commencement Will spoke on the importance of woman's suffrage. If his parents were disappointed in his standing (why not first?), they can't have opposed his stand.

Emulating his father again, Will went off to Yale, probably feeling both apprehension and anticipation. Pringle describes Will during his years at Yale as, naturally enough, "big and heavy," with "fair skin, blue eyes, and light hair. He was good-natured, but authority marked his bigness and integrity his personality." In his twenties he already started to grow his trademark flowing mustache and looked much as he would throughout his life. Stephen Hess describes Will in later years: "His face was ruddy with a blondish mustache and dark hair. Despite his great bulk he was light on his feet and a great dancer." Unlike pictures of his father, photographs of the mature William Howard Taft frequently show him smiling and almost invariably looking benign.

To his classmates, who envied Will's receipt of so many letters from home, he explained that his father viewed letter writing as a "recreation." Nor had he forgotten his extraordinary mother. Impressed by her knowledge of the stock market, he wrote to her jocularly while still at Yale, "When woman's field widens, Mother, you must become President of a Railroad Company. I am sure you would be a success." Alas, even late in the nineteenth century, "woman's field" had not yet widened very far. He also wrote her more earnestly, in a message meant equally for his father, "You expect great things from me, but you mustn't be disappointed if I don't come up to your expectations." Taft came in second in the final academic evaluation, as he had in high school. His senior oration was on "The Professional and Political Prospects of the College Graduate." Will pondered his own. Only second again. Had he let his parents down? Still, in a lighter moment after feeling the biceps of heavyweight boxing champion John L. Sullivan, Alphonso Taft was reputed to have said, "My Will is the better man." Certainly, he was the bigger man.

Will went on the prescribed professional path but in a less intensive environment than Yale. In 1878 he entered the relatively slow-paced Cincinnati Law School, which allowed him to lapse into at least a measure of recreational lethargy not previously possible. He read law in his father's office, enjoyed an active social life, and passed the bar, but then worked for a time as a newspaper reporter covering the law courts. In 1880 he finally settled into public life, with his appointment as assistant prosecutor of Hamilton County.

Defeated in his final quest for the Republican nomination for governor of Ohio, his father withdrew from private practice, the end of Alphonso Taft and Sons. Will's future, however, preoccupied him even more. "I do not think you have accomplished this year as much as you ought," Alphonso wrote him. "Our anxiety for your success is very great and I know that there is but one way to attain it, and that is by self-denial and enthusiastic hard work in the profession. . . . This gratifying your fondness for society is fruitless."

Nonetheless, such "fondness" was enjoyable to Will, and he wasn't about to give it up. In 1886 he married bright, strong-willed Helen Herron, whom everyone called "Nellie," whom he had pursued for years. If possible, she was even more ambitious for Will's success than were his parents, of whom she was very fond.

From 1880 on, Will Taft was employed in public service of one kind or another for most of the next thirty-two years. In 1887, he was made a judge on the superior court of Ohio, as his father had been. In 1890 President Benjamin Harrison appointed him solicitor general of the United States. Two years later he was named a judge of the United States Circuit Court of Appeals. Perhaps he was "foremost" after all. "I like judicial life," he confided to his father, who by now must have recognized his son's similar temperament.

Eventually, Louisa Torrey Taft also came to a reluctant acceptance that her Will was in fact temperamentally very much like his father—a hard-working, deliberative man meant for the law, who neither enjoyed nor was intended for a political career. Ultimately, after Louise was widowed, she and Delia, lifelong friends, lived together in the old Torrey household in which they had been raised and managed to travel more extensively than they ever did in their youth. Louise had not totally changed.

Indeed, in her sixties, her children grown, Louise had already managed a world tour even she and Delia had scarcely dreamed of. Alphonso, at seventy-two, his career seemingly coming to a close, had received astonishing news. He had been named American minister to the court of Austria-Hungary. Why? He had no prior diplomatic experience. Louise had quietly written to President Chester Arthur to consider her husband. At last she would have the opportunity to preside over festive social events and mingle with people of the highest quality and taste. Alphonso could not disappoint her. After all, her life had been circumscribed for so long by caring for her husband and family. Didn't she deserve this?

In regal Vienna, Louise blossomed, her grasp of languages and enduring vivacity a great asset in diplomatic and social circles. How Delia would have loved it. Alphonso may have become a rather bemused appendage in his wife's wake, but he was genuinely happy for her. Hadn't they embarked so long ago on a marriage of shared interests? He was subsequently named ambassador to Imperial Russia, where Louise similarly dazzled official St. Petersburg. Will came over to see them. Nellie was pregnant with the second of their three children. The first, Robert Alphonso Taft, born in 1889, would become a prominent U.S. senator. "I am very happy in your prospects," Alphonso told Will.

After a particularly severe Russian winter, Alphonso's health began to fail. He and Louise returned to lengthen their final days together in the warm California sun. Louise wrote Will from San Diego with perceptive reflection, "What a resource is a cultivated mind. What can people do when old and sick without intellectual resources?" They still had much to talk about, the hallmark of a good marriage. Alphonso wrote Will with wry poignancy that he should consider "the fate of an old man who has to be across the continent from the best children in the world."

Finally, in the spring of 1891, sitting by Alphonso's bed, Will saw his father, who had been drifting in and out of consciousness, look up at him, "and in the sweetest way imaginable" smile and say, "Will, I love you beyond expression." It was all he had ever hoped to hear. Alphonso died peacefully shortly thereafter, on May 21, 1891, at the age of eighty. His body was brought back to Cincinnati, as he had directed. In tangible form he had little to leave his family after a lifetime of labor—a good name, their home, and $482.80.

As Alphonso had once said, the Tafts bred "men who knew how to get rich and men who dared to be poor." He had spent his substance bringing up his family. Will had written him in appreciation of the education and travel he had afforded them, "Certainly that is something for you to be proud of and for us to be thankful to you for."

It was Will's potential political career that put his wife and mother in divergent directions. Theodore Roosevelt had ordained that a reluctant Taft succeed him in the presidency, faithfully continuing and expanding on his own policies, a path supported by Will's highly ambitious wife. Whatever his misgivings, how could he say no? To build up Taft's international credentials, Roosevelt proposed that he go on a delicate mission to Rome for the administration. Louise couldn't resist going along.

Nellie had been delayed because of the illness of their oldest son, Robert. When she arrived in Rome, despite her growing differences with her mother-in-law, she couldn't help admiring Louise's sheer spunk. Once more, she was having the time of her life, being a vivacious diplomatic hostess and the center of attention. When the Pope asked young Robert Taft what he hoped to be when he grew up, the boy replied that his ambition was to become chief justice of the Supreme Court. He must have had conversations with his grandmother. Indeed, Alphonso had told Will when he was still quite young that "to be chief justice is more than to be president."

In terms of Roosevelt's intentions, however, perhaps a cabinet post might be a helpful stepping-stone. Taft was named secretary of war in 1904. Louise had come to understand that, like Alphonso, her son was simply too guileless to carefully plot a political future in this way, but now others were doing it for him. She sent Will this succinct observation, "Roosevelt is a good fighter and enjoys it, but the malice of politics would make you miserable." Later, she even came out publicly, stating, "I do not want my son to be president. His is a judicial mind, and he loves the law."

Still, when Taft was asked by Roosevelt to undertake an around-the-world tour to further enhance his pre-presidential stature but hesitated because of his mother's declining health, she told him firmly that he must go. Although Louise opposed its purpose, she was as firm with Will at fifty as she had been when he was fifteen. She told her son in words that still resonate, "No Taft, to my knowledge, has ever yet neglected a public duty for the sake of gratifying a private desire." Alphonso couldn't have said it better.

Louisa Maria Torrey Taft did not live to see either her son's earnest but unhappy presidency or his subsequent career as a distinguished chief justice of the United States, the only man in American history to hold both positions. She died on December 7, 1907, in her eightieth year, the same age as her husband when he passed away. William was still at sea, anxious to return to see his mother at least once more. His career would not be capped until 1921, fourteen years after Louise's death, when President Harding finally named him chief justice.

No one would have appreciated better than Louise Taft this exchange between Supreme Court Justice Louis Brandeis and future Justice Felix Frankfurter. "It's very difficult for me to understand," Brandeis said, "why a man who is so good as chief justice . . . could have been so bad as president." Frankfurter replied, "The explanation is very simple. He loathed being president and being chief justice was all happiness for him." His measured, judicial temperament was so like his father's, a recognition ultimately shared by both his parents. William Howard Taft, who died on March 8, 1931, left an estate a thousand times larger than his father's but shared a more significant legacy from both demanding parents—their values.

CHAPTER 11

The Scale of Salvation—Jessie and Joseph Wilson

—❦—

For a short span, between 1917 and 1920, Woodrow Wilson would be admired to an extent few statesmen in history have experienced. The only academic to ever occupy the White House, the cerebral self-confidence he brought to the presidency, however, masked inner turmoil. Wilson seems to have had a breakdown of one kind or another at almost every pivotal juncture of his life. His relentless drive to excel came from both within and without. Thomas Woodrow Wilson's father always encouraged him. His mother simply adored him. Her "Tommy" could do no wrong.

Near the end of her life, Jessie Woodrow Wilson wrote to her son, "God bless you, darling boy. You have never been anything but a comfort to me all your life!" To Woodrow's more demanding father, the imposing Reverend Dr. Joseph Ruggles Wilson, "Tommy" *could* do wrong, but only if he went against his nature or compromised his standards. He was simply destined for greatness. Wilson himself, at least publicly, never doubted it—a different form of pressure.

It is impossible to overestimate the importance of the certainty of his father's Covenanter Presbyterian faith on Woodrow Wilson. Indeed, his family on both sides is the most thoroughly ecclesiastical in presidential history. As Wilson informed incredulous political associates in 1912, "I am a Presbyterian and I believe in predestination. . . . God ordained that I should be the next president of the United States." In 1919, seeking unqualified approval of the Treaty of Versailles and his vision for a League of Nations, Wilson intoned to the U.S. Senate, "The stage is set, the destiny disclosed . . . the light streams upon the path ahead and nowhere else." One doesn't compromise with destiny. Given the influence of his father, it is not surprising that Wilson ultimately set out to redeem the world, finally giving up any semblance of policy for prophecy.

The Wilsons had been Americans for only a generation when they became Southerners by choice. Woodrow's father was born in Ohio, his mother in England. All four of his grandparents had been born abroad. In 1807, at the age of twenty, Woodrow's paternal grandfather, the gregarious, enterprising James Wilson, arrived in Philadelphia from Scotland by way of Ireland, driven more by ambition than destitution. After marrying a devout young woman named Anne Adams, whom he had met on board the ship, and learning the printer's trade, James set out for Ohio in 1815. He settled in Steubenville and rose quickly to both affluence and prominence, eventually becoming the proprietor of newspapers in both Ohio and Pennsylvania. Wilson was named a justice of the peace, was elected to the state legislature as a Whig, and became an elder of the Presbyterian church. The Wilsons had ten children, their parents ambitious for them all. Joseph Ruggles Wilson, their last child and seventh son, was born in Steubenville on February 28, 1822. Within only a few years it became clear to his parents that this last of their progeny was probably their brightest and best. Joseph was dutiful and studious, excelling at the local Male Academy, as religious as his mother and as outgoing and forceful as his father.

James was intent that this son must have a college education, which fortuitously he had the means to provide. Joseph didn't disappoint him, graduating in 1844 as valedictorian of his class at Jefferson College (later Washington and Jefferson) in Canonsburg, Pennsylvania. He became a schoolmaster for a time, studied at a Pennsylvania seminary, and then

An idealized print showing a young George Washington with his father. Such earlier illustrations of presidential parents were largely individual portraits with little relevance to their sons. (Courtesy of the Library of Congress)

"Thee" Theodore Roosevelt Sr. (Courtesy of the Theodore Roosevelt Collection, Harvard University)

"Mittie" Martha Bulloch Roosevelt. (Courtesy of the Theodore Roosevelt Collection, Harvard University)

"Teedie" Young Theodore Roosevelt Jr. (Courtesy of the Theodore Roosevelt Collection, Harvard University)

The Reverend Dr. Joseph Ruggles Wilson. (Courtesy of the Woodrow Wilson Presidential Library)

Wilson family; Woodrow on left. (Courtesy of the Woodrow Wilson Presidential Library)

Young Herbert Hoover. (Courtesy of the Herbert Hoover Presidential Library)

James Roosevelt holding baby Franklin. (Courtesy of the Franklin D. Roosevelt Presidential Library)

Young Franklin with his mother, Sara Delano Roosevelt. (Courtesy of the Franklin D. Roosevelt Presidential Library)

President Franklin D. Roosevelt with his mother. (Courtesy of the Franklin D. Roosevelt Presidential Library)

Wedding photo of John and Martha Truman. (Courtesy of the Harry S Truman Library)

Harry S Truman with his mother. (Courtesy of the Harry S Truman Library)

Wedding photo of Ida and David Eisenhower. (Courtesy of the Dwight D. Eisenhower Presidential Library and Museum)

Eisenhower family, with "little Ike" on left. (Courtesy of the Dwight D. Eisenhower Presidential Library and Museum)

General Dwight D. Eisenhower with his mother. (Courtesy of the Dwight D. Eisenhower Presidential Library and Museum)

Rose Fitzgerald Kennedy. (Courtesy of the John F. Kennedy Presidential Library and Museum)

Young John F. Kennedy. (Courtesy of the John F. Kennedy Presidential Library and Museum)

The Kennedy family at Hyannis Port. (Courtesy of the John F. Kennedy Presidential Library and Museum)

Joseph P. Kennedy Sr., flanked by his two oldest sons. (Courtesy of the John F. Kennedy Presidential Library and Museum)

Campaigning together—
JFK and his mother, Rose
Fitzgerald Kennedy.
(Courtesy of the John F.
Kennedy Presidential
Library and Museum)

Young Lyndon Baines Johnson. (Courtesy of the Lyndon B. Johnson Library)

"Lady Bountiful"—Rebekah Baines Johnson. (Courtesy of the Lyndon B. Johnson Library)

Sam Johnson, flanked by his sons. (Courtesy of the Lyndon B. Johnson Library)

The Frank Nixon family, Richard on right. (Courtesy of the Richard M. Nixon Presidential Library)

Richard M. Nixon with his mother, Hannah. (Courtesy of the Richard M. Nixon Presidential Library)

Young Jimmy Carter.
(Courtesy of the Jimmy Carter
Library and Museum)

President Carter with his mother, "Miss Lillian." (Courtesy of the Jimmy Carter Library and Museum)

The John Reagan family with "little Dutch" on right. (Courtesy of the Reagan Presidential Library)

Ronald Reagan with his parents, John and Nelle Reagan. (Courtesy of the Reagan Presidential Library)

Wedding dress of Mrs. Leslie Lynch King.
(Courtesy of the Gerald Ford Presidential
Library and Museum)

Young Gerald Ford with his mother, Dorothy.
(Courtesy of the Gerald Ford Presidential
Library and Museum)

Enterprising Gerald
R. Ford Sr. (Courtesy
of the Gerald Ford
Presidential Library
and Museum)

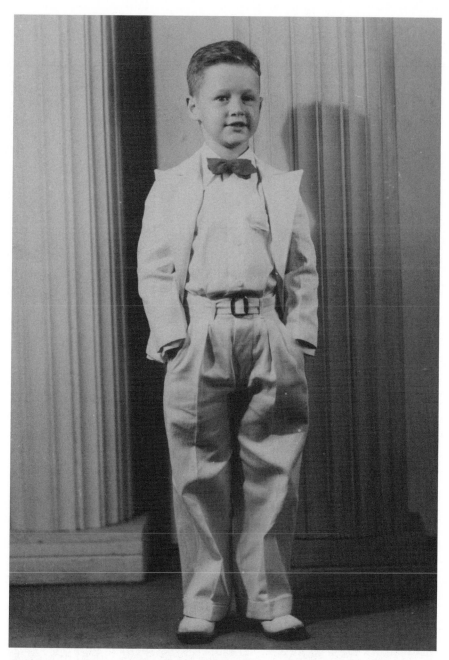

Confident young Bill Clinton. (Courtesy of the Clinton Presidential Library)

Bill Clinton with his mother, Virginia, and brother, Roger. (Courtesy of the Clinton Presidential Library)

Young Dorothy Walker Bush. (Courtesy of the George Bush Presidential Library and Museum)

Prescott Bush with son George H. W. Bush. (Courtesy of the George Bush Presidential Library and Museum)

Barbara Bush with little George W. (Courtesy of the George Bush Presidential Library and Museum)

George H. W. Bush and family in a familiar setting. (Courtesy of the George Bush Presidential Library and Museum)

Two American presidents in stride. (Courtesy of the George Bush Presidential Library and Museum)

Young Barack Obama with his mother, Stanley Ann. (Courtesy of Polaris Images)

Barack Obama with his father, Barack Obama Sr. (Courtesy of Polaris Images)

Obama with his stepfather, mother, and sister in Indonesia. (Courtesy of Polaris Images)

went on to graduate from Princeton Theological Seminary, as had Richard Cleveland. Before being ordained, Joseph returned to teaching at his old school in Steubenville. Teaching and preaching were both of interest to him. He had grown into a strikingly good-looking, sturdy six-footer, with thick brown hair, regular features, and the penetrating gaze of someone confident of what he wants.

There was also a companion Female Academy in town. One of its students was Janet Woodrow, whom everyone called "Jessie." She was slender and almost painfully shy, but her keen intelligence had so impressed her father, the Reverend Thomas Woodrow, that he determined to enhance her education, entering her in the academy in her teens. She is described by Doris Faber as "whispy-haired" and "possessing an ethereal quality that substituted quite effectively for mere earthly beauty." Eventually, Jessie made the acquaintance of young Joseph Wilson, who was already regarded as a preacher of promise and a teacher of uncommon ability. He was also the handsomest man she had ever laid eyes on. Even as his "incomparable father" aged, Woodrow Wilson would say of him, "If I had my father's face and figure, it wouldn't matter what I said."

As John Mulder writes, the Woodrows were a more distinguished family than the Wilsons, "tracing their ancestry back to prominent Scottish divines across six generations." Jessie's close-knit family emigrated to New York when she was five, then moved to Ontario and finally to Ohio. The fifth of eight children, Jessie's ties with her siblings became even stronger after the early death of her mother. Her father was the scholarly pastor of an independent Congregational church, and her brothers continued in the family tradition, becoming learned Presbyterian ministers in both the northern and southern United States.

Jessie was utterly smitten with Joseph Wilson, and the attraction was mutual. On June 7, 1849, only a few weeks before his ordination by the Presbytery of Ohio, twenty-seven-year-old Joseph Ruggles Wilson married twenty-two-year-old Jessie Woodrow in Chillicothe, Ohio. The nuptials were performed by Jessie's father, who could not have been more delighted. It must have seemed to the Woodrows as much a fortuitous merger as a marriage, but in coming years there would be little doubt of the couple's devotion to each other. If Jessie's love for Joseph was perhaps tinged with a touch of adoration, well, that was fine with him.

Joseph Wilson would always feel most fulfilled when he was enabled to both teach and preach. After his wedding, he served as an instructor in rhetoric and at the same time was pastor of a small Pennsylvania church. Word of his erudition spread. In 1853 he was offered a promising professorship at Hampden-Sydney College in Virginia. A measure of the breadth of his knowledge was that he taught chemistry as well as natural science. For the remainder of their lives together, by preference as well as residence, Joseph and Jessie Wilson lived in the South, and their children would think of themselves as Southerners. Wilson scholar Arthur Link notes that when news reports surfaced that President Wilson was the son of an old Virginia family, he replied, "I wish it were true." He also never quite forgot his English heritage, admiring the parliamentary system. His earliest political heroes were English, particularly the great Liberal Prime Minister, William Gladstone. Young Woodrow thought perhaps one day he might become a distinguished statesman himself.

In 1854, Joseph Wilson was called to the pastorate of the First Presbyterian Church of Staunton, a lovely town nestled in the Shenandoah Valley of Virginia. He and Jessie already had two children, both girls. In their spacious manse, which still stands, on December 28, 1856, their third child and first son was born. He was not named Joseph Ruggles Wilson Jr. but Thomas Woodrow Wilson, for his mother's favorite brother and her father. Years later, he would drop the "Thomas," to his mother's disappointment, and her maiden name became his first name. There would finally be a "Junior" about a decade later, when the Wilsons had their second son and final child.

From the start, Jessie was effusive about her "Little Tommy," writing everyone within her family circle about this "fine, healthy fellow." He was "just as fat as he can be" and "as little trouble as it is possible for a baby to be." Had Tommy been as homely as Theodore Roosevelt, it would likely have made little difference. As it turned out, the unique appearances of both men, the sons of strikingly handsome fathers, would become grist for cartoonists—Roosevelt with his bespectacled, owlish face, Wilson with his long professorial chin, both with prominent teeth.

"A boy never gets over his boyhood," Wilson would later write. His was dominated by the Civil War and its immediate aftermath. He did not enter school until he was nine. His first recollection was from when he was four, standing at the gate of his parents' home, hearing a passerby tell his father that Mr. Lincoln had been elected and "there was to be war." In 1857, the same year that Joseph Wilson received his doctor of divinity degree, he had ventured down to the larger community of Augusta, Georgia, to officiate at the wedding of his brother-in-law, Thomas Woodrow. While in town, he was asked to preach at the First Presbyterian Church, whose prominent pulpit had recently become vacant. Wilson's eloquence made such a strong impression that he was invited to become their minister. The offer was enhanced by the construction of a handsome new brick parsonage. He and his family spent the next twelve years in Augusta, the most productive of his career.

His father's decision to side with the South colored many of young Woodrow's later convictions. Presbyterian Covenanter theology, founded in Scotland in 1638, affirmed that God's will *could* be determined and His grace received by an imperfect humanity. Through prayer and reflection, Joseph Wilson discerned that the Lord's will ordained the preservation of the established order, even if it resulted in secession, war, and the continuation of slavery. The First General Assembly of the Presbyterian Church of the Confederate States of America was held in Wilson's church in Augusta, and he was elected permanent clerk of the Southern Presbyterians. Aside from the sadness of separation from his Northern brethren, it was an extraordinary distinction for such a young clergyman. Yet only a few years later, Wilson's Covenanter conclusions made him rejoice in the final failure of secession. By then, continued suffering and destruction was insupportable. Like a loving parent, the Lord might permit such revision, but not a fundamental compromise with unbelief.

Despite Augusta's status as a major supply center for the Confederacy and a good deal of fighting in the vicinity, tangibly the Wilson family suffered surprisingly little in the Civil War. Relations with Northern kin were strained, but only for a time. The church building was damaged; later its sanctuary served as an emergency hospital and its grounds as a stockade for Union prisoners. It must have been an exciting time for a young boy, but Woodrow tended to be rather removed from it all, a dreamy and solitary child.

Perhaps it is most accurate to suggest that Woodrow's father was the more influential in molding his public life, his mother in shaping his inner life. When they were apart, correspondence between father and son was constant, advice mingled with encouragement. Even when critical of his "precious son" for some perceived lapse, Joseph Wilson would conclude, "You have only to persevere. . . . It is just because of my love for you that I have always tried to be faithful in telling you the truth about yourself." Or, on a happier occasion, "My dearest boy—How much we all love you cannot be put into words, and we are proud of you besides." Not just fulfillment but happiness came from high achievement.

That both mother and son suffered from a series of sometimes mysterious ailments may have helped cement their special bond. Rev. Wilson was often obliged to be away during the time that Jessie was pregnant with their last child. Young Woodrow was especially solicitous during this period, doing all manner of household chores. Later, he would recall those days with his mother, saying, "I remember how I clung to her (a laughed at 'mama's boy') till I was a great big fellow; but love of the best of womanhood came to me and entered my heart through these apron-strings."

Some historians believe that the reticent Jessie's influence on her Tommy was greatest during the first decade of his life, and his gregarious father dominant thereafter. But the pervasive influence of both parents overlapped. It was simply different, and exercised differently, just as the Christian piety they shared could be seen more clearly through compassion on the mother's part, and certainty on the father's. As a family retainer said of young Wilson, "Outside, Mr. Tommy was his father's boy, but inside he was his mother all over." She was the foundation of his emotional life.

Finally being able to attend school brought Woodrow out a bit. He learned to play with others and found that he loved baseball. Even more, he enjoyed organizing the games. Yet why did he have such difficulty learning to read? Even after the dislocations of war, it was a perplexing question. Thomas Woodrow Wilson had what today would be called a learning disability, probably dyslexia, which took a great deal of effort to overcome. It is likely that Woodrow couldn't fully comprehend what he read until he was eleven or twelve years old. One result was his interest in shorthand, which he could understand more readily than Greek or Latin, or initially English.

In 1870, although the Rev. Dr. Wilson retained his position as "stated clerk" of the Southern Presbyterians, he received two prestigious appointments that seemed the capstones of his career. He was called to become minister of the much larger First Presbyterian Church in Columbia, South Carolina, and at the same time was asked to accept a professorship in pastoral theology at Columbia Theological Seminary. Wilson fully expected to remain in these dual capacities, always his preference, for the remainder of his active professional life. Instead, they lasted only a tumultuous four years.

Young Woodrow had his own decision to make. In 1873, at the age of eighteen, he left the safe haven of his parents' parsonage for Davidson College in North Carolina, closely affiliated with the Presbyterian church, with the intention of becoming a distinguished divine like his father. Being on his own for the first time, however, opened new vistas for reflection. To win the world one must be *in* the world. His father had stressed the power of forceful rhetoric. How much more might he ultimately accomplish in meaningful temporal reform, as an American equivalent of someone like Gladstone? He finally decided not to pursue the ministry. By all accounts, Wilson loved Davidson and did well there, both within and outside the classroom, developing a lifelong affection for the college. His father may have been disappointed when Woodrow told him of his change in vocational plans, but he could also see the potential of a broader career.

Both parents continued to pour out their thoughts to their increasingly independent son. When Wilson finally decided to discard his first name as not quite mature enough, his mother wrote, "My darling Woodrow, I am going to make a desperate effort to call you Woodrow from this time on. . . . I have learned to love the name we have called you ever since your baby-hood, that I have found it hard to resolve to give it up. But 'Tommy' is certainly an unsuitable name for a grown man." As noted, there have been many presidents whose middle names were their mothers' maiden names, but Wilson was one of only two who made it their first name.

His father's letters were equally supportive but also began increasingly to share his own problems. Joseph Wilson's promising dual career in Columbia was simply not working out. The church wanted a full-time minister. Someone less stubborn and more flexible than the Rev. Dr. Wilson might have promptly dealt with and resolved such understandable concerns equitably; Wilson could not. In this, as in other areas, father and son surely were similar, neither prone to compromise.

Despite his positive adjustment to Davidson, around the end of his freshman year Woodrow suffered the first of his rather mysterious breakdowns—physical, emotional, or both—that took over a year of recuperation at home to get over. Perhaps it was partly influenced by the stress of the decision to change his career path. In any case, he did not return to Davidson for his sophomore year. Wilson followed his father's advice in 1875 to return to college at Princeton (it became Princeton University in 1896) in New Jersey. He flourished there, not only in academics but also in a variety of activities, from debating to baseball to editing the new college newspaper and joining a convivial eating club. Most important, before graduating in 1879, he resolved the general outline of his future. He would do the Lord's work outside the ministry, hopefully eventuating in public service. Woodrow decided to initiate his new career, after graduating from Princeton, by going to law school at the University of Virginia, but that led to another crisis of confidence.

He found the curriculum dry and didactic but persevered, until concluding that perhaps the legal profession was not the best path to choose.

Both mother and son fell ill. They tried to keep the details of their ailments from distracting Joseph, who had his own problems to cope with. Woodrow was permitted to finish his law studies at home, passed the bar, and set up a practice, but his heart was never in it. The highlight of his brief legal career was meeting and courting bright-eyed, auburn-haired Ellen Louise Axson, daughter of a Presbyterian minister, from Rome, Georgia. He was married to "Ellie Lou" in Savannah, on June 24, 1885, by his father and her grandfather.

Once Woodrow focused on his true path to prominence, his meteoric career was little short of astonishing. He became a scholar and teacher, particularly of government, and then went on to "effectual public service," ultimately to its highest level. In only seven years, Wilson rose to the heights of academia. Despite diminished financial resources, his father supported him unreservedly, financing his graduate studies. Between 1883 and 1890 Woodrow Wilson earned his PhD at the Johns Hopkins University, taught at Bryn Mawr and Wesleyan colleges, and finally joined the faculty of Princeton University. In 1902 he was named Princeton's president. In 1910, a Democrat, he was elected governor of New Jersey, and in the dramatic three-way race of 1912, as he had preordained, he was elected president of the United States and was headed for a momentous two-term tenure.

With her husband still battling for the Lord on lonelier ground, Jessie Woodrow Wilson died on April 15, 1888, in Clarksville, Tennessee, at the age of sixty-two. Writing to his wife from his teaching assignment at Bryn Mawr, Woodrow found his grief all but inexpressible. He later wrote, "As the first shock . . . of the irreparable blow passes off . . . my heart is filling up with the tenderest memories of my sweet mother," adding, "If I had not lived with such a mother, I could not have won and seemed to deserve . . . such a wife—the strength, the support, the human source of my life." It was to his mother that Woodrow dedicated his essay on the obligations of youth: "Your mother, who brought you forth, nourished you in your helplessness, loves you as only a mother can—who will trust you when all others forsake you, is ready to give her all to make you happy—are you to do nothing for her?" In 1885 Wilson had written his first major work, *Congressional Government*, to much acclaim. It was dedicated to his father, "the patient guide of my youth."

After the death of his wife, now lonely as well as depressed, his health in decline, Joseph quit his final post and traveled from place to place, often serving as a guest preacher on Sundays. In 1901 Wilson finally gave up his wanderings and his lifelong fight for faith and went to stay with Woodrow and his family. He lived long enough to witness his son's ascension to a presidency, even if it was only of the university. The Rev. Dr. Joseph Ruggles Wilson died at "Prospect," the Princeton president's home, on January 21, 1903, at the age of eighty. His body was taken to Columbia, South Carolina, where he was buried in the churchyard of his most prominent parish, next to his wife, both Southern by preference in life and death.

Woodrow Wilson aptly memorialized his father as a "master of serious eloquence, a thinker of singular power, a lover and servant of his fellow man, a man of God." As August Heckscher notes, Joseph "had instructed the boy in his youth, counseled him with rugged good sense, until without envy he had seen his son surpass him in worldly success." Woodrow's younger brother observed in 1919, "Our parents made companions and friends of their children, thus holding us to them in the bonds of strongest love and mutual confidence." There was a difference in the attitudes of the two parents, however. To Joseph, it was necessary that Woodrow always strive to be the best. To Jessie, her oldest son could not possibly be less. Given his upbringing, it is not surprising that Woodrow Wilson would try so earnestly to redeem the world, and when he failed, turn from compromising policy to the solace of prophecy. His strength and shield had been his faith, but his inflexibility denied him a statesman's measured success. Wilson's greatness had been foreseen by his father, but not necessarily its final fulfillment. Few prophets die fulfilled.

CHAPTER 12

Unlikely to Unlucky—Hardings, Coolidges, and Hoovers

Phoebe and George Tryon Harding II

One thing about Warren Gamaliel Harding: he really *looked* like a president. Six feet tall, chiseled features, noble bearing, silver hair. His appearance, his amiability, and his availability, in the opinion of many observers, constituted the bulk of his qualifications for high office. Harding found it so hard to say no that his father, George Tryon Harding II, suggested that had he been born a girl, he would always be in the family way.

On the other hand, Tryon, as he liked to be called, bore rather a noble-sounding name, but little else about him seems very notable. Physically, as described by Frances Russell, he "was small for his age—his height at maturity would be below average—dark-complexioned, with dark curly hair and over-large ears. Some would call him ferret-faced." Charles Mee's description is equally merciless. Tryon "was a small, idle, shiftless, impractical, lazy, day-dreaming, cat-napping fellow whose eye was always on the main chance." Yet he was energetic enough to pursue success in a dozen different directions and to induce the grounded Phoebe Dickerson to elope with him.

Both families grew from immigrant roots, English or Dutch, in the seventeenth century. Puritan Richard Harding, "a mariner engaged in fishing," arrived in Braintree, Massachusetts, in 1623. Around forty years later, Phoebe's maternal grandparents, the Van Kirks, came to Long Island. The Hardings, Dickersons, and Van Kirks replicate the familiar rise in status from farmers and blacksmiths to sea captains and frontier lawyers to doctors and legislators. Each family was active in the American Revolution, one of the Van Kirks reportedly supplying seven sons to the cause, and in the War of 1812. After that conflict, like so many others in New England and New York, Harding's forebears sensed greener pastures to the west and set off to Ohio.

So it was that barely a century before Warren Harding's inauguration as president—the seventh chief executive from Ohio—his great-great-grandfather Amos built his log cabin on the frontier that was already America's breadbasket. Here the first Tryon Harding was born in the "Harding Settlement" around the town of Blooming Grove. Two generations later, George Tryon Harding II was born nearby on June 12, 1843. Although smaller than prior Hardings, Tryon shared their generally swarthy complexion, leading to rumors that there had been Negro blood somewhere down the line. The Hardings were now secure enough to donate land, in the New England tradition, for a schoolhouse. On Sundays it could be converted to community worship.

Later that year, on December 21, 1843, on the adjoining farm, Isaac and Charity Dickerson had a daughter they named Phoebe Elizabeth. She was the youngest of their nine children, the eighth girl, and the liveliest. Early on, Tryon noticed his new neighbor at school. The little girl in pigtails who excelled at recitations was becoming a slender, self-assured young woman.

Although obliged to go back to it from time to time, Tryon would find farming less than fulfilling. Fortunately, it was possible to "read" any profession—teaching, law, even medicine—especially on the frontier, so long as some education preceded it. In 1858, at the age of fourteen, Tryon entered Iberia College (later Central Ohio College), a few miles from home. In three years, he had his bachelor's degree and was enabled to at least start his career by teaching in a rural school. Phoebe was never far from his mind. Now, however, the nation was engaged in civil war. Despite his short stature, Tryon longed to fight for the Union. Despite his youth, he also longed to get married. He was able to do both. Fortunately, Phoebe reciprocated his feelings and admired his ambition.

Harding's military career, however, turned out to be more musical than martial. He enlisted as a "fifer" and was later a "drummer boy" in the Ohio National Guard.

In the spring of 1864 Harding drove his wagon, hitched to a team of horses, to the Dickerson homestead and asked if he might take Phoebe and her older sister Deborah out for a ride. They went directly to the Methodist preacher in the next town, who married Phoebe and Tryon in a swift ceremony, witnessed by an equally excited Deborah. When their marriage was finally revealed, neither family was particularly upset. Here were two young people who seemed uncommonly well suited. Like so many other first fathers, at the outset George Tryon Harding II hardly lacked for energy or ambition, whatever later critics might conclude. Unfortunately, his shifting plans would never quite work out.

Like so many other first mothers, Phoebe Dickerson Harding's own plans would eventually center on her first son. On November 2, 1865, he was born—the customary large, healthy boy. Phoebe wasn't overjoyed with the imposing name—Warren Gamaliel Harding—selected by her husband, but she went along. Phoebe soon started calling her boy "Winnie." She had seven more children, but none who fueled her expectations as Winnie did.

Tryon's new career goal was to become a country doctor. After completing two semesters at the Homeopathic Hospital College in Cleveland, Tryon was entitled to put out his own shingle as an MD. His practice, such as it was, actually prospered, although his rural clientele too often paid him in produce rather than money. Tryon would buy, sell, or swap almost anything. But it was his purchase of the town's struggling newspaper, the *Caledonia Argus*, that would mean the most to young Warren. While still in school, he learned the business from the ground up. However bold Tryon's investments were, however, they never led to sustained financial security.

Phoebe became her family's salvation by becoming a professional midwife. She even managed to find the time to take courses in obstetrics and began specializing in the treatment of women's ailments in their own homes, eventually obtaining a state license as a "homeopathic." The

Methodist church was always her bulwark. She loved scripture and poetry with equal ardor. Her Winnie, "bright beyond his years," whom she had personally taught to read and calculate at an early age, stood out at Sunday school. By the age of four, prepared by his proud mother, he was declaiming in public. Russell says about Phoebe, "Except for her religious zeal, she was a quiet, dark woman, always ready to help with self-acquired efficiency when any Blooming Grove mother was in labor." Charles Mee describes Phoebe at about thirty: "Her hair pulled tightly back, her eyes calm and gentle . . . both austere and lovely." She particularly enjoyed gardening, as the adult Warren Harding never forgot. Every Sunday he brought or sent her flowers.

In high school Warren was encouraged by his mother's energy and his father's enterprise. However, his success there would prefigure his later dilemma in public life. He sought to fit in but also to stand out, to excel without seeming to exert too much effort. At the age of fifteen he went on to Ohio Central College in Iberia, where he proved to be a most versatile student leader and the most congenial. Handsome, robust, and over six feet tall, he towered over his father, who was already on the way to new enterprises.

Reinvigorated by a modest inheritance from his father, Tryon moved a few miles to the west, to the larger town of Marion, Ohio, the county seat. Warren always viewed it as his home, more than Blooming Grove or Caledonia. Here his irrepressible father continued his venturesome proclivity, encouraging Warren and two friends to purchase the bankrupt local newspaper, the *Marion Star*. Installed as its editor, Warren had been doing some drifting himself, uncertain what profession to pursue, and enjoying "bloviating"—or simply hanging out with his friends. Journalism led to politics, as Warren's new wife, the formidable Florence Kling, put the paper on a firm financial footing. Although she was the daughter of the richest man in Marion, why Warren married such a strong-willed woman five years his senior, whom he would justifiably call "The Duchess," remains something of a mystery. She had been married and divorced previously, and her father was not more favorably disposed to the Hardings. During this period, they endured a wrenching tragedy. Warren's younger brother and sister died of a severe form of jaundice that Phoebe had been powerless to prevent. It led her to move from her firm Methodism to try to find some solace in a fundamentalist certitude of the Seventh Day Adventist faith.

With his political career on the rise, Warren started attending Republican conventions and in 1898 was elected to the state senate. On May 20, 1910, after her wonderful Winnie had been elected lieutenant-governor of Ohio, Phoebe Dickerson Harding died at the age of sixty-six. She had been bedridden after a severe fall. With his father and siblings, Warren had been by her bedside when the end came. Near the end, asked whether she was praying, Phoebe replied, "No, I am trusting." Warren observed, "She had the right to trust. . . . Surely there are for her all the rewards in eternity God bestows on His very own."

Tryon was, of course, devastated. His wife had held the family together in three locations, while he tore about the countryside seeking new schemes for success that always proved elusive. From 1910 on he was largely supported by Warren. In his old age he finally became the indolent figure later pictured by biographers, and he made several imprudent and ill-timed marriages. Father and son shared that weakness. Warren's most noted affairs, so luridly publicized after his death, were with comely Carrie Phillips, the true love of his life, who was also married at the time, and fetching young Nan Britton, who might be called the leading lust of his life, with whom he had a child, Elizabeth Ann. It all came out in Nan Britton's book, *The President's Daughter*, published four years after Harding's death. It is doubtful, however, that he would ever have left the Duchess. He needed her in practical terms as much as his father had needed Phoebe.

The passion that most sustained Tryon in his old age was sharing in his son's success. Human-interest articles were written under Tryon's name about "My Boy Warren." He took to wearing a replica of his old Civil War uniform, haunting reunions of the Grand Army of the Republic. Warren Harding was the first American president to have been born after the Civil War. To Tryon's delight, the press rediscovered him when Warren ran for the presidency in 1920, announcing to a receptive nation that what was needed was "not nostrums but normalcy," his rhetoric reassuringly devoid of substance.

Harding seems more to have been swept along by a wave of good feelings than to have actually campaigned, writing to friends that the exercise of power had never really appealed to him. It was some of these friends who were keeping him awake nights. He appointed too many of them and supervised them too little. From Teapot Dome to the Veterans Bureau, Harding's "Ohio Gang" formed probably the most corrupt administration in American history, leading to indictments and even suicides. It took a terrible toll on the president. "Normalcy" couldn't cover outright theft. Yet, despite his personal and political lapses, Warren Harding was a man of honorable instincts. It was his august secretary of state whose treaty reduced the navies of the great powers. It was Harding who expressed his belief in free speech by releasing the Socialist Eugene Debs from prison. It was Harding who promoted an eight-hour workday. It was Harding, not the segregation-supporting Woodrow Wilson, who spoke in the South in favor of full legal equality for all the nation's citizens, black as well as white, not because of his complexion but his convictions. It is not too much to suggest that the best moments of Warren Harding's presidency were a reflection of the influence of his mother's values.

Done in more by his supposed friends than his enemies, Harding decided to overcome the sordid details deals of his old cronies, many of which had not yet been made public, by embarking on his own "Journey of Understanding" by train across the nation. He also wanted to get out to see more voters personally, to talk in favor of the World Court, perhaps even in preparation for a reelection campaign in 1924. He seems to have revised his earlier views about the appeal of political office. However, many who observed him noted that he seemed terribly worn out. In Seattle, after visiting Alaska, he contracted what appeared to be indigestion or food poisoning from some tainted seafood. Physicians insisted that he rest completely. After a few days he said he felt better but was still "so tired, so tired."

On the evening of August 2, 1923, in San Francisco, after his wife, who had been reading to him, went to her own compartment, Harding's nurse left his side momentarily to bring a glass of water for his medicine. He was sitting up. She arrived back just in time to see him twitch and slump over suddenly, his mouth open. The cause of death was probably a cerebral hemorrhage or a blood clot after a massive heart attack. His wife did not permit an autopsy. Perhaps she had finally endured one too many of her husband's blatant affairs, but it is difficult to believe the recurring rumor that she hastened his demise with poison. After all, she had worked so hard on his behalf. Warren Gamaliel Harding was only fifty-seven. Most of the nation had believed he was on his way to recovery, including his profoundly dissimilar vice president, Calvin Coolidge.

Tryon, the first father of an American president to outlive his son, for once was silent, mute with grief. The final of four funeral services, from Washington to Ohio, took place in the stifling midsummer heat of Marion Cemetery, as taps sounded and Tryon stiffened to a twenty-one-gun salute. Whatever the revelations to come, there have been fewer presidents more personally popular while he lived than Warren G. Harding. The outpouring of public emotion was exceptional.

George Tryon Harding II died in desired obscurity at the age of eighty-five on November 19, 1928, in Santa Ana, California. His prior life had been limited to Ohio, but his dreams were not defined by its dimensions. So many years before, he had eloped with a young woman who would endow their children with more elevated dreams.

Victoria and John Coolidge Sr.

The knocking on his front door grew louder. It was after midnight on August 3, 1923. John Calvin Coolidge had been sleeping soundly since 9 p.m., his normal time to retire, in the small first-floor bedroom of his modest Vermont farmhouse. His son, Calvin, and daughter-in-law, Grace, were visiting at the time, enjoying a pleasant escape from Washington's high humidity. After determining who was at the door and reading the telegram he brought, John called up to his son. He and his wife dressed quietly, said a brief prayer, and went downstairs. John Coolidge was the first person to address his son as "Mr. President."

Later, at precisely 2:47 a.m., by the light of an oil lamp, the senior Coolidge, a notary public, using the family Bible, administered a hastily typed oath of office to his son. Grace Coolidge was overcome with emotion. Her husband's first reaction, after kissing the Bible, grasping his father's hand, and embracing his distraught wife, was customarily calm: "I think I can swing it." Warren G. Harding had died suddenly the preceding day in San Francisco, and the Coolidges of Plymouth Notch, in Plymouth Township, one of the more remote regions of Vermont, were likely among the last Americans to learn of it. Although his son was vice-president of the United States, John Coolidge had not previously felt the necessity to have a telephone installed in his home. Intrusiveness was never in his nature.

Nor was it in his son's. For a man immersed in public life for almost thirty years, "Silent Cal" seemed taciturn even by the standards of rural New England. Yet there was nothing reserved in his appreciation of his father, recognizing all that he owed the man everyone in the region called "Colonel Coolidge." He had earned that title in 1900 as an aide to the governor of Vermont and had just enough ego not to mind being addressed by it.

Of course, many other presidents similarly esteemed their fathers. Calvin Coolidge went a step further. "My father," he would write, "had qualities greater than any I possess." Given their emotional attachment, it is not surprising that Woodrow Wilson and his father embraced upon encountering each other, even in public. Given their customary reserve, that Calvin and John Coolidge would kiss whenever *they* met was viewed with astonishment by reporters and onlookers alike. The quality that most separates John Coolidge from other memorable first fathers is entirely consonant with Coolidge's character—restraint. He never pressured his son. John understood that Calvin would do his best. He patiently supported him into his thirties. Sensitive, shy, and sometimes uncertain, but ambitious nonetheless, Calvin needed no spur to find his way, and cherished his father all the more for understanding.

Before returning to Washington to take up his new duties, as William Allen White writes, Calvin Coolidge "went across the field to the little family cemetery . . . where he paused for a time in front of the marble headstone where his mother lay buried." Her image had been with him every day since her death, and would be every day until his own. Robert Sobel adds, "As close as Calvin was to his father, he was still closer to his mother, Victoria Moor Coolidge." Already an invalid when she bore him and his younger sister, Abigail, Calvin's mother died when he was only twelve. "The greatest grief that can come to a boy came to me," he later wrote. "Life was never to seem the same again."

The autobiography that Coolidge wrote almost a half-century after his mother's death, not surprisingly the shortest by any twentieth-century president, is surprisingly eloquent for its loving description of his mother and the Vermont of his childhood. Victoria Moor Coolidge "was of a very light and fair complexion with a rich growth of brown hair that had a glint of gold in it. Her hands and features were regular and finely modeled. The older people always told me how beautiful she was in her youth. Whatever was grand and beautiful in form and color attracted her. . . . When she knew that her end was near she called us children to her bedside, where we knelt down to receive her final parting blessing. In an hour she was gone. It was her thirty-ninth birthday [March 14, 1885]. . . . It always seemed to me that the boy I lost was her image." Coolidge carried her portrait inside the watch case next to his heart for the rest of his life.

Coolidge was proud of his "English Puritan stock" and their "courageous pioneer spirit." His autobiography begins almost lyrically: "The town of Plymouth lies on the easterly slope of the Green Mountains, about twenty miles west of the Connecticut River." In Coolidge's case, country life not only had depth, it had continuity. The Coolidges went back to the Massachusetts Bay Colony that the first American John Coolidge found in 1630, and where others later achieved distinction. It was the grandfather of Calvin's grandfather who founded the family's first farm in Vermont, near the town of Plymouth Notch. The region was largely wilderness until the French and Indian War, when a military road was cut through by Lord Jeffrey Amherst. Settlers began arriving in numbers only after the Revolution. A Captain Coolidge's service entitled him and his five children to five homesteads. By 1840 the town and surrounding farms had over 1,400 inhabitants.

John Calvin Coolidge was born in Plymouth Notch on March 31, 1845. The son of fun-loving Galusha and pious Sarah Coolidge, he seems to have come into the world running. His younger brother, rather surprisingly named Julius Caesar Coolidge, probably at the inspiration of Galusha, died at the age of twenty in 1870. Despite the bracing climate and fresh air of Vermont, as Sobel points out, life expectancy was little more than forty years. Tuberculosis was especially feared. It had taken the lives of many in the Moor family, as it would Calvin's mother.

John's education, beyond that provided by his parents, was limited to the local schoolhouse and a few terms at the boarding school of Black River Academy in nearby Ludlow. When home, John was always working—"burning out" some of the diminishing supply of local lime, helping on his father's farm, working for the village wheelwright, and learning carpentry, bricklaying, masonry, and carriage making. Calvin would write of his father, "If there was any physical requirement of country life which he could not perform, I do not know what it was." Claude Fuess adds, "He pitched the hay onto the oxcart; he owned and knew how to use the tools for mending water pipes and tinware; he could even help a blacksmith at the forge." When a visitor suggested that John seemed to serve his community as everything but an undertaker, he replied that, yes, he had made coffins, as well. He even taught school for a time, at nearby Pinney Hollow.

By the time he'd reached his teens, John was nearly the height of his father, with an impressive physique hardened by physical labor—as Sobel writes, "a powerfully built man with an impressive face." Somehow he had found time to become acquainted with a lovely but delicate young woman named Victoria Josephine Moor. Although apparently named for both a queen and an empress, she came from a family as Puritan as the Coolidges. Her mother, Abigail Franklin Moor, and her father, Hiram Dunlop Moor, were of Scotch, Irish, and Welsh descent.

She was born on a Vermont farm in 1846 but moved at the age of two to the more populous hamlet of Plymouth Notch. Her parents had prospered, and they lived in the largest house in town.

At Black River Academy, Victoria was similarly attracted to energetic John Coolidge. On May 6, 1868, when she was twenty-two and he twenty-three, they were wed, and moved into a relatively spacious five-room, two-and-a-half-story cottage. It was attached to the village post office that Coolidge managed, and the general store that he, of course, ran profitably. Later, he would become involved in insurance, real estate, and preparing credit evaluations, even operating the local pound.

The couple's first child, a boy they named yet another John Calvin Coolidge, was born on a date that would always bear a special significance to him—July 4, 1872. By the time, three years later, that his sole sibling, Abigail, dear "Abbie," arrived, the family had moved to a larger house across the street on two acres of land, with several outbuildings. But Calvin's mother was already an invalid. She would live always in his memory after her death in 1885, but his grieving father remained a sustaining physical presence. Many future presidents, of course, highly esteemed their fathers. Calvin Coolidge was in awe of his. The Colonel could do just about anything. Calvin eventually gave up his first name; he preferred to be plain Calvin Coolidge, not a junior version of such a formidable father.

In addition to all his business activities and practical skills, John Coolidge served as township constable, justice of the peace, and tax collector; he would later be elected to the state legislature and senate, and was named a "colonel" on the staff of the governor—his considered judgment respected by virtually everyone. In a way, he was a throwback to the fathers of presidents in the earliest days of the republic, who were invariably the first citizens of their communities, however modest those communities might be.

Unfortunately, Calvin was not at all like his robust father physically. He grew to be as tall, but his frail-looking slender frame was more like that of his mother's family than the hardier Coolidges. He was frequently and alarmingly ill with severe colds and asthma, the threat of tuberculosis ever present. Medical treatment was still rudimentary and remote in the highlands of Vermont. "The only thing close to flamboyant" about Calvin Coolidge, Sobel writes, "was his bright red hair, which contrasted with his pale, freckled face." Despite his unimpressive physique, as Donald McCoy details, Calvin pulled more than his weight on his father's farm. His closest companion and playmate was his cheerful, outgoing, and seemingly healthier younger sister Abbie, who also had bright red hair. She died of appendicitis at the age of fifteen. Three of the people Calvin loved best were lost to him early, at five- to six-year intervals: his grandfather, his mother, and his sister. William Allen White writes that Coolidge's losses were suffered largely in silence, although no less deeply felt.

Of course, such losses only brought him closer to his devoted father, who knew what it was to be a sole surviving child. John Coolidge worried not only about his son's physical health but also about his emotional well-being. Years later, Calvin would say to his wife, "I am as much interested in human beings as one could possibly be, but it is desperately hard for me to show it." He would always be uncomfortable meeting new people. In that sense, as he admitted, "I've never really grown up."

Calvin was excited, at least for him, when he learned in 1887 that he would be going, as had his mother, father, and grandmother, twelve miles down the hill to Black River Academy in Ludlow. Colonel Coolidge, however, who now served on the school's board, intended that Calvin would stay to graduation, and then—the first in his line of Coolidges—go on to college. The ultimate profession he might follow didn't matter to his father; his education did. It is certain that both father and son were terribly lonely after the boy's departure. Despite his abiding affection for his mother, Calvin could appreciate why his father, seven years a widower, would marry Carrie Brown, who had been one of his early teachers. She would prove to be a loving stepmother to Calvin, but by then he was off to college. Unfortunately, John Coolidge would outlive his second wife, as well.

It was not until his senior year, his fourth at Black River, that Calvin, still a gawky, rather solitary teenager, discovered Latin, classical literature, and rhetoric and found that he actually enjoyed recitation and debating. He also filled out a bit physically. The childhood freckles faded, the red hair toned down. According to White, "He was slight but not skinny. His muscles were hard and his jaw was well set, his features clear cut"—more like his father. He spoke at graduation on "Oratory in History."

After initially failing Amherst College's entrance exam and attending a preparatory semester at prestigious St. Johnsbury Academy, Calvin was admitted to Amherst. That is all it took in those halcyon days. "I hate to go away," Calvin would say, always fondest of the people and places closest to him, but still he came to love Amherst. By his senior year, as Fuess writes, he was recognized for "his intrinsic character and ready wit." He didn't drink, smoke, or play cards, and he had never danced before going to college, but he finally joined a fraternity and was chosen "Grove Orator"—to give a humorous address on Class Day. His pride in being selected, something that would have been inconceivable for Coolidge only a few years before, was undoubtedly shared by his father. Calvin graduated cum laude, just short of Phi Beta Kappa.

Two prominent Amherst alumni practicing law in Northampton, Massachusetts, invited him to "read" the profession in their offices. It was still possible to pass the bar without going to law school, and Calvin did so in 1897. He also got involved in local politics, initially by handing out literature for one of the firm's partners, who ran successfully for mayor, and started attending state Republican conventions. At the end of 1898, after opening his own law office, Calvin won his first election, to the city council. From the start, he demonstrated surprisingly shrewd political instincts, working smoothly with local Democrats as well as the GOP faithful. Throughout, as Sobel writes, he had the advantage of "a loving, generous father on whom he could count for anything he needed."

Calvin's first meeting with Grace Goodhue sounds like a scene from a Mack Sennett silent comedy. She saw him standing in the open window of the Northampton house in which he roomed, shaving himself while dressed in his long underwear and wearing a derby hat, perhaps intended to keep his hair in place. Calvin also saw *her*, and despite his embarrassment, with uncommon impulsiveness, he fell in love with the vision. Despite so inauspicious a start, he managed to meet her. Gradually, Grace perceived qualities in Calvin visible only to a discerning eye. They made an unlikely couple, this "odd stick," as Calvin called himself, and his gracious Grace. Vivacious, dark-haired, attractive, and stylish, Grace Goodhue may have seemed lighthearted, but she was hardly lightheaded. After graduating Phi Beta Kappa from the University of Vermont, she learned sign language and took a position in 1903 teaching the deaf at the Clarke School in Northampton.

Not long afterwards, in Burlington, Vermont, Andrew Goodhue looked up from the magazine he was reading to see a surprise guest in his living room. "Hello, Calvin," he said, "What are you doing in Burlington? Got some business here?" "No," Calvin replied, "came up to marry Grace." Or so the story goes. Apparently, Mr. Goodhue suggested that Calvin might want to ask the young lady herself. According to Grace, when Calvin got around to it, his proposal consisted of, "I am going to marry you." Coolidge put it more tenderly in his autobiography, "We felt we were made for each other. For almost a quarter of a century she has borne with my infirmities, and I have rejoiced in her graces."

They were married at her parents' home in Burlington on October 4, 1905. He was thirty-three and she was twenty-six. His pleased parents were among the fifteen or so guests. At a larger party the night before, a friend of the Goodhues who had not yet met Calvin, seeing him standing alone and silent in a corner, mistook him for one of Grace's students. Later, according to McCoy, a wag suggested that since Grace had taught the deaf to hear, she might one day teach Calvin to speak. Grace soon became accustomed to this sort of comment. Years later in Washington, when she was complimented as a stimulating conversationalist, Grace responded that, after all, she'd had to learn to speak for two. The fact is, she was precisely what Calvin Coolidge needed, and he was smart enough to realize it. After a frugal honeymoon in Montreal, they moved into a modest duplex in Northampton, where they continued to live long after they could afford more luxurious accommodations. The first of their two sons, John, was born in 1906. Despite his growing legal practice and political progress, Calvin still reluctantly needed to call on his father for financial assistance. It was never given with reluctance.

No less an authority than Will Rogers considered that Calvin Coolidge "had more subtle humor than almost any public man I ever met." There is little doubt that he eventually turned his wry, cryptic, straight-faced comments into a sort of art form, relishing, in the current parlance, "putting people on." The most celebrated instance was at the sort of dinner party Coolidge detested. When a society matron gushed that she had wagered that she could get "Silent Cal" to say more than two words, he replied, "You lose." Once, when asked the subject of a minister's sermon, Coolidge replied, "Sin." When pressed for more details, he added, "He's against it." His father's comments were equally succinct. When a reporter told Colonel Coolidge, "We expect great things from your son," his deadpan response was: "I hope you won't be disappointed." Invited to attend a dinner to promote Calvin's political prospects, he replied, "Gentlemen: Can't come. Thank you, John Coolidge."

In his entire political career Coolidge lost only one election, for an unpaid post on the Northampton school board. It was before the birth of his own children. When a friend said that he would have voted for him had he had a child in the public schools, Calvin ruefully replied, "Might give me time." It wasn't many years later that, with the support of some four hundred Democratic voters, Coolidge was elected mayor of Northampton. At his Amherst reunion in 1910 he told classmates, "I got the job by keeping my mouth shut so they wouldn't know what a fool I was." To his father he wrote more seriously, "I could not have been Mayor without your help." For nearly the next thirty years, this seemingly unlikely politician held public office until his surprising, laconic announcement, "I do not choose to run for president in 1928."

It was a somewhat lengthier pronouncement that launched him into the national spotlight. In 1919, as governor of Massachusetts, Coolidge, after some deliberation, ordered the State Guard to intervene in a Boston strike by policemen that had opened the way for heightened criminal activity. When labor leader Samuel Gompers objected, Coolidge responded by declaring, "There is no right to strike against the public safety by anyone, anywhere, anytime." For the first time, Republicans across the nation envisioned Coolidge as a potential presidential candidate. Although hardly a crony of Warren Harding, he was nominated, with considerable enthusiasm, as his running mate in 1920. Those who characterized colorless Calvin Coolidge as a chief executive with the sedentary instincts of a domestic feline probably never spent much time with him. Coolidge believed that "it is much more important to kill bad bills than to pass good ones." The prospering nation didn't seem to require an activist president. He was not so old-fashioned, however, that he didn't relish talking to the electorate over the radio.

When his son was elected vice president in 1920, the Colonel's satisfaction had been tempered by Carrie's death. Once again he was a widower. Within three years he would swear in Calvin as president, and only nineteen months later, on March 4, 1925, sit as an honored guest at his son's inauguration after Calvin won the office in his own right. Yet even that occasion was diminished by an inexplicable tragedy. If possible, it brought John Coolidge and his son even closer together.

In the summer of 1924, Calvin's younger son, Calvin Jr., had developed a blister on his toe while playing on the White House tennis court. It became terribly infected, and despite every medical effort, the boy passed away on July 7. He was the first child of a president to die in the White House since Willie Lincoln. "When he went," he wrote of his son, "all the power and glory of the Presidency went with him." In November 1924, after the election, Grace Coolidge crocheted a bedspread with one square for each month she and her husband must remain in Washington, literally counting the days until their departure. Although it may have come to the nation as a surprise, it is little wonder that Calvin Coolidge did not choose to run again in 1928.

Later, in 1925, his father, still in Plymouth Notch, was ailing, almost an invalid after undergoing a prostate operation. His condition worsened after a heart attack. Calvin had finally installed a direct telephone line and called every day, upset that the press of work made him "resort to the poor substitute of a telephone. . . . I wish you were here where you could have every care and everything made easy for you, but I know you feel more content at home. . . . I suppose I am the most powerful man in the world, but great power does not mean much except great limitations."

John Calvin Coolidge died on March 18, 1926, late in his eightieth year. Not since John Adams had a first father died while his son was in office. When informed that the Colonel was failing, Calvin and Grace rushed by a special train up to Vermont, but they were too late. "When I reached home," Calvin wrote, "he was gone. It costs a great deal to be president."

After the simple Episcopal service he had requested, John Coolidge was borne from his farmhouse in the place where he had always lived and laid to rest next to those he loved best—all but Calvin, who would join him seven years later. Colonel Coolidge left an estate of over $70,000, a substantial sum for the times, but then profligacy was never in his nature. Generosity was. It was his hand that Calvin had first grasped after receiving from him the oath of office. After that, John Coolidge's life had never been quite the same, his treasured privacy shattered by hordes of visitors.

In a letter to his father on August 2, 1925, Calvin recalled, "It is two years since you woke me to bring me the news that I was president. . . . I am sure I came to it largely by your bringing up and your example." And, he may have added, your uncommonly patient perception.

Hulda and Jesse Hoover

Has any prominent American ever undergone so swift a transition from admiration to vilification as President Herbert Clark Hoover? He came into office hailed as the "the Great Engineer," a benefactor of humanity, who had saved millions abroad from starvation. Yet he had run out of miracles when obliged to confront the Great Depression, particularly as it affected millions of Americans. To Forrest McDonald, this ostensibly publicity-shy president had been in fact "so adept at image management that it can be said that he engineered his own demise." The shantytowns that emerged throughout the nation were dubbed "Hoovervilles." A popular slogan: "In Hoover we trusted. Now we are busted." This progressive Republican, who as Harding's and Coolidge's commerce secretary had opposed child labor and promised workers' rights, became the somber-faced image of national catastrophe.

Fortunately, he lived long enough to earn a more balanced evaluation as a survivor called upon to work again in famine relief after the Second World War and to streamline the federal bureaucracy from the late 1940s through the 1950s. Despite his seemingly dour demeanor and uninspiring rhetoric, he remained a featured attraction at Republican conventions. Hoover died at the age of ninety on October 20, 1964, with at least his reputation for laudable works restored.

His memoirs are as surprising as (and, of course, longer than) those of Calvin Coolidge, not only for their forceful writing but also for a touch of actual humor. In fact, his earlier business career had been replete with the kind of adventure experienced by few chief executives. Had his parents only lived longer, they would have merited far more than a mention in nurturing such ambitions.

Jesse's great-great-grandfather, Andreus Huber, who arrived in Philadelphia in 1738, was from a Swiss family that had moved to the German Palatinate. As George Nash writes, the Hoovers had a "habit of migration," continuing in the New World. Somewhere between Lancaster County, Pennsylvania, and Maryland, where he farmed, and North Carolina, where he opened a gristmill, Andreus Huber became Andrew Hoover. Andrew's son John, both a farmer and a millwright, took his family to the more abundant acreage of Ohio, settling in Miami County. He married a member of the Religious Society of Friends and soon joined it himself. These Quakers were also expanding westward. In the mid-nineteenth century they established a settlement in West Branch, Iowa, which grew quickly. John Hoover's grandson, Eli, joined the migration, establishing his farm outside West Grove. His large family included his son, Jesse Clark Hoover, who had been born in West Milton, Ohio, on September 2, 1846.

Jesse's childhood in his new home was divided between terms at the local "select school" (which was not selective, but open to all), the seasonal recreations of fishing and sledding, and chores on his father's farm. Christmas was popcorn balls cemented with sorghum molasses. They wore homespun clothes dyed with butternuts, and no shoes in the summer. Self-sufficiency was essential. Nothing was wasted. The women of West Branch canned their own fruits and vegetables and made everything from rugs to soap. Local men constructed the spare furniture that went into their homes of unadorned, whitewashed wood. The Hoovers' house had only two or three rooms, its overall dimensions not much larger than John Coolidge's sitting room.

The Indians who still resided nearby taught the local children how to hunt with bows and arrows, in the absence of firearms. West Branch was different in only one significant respect from dozens of other rural towns in the growing Midwest—it was a thoroughly Quaker community. There was no saloon in town. Nor would there be a jail until the railroad brought in interlopers. Friends in the Midwest would encourage something of a compromise between the restraint of traditional meeting for worship in the East and the churches of the Far West. However, whether in Iowa, Pennsylvania, or California, Friends were all committed to pacifism, temperance, abolition of slavery, and the rights of Native Americans. Dress was sober and restrained; women wore bonnets, and men wore broad-brimmed hats and dark, collarless coats. "Thee" and "Thou" were still forms of salutation, and frivolity of all kinds was discouraged.

Jesse's childhood may have been unexceptional, but he early evidenced two distinctive characteristics: one of temperament and one of skill. He was extremely cheerful and outgoing, and he was a natural-born tinkerer and promoter. They combined to make him exceptionally ambitious. His plans centered on bright, devout Hulda Minthorn, whom he had encountered at the meetinghouse. He had also heard her, for the spirit often moved Hulda to speak, with uncommon eloquence for one so young. The Minthorns were also a pioneer family. Hulda had been born on a farm in Ontario, Canada, of old New England stock, but moved with her parents to Iowa when she was only eleven. Most of the community shared the opinion of Hulda's sister that "she was such a gifted girl." Hulda had attended the University of Iowa when higher education for women was still rare. She taught school for several years and wrote verse and music. Ahead of her time, and perhaps even of her place, she gave every evidence of future leadership.

It is little wonder that these two were attracted to each other. Jesse Clark Hoover, twenty-four, married Hulda Randall Minthorn, twenty-two, in the West Branch meetinghouse in 1870. They would have three children—Theodore Jesse, called "Tad," in 1871; Mary, called "May," in 1876; and, in between, Herbert Clark Hoover, called "Bert" or "Bertie," on August 10 or 11, 1874. The confusion results from his having been born just before or just after midnight in their small frame cottage.

Little Bertie almost didn't survive. At the age of two he had such severe croup that he nearly choked to death. The village doctors were unable to keep him conscious, but, by a stroke of fortune, Hulda's uncle, Dr. John Minthorn, came by just in time and brought the child back to life through artificial respiration. For days his parents never left his side, taking turns monitoring his temperature. Reportedly, his Grandmother Minthorn predicted, "God has great work for that boy to do. That is why he was brought back to life." His childhood was much like his father's— a mix of meetings, school, and chores, but with a good measure of mischievous fun, as well. Yet one of his earliest memories was of his mother taking him to a local polling place to explain how it all worked, even though she herself could not yet cast a ballot—if only she had been born later and lived longer.

For some reason, Jesse Clark Hoover decided to grow a beard. It would eventually become the longest of any first father, making him look like an Old Testament prophet. He was still thin, almost gaunt, but had grown tall and quite strong. By 1878 he was doing well enough to sell his blacksmith shop and start devoting all his business efforts to a farm-implements store. He moved his family of five to a far more spacious trim white five-room home. Jesse was also named town assessor and councilman, although to many he seemed a bit too worldly. Despite all of Hulda's activities as a community leader, which often took her to other localities, her home, as her sister noted, was "always so clean and neat"—high praise in West Branch. Hoover's depiction of rural Iowa, as idyllic as Coolidge's of Vermont, recalls the abundant surrounding fruit trees and fragrant flowers, undimmed by time. His cousin, Harriette, described the Hoover household as a "merry place," the parents involved and the children very lively.

Jesse sold everything an up-to-date farmer could use, including his own inventions and those of his father. His sons would be the third generation of inventive Hoovers (although, no, they did not develop the vacuum cleaner), and Jesse patented many of his inventions. His catchy newspaper ads stressed the promotional side of his enterprise: "Why go to Iowa City to buy Sewing Machines when you can get any kind you want [at] J.C. HOOVER and save FIVE DOLLARS." The innovative business was really gaining momentum. It was an exciting time for all the Hoovers.

Unfortunately, as Herbert continues in his memoirs, "Medical science was still almost powerless against the contagious diseases which swept the countryside. My own parents were among the victims." When Herbert was only six, his father died of typhoid fever on December 13, 1880. Jesse Clark Hoover was only thirty-four. The local newspapers praised his "pleasant, sunshiny disposition," his kindness, and his contributions to the community. Heartsick but stalwart, Hulda invested all the effort she could muster to try to sustain her close-knit family. As Hoover later wrote, "My recollections of my mother are more vivid and are chiefly of a sweet-faced woman who for two years kept our little family of four together. She took in sewing to add to the family resources. To relieve some of the pressures on Hulda, kindly relatives took the children to live with them for months at a time. With so much support, it appeared as if Hulda might succeed in keeping her family intact. Then she, too, was gone, dying of pneumonia on February 24, 1884, also at the age of thirty-four, a promising life extinguished. Ideas and ideals were both combined in Herbert Hoover's inheritance from each of his parents. Only their time was limited.

After his mother's death, a council of concerned relatives and friends took over the rearing of the three Hoover children. Herbert, raised by an uncle in Oregon, had nothing but praise for their compassionate efforts, yet his most extensive family would probably be the Stanford University community. He was admitted as part of its first freshman class in 1891, more in terms of potential than actual academic preparation, and worked his way through. Although a very quiet, self-contained youth, he excelled as a student leader, met his future wife, the highly intelligent Lou Henry Hoover, found his vocation in engineering, and launched his career. Hired in 1897 as an engineering assistant by an international mining company, during the next seventeen years he managed mines on five continents and before the age of forty was more than a millionaire. The advent of World War I in 1914 initiated his notable second career of working in the nation's service, initially for private charities and then for the government itself.

He never forgot the memory of more arduous times, though, revealing both a practical dimension and that unsuspected wit when he recalled, "On leaving college I needed at once to find some person with a profit motive who needed me to help him earn a profit. At the risk of sounding counter-revolutionary or a defender of evil, I am going to suggest that this test for a job has some advantages." Both Hoover's humanity and ambition, submerged under his shy surface, might have been more evident had his remarkable parents lived only a few more years to nurture them. Even suffering so traumatic a transition—from the most admired American to the most reviled—Herbert Clark Hoover was in the end more fortunate than they had been.

CHAPTER 13

Smothering Mothering?—Sara and James Roosevelt

⋘

The contrast could not have been more marked. There, in the rear of an open car, sat Franklin Delano Roosevelt and Herbert Clark Hoover, side by side. Roosevelt was smiling that confident, incandescent smile, head thrust back, waving vigorously to the immense crowd that lined Pennsylvania Avenue as the motorcade drove slowly past. Alongside him was Hoover, settled in his seat, glum and absolutely still, staring straight ahead as if he wished to be anywhere but there. It was March 4, 1933, Roosevelt's first presidential inaugural day. He had beaten Hoover in the election of 1932 by more than seven million votes, 472 to 59 in the Electoral College. Even with the Depression at its darkest, with some fifteen million people unemployed, Roosevelt had declined Hoover's invitation to work on recovery programs together between the election and the inauguration, preferring to launch his "New Deal" as a fresh start.

His mother had always known that he was meant for great things. To most contemporary Americans, Theodore and Franklin Roosevelt seem to belong to separate eras. Their mothers, however, were born less than twenty years apart. Beyond affluence and social standing, Sara

211

Delano Roosevelt had little in common with her predecessor, Martha Bulloch Roosevelt. While Martha had been the radiant daughter of a landed Georgia squire, Sara was the strong-willed but circumspect product of a Hudson Valley hierarchy built on acquisitive commerce. While Martha was vigorous and outgoing but delicate, dying at the age of forty-nine, the physically robust Sara lived to be almost eighty-seven. In one significant respect, however, the two mothers were similar. Both were utterly devoted parents, "Mittie" with her joyous hugging "melts" when her children were young. Sara, on the other hand, had only one child, and wanted only one, who virtually on the day of his birth became the focus of all her considerable energies. Her advice to Franklin continued ceaselessly as long as she lived, despite the often competing counsel of his wife, Eleanor, his cousin from the Theodore Roosevelt side of the family.

There was nothing diminutive or delicate about "formidable" Sara Delano. One of eleven children, nine of whom survived into adulthood, she stood a very erect five-foot-ten. Called "Sallie," as one of "the four beautiful Delano girls," Sara may have been the least comely, but she had a good mind, a hearty constitution, a will so strong that it could be intimidating, and a zest for life joined with impeccable manners. She dressed faultlessly, traveled widely, took part in no shortage of diversions, and was handsome enough to attract her share of admirers and suitors. But why settle for the sort of listless inheritors of family wealth who inhabited her circle? In her mid-twenties, Sara was in no hurry to wed. Nor was she pressured to do so by her father, whom she admired above all other men. He rather liked having this most spirited but still very respectful daughter, his favorite, at home.

Warren Delano II was no bloodless specimen of the landed gentry. He was a bold, risk-taking entrepreneur, with more than a touch of the buccaneer. As Frank Freidel writes, Delano prided himself on being capable of captaining his own sailing ships. He won, lost, and rewon fortunes in the China trade, including importing opium, supplemented by domestic investments. Delano's wheeling and dealing did not inhibit the social standing of his family. By Victorian times, heredity mattered more than enterprise. The Delano name had been anglicized not long after the 1621 arrival in Plymouth Colony of a young Huguenot émigré named Philippe de la Noye. As Ted Morgan notes, the Delanos encompassed thirteen bloodlines that could be traced back to the Mayflower. When Sara was born on September 21, 1854, her father's fortunes were at their height. The family was ensconced in a spacious Newburgh mansion called "Algonac," commanding a magnificent view of the Hudson River.

Only three years later, however, a financial panic wiped out her father's wealth. Naturally, Warren Delano promptly sailed off to Hong Kong to seek a second fortune. Eventually, in 1862, his family, headed by Sara's resilient mother, Catherine, and including six brothers and sisters, followed him. Sara was eight, and interested in everything. The family didn't return to Newburgh for three years. Sara's practical education was not limited to the lessons of proper governesses at Algonac and a brief stint at a school in Dresden. In Asia, and later in Europe, she was exposed to other cultures. Even though she found most foreigners "horrid," at least she had seen them at first hand.

At home, her acquaintance encompassed the liveliest of those who were suitably placed socially. One of Sara's favorite people was young Theodore Roosevelt, whose zest for life was no less than her father's. At a dinner party given by Roosevelt's widowed mother at their Manhattan mansion, Sara was impressed by another guest, a cousin of Theodore's named James Roosevelt. At fifty-two, tall, blue-eyed, whiskered, and widowed, James retained a mature bearing that set him apart from her younger admirers. But Roosevelt was twice Sara's age. Indeed, "Rosy," his only child by his first wife, had been born on the exact day and year as Sara herself.

Descended from the same Claes Martenszen van Rosenvelt (the original family name meant "from the rose field") as the Theodore Roosevelts, by the nineteenth century the Hudson Valley branch was as much English as Dutch and was among the leading Knickerbocker families. Originally proprietors of a prosperous mercantile business and later sugar refiners in the West Indies, the Roosevelts by the time of the

American Revolution were staunch, if rather conservative, patriots. The most prominent, Isaac Roosevelt, eventually presided over the Bank of New York, served in the state senate, and helped assure New York's ratification of the Constitution.

On July 16, 1828, James Roosevelt was born at "Mount Hope," his family's home near Poughkeepsie, on the heights overlooking the Hudson River. His father, one of several subsequent Isaac Roosevelts, was surely the most eccentric—a reclusive, hypochondriac physician. Fortunately, James's doting mother was a good deal more normal, and he had additional relatives nearby. As Geoffrey Ward writes, "He was free to roam with his black dog Billy; he hunted and fished, built a water wheel on the ice pond; learned to ride and care for the fine horses his grandfather bred and trained." He seemed a rather serious child, but there was already a streak of rebelliousness, resulting in a succession of schools.

Somehow James persuaded his father to let him attend New York University, but the blandishments of the metropolis proved too tempting. In May of his freshman year he was reprimanded for causing "disorder," and the following year he was transferred to small but well-regarded Union College in upstate Schenectady. James continued to lead an active social life, joining a fraternity that, to his father's dismay, met in a tavern. Although he may have majored more in carousing than serious scholarship, he did manage to graduate in 1847. Rewarded with a grand tour of Europe, for eighteen months James traveled from Europe to the Middle East, even spending time in Italy as a volunteer with Giuseppe Garibaldi's "Red Shirts." Upon his return, he entered Harvard Law School, did surprisingly well in his studies, and graduated in 1851 on his twenty-third birthday. As evidence of the esteem in which he was held, he was made an honorary member of Porcellian, the most prestigious of Harvard's clubs.

Attaining a coveted position with a major New York law firm, James found its routine dry and tedious. Fortunately, through the firm's corporate clients, James launched his career as what Ward calls a "genteel gambler." He was elected to the board of the Consolidated Coal Company of Maryland, the first of several increasingly ambitious business ventures.

James was equally active in the romantic realm. He met, courted, and married his lovely twenty-two-year-old cousin, Rebecca Brien Howland. He had inherited Mount Hope, viewing it less as a showplace than as a working farm that should be self-supporting. He bred cattle, raised a variety of crops, and attended to local events and charities so energetically that he earned the warm regard of his neighbors. When his wife gave birth to a lively, healthy son, he and Rebecca settled on the peculiarly redundant name of James Roosevelt Roosevelt. The boy would always be known as "Rosy." James delighted in teaching his receptive son horsemanship, hunting, fishing, and a love of the outdoors that decades later he would also impart to a second son. Such idyllic times as a country gentleman in verdant Dutchess County alternated with James's other life in the great metropolis. He invested in railroads, banks, and trust companies.

When a fire of mysterious origins burned his home to the ground, James bought and greatly expanded a much larger estate with a home he called "Springwood" in the nearby town of Hyde Park. He became, in effect, the community's benefactor. In time he would oversee virtually every local institution, serve as town supervisor, and become the senior warden of St. James Episcopal Church. One day a window there would memorialize him. But to his wife's great relief, when President Cleveland wanted to name him an ambassador, he declined. His domain might be relatively modest, but it was his own.

In New York City, however, he continued his efforts to become a multimillionaire, but it never happened. His venture in coal fell victim to the Panic of 1873. His attempt to gain control of the railroads of the Southeast also failed. His most ambitious venture, to build a canal through Nicaragua, never materialized. Ironically, it would be his cousin Theodore who would develop a more viable route, through Panama. He was still quite wealthy, but in the future his business activity would largely be limited to consolidating his holdings.

When his supportive wife, Rebecca, died of a massive heart attack in 1876, James's productive life seemed to be over. Eventually emerging from mourning, at a small dinner party in 1880 James met the stately Sara Delano. Doris Faber describes "Sallie" Delano's imposing appearance at the age of twenty-six, "with her brown hair coiled into a dignified chignon, she looked rather regal already." James may not have been looking for an empress, but he saw in Sara the perfect consort to help him preside over his compact domain. Despite the difference in their ages, he sensed that she might reciprocate his sentiments. James invited her to a weeklong house party at Hyde Park, and she accepted. In the minuet of Victorian courtship, when James asked Sara to arrange the flowers on his luncheon table, both appreciated the significance of such an invitation. Perhaps James Roosevelt at fifty-two reminded her of a more sedate version of her father. She knew he had a son her age, but at twenty-six was she content to wind up as simply sad "old Miss Delano"?

Warren Delano couldn't understand why Mr. Roosevelt started visiting him with such frequency. True, he liked the fellow well enough, even allowing that James made him "realize that a Democrat can be a gentleman," an anomaly in the Hudson Valley aristocracy. They'd served on some business boards together and were already acquainted, but when James finally came to the point, Warren was thunderstruck. It wasn't that the Delanos' resources dwarfed those of the Roosevelts. James was presentable enough. But what of the age difference? Yet, if not totally captivated, Sara had been deeply impressed by James Roosevelt. After some discreet but persistent urging, Warren Delano finally, if still reluctantly, granted his consent.

The couple was married in the resplendent setting of "Algonac," the Delano estate. Sara found James to be the cheerful, considerate, and generous husband she had anticipated. He welcomed the prospect of another child. Perhaps an extension of the bloodlines of two notable families was in Sara's mind, as well, when she agreed to marry him. Franklin Delano Roosevelt was conceived in Paris during a ten-month honeymoon that was more like another grand tour. He was born in an upstairs bedroom at Springwood in Hyde Park on January 30, 1882. It was a most difficult delivery, taking well over a day, and James stayed by his wife's bedside all night. There was nothing restrained about his reactions the following morning. "At a quarter to nine," he wrote in his diary, "my Sallie had a splendid large baby boy. He weighs 10 lbs. without clothes."

Much has been written about the impact of this special child on Sara, a transformation that would dominate future interest in anyone or anything else—"her reason for being," as Ted Morgan puts it. However, during the two remaining decades of their life together, Sara and James had a most amiable relationship. Affection may not have been so overt as with the Theodore Roosevelts, but everything was ordered and congenial, the love of both his parents evident to Franklin, who had no siblings at home vying for their attention.

However, from the first, although not yet certain of the ultimate goal for this special child, Sara ordered every aspect of his life. As Frank Freidel writes, Sara herself bathed and dressed her baby and breastfed him for over a year. He was eight years old before he was able to take a bath alone. Until he was in his twenties, she kept the most minute diary of his activities. Franklin wore dresses until he was five and had long blond curls his mother could not bear to have cut. When it finally became necessary, locks of his hair were placed in a satin-lined box that contained other mementos of Franklin's childhood. Sara saved everything.

Although she employed tutors to supervise Franklin's carefully structured education, Sara personally taught her son reading and geography. At the age of three, he made his first extended trip to Europe. Until he was fourteen, his only playmates his own age were relatives and a few similarly privileged children from surrounding estates.

He did have one notable companion, however, who kept Franklin from becoming overwhelmed by what I called, in a prior book, Sara's "smothering mothering"—her conviction that he was meant for something special. Even at fifty-four, James Roosevelt, who had eased back from his earlier attempts at business enterprise in favor of Hyde Park paternalism, was able to devote every available hour to Franklin. Sara recalled the healthy equity of their relationship, "His father never laughed at him. With him, yes—often." When discipline seemed called for, James would sternly remonstrate to Franklin, "Consider yourself spanked."

James taught Franklin to hunt, fish, and skate, to swim and sail, to go ice boating, to learn to control a sled and ride a thoroughbred. James loved horses, and his special pride was a matched pair, "Top Mast" and "Top Royal." Father and son would travel together in James's private railroad car, a reminder of past ventures and a special pleasure to a young boy. They would ride together over the estate, Franklin learning to appreciate the natural world. Franklin's son Elliott relates, "James taught his son to recognize the various birds whose habitat was the Hudson Valley and to make a collection of them. . . . With their favorite dog they would go together, Frank and his 'Popsie,'" a companion he could never replace, but a relationship Franklin would try to replicate with his own children.

At their summer cottage at Campobello Island in Canada, just off the Maine coast, a splendid place for sailing, Franklin learned to cruise on his father's prize auxiliary cutter, the *Half Moon,* and later to sail his own knockabout in the chill waters. He embarked on a lifelong love of the sea, collecting ship models along with his stamps and birds. Ward writes, "Mr. James was never distant, and for the first half of their lives together . . . he and Franklin were vigorous and almost inseparable companions."

At least the spontaneity of their relationship ended when Franklin was eight. In 1890 his father had a heart attack. The bond with his son remained as close as ever, but James was never to be so energetic again. The three Roosevelts traveled to Europe together a total of nine times, but during the final decade of James's life it was particularly to seek out the curative potential of spas. The daily connection, if not the constant communication, would conclude when at the age of fourteen Franklin went off to Groton, the highly regarded new boarding school in Massachusetts. Despite their imposed isolation, Franklin's parents understood that to become a self-confident adult he had better learn to mingle with others before going off to college. Although Sara wrote in her diary, "It is hard to leave my darling boy," at least Groton was administered by Episcopalians. Always cognizant of her Delano heritage, Sara, ever a staunch member of the socially acceptable Protestant Episcopal Church, sometimes termed the faith of many of her husband's relatives "Dutch Deformed." When prominent presidents became identified by their initials alone, an aid to the media, it would be "TR" but later "FDR," keeping that Delano connection prominent.

As an adult, Franklin lauded his father as among "the most generous and kindly of men," adding, "My father was no snob"—an evaluation that was less than entirely accurate. One almost senses the protestations of subsequent presidents whose mothers seemed the more dominant figures in their lives—"Now, don't forget my father." Ward goes so far as suggesting some temperamental similarities between James and Franklin Roosevelt: "The conservative and the gambler warred within James Roosevelt all of his life, just as they would later within his son." The elder was not solely a settled, self-satisfied, English-aping sedentary country squire, muttonchops and all, implied in brief accounts of his influence on Franklin.

Based on the Rugby School in England, Groton combined the concepts of Christian commitment and public service, expressed in physical and intellectual rigor. It was the obligation of the well-educated sons of leading families to not only lead the nation but to devote their efforts to the less fortunate. Groton's founder and headmaster, Endicott Peabody, was to Franklin Roosevelt what Theodore Roosevelt Sr. had been to Theodore Roosevelt Jr.—the true father of his ambitions. At first, not surprisingly, Franklin, who had been entered a year late, had difficulty adjusting to this new environment, although there was nothing lacking in his deportment. At home, Franklin gave his parents little reason to complain. But he had no experience with meeting people, even young people, on his own. By his senior year, however, Roosevelt had not only embraced Dr. Peabody's commitment to help the underprivileged, he had made fast friends and was active and well liked. He had learned to cope.

Perhaps, however, he had tried too hard. When he went on to Harvard, his self-confident enthusiasm may have struck some of his more elitist classmates as excessive. Although he was elected editor of the *Crimson* and was very popular on the campus, Roosevelt was not tapped for Porcellian, the most prestigious club, of which his father had been made an honorary member. In a residue of his patrician upbringing, he is said to have considered this the greatest disappointment of his life.

His letters from Groton, and later from Harvard, are not quite as spontaneous as were Theodore Roosevelt's letters to his parents. They read almost as if Franklin carefully worded his reports to "Dearest Mummy and Papa" to tell them what they wanted to hear—that all was well and would continue to go well. Doris Kearns Goodwin considers that from the time of his father's first heart attack, Franklin feared "that if he ever appeared other than bright and happy it might damage his father's already weakened heart."

Even as James lapsed into invalidism, his letters to Franklin remained frequent, solicitous, and tender. In his last semester at Groton, Franklin heard from his father, "Do you realize that you are approaching manhood and next year, when you begin your university life, you will be away from the safeguards of school and will have to withstand many temptations? . . . But I always feel your character is so well formed and established I have no fear as to your future career."

On January 30, 1898, he had sent a telegram to his son: "My Dear Franklin, Only a few lines before we leave for church to wish you many happy and prosperous birthdays in your future life, and may you always bear in mind that in the past on both sides of your ancestors they have a good record and have borne a good name. God bless you my dear boy. We shall think of you often today and drink your good health at dinner this evening. Your affectionate father, James Roosevelt."

More and more, in 1899 and 1900, Franklin's letters from Harvard were solely to his "Dear Mummy," inquiring after the state of his father's health. She had taken her "beloved invalid" to the softer climes of South Carolina, where he insisted on continuing to ride, however slowly, his wife by his side. He even dashed about, despite her protestations, on a motorized tricycle and later an unreliable "locomobile" auto, alarming horses and nearby spectators alike. In November 1900, however, back at

Hyde Park, he suffered a more severe heart attack. His son Rosy hastened over from next door, and Franklin hurried home from college. Eventually, James was taken to New York City to be closer to his doctors. A nurse moved in with them, and the vigil began. Franklin came back from Cambridge on December 5, sat for hours with his father, and ran errands for his mother. "James was so glad" to see him, she wrote to relatives. Sara and both of James's sons were with him when he died of heart failure on December 9, 1900. His last words to his wife were, "Only tell Franklin to be a good man." James was seventy-two.

Franklin and his distant cousin Theodore were about the same age (and both were sophomores at Harvard) when their fathers died, but the senior Theodore Roosevelt had been only forty-six. His wife died six years later. But Sara, only half her husband's age when they married, outlived James by forty-three years. She despaired in her diary that "all is over" when he died, and her feelings for him were undoubtedly genuine, but how could all be over when the son they both cherished was not yet twenty? Sara missed Franklin so terribly that she visited Cambridge to be near him. She even considered taking courses at Harvard to "improve my mind." When her son turned eighteen, she had written him, "What a difference in our lives you have made and how I thank God daily for having given you to me." As she grew older and Franklin turned to a career in politics, Sara tried to transcend the limitations of her husband's world and her own bias. Their lives had been rooted in certainty. She had imparted to her son an appreciation of his lineage, but she understood that now he was looking more to the future than the past. A letter from an uncle reinforced what Franklin had absorbed at Groton, "We are proud of our ancestors. Will our descendants be proud of us?"

Even with Franklin out of college, Sara's advice never slackened. In part, her continued influence was based on the pragmatic reality that she still controlled the family purse strings. Beyond her own Delano inheritance, James had signed over to her all his resources, certain she would use them judiciously. Franklin's streak of independence had long been apparent to her, inheriting something of her own self-confidence. Even his "Dearest Mama" letters, telling her what she wanted to hear, were a precursor of the calculation and avoidance of confrontation that would characterize his relationships in later life.

His engagement to his less-than-glamorous fifth cousin Eleanor came as a surprise to almost everyone. Although she was equally a Roosevelt, her childhood had been blighted by the death of the alcoholic father she had adored and the disdain of a beautiful mother who called her "Granny" but who also died young. Sara succeeded in having her son at least delay the announcement, perhaps hoping for some second thoughts. Franklin was twenty-one, Eleanor only eighteen. After all, Sara had been twenty-six when she wed; her father married at thirty-three. But the wedding was only postponed. When Franklin and Eleanor married in 1905, it moved him closer to Theodore Roosevelt, Eleanor's uncle, who gave the bride away and was inevitably the center of attention. Sara had to accommodate to new realities.

Eleanor had initially viewed her handsome, fun-loving husband as something of an insubstantial "feather duster," and others considered him more than a bit arrogant, but his career moved inexorably toward public service. After Harvard, he studied law at Columbia. Although not taking a degree, he managed to pass the bar. By 1910 he was elected to the New York State senate as a reform Democrat. Reelected in 1912, he gave up his seat when asked by President Woodrow Wilson to serve as assistant secretary of the navy, a position previously held by his cousin Theodore.

As Franklin's career took off, Sara must have felt a mixture of pride and apprehension. She wrote him in much the same tone as Abigail Adams had used to address her son, John Quincy. "Everything is so new," Sara commiserated, "that it will take time to fit *into* it. Try not to write your signature so small." In future years, Sara continued to offer counsel as if he were still a schoolboy, later reassuring him that, if need be, she would supplement his salary. The uncertainty in her mind was not easily resolved. Her adored son might well be happier duplicating his father's comfortable life, but had she not raised him for something more elevated, some grand achievement? Yet politics led inevitably to associating with such unsuitable, unkempt characters as Franklin's new adviser,

Louis Howe. It meant stress, controversy, publicity—the antithesis of a gentleman's values.

When years later Franklin was urged to run for governor, Sara did not really want her son to run—or did she? Whatever her conflicted emotions, in the end the competitive fire of the daughter of Warren Delano won out. If her son was intent on running, she told him, "I do not want you to be defeated." She would always support him unreservedly, whether or not she agreed with all his positions or decisions. She might argue with him in private, but in public she uttered no discouraging words.

In the prism of her difficult relationship with her daughter-in-law, Eleanor, Sara *was* domineering, and she could certainly be tactless, thoughtless, or even cruel, but her motivation was invariably whatever she thought would be best for Franklin. Her substantial wedding gift to the couple was a New York townhouse adjoining her own on Sixty-Fifth Street, completely furnished to Sara's taste, with a passageway between the two. The arrangement reduced Eleanor to tears. At Hyde Park, Sara continued to sit at the head of the table. She still presided over her son's domiciles even after his marriage, just as she continued to control his finances.

Somehow, Franklin had difficulty understanding why his sensitive wife, both of whose parents had died when she was young, resented her subservient status. As children came, five in all, Sara undertook to direct their upbringing as well, increasingly disdaining her daughter-in-law's parenting skills. Eleanor came to feel, in the words of biographer Blanche Wiesen Cook, like "an outsider in a land of strangers." In time she would learn to assert both her independence and her own influence on her husband, but first two serious crises had to be overcome. Either could have wrecked Franklin Roosevelt's political career.

In the fall of 1918 Eleanor found a packet of love letters to Franklin from her vivacious social secretary, Lucy Mercer. The discovery of their affair, so devastating to Eleanor, nearly led to her divorce from Franklin. Public divorce seemed more scandalous in those days, particularly in the upper classes, than a discreetly amorous relationship. Sara simply forbade a divorce, threatening—although it must have hurt her—to cut off all financial support. Moreover, Lucy was Catholic. The ultimately reluctant reconsideration by the parties involved at least formally preserved the marriage as well as Franklin's political career, but it widened the gulf between him and his wife, as she pursued a more independent, increasingly separate life of her own. It also sustained Sara in uneasy alliance with Louis Howe, who had already envisioned Franklin as a future president of the United States.

In the second, more sustained crisis, they would be at odds. In 1921, while vacationing at Campobello Island, Franklin contracted crippling poliomyelitis. After years of strenuous but fruitless attempts at recovery, he determined to continue his political career. In 1924 he nominated Al Smith for president in a dramatic appearance at the Democratic National Convention, and in 1928, supported by Smith, Howe, and Eleanor, Roosevelt agreed to run for governor of New York. In a difficult year for Democrats nationally, he won. Franklin Roosevelt would serve in political office for the rest of his life.

Almost from the first diagnosis of polio, Sara remonstrated with her son to return to Hyde Park under her attentive care. Instead, he ventured from time to time to Warm Springs, Georgia, where he had purchased and expanded a spa in the vain hope that its waters might have a curative effect on his immobile legs and might help in the treatment of others. Sara had hoped that a period of relative repose at Hyde Park, with consistent exercise but away from the excessive demands of public life, might hasten even the remote possibility of her son's recovery. Sara had long accepted Franklin's choice of a career and had even come to rather enjoy it. Whatever her hopes, she had always championed what she thought was best for her son.

However, others prevailed at this critical juncture. As Franklin painfully learned to make periodic use of his metal "legs," and the public was kept as unaware as possible about his crippled condition, Eleanor came into her own. They may never have fully reconciled personally, but she would always believe that Franklin's more compassionate nature had derived from his own suffering. She ultimately became his energetic eyes, ears, and legs, traveling everywhere—and a trusted, if sometimes overly persistent, sounding board. Often, her progressive ideas were well in advance of his, which were more inhibited by political realities.

Sara, of course, remained intrusive—she could hardly be otherwise—but she accommodated her dignified demeanor to be as supportive of her son as possible. She endured interviews and managed to say nothing controversial. She appeared in newsreels, a striking figure in her long dresses. She even shook hands with cigar-chomping politicos. Sara had become a national celebrity of sorts, a dignified, reassuring reminder of traditional verities. When her son finally won the presidency in 1932, she issued a poignant plea, "I shall be glad if every mother will pray God to help and preserve him." As Anthony writes, Sara eventually came to relish "her public status, reigning over fund-raisers and balls, the grande dame of a historic era." She even wrote an eminently forgettable book, *My Boy Franklin.*

In 1939, Sara very visibly helped Eleanor and Franklin host a historic visit from the king and queen of England, although the hot dogs that were served at a Hyde Park picnic would not have been her choice of fare. Sara presented a rather regal figure herself, and even Eleanor came to admire her indomitable fortitude as she aged. She may not have been an easy person for anyone to live with, but she was dedicated, constant, and even cheerful. One of her favorite expressions was "Every day is a good day."

Sara was neither an ideologue nor an intellectual. Her contribution was not in what her son did or tried to do but in who he was—his air of confidence and his underlying tenacity. In the end, he was not so much smothered by her devotion as sustained. Franklin Delano Roosevelt was a most complex man—both charming and devious. But most objective observers likely agree that his immense contribution in 1933, whatever his own doubts, was to impart a sense of hope to a nation on the verge of upheaval. Through the changing configurations of the New Deal, both our political and free-enterprise systems endured, although only preparing for war finally brought the nation out of the Great Depression Roosevelt had inherited.

Nearing her eighty-seventh birthday, finally confined to a wheel-chair, Sara Delano Roosevelt came home from Campobello to Hyde Park to be with her son. She died on September 7, 1941, and was buried on September 10. It was a windless day, yet minutes later the largest oak tree on the estate toppled over. Franklin would die less than four years later. When Franklin, alone in his office, looked through his mother's things and opened the box containing the locks of his baby hair she had cut, he broke down and cried uncontrollably. Later he wrote, "Those of us who enjoy the companionship of our mothers beyond the average number of years are indeed fortunate, for we know the good influence they exert. . . . The greatest pleasure we can get is to observe them rejoicing in our achievements." There is no doubt to whom he was referring.

7

CHAPTER 14

From the Heartland—Trumans and Eisenhowers

Mattie and John Truman

Supreme Allied Commander Dwight David Eisenhower, when honored by the British after World War II, spoke equally for President Harry S Truman when he said, "I come from the very heart of America." Their mothers put it plainly. When a reporter ventured into that heartland to the modest Kansas home of eighty-three-year-old Ida Stover Eisenhower and asked if she were proud of her son, she replied, "Which one?" Arriving at the White House from Missouri on Mother's Day, after her first airplane ride, ninety-three-year-old Martha Ellen Young Truman deplored the fuss over her visit, insisting, "I wouldn't have come if I'd known all these people were going to be here." Feisty or gentle, both mothers voiced the same unpretentious values. Take your work seriously, not yourself. Keep your word. These values were imparted to all their children, not only the ones history would honor.

Speaking for his brothers as well as himself, Eisenhower said, "Mother was by far the greatest influence on our lives." Of his own upbringing, Truman recalled, "She was always a mother who did the right thing, and she taught us, my brother and sister and I, that too." Both fathers, from similar towns in similar states, although denied the success they had sought for themselves, made their own contributions. Pugnacious John Truman inspired Harry's interest in politics. Stubborn David Eisenhower toughened his sons to fear failure even more than they feared their father.

When his father died, Eisenhower expressed regret about how difficult it had been "to let him know the great depth of my affection for him. . . . I'm proud he was my father." There is a similar sense of defensiveness in Truman's insistence that both his parents were "sentimentalists" who encouraged his ambitions, insisting to Merle Miller that his father had exercised "every bit as much influence" on him as had his mother. It wasn't true, but the desire that John Anderson Truman not be overlooked was genuine enough.

Truman's daughter, Margaret, his only child, stressed the "extraordinarily strong intellectual-emotional bond" between Harry Truman and his mother, encouraging an appreciation of history, literature, and music. Widowed for thirty-three years, Martha Ellen Truman became her son's closest confidant—indeed, his best friend until his marriage. The great contribution of his father was to share his enthusiasm for politics, ultimately leading to his first son's professional career. Harry Truman also relished a desired similarity in persona. His father, he proudly proclaimed, "would fight like a buzzsaw," sometimes even physically, for what he believed in. Harry, who never had a fistfight in his life, would contest issues with equal vehemence, only with words. How John Truman would have relished his son's "Give 'em Hell!" campaign of 1948.

John Anderson Truman's whole life was a struggle for stature. He couldn't do much to heighten his physical size, five-four and perhaps 140 pounds, although no one dared call him "Peanut" to his face. But size alone need not inhibit success. The Trumans were "yeoman gentry" in the New World as in the Old. Their English roots mingled with Germanic and French origins. The lure of abundant land brought them west from Virginia to Kentucky to Missouri. John's congenial parents, Anderson Shippe (or Shipp) and Mary Jane Holmes Truman (related to President John Tyler), were a hardworking, soft-spoken, pious, respectable, and respected couple. They loved their fertile, modest, but prosperous Jackson County farmland and never saw reason to leave it. The third of their five children, John Anderson, was born on December 5, 1851. Although he loved his gentle parents, his role model for life was the less easily contented Solomon Young, his future father-in-law.

Perhaps being orphaned early fired the ambition of both Solomon and his equally formidable wife, Harriet Louisa Gregg Young. While Louisa oversaw farms that grew to thousands of acres, risk-taking stock-dealer Solomon led cattle drives and wagon trains all the way to the West Coast. He is reputed to have owned much of Sacramento, California. He was as much at ease on the Santa Fe Trail as at home in Missouri, where the clouds of conflict were already gathering in the 1850s.

The Civil War came early to Missouri. John was only five when the first "bushwhackers" and "redlegs" came over from "bleeding Kansas" to terrorize any who dissented from their views. Both Anderson Truman and Solomon Young owned slaves, but their Southern sympathies were more by heritage than conviction. Taking oaths of loyalty to the Union didn't help. The Young homestead was particularly devastated by the boys in blue and their partisans. Until her dying day, Harriet Louisa Young viewed the Republican Party as the embodiment of evil. Her unreconstructed sentiments were imparted to her children, and to their children. Eighty years later her daughter would refuse to sleep in the Lincoln bedroom of the White House. The Trumans would always be Democrats.

After the war, the Youngs' prosperity returned, and they moved to a larger farm around Grandview. Their daughter, Martha Ellen, next to the last of their nine children, was born on November 25, 1852. Called "Mattie" by everyone, she would turn into a lively, self-confident, accomplished young woman. David McCullough describes her as about five-foot-six, striking and slender, "with dark hair, a round bright face, and a way of looking directly at people with her clever gray-blue eyes." One of those she looked directly at (or down on, since she was two inches taller) at the frequent socials for young people in the area was John Anderson Truman. In this company he was unfailingly polite, if somewhat somber, and took great care with his appearance. He combed his thick dark hair over to one side. His shoes were brightly polished, his clothes immaculate. Although he was generally sunburned from all those hours helping his father in the fields, his facial features were delicate, almost feminine. He had a long, thin nose and mouth and heavy-lidded eyes. He was always clean shaven.

Both the Trumans and Youngs had come from the same part of Kentucky and had become neighbors in Missouri, the Youngs having contributed the land for the Blue Ridge Baptist Church, which both families attended. Unlike John Truman, Mattie Young never did farm chores, was attended by servants, and learned outdoor as well as indoor skills—to ride, shoot, play the piano, crochet, and cook—gaining an appreciation of art and literature at the Ladies' Baptist College. Although she invariably rose early and worked hard, helping her mother supervise some twenty hired hands, she was indulged by both her parents. Mattie particularly loved to dance, describing herself as "what you might call a lightfoot Baptist," and had no intention of marrying until she was good and ready.

She also enjoyed playing the piano, and soon she was accompanying John, who had a fine singing voice, at their community socials. Although concealing his truculence in such settings, John was tenacious in going after what he wanted, and it was trim, captivating Mattie Young he wanted now. It didn't matter that she was twenty-nine and taller than he (as who was not?). John had proved to be a very competent farmer and a great help to his parents, but he had far bigger plans, and a role model before him—Solomon Young, the father of his intended. He, too, would be an entrepreneur, succeeding by instinct, grit, and determination, trading and investing until he also became rich.

To the surprise of many, his first campaign bore fruit. Mattie Young and John Truman were married in the Youngs' spacious parlor near the end of 1881. Truman wasted no time, setting out in a carriage borrowed from Solomon Young, to the town of Lamar, some ninety miles away, to start accumulating his fortune by trading in horses and mules. He would move his family many times in pursuit of his elusive goal of prosperity.

Their first child was stillborn, but on May 8, 1884, in their tiny cottage, Mattie gave birth to a healthy son. They named him Harry after

Martha Ellen's favorite brother, Harrison. "Don't call him Harrison," John insisted, "They'll call him Harry anyway." For a middle name they wanted to honor both their fathers. Unable to decide between Shippe and Solomon, they settled on just the letter "S" (with no period).

Two years later, when the Trumans' second son was born, named John Vivian for his father and a Confederate cavalry officer, the family had moved to Harrisonville. By the time their third child and only girl, Mary Jane, arrived three years later, the entire family was back on the Grandview farm of the Youngs. John Truman had reluctantly temporarily returned to the calling he was actually suited for. Solomon Young's vast holdings, once over 5,000 acres, were down to a manageable 600. Still, he needed help to run it. Harry Truman remembered his mother's father as a "gentle . . . great big man with a beard" who took him riding to county fairs and gave him gifts and candy, "the best time a kid ever had." His appreciation of both grandfathers would only grow with the years. Early in 1892, Solomon Young quietly died at the home from which he had so often departed in the past. Young Harry pulled on his beard, imagining he must recover. Solomon's restless son-in-law, after setting things in order, moved his family again.

Mattie taught Harry to read before he was five. She could see his potential, but she discerned that something was not quite right. Harry could readily read the large print of the family Bible but not the small print of a newspaper. At a Fourth of July celebration, as the fireworks exploded above Grandview, she learned what was wrong—his eyesight. Harry responded only to the noise, not the dazzling display overhead. He really couldn't quite see it. As soon as she could, Martha Ellen put her son in the family buggy and rode straight to an eye specialist in Kansas City. The diagnosis was that Harry had a serious affliction called "flat eyeballs." If he were to see clearly, he needed to wear very thick, very expensive glasses and keep them on whenever he was awake. He could not roughhouse or play competitive games with other boys for fear of damaging his glasses or himself. Mattie Truman was not about to have her promising son ridiculed as "four eyes" by rustic ruffians, and the local school was not all that exceptional, anyway. They would move to the county seat of Independence, with its superior schools and at least a veneer of cultivation.

Harry's father, who had always viewed farming as a temporary expedient, was all for the move. His prudent father had left him an inheritance of a few thousand dollars, and he was anxious to explore business ventures again. Perhaps he would return to livestock trading or invest in real estate or speculate in grain futures. Somehow, something had to succeed. Moreover, both parents looked forward to the amenities of life in Independence and to a more fulfilling life for themselves as well as for their children.

Although Independence was viewed as a sophisticated metropolis by many of its residents, it had a colorful, eventful past. Both the Oregon and Santa Fe Trails had started in Independence, and it had witnessed raucous days as a jumping-off place for the 1849 California gold rush. It had been the Mormons' original Zion, although they were obliged to depart, and the James Boys had robbed banks in the vicinity, with somewhat greater success. Now it was an incorporated city of six thousand, settled and prosperous. Families who had arrived from places like Kentucky only a generation earlier than the Trumans viewed themselves as the local gentry and were none too hospitable to newcomers. At the top were the Wallaces, presided over by a haughty widow, whose daughter, Elizabeth Virginia, was called "Bess" by her friends. From the time Harry shyly spied her at the local Sunday school, he longed to be among them. Bess Wallace would be the love of his life.

John Truman was at his most productive during this period, even showing an inventive bent, designing labor-saving devices. John had met a notably successful investor from Kansas City named William Kemper and was busily engaged in emulating his example. Through Kemper he also became acquainted with the emerging Pendergast political machine that was being developed by three ambitious brothers. Business and politics went hand in hand. Jackson County, Missouri, at the center of the United States, was a microcosm of the evolving nation, its diverse western end anchored by burgeoning Kansas City, its homogeneous eastern end rural and settled. To the Pendergasts, Truman looked like an ideal representative for that region, seemingly related by birth or marriage to half the electorate out in the boondocks. The whole of Jackson County could be pivotal statewide to many elections. It was primarily Democratic, but factions were emerging that would affect both Trumans, father and son.

Encouraged by his mother, Harry was doing well in school. He particularly loved history and was reputed to have read every book in the Independence public library. Truman always insisted that he had enjoyed the happiest possible childhood. To his no-nonsense father, however, his bespectacled older son might seem a less natural companion than his tough younger son, Vivian, who wanted nothing more than to be a good farmer. Except for politics. Like his father, Harry was fascinated by the compelling entertainment of all-day picnics, rallies, and parades, of seemingly endless campaigning. Politics was their shared enthusiasm, their bond. John was particularly thrilled with Grover Cleveland's return to the White House in 1892. Harry recalled his father riding "a beautiful gray horse in the torchlight parade" and decorating a weathervane on the roof of their home with a flag and bunting. At the Democratic National Convention in Kansas City in 1900, while his father sat proudly in Kemper's private box, Harry served as a page, overwhelmed by the dramatic oratory of William Jennings Bryan.

But even with his emerging relationship with the Pendergasts, for himself, John Truman viewed political activity more as an avocation than a profession. He remained intent on investing, and for a time he was actually doing it profitably. His run of good luck enabled him to buy a spacious home on Crysler Street on a large lot. Although the family was still not quite among the social elite of Independence, as Harry recalled, "Our house soon became headquarters for all the boys and girls around." The property not only contained an extraordinary menagerie of cows, ponies, goats, chickens, and all manner of household pets, but also a barn and hayloft, ideal for children's adventures. Whatever the neighbors may have thought, Truman never forgot those "wonderful times."

By sheer effort, the shy bookworm won over his classmates. If he could not participate in their sports and games, he would become their impartial arbiter. Harry Truman couldn't recall ever having had a bad teacher. No one considered him brilliant, except perhaps his mother, but everyone was impressed by his conscientiousness. Martha Ellen Truman widened Harry's world. As Margaret Truman writes, "His life revolved around her." All that reading, especially of history, was at her behest. His relationship with his mother was so close that sometimes it seemed to her other two offspring as if Harry were an only child.

By the time Harry was in high school, such acquaintances as Charlie Ross, the brightest student in his class, had become lifelong friends. They were each contemplating college. Popular Bess Wallace, also a classmate, would represent Harry's lengthiest campaign. He had worked part-time since the age of fourteen at a local drugstore, but his parents had agreed to terminate that employment so that he could focus on continuing his education. In particular, he was contemplating taking entrance examinations for the service academies until he realized that his eyesight precluded any such possibilities.

Then, late in 1902, the blow fell. John Truman took his largest risk, and his luck turned once again. He lost everything in grain futures trading—all his inheritance, even the small farm given to his wife by her parents. Now college of any kind for Harry was out of the question. First, the family moved to a more modest house, then to Kansas City, where, after trying a number of other alternatives, John endured the indignity of working for wages as a night watchman. Alonzo Hamby writes, "Still a tough, feisty man, he seems never to have recovered."

Harry held a succession of jobs, ultimately working as a clerk and bookkeeper at major banks, where his industry and demeanor were highly praised. Kansas City became his college. On his own for the first time, he lived in a lively boardinghouse. Another resident was named Arthur Eisenhower. The bright lights of the city held an immense attraction for young Harry, especially its music halls and theaters. He overcame his shyness by playing the piano at parties, although it was not quite the Chopin his mother would have preferred. With his friends he joined a newly formed National Guard unit, one not overly concerned with his poor eyesight. A lifetime later, at his presidential library, Truman would tell surprised groups of students that the three best preparations for a career in public service were farming, business, and the military, corresponding to his own path.

It must have been a great disappointment when the call came in 1905 to return to Grandview, but Harry complied. John had heeded the request of his aging mother-in-law and her bachelor brother Harrison to return to Grandview and again take over management of their farm. To the surprise of his Kansas City friends, Harry joined him, and the Grandview farm truly became "J. A. Truman and Son." In his twenties, Harry grew stronger physically, five inches taller and twenty muscular pounds heavier than John Truman. The two became closer and, as Robert H. Ferrell writes, father and son debated politics with even more fervor than before. Harry also renewed his acquaintance with Bess Wallace.

Somehow Harry managed to spend so much time off the farm it is almost as if he were already running for office. Richard Lawrence Miller observes that Harry's extra activities during this period already made him "a community leader with connections throughout the business and political circles of western Missouri." One of these key contacts was Mike Pendergast, the brother consigned to this region.

Although he viewed politics as secondary to investing, John Truman had held a number of part-time posts at the behest of the Pendergasts. In 1912, he agreed to become the local road overseer. The condition of rural roads in Missouri was critical to the prosperity of local farmers. Many overseers used these coveted political appointments to line their own pockets. Not John Truman. He became renowned for demanding as much from his road crews as from himself. As Harry later wrote, he learned from his father that "the expenditure of public money is a public trust. . . . Grandview had the best roads in the county."

Characteristically, it was John's stubbornness that led to his death. Impatient with a workman's hesitation to remove a large boulder, John did it himself. The strain caused an intestinal blockage. After months, he finally agreed to an operation, but he never really recovered. On the morning of November 2, 1914, his family by his side, John Anderson Truman died, shortly before his sixty-third birthday. The Independence

Examiner eulogized him under the headline, "An Upright Citizen Whose Death Will Be a Blow to His Community," but a few days earlier, to visiting friends, John had pronounced his life a failure.

His son disagreed. John Truman "worked from daylight to dark all the time," Harry recalled, "and his code was honesty and integrity. His word was always good . . . and he raised my brother and myself to put honor above profit. He was quite a man, my dad was . . . a doer, not a talker." Harry Truman would do more talking, but he viewed himself, as would others, as a plain talker, and as straight a shooter as his father.

Emulating him, he invested everything he could scrape together in a series of entrepreneurial ventures. Remarkably, the last of these, an oil-drilling enterprise, would have made him a millionaire, had he been able to stay around and retain his shares. By then, however, Truman was in France. When the United States entered World War I, Harry, at the age of thirty-three, was under no obligation to serve, but there was no way he could stay on the sidelines. According to his brother, Vivian, he managed to memorize the eye chart at the recruiting office.

Entering as a lieutenant but promoted to captain within a year, Truman was put in charge of the unruly Battery D of the 129th Field Artillery. He came of age in the regular army, making the astonishing discovery that he could actually lead other men, even into combat. The veterans of Battery D would be with him in every future political campaign. He later wrote, "My whole political career is based on my war service and my war associates."

Mustered out as a major in 1919, a newly confident Harry Truman sold his share of the farm and finally married Bess Wallace on June 28, despite the opposition of her snobbish mother who had always insisted that the Trumans were no more than dirt farmers. Harry had been courting Bess, in a manner of speaking, since she was five and he was six. After a haberdashery that Truman launched with an army buddy, initially a success, failed in the postwar recession, he was induced to run for a judgeship in 1922. Through many highs and lows, politics became his profession.

Martha Ellen Young Truman never lost her intimate interest in her children, especially her first son's career. At eighty-two she campaigned for Harry's first Senate race, claiming as one qualification that he had "plowed the straightest furrow in Jackson County." She even chaired a meeting of women campaign workers in 1944 when Harry became Franklin Roosevelt's running mate. He wrote her constantly, his "Dear Mama" letters a testament to his continuing regard for her counsel.

She died on July 26, 1947, at the age of ninety-four, undoubtedly looking forward to Harry running for the presidency on his own in 1948. For, as Margaret Truman Daniel recalls, it was to his mother, more than anyone else, that Harry Truman "turned again and again for the emotional support he needed."

Ida and Jacob Eisenhower

Hadn't he been right all along? Here were all six of his sons, reunited back in Abilene, Kansas, every one a success. Arthur, the oldest, who had lived in that lively Kansas City boardinghouse with a young Harry Truman, was now vice president of a major bank. Edgar, despite his parents' antipathy to lawyers, had persevered to become a prominent attorney. Roy's pharmacy was flourishing. Earl was an engineer. Milton, the youngest, who would go on to become president of three major universities, held an important position in the Department of Agriculture.

Dwight, a major in the United States Army, made less money than any of his brothers, and his prospects in the glacial peacetime military seemed the least promising. Yet he had recently graduated at the top of his class at the elite Leavenworth Command and General Staff School. At thirty-six he was noticeably more tanned and fit than the others, who ranged from twenty-seven to forty, and his natural optimism hadn't diminished. He admired but didn't really envy any of his brothers.

It was June 1926. Their proud father, David Jacob Eisenhower, still the picture of Teutonic stolidity at sixty-three, had to smile for once. Here were the living results of his harsh patrimony. He had beaten even the possibility of failure out of his sons. None would be denied the career of his choice, as he had been.

Why hadn't David's father, that good, generous, pious Dutchman, Jacob Eisenhower, understood his children as David did? He was never cut out to be a farmer like his forebears or brothers, but an engineer. Even though the family was originally named "Eisenhauer" for "iron hewer," their vocation had been tilling the soil, generation after generation.

General Dwight David Eisenhower may have "come from the very heart of America," but his family had emigrated from a different heartland, the "Heimat" of the land their martial descendant would one day be called upon to subjugate. Although related to respectable Lutherans, they were Mennonites, religious dissenters from the Rhineland. They had fled to Switzerland and then to Holland, finally embarking for America in the 1740s. Settling in the rich agricultural region around Lancaster, Pennsylvania, they joined those who had come before, establishing their community of Brethren in Christ. Known as "River Brethren" for their practice of freshwater baptisms, these Pennsylvania Dutch, like their successors, were devout pacifists who feared only God and were renowned for their self-supporting industriousness and the productivity of their farms. As journalist Marquis Childs writes, they believed in "hard work, temperance, self-denial, simple living, and ordered, almost Biblical simplicity." Their disdain for the worldly trappings of materialism, however, did not deter their own prosperity. Their families were as fertile as their farms. Jacob Eisenhower, both their temporal and their religious leader, expected his young son, David, to follow in that tradition. Born on September 23, 1863, he was one of the fourteen children of Jacob and Rebecca Eisenhower.

The Civil War had come much closer to a community of similarly Germanic origins in the Shenandoah Valley of Virginia. It destroyed the farm of the Stover (originally Stoever) family. In its aftermath, Ida Stover, the only daughter amidst seven sons, became an even more fervent pacifist. She was born on May 1, 1862, in the midst of the conflict, and blamed the early deaths of her parents on the stress of the war. At the age of sixteen, Ida decided to move west on her own.

Jacob Eisenhower had induced his whole community of River Brethren to move with him to Kansas, with its cheap, abundant land—an extraordinary migration. His sturdy, thrifty folk adapted well, duplicating their prior abundance. Perhaps such success encouraged Jacob to indulge his son. In Kansas as in Pennsylvania, David hated the dawn-to-dusk monotonous drudgery of farming. The only thing he enjoyed about it was working with its primitive machinery and trying to improve it. As Stephen Ambrose writes, "He was, according to neighbors, a 'natural-born' mechanic," but he wanted to become more, a professional engineer. His father permitted David to attend the nearby Brethren college in Lecompton. Although it mixed mechanics with classics, the modest establishment was hardly the school of engineering David had desired. By his sophomore year, however, his attentions had been diverted to another student, vivacious, enterprising Ida Stover, who had come all the way from Virginia in search of higher education.

Ida had a longing for learning, wanting to use the English she had been taught for reading more than only the Bible. She also loved music of all kinds. She wound up in Staunton, the Virginia town that would be identified with Woodrow Wilson, finding a family willing to provide room and board in exchange for cooking and cleaning. Finally able to attend high school, Ida did so well that soon she was teaching children herself. At twenty-one, she invested the first $600 of a modest inheritance in a piano she would prize for the rest of her life. Then she joined an aunt heading west with another group of Brethren. Ida had heard that the sect had established a small college in Kansas and that—wonder of wonders—it accepted female students.

There was a similar streak of nonconformity in Ida Stover and David Eisenhower. They made an attractive, if contrasting, couple. Ambrose describes David, still clean-shaven, as darkly handsome, "tall, muscular, broad-shouldered . . . [with] a thin, hard-set mouth, thick black hair, dark eyebrows, deep set, penetrating eyes, and a large rounded chin. His legs were long, his hands large and powerful." He was stocky, stolid, and silent, even more so as his dreams diminished. Ida was slender, fair, with lustrous brown hair, cheerful and outgoing, not so much beautiful as glowing, with a ready smile that her sons, one in particular, would inherit. She was sixteen months David's senior. Neither would graduate, but they were married in the Lane University chapel on September 23, 1885, David's twenty-second birthday. In their wedding picture, unlike the John Trumans', both were standing, David at least a bit taller than his wife.

Ida may have regretted not receiving her degree, but she truly loved learning for its own sake. She exuded joy and was anxious to fulfill it in motherhood. But she couldn't quite contain her husband's violent temper, never overtly directed toward her but later more vigorously on their sons. Perhaps it was a manifestation, at least in part, of his own bitterness at being denied the opportunity to pursue the engineering career he had sought. Austere David Eisenhower may have been the undisputed head of his household, but Ida was its heart. She must have understood, as would her children, the unspoken truth that she was not only the more compassionate but also the stronger of their parents.

Perpetually hopeful, David's father gave the couple $2,000 and a 160-acre farm of their own, his customary wedding gift to each of his sons. David promptly mortgaged the farm to his brother-in-law and opened a general store in the town of Hope, south of Abilene. Anything was better than agriculture. The couple lived above the store. Arthur, the first of their six sons (a seventh died in infancy), arrived in 1886. David demonstrated little talent for retailing, and enjoyed less luck. He took on a more experienced partner named Milton Good, who turned out to be a swindler. As Brendon observes, Hope did David "no good, and neither did Good." Moreover, a rural depression in 1888 severely hurt retail businesses of all kinds, and the venture was a disaster. A lawyer hired to clean up the mess took everything but Ida's piano, motivating the couple's antipathy to the legal profession.

David was obliged to move four hundred miles away, to Denison, Texas, where he had been able to find work at ten dollars a week as a railway mechanic. After giving birth to their second son, Edgar, Ida joined him. They lived in a tiny frame house, little more than a shack, near the railroad tracks. Here, on October 14, 1890, she gave birth to their third son. He was named David Dwight, but his parents soon decided to reverse the order to avoid confusion. By now it must have been clear even to Jacob Eisenhower that this son simply wasn't cut out to be a farmer, but the Brethren looked after their own. They needed a plant engineer to take charge of the machinery at their creamery back in Abilene, an ideal job for a man with David's skills. The pay was modest and the hours long, but he was happy to bring his family home from Texas after two trying years. Dwight Eisenhower would always view himself as a Kansan.

The Abilene he knew was not unlike the Independence, Missouri, that Truman called home. It was a comfortable, rather placid town of some four thousand residents, surrounded by wheat fields, but it had a lurid past. Railroads and cattle drives had brought every variety of frontier roughneck and adventurer to this terminus—to drink, fight, consort with loose women, and raise hell generally, all under the watchful eye of Sheriff "Wild Bill" Hickok. By the 1890s, however, respectable folk already preferred to view Abilene's embarrassingly recent heyday as colorful mythology. The more affluent lived on the north side of town, separated by railroad tracks from the equally proud families of working men on the south side. That is where the Eisenhowers resided, in a tiny cottage. During Ida's first seven years in Abilene, her logistical talents emerged. Somehow, despite too many people jammed into too little space and supported by too little money, she managed to create a harmonious family life, leavened with her own good cheer.

Ida's unquenchable optimism was finally rewarded when a relative offered an alternative of palatial proportions. The family could reside in a much larger house on a three-acre lot for a modest rental, with an option to buy, if they would care for David's father. They accepted with alacrity. Ida's goal was virtual self-sufficiency. To the barn and apple orchard she added a vegetable garden, a cow, chickens, ducks, pigs, and anything else that might contribute to the family larder. Daily chores, indoors and out, were rotated to give every son equal experience at everything. Among Dwight Eisenhower's earliest memories was his avoidance of the most onerous tasks, to his parents' consternation. They were still poor, but as he would recall, "We didn't know it then. All we knew is that our parents—of great courage—could say to us: 'Opportunity is all around you. Reach out and take it.'"

Ambrose describes Dwight at nine or ten as normal-sized, wearing clean but hand-me-down clothes, generally barefoot, "with a shock of light-brown hair, blue eyes, a friendly disposition, and his mother's grin." The most striking quality was his restless energy. He was never still, always on the go. He already loved sports and had inherited something of his father's temper. He would fight readily, no matter what the size of his opponent, seemingly as much to burn off energy as for any specific reason. In the growing solidarity of the brothers, by twelve he was already showing signs of a sort of instinctive leadership. As a teenager he would be called "president of the roughnecks." He would be "Little Ike"—his older brother Edgar was "Big Ike." At school, Dwight liked arithmetic, spelling, and history—especially military history, which didn't sit particularly well with his mother.

It must be said to the credit of both parents that they encouraged their children to think for themselves, more independently as they grew older. Their future lives, their ultimate professions, would be based on their own preferences, not the well-intentioned coercion their father had faced. Although dissimilar in personalities, David and Ida were of one accord in this regard. Still, all six sons were frightened to death of their father. As an adult, Dwight still recalled this singular difference between his parents. His sullen father, who communicated with his strap or a switch, "had quick judicial instincts." His sensitive mother, "had, like a psychologist, insight into the fact that each son was a unique personality and she adapted to the methods of each." Dwight's youngest brother, Milton, the future college president, put it this way, "Father and Mother complemented each other. Mother had the personality. She had the joy. Dad had the authority." Ambrose adds, "David hardly ever smiled; Ida smiled as easily as she breathed. She was quick to laugh; quick to give sympathy. Like David, she demanded much of her sons; unlike him, she gave much."

There is no doubt that by high school Dwight was one of the most popular young men in Abilene. Possessing his mother's outgoing personality and overcoming the combative inheritance from his father, he made friends easily. He still loved roaming, hunting, and fishing, but sports were at the center of his life and helped establish him as a student leader. Despite weighing only 150 pounds, he excelled in football and baseball. His average grades seemed to have improved without excessive effort, but he still enjoyed reading history and biography by the hour. He had also discovered girls, although he was extremely shy around them. It didn't hurt that the young lady he would marry in 1916, Marie "Mamie" Geneva Doud, considered Dwight "the handsomest man" she had ever seen.

Dwight's most traumatic experience came when he was a fourteen-year-old high school freshman. He had scraped his knee, it became infected, and the infection spread to the extent that doctors wanted to amputate his leg. Dwight insisted that he would rather die. In an illustration of the kind of loyalty their parents had instilled, Edgar stood guard at his bedside in case he lost consciousness. While his parents prayed and specialists were called in, the leg was saved, but it was a close thing. Having to repeat a year gave Dwight time to think things over. His high school yearbook predicted that Edgar would be president of the United States one day and Dwight would eventually teach history at Yale. When Edgar, "Big Ike," went off to study law at the University of Michigan with the aid of an uncle's loan, the ultimate validation of his parents' vow that each son follow his own path, Dwight became simply "Ike." His friends noticed a heightened seriousness and self-confidence. He had also bulked up physically.

In rural towns at the turn of the century, only the brightest, most affluent, or most motivated young people finished high school, let alone college. Ike understood the financial realities, and he took a cram course to apply for the Naval Academy. It provided a first-class education, it was free, and he could continue playing football. At twenty, however, he was too old, and the local appointments had already been made. Instead, he arranged to take the test for West Point. Coming in second in the exam, he won a cherished appointment. The train trip east would be by far the longest he had yet experienced, but only the prelude to an unimaginable journey.

His brothers were excited. His father revealed little emotion. His mother said only, "It is your choice." When he took his suitcase and walked the few blocks to the Union Pacific depot, she waved to her departing boy from the front porch. Then, Milton recalled, she could no longer restrain her tears. It was the first time he had ever seen her cry. She ran to her room and did not leave it that day. Lawyers only cheated people; soldiers may have to kill them. Yet in time Ida Eisenhower, whom Ike viewed as the most sincere pacifist he had ever known, learned to accept her son's career and even take pride in it. But, of course, she was proud of all her sons.

As adulthood approached for each son, their father loosened the bonds of discipline and their mother the restraints of tradition. Bible readings and prayer sessions became less frequent. As Doris Faber writes, "Cards made their appearance and in time cigarettes were allowed; music, secular as well as devotional, tinkled from Ida's still prized piano in the parlor." All this was in preparation for the environment that each son might face in his future. When Ike went off to West Point, although his aim was most of all to play football, an opportunity later precluded by injury, his parents' acceptance of his decision was still a confirmation of their constancy.

Dwight managed to come home at least once a year, even as his army career took him to foreign postings. A highlight was in 1935, as the Eisenhower boys returned again, this time with their wives and families, to celebrate David and Ida's golden wedding anniversary. David had taken a better paying job at the local utility company, and even in the midst of a national depression, times for his family were better than they had ever been. When David Jacob Eisenhower died at the age of seventy-eight on March 10, 1942, after recurrent illnesses, General Dwight David Eisenhower, immersed in the War Plans Division in Washington, was unable to attend his father's funeral. All Ike could do was reflect in his diary, "I have felt terribly. I should so like to be with my mother. . . . But we're at war! And war is not soft. . . . I loved my dad." The following day, as the burial was taking place, he eulogized his father, "I've shut off all business and visitors for thirty minutes—to have that much time by myself, to think of him. He had a full life. . . . He was a just man, well liked, well educated, a thinker. He was undemonstrative, quiet, modest, and of exemplary habits. . . . His finest monument is his reputation. . . . His pride in his independence earned for him a reputation that has profited all of us boys." It was not the occasion to reflect on his father's complexity.

As she aged, Ida's memory began to lapse, and she needed help getting about, but she readily recognized her soldier son when he paid her a surprise visit on a brief leave home in 1944. This time laughter mixed with the tears. Then, on May 1, 1946, nearing her eighty-fourth birthday, Ida Stover Eisenhower passed away. Ike praised "her serenity, her open smile, her gentleness with all and her tolerance of their ways." There was no challenge in finding the words to express her son's boundless affection for her, the light of all their lives.

Whatever view one takes of these two very different presidents from the American heartland, whose relationships with each other fluctuated, the striking similarity was the pivotal influence of their mothers. Not long before Martha Ellen Young Truman died in 1947, she feared that her least favorite Republican, Senator Robert A. Taft, would be nominated for president the following year and that her son might not choose to run against him. "Don't you think it's about time you made up your mind?" she demanded of Harry Truman. Ida Stover Eisenhower would not have been so concerned about politics, but she had also insisted that her sons make up their own minds. Both mothers had laid a strong foundation for them to do so, buttressed by a buoyancy that balanced their husbands' concurrence with the same conclusions.

CHAPTER 15

Losers Need Not Apply—Rose and Joseph Patrick Kennedy Sr.

※

Joseph Patrick Kennedy Sr.'s first choice for our first Catholic president was himself. His original intention to run in 1940 vanished with Franklin Roosevelt's decision to seek a third term, and their irrevocable disagreement about foreign policy. His second choice, the outstanding son named for him, dissolved with his death in a near-suicidal mission over English skies late in World War II. The mantle then fell to the second son, John, whom everyone called "Jack," a more bookish Kennedy, who initially had seemed a far less likely candidate for high political office. Others may have come close, but Joe Kennedy was the only first father who specifically sought a political career for his son.

What biographers often overlook in their emphasis on Kennedy's obsessive ambition, and the wealth accumulated to achieve it, is a kind of personalized patriotism. He believed that all Americans, irrespective of their religion or ethnic origins, share a birthright of aspiration to even the nation's highest office. However, Kennedy also felt that because of how *his* sons were raised, they should be especially qualified for national leadership. In business, Kennedy was a combination of lone wolf and buccaneer, in politics an advocate of overkill, yet his own views on issues tended towards the conservative. But that is not what mattered. A well-prepared president should find the right path to meet the challenges of his own times.

It was ambition more than destitution that brought the Kennedys to these shores in the first place. County Wexford, from which they came, was not as afflicted by the terrible Irish potato famine as was most of the Emerald Isle. The Fitzgeralds, with whom the Kennedys would be inextricably intertwined, had come over a few years earlier from the same locale. They had been in Ireland for eight centuries. What is extraordinary is that from the year they arrived, it took the Kennedys of Massachusetts no longer to achieve the presidency than it had the Washingtons of Virginia.

In only their second generation in America the patriarchs of the Kennedy and Fitzgerald families were already wealthy and powerful. In every other way, however, "P. J." Kennedy and "Honey Fitz" Fitzgerald were so different from each other as to destroy anyone's ethnic stereotypes. It is not surprising that they also profoundly disliked each other.

Tall, handsome, deliberative Patrick Joseph Kennedy Jr. had risen from working the Boston docks to owning saloons, importing liquor, investing in a hotel and a coal company, and becoming a banker. In 1887 he married Mary Augusta Hickey, the bright, assertive, socially ambitious daughter of one of Boston's most prominent Irish families. On September 6, 1888, she gave birth to the first of their four children, a boy they named Joseph Patrick. Dapper, gregarious, lively John Francis Fitzgerald, who had the advantage of an education at the elite Boston Latin School and studied medicine at Harvard, owned an immensely successful insurance business and later his own newspaper. In 1889 Fitzgerald married his attractive but extremely shy and devout second cousin, Mary Elizabeth Hannah. The first of their six children, a girl, was born on July 22, 1890. They named her Rose Elizabeth Fitzgerald. She would always be her father's "shining star."

All P. J. and Honey Fitz had in common, beyond heritage, was wealth, energy, and politics. P. J.'s real interest was in exerting power behind the scenes. Honey Fitz was an instinctive, irrepressible politician whose goal was to be mayor of Boston, by then considered the "Irish presidency." The polo-playing proletarian was already assuming the role of vaudeville "stage Irishman" on the hustings—in James Hilty's words, the "back-slapping, quintessential Irish politician who knew every voter's name." By his side at every rally was not his reticent wife but his vivacious fifteen-year-old daughter, Rose. Slender, dark-haired, and poised, she had been acclaimed "Boston's prettiest high-school senior" and added a touch of class to the crass. After his election, she became in effect the official hostess of Mayor Fitzgerald. Rose had hoped to go on to Wellesley College, but Boston's archbishop prevailed on her father to set the right example. She went instead to Manhattanville College of the Sacred Heart.

At Boston Latin Joe Kennedy excelled at sports and was elected class president, but it still wasn't sufficient to get him invited to the parties hosted by his classmates' snobbish parents. As Rose later put it, there were parallel social circles in Boston, "one for them and one for us." At Harvard Joe enjoyed success, if not enough to suit him, but also absorbed a grasp of investing profitably on his own.

Despite the political differences between the Fitzgeralds and the Kennedys, the families vacationed together at Old Orchard Beach in Maine. As they got to know each other better, there was nothing tentative about the attraction between Rose and Joe. Rose viewed bright, lean, sandy-haired, freckle-faced Joe Kennedy as "open and expressive." He had a "youthful dignity . . . neither drank nor smoked. . . . He was serious but with a quick wit and a spontaneous infectious grin. . . . Even then he had an aura of command." Joe was similarly smitten. Although it took some time to reach fruition, their summer romance had a happy ending, or at least a happy beginning.

On October 7, 1914, twenty-six-year-old Joseph Patrick Kennedy married twenty-four-year-old Rose Elizabeth Fitzgerald in the private chapel of William Cardinal O'Connell, merging Boston's two most prominent political families. Their expansive house in the comfortably middle-class suburb of Brookline would soon be full of little Kennedys. Rose's "precious package," Joseph Patrick Kennedy Jr., arrived on July

15, 1915; John Fitzgerald Kennedy on May 29, 1917; Rose's first "dainty daughter," Rosemary, christened "Rose Marie," in 1918; Kathleen, called "Kick," in 1920; Eunice in 1921; Patricia in 1924; Robert Francis, called "Bobby," in 1925; Jean in 1928; and finally Edward Moore Kennedy, called "Teddy," in 1932.

Meanwhile, their father set out to achieve his initial goal, to make his first million within the next ten years. After managing a shipbuilding facility during World War I, Joseph Sr. joined a well-established Boston investment house. By 1923, however, he was on his own. At his Harvard reunion he listed his profession as "capitalist." There followed two decades of often-mysterious machinations, from Wall Street and real estate to liquor importing and investing in Hollywood. Well diversified, Kennedy adroitly got out of the stock market before the crash of 1929, making more than his first million well ahead of time. He would be self-employed for the remainder of his business career.

Rose had a more immediate problem. In 1913, another colorful, ambitious, canny Boston politician named James Michael Curley had challenged Honey Fitz for the mayoralty. Curley threatened to expose Fitzgerald's affair with a comely young "cigarette girl" named Elizabeth "Toodles" Ryan, and this was hardly his sole indiscretion. Rose was horrified, yet her mother had volunteered nothing. Had she looked the other way, or inward? "At the heart of Mary Fitzgerald's life," writes Thomas Reeves, "was the Roman Catholic church, and she instilled an intense devotion in her children." Her mother's example of grace under pressure would impart in Rose a lifelong legacy of admiration, if not imitation.

With his father so often away, Jack reflected that Rose Kennedy became "the architect of our lives," the "glue" that held their family together. Still, he added that, present or not, their father "made his children feel that they were the most important things in the world to him. He was so terribly interested in everything we were doing. He held up standards for us."

Soon, however, Rose Fitzgerald Kennedy faced a shocking reality of her own. If alcohol was the curse of the indigent Irish, was infidelity the affliction of the affluent? To Joseph P. Kennedy, life was composed of compartments. One *could* be a devoted husband and father, even attend church regularly, yet carry on virtually public affairs with such luminaries as Hollywood sex goddess Gloria Swanson and no end of lesser mistresses too public to ignore. In a contemporary marriage, a strong man could do just about whatever he wanted, without compromising his harmonious home. They were simply separate spheres. This from the man who had pursued Rose Fitzgerald so avidly. To Joe Kennedy, "The measure of a man's success in life isn't the money he has made—it's the kind of family he has raised." Two decades later, he reiterated, "My wife and I have given nine hostages to fortune. Our children . . . are more important than anything else in the world."

Would they, particularly the boys, follow their father's example, or the faith-driven fidelity of their mother? Yet how could Rose continue to live with Joe Kennedy? In 1920 she left her family and embarked on a lengthy religious retreat. Divorce seemed the only option to retain her self-respect. Her resolution, however, was also to put their children first. She and her husband would retain a partnership of shared interests, with regard replacing romance, built around raising their children, but Rose would also pursue a vibrant life of her own. During the first six years of the Great Depression, she went to Europe seventeen times, buying everything in sight from the foremost couturiers in Paris. Although becoming less accessible, Rose continued to impart not only Catholic piety but also, Hilty notes, "neatness, social grace, gentle behavior, proper grammar and diction, dutiful obedience . . . [all within] a prescribed and regulated family life." Rose and Joe Kennedy might have invented the concept of "quality time."

So often away, Joe Sr. sent an endless stream of letters to each child. Joe Jr., the eldest, became a sort of surrogate father, teaching the others how to swim and sail, how to play almost every sport. However, when he was home, Joe Sr., sitting at the older children's table, dwelled on national and international affairs and issues, grilling everyone as in a free-flowing debate. Money and business were never discussed. Toughness was a virtue, competition a constant, their father's mantra drummed in daily:

"We don't want any losers around here. In this family we want winners." Arthur Schlesinger Jr. writes, "No child could doubt the order of priority." To Bobby Kennedy, at the younger kids' table, public life was "really an extension of family life." Specifically, Jack Kennedy recalled, "My father wanted his older son in politics. He demanded it. . . . It was like being drafted."

Of course, it was all supplemented by the advantages of wealth— travel, education, exposure to the world of ideas. All the Kennedys would be prepared for leadership, not only the eldest boys. The Kennedys are viewed as a Boston family, but Joseph Sr. had decided that Boston, even Brookline, was "no place to raise children," or at least not *his* children, because of the impenetrable snobbery of its self-appointed Protestant "Brahmin" elite. "You can go to Harvard and it still doesn't mean a damned thing."

They moved to Riverdale, north of Manhattan, then to an immense estate in Bronxville, Westchester County, and established summer residences in Hyannis Port, Cape Cod, and Palm Beach, Florida. Wherever they settled, even for a season, became their *own* exclusive enclave, outsiders admitted only as they accommodated to the Kennedys. The closest to a real home centered on Hyannis Port. In the most active years there, with the church of her childhood becoming even more of a refuge, Rose determined that she might provide each of her children with a moral foundation firmer than their father's pragmatism. However, if her own relationship with Joe Sr. had evolved into a combination of cooperation and competition, there is little doubt who won. As Reeves writes, except for Bobby, who was closest to his mother, "Each of the boys would strongly identify with the church and always attend weekly mass, while doing what was to their advantage . . . with little or no regard to its moral content." As for the girls, Rosemary suffered from retardation or mental illness. After an experimental lobotomy that was ordered by her father failed, she was shut away in an institution. She could never be a winner. Kathleen, her parents' favorite, bright, lively, and independent, would go her own way, first falling in love with a Protestant English peer who died during the Second World

War, and then planning to marry another, but eventually dying in an airplane crash.

At Cape Cod, Rose reverted to her role as family activities director, managing to be self-indulgent and intrusive at the same time. She continued to try to regulate every aspect of her children's lives. Peter Collier and David Horowitz write, "It was a regimen that abhorred weakness and tolerated no slackers. The children learned that their mother's apparent distraction was protective coloration for a character that was actually strong-willed and durable." All that competition, of course, coincided with Joseph Kennedy Sr.'s role as debating coach and instructor in world affairs.

What would be next for himself, still relatively young and wealthier than ever? With a Democratic administration likely in 1932, government service seemed a likely next step, leading directly to politics. In 1928 Al Smith had been simply "too Irish," too New York, too unlettered to be elected president, and the Depression was yet to come. It would take someone more like himself, or polished Joe Jr., to become the first Catholic president of the United States. It was no more improbable a goal than earning one's first million by the age of thirty-five.

Although young Joe was an exemplary student, athlete, and leader at Choate, the establishment prep school his father had chosen, Jack just seemed to be plodding along there. "You have the goods," his father assured him, "Why not try to show it?" Yet even Joe Sr. could see the potential in Jack, so different from the Irish American stereotype still at least personified in part by Joe Jr.'s gregariousness. Although reticent, Jack would become, as Schlesinger writes, "patrician, bookish, urbane." Massachusetts governor Paul Dever called him "the first Irish Brahmin."

A Democrat by inheritance, Joe Kennedy put his money on Franklin Roosevelt in terms of 1932. He also raised substantial contributions from others and got as close to the candidate as possible. Many in Roosevelt's camp, however, viewed Kennedy suspiciously as arrogant, headstrong, and anything but a team player. After the election, Kennedy was made the first chairman of new Securities and Exchange Commission. However, late in 1937, President Roosevelt made an extraordinary and perhaps rather whimsical decision. Even though, as Kennedy's grand-daughter Amanda Smith notes, Joseph P. Kennedy Sr. "lacked both dip-lomatic experience and a diplomatic nature," the president named this son of an Irish saloonkeeper to become American ambassador to the Court of St. James.

To both Rose and Joe (and a good many others), it was hard to believe. It not only brought them back closer together, to Rose this too-brief time in Great Britain would be "by far the happiest years" of her married life. As Joe Sr. said to her while dressing for dinner at Windsor Castle, "Well, Rose, this is a helluva long way from South Boston, isn't it?" The whole handsome, photogenic family, an early example of celeb-rity, was warmly embraced not only by the British media—"eleven ambassadors for the price of one"—but throughout the entire United Kingdom, from the king and queen to commoners. Invitations flooded in from the cream of English society. Ironically, full social acceptance came not in Boston or New York but in class-conscious England, greet-ing these refreshing American representatives with genuine enthusiasm. In the spotlight as never before, slender Rose Kennedy—who with her lovely "agate" eyes, fine-featured face, and strong chin had in truth the look of a New England aristocrat—was in her glory. Attired as fashion-ably as any duchess, she became an acclaimed hostess. The family trave-led throughout Europe, making a similar splash in Paris.

Encouraged by his father, Jack took full advantage to soak up all he could about current events. He even studied for a time with Harold Laski at the London School of Economics and served as his father's sec-retary at the embassy. Forced to leave Princeton because of illness, he later transferred to Harvard, where his senior honors thesis was adapted to a well-received book, *Why England Slept,* reportedly revised by his father's journalist friend Arthur Krock. For the first time, Joe Jr., now at Harvard Law School, may have experienced a touch of sibling rivalry.

Ambassador Kennedy had made a strong start in his new post, his refreshing candor appealing to the English. Unfortunately, the aristo-crats Joseph Kennedy seemed to admire most were from the "Cliveden set," who felt at least some affinity for fascism. He not only became a personal friend of Prime Minister Neville Chamberlain but an overt supporter of his policy of "appeasement" of Nazi Germany. By 1938 he was an ardent isolationist, his defeatist tone becoming deeply distressing to President Roosevelt and his associates.

At the outbreak of war in 1939, Rose and the children returned to the United States. Joe's letters to his "Rosa" were particularly tender during this time, recalling the days of their courtship, as if he had never strayed. "I love you devotedly . . . more every day," he wrote her in 1940. Soon Kennedy himself would be called home for "consultations." He would not return. He was permitted to resign, at his own request.

Kennedy had long considered making a run for the presidency himself in 1940, or perhaps 1944, with Joe Jr. a likely candidate for governor of Massachusetts. However, newly branded as a misguided isolationist—or worse—he realized that he would never have a political career of his own. He was now free to promote his oldest son in his stead. Although he shared his father's views, Joe Jr. had volunteered to be a naval aviation cadet. Jack had a bad back and potentially fatal Addison's disease, later hidden from the public, but his father pulled strings to get him a commission as an ensign in the navy. As for Rose, the few lovely years were over far too soon. With Rose Marie separated from the family, and her beloved "Kick" dead, Rose had an early acquaintance with grief.

In August 1943 as commander of PT-boat 109 in the Pacific, Jack would be acclaimed as a naval hero, a perception that would be perpetuated by his father's publicity machine, resulting in a book and, in 1963, a film. After his boat was rammed and cut in two by a Japanese destroyer, killing two crewmen, Kennedy personally saved the life of another while leading the rest of his crew to the safety of an island. Joe Jr., in England, was as relieved as the rest of the family that Jack had survived, but he wasn't about to be upstaged by his younger brother. In August 1944 he volunteered to fly a plane loaded with explosives to destroy a German rocket site in France. There could hardly have been a more hazardous mission. He was to bail out early, the plane continuing to its target by remote control, but it exploded too soon, and Joseph Patrick Kennedy

Jr. was killed instantly. It nearly killed his father, as well, who lamented, "All my plans for my own future were tied up with young Joe."

As he gradually overcame his grief, insisting, "We've got to carry on. We must take care of the living. There is a lot to be done," an admiring Joseph Kennedy also wrote that his wife was "ten thousand percent better than I am. Her terrifically strong faith has been a great help to her, along with her very strong will and determination not to give way." The renewed affection of their years in Europe seemed to sustain them both. When apart, she signed her letters "All my love, Rosa." As her children grew and scattered, Rose's round-robin communications to all of them became more frequent. Jack wrote his mother, "I'm saving them to publish."

If there was still "a lot to be done," it was understood who must be next in line to start doing it. As Jack recalled, "I could feel Pappy's eyes on the back of my neck." His father concurred in a candid interview, "I got Jack into politics. . . . I told him he had to." How anxious the potential journalist was to pick up the family banner remains a matter of conjecture, but in 1946 he ran for the House of Representatives.

The same year, the Joseph P. Kennedy Jr. Foundation was launched, with Jack composing a moving memorial tribute, "As We Remember Joe." The whole campaign stressed continuity, with Joe Sr. leaving nothing to chance. Although vowing to "sell Jack like soap flakes," his real theme was a war hero inheriting his brother's mantle. The surprise was not that Jack won, but that, as biographer Nigel Hamilton points out, he already demonstrated the boyish charm and magnetism of a natural campaigner. Foreshadowing future campaigns, Rose and her daughters invited thousands of starstruck ladies in the district to take coffee or tea with them. Every campaign was a family affair.

Jack would hardly prove to be the most conscientious congressman, although his father pulled strings to have him placed on the most prominent committees. Joe also used his publicity machine to place stories about Jack as "America's most eligible bachelor." The new congressman made friends with other freshman "comers" in the class of 1946, including a Republican from California down the hall named Richard M. Nixon.

Rose had always viewed herself as more a Fitzgerald, the family that came first to American shores, than a Kennedy, and there were conflicted convictions in her merger of faith and politics. She had once imagined Bobby, the son closest to her, whom Paul Dever had dubbed "the last Irish Puritan," as perhaps a candidate for the priesthood. When, instead, he emerged as his older brother's "ruthless" campaign manager and later a candidate himself, she supported him just as visibly and vocally as she had Jack. When Jack ran for president, she won the crowds by telling them how she had rocked him to "political lullabies." Behind the scenes, his father was still very much a force in that campaign. When the subject of religion was raised, with Jack pointedly remarking that no one had ever asked about it in the South Pacific, Adlai Stevenson memorably remarked that his fear was "not the Pope, but the Pop."

In 1953, Jack Kennedy had triumphed again, winning the hand of lovely, stylish Jacqueline Bouvier, in the wedding of the year. Others in the family may have questioned how delicate "Jackie" Kennedy would fit into the rough-and-tumble of touch football at Hyannis Port, but Joe Kennedy knew better. Jackie was just what Jack needed to help forward his political career, adding to his vigor her almost regal elegance.

Culminating in the 1960 presidential election, there was no refuge remote enough for Joe Kennedy to escape being a campaign issue. The founding, funding father finally emerged on the morning of November 9, 1960, joining the other exhausted Kennedys at the armory in Hyannis Port. His son Jack said with utter accuracy, "The margin is thin, but the responsibility is clear." Joe Kennedy for once couldn't contain his glee. Even if not as originally planned, it was the fruition of everything. He had only two requests to make, neither of them negotiable. A reluctant Bobby Kennedy, only thirty-four, the confidant Jack could most trust, must be his attorney general. Ted Kennedy, who had worked so hard in the campaign, must, as soon as he reached the legal age of thirty, take Jack's place in the Senate. "You'll learn together," Joe said. "You know my father," Jack explained to friends.

On December 19, 1961, little more than a year after the election, seventy-three-year-old Joseph P. Kennedy suffered a massive stroke.

Although he rallied, Joe Kennedy would be incapacitated for the rest of his life, paralyzed on one side, and unable to speak intelligibly. In this agonizing state he lingered for eight years, his mind apparently still capable of comprehending whatever he was told. Much of the news would be tragic—the violent deaths of two more of his sons and the humiliation of the third. "The New Frontier" would be reached, if at all, by others. "Camelot" had proved to be as ephemeral as the stage play on which Jackie Kennedy's fantasy had been based. During the Cuban missile crisis Rose Kennedy lamented, "My son, my poor son, so much to bear, and there is no way now for his father to help him."

Joseph Patrick Kennedy Sr. died at the age of eighty-one on November 19, 1969. He outlived four of his nine children, and a fifth he had put away, finding no other solution to her plight. When, perhaps, in a rare moment of uncertainty, Joe Kennedy asked Jack why he wanted to undertake the "appalling burdens" of the presidency, his son replied with a question, "Who can do it better?" The tables had been turned. That had been his father's original justification for the quest.

If Rose Fitzgerald Kennedy came to believe at least as much in the forms of her Roman Catholic faith as in the substance, as some biographers suggest, it is surely understandable. She lived with ambivalence both before and after her marriage. Her flamboyant father, her ambitious husband, and her most successful son were all blatantly unfaithful to their wives. Yet she never gave up, reminding everyone of their religious obligations, even in the heat of political combat. As late as 1959 the entirety of a communication to Jack reads, "This is a note to remind you of church. Mother." Still, politics was simply in her Fitzgerald blood. In 1968 she gracefully greeted Bobby's Democratic primary rival Eugene McCarthy with: "Have fun in the campaign." And then Bobby, too, was gone.

There is little doubt that Rose's most enduring gift to each of her children was in the realm of inspiration. As Reeves writes, Rose reflected at Jack's inauguration, "I said to myself, drawing on Cardinal Newman's words, 'He will do good, he will do God's work.'" The escalating tragedies she endured seem too much for anyone to have to bear. Yet Rose

Elizabeth Fitzgerald Kennedy went on to be the matriarch of a new generation, facing its own personal challenges. She lived to be 104, passing away on January 23, 1995. Her extraordinary strength, whatever its source, can only be lauded. Despite the good times they shared, her unalloyed joy was perhaps the first victim of her husband's insatiable ambition.

CHAPTER 16

Politics as a Profession—Johnsons and Nixons

Rebekah Baines and Samuel Ealy Johnson Jr.

Compare father and son: the same pale skin, the same slicked-back hair, the same bulbous nose, the same enormous ears, the same penetrating eyes and tight mouth. Both over a slender six feet. Both walked angled forward, the same confident strut, the loping strides. Their clothes, cowboy or cosmopolitan, were cut with care. Imagine them in action, their "treatment" enveloping whoever must be convinced, constituent or congressman, one long arm over his shoulders, the other hand grasping his suit lapel or the strap of his overalls, chin lowered to chest, eyes narrowed, nose almost in the face of the prey, yet a slight conspiratorial smile, "We know we can count on you. . . . We need you to come through." This was the picture of Sam Ealy Johnson Jr. and his son Lyndon Baines Johnson, each viewed at the age of, say, thirty-five or so, both professional politicians in midcareer. Lyndon Johnson didn't merely resemble his father physically. In his childhood he wanted nothing more than to be like him. Yet after Sam lost everything, proving he had more scruples than sense, it all changed. Finally, near the end of Sam's life, there was a welcome reconciliation.

The Hill Country was in the blood of both. However, Sam's political and business ambitions never really went beyond it. Lyndon's would encompass not only the whole of Texas but the nation—and ultimately the entire world. At the end, Lyndon too was undone, but not by anything so trivial as the fall of cotton prices. Lyndon's fall was that of a giant, brought down as the world watched.

Sam Ealy Johnson Jr., born on October 11, 1877, the first son after four girls, was his father's special joy. Bright "Little Sam" grew up listening to the older Sam, who had known boom and bust, swapping Civil War stories with his neighbors and sharing their plight as small farmers and ranchers unequally ranged against the domination of "the interests." Populist politics was in his blood, but also enterprise. Sam earned a teaching certificate and taught for several years. In 1904 he won a seat in the Texas House of Representatives, the first of his six successive terms in the legislature. At least in appearance he seemed the prototypical Lone Star State lawmaker of the old school. Robert Dallek describes Sam as "six foot two, with coal black hair, a big Stetson hat, hand-tooled boots, into which he stuck his pants." He was convivial, a hearty backslapper, and was a frequent patron of the Congress Avenue bars in wide-open Austin. Biographer Robert Caro writes that Sam also frequented the lively street's bordellos. Ubiquitous lobbyists "dispensed the 'three Bs' favored by legislators—beefsteak, bourbon, and blondes." But everyone soon discovered what Sam's father already knew. His son was different. He paid his own way for everything.

Many of the causes that Sam Johnson Jr. championed were hardly popular with the powerful—the eight-hour day, pure food and drugs, taxing corporations, equitable justice, regulating utility rates—the whole litany of Lone Star liberalism. Politics came first, but Sam was hardly averse to making money. He expanded his ranch, bought and sold livestock, invested in real estate, and traded in high-risk commodities futures. When the bottom dropped out of the market, and he was all but wiped out, he started all over again.

One of those who admired him was his predecessor in the legislature, a highly literate lawyer named Joseph Wilson Baines, who was down on his luck. The Baines heritage of learning and piety originated in Scotland and was transported almost seamlessly to the New World. The Reverend George Washington Baines, who brought the family from North Carolina to Texas, was a highly regarded Baptist minister who became president of Baylor University. Of his six sons, none excelled in so many areas as Joseph. A lay preacher and pillar of his church and community, he served in the Civil War, taught school, put out a newspaper, and by the 1870s was a very successful lawyer. He was named Texas secretary of state at least in part because of his writing talents. He had married the agreeable daughter of a country physician when she was not yet fifteen, which raised only a few eyebrows at that time and place.

It was twelve years before they had their first child, on June 26, 1881, a girl who grew up to look much like her mother. They named her Rebekah, after the wife of Isaac in the Old Testament. Joseph taught Rebekah to read and appreciate the works of great writers and poets, to love the natural world, and to pursue a life committed to others. She went on to Baylor, one of few Texas women in those days to pursue higher education. Thrilled, as Doris Kearns writes, by her father's "eloquent speeches on the rights and duties of mankind" in the state legislature, she was stunned when somehow he lost his bid to be elected to Congress.

Disaster followed defeat. Joseph Wilson Baines had made one serious lapse that had gone bad—a land speculation involving overgenerous rentals to tenant farmers. The droughts devastated their crops. Hoping to stay at Baylor, Rebekah gave elocution lessons, taught English to the German-speaking residents of Fredricksburg, and wrote articles about Hill Country happenings as a "stringer" for major Texas newspapers. She hoped someday to make her living as a writer. Baines suggested to his daughter that Sam Johnson might be an interesting subject for an interview.

She didn't get much of a story. Sam's manners were rough, his language no more literate than that of his back-country neighbors, and he was very "cagey" about answering any specific questions. Yet, despite everything, she sensed something "dashing and dynamic" about him. Most of all, his political credo emulated her father's. As for Sam, while he wasn't about to broadcast it, he was absolutely bowled over by the bright and beautiful Rebekah Baines. He had never met anyone like her, a lovely, delicate-looking young lady of quality who actually enjoyed talking about politics. Her slender body was shapely, her eyes a deep blue, her hair ash blonde. Caro describes her as a "soft-spoken, gentle, dreamy-eyed young lady who wore crinolines, and lace, and lovely bonnets." Rebekah's daughter would recall her mother's "flawless, beautiful white skin, protected from the sun." Soon Sam seemed to be showing up almost daily, on one pretext or another, at the Baineses', some twenty miles from his isolated cabin on the banks of the Pedernales River. And Rebekah's father genuinely liked Johnson, viewing him as a young man with promise, and fostered the relationship.

However, in November 1906, Joseph Wilson Baines died. Grief-stricken Rebekah memorialized him as "the dominant force in my life as well as my adored parent, reverenced mentor, and most interesting companion." Perhaps her distracted state after the death of her father made Rebekah more amenable, but during Sam Johnson's whirlwind courtship her curiosity about him had turned into something closer to affection. It would be put to the test almost immediately. On August 20, 1907, she became Mrs. Sam Ealy Johnson Jr.

Moving to Sam's three-room shack—it wasn't much more than that, although he painted it a bright yellow to cheer her up—wasn't so much going to a new locality as to a new planet. Everything around her reflected desolation—the cabin itself, the bleak, dusty landscape, her neighbors, raucous farmhands and their wives, no less coarse. Worst of all, when Sam drank he could become uncontrollable. Perhaps he harbored some inner demon.

Yet she coped. Delicate Rebekah loved to cook. Even though there was no electricity, she managed to prepare meals in harvest season for as many as twenty workers at a time. She waged an unrelenting campaign to keep the cabin clean. She never gave up hope for something better, keeping her good china and linens in readiness, should Sam bring back someone prominent from Austin. For all Rebekah's pretensions, Sam understood that she, whose complaints had been limited to wistful looks and sighs, was the best thing that had ever happened to him. And with all his faults, he was the best company she had.

On an August morning little more than a year after they had married, as Doris Faber puts it, Rebekah "discerned the reason she had been brought forth on this earth." When she went into labor, the local creeks were rising and Sam was away. His father, who lived nearby, saddled up his horse to bring back a midwife. It was hours before a doctor was able to make his way to the Johnson cabin. "It was daybreak, On Thursday, August 27, 1908," as Rebekah put it in her rather florid style, "The light came in from the east, bringing a deep stillness . . . and then there came a sharp compelling cry—the most awesome, happiest sound known to human ears—the cry of a newborn baby, the first child of Sam Ealy and Rebekah Johnson was 'discovering America.'" After hearing the news, white-bearded old Sam Johnson, oblivious to the weather, mounted his horse and rode wildly from farm to farm, proclaiming, "A U.S. senator was born this morning!"

Rebekah's focus was on the lower house. She looked into the infant's eyes and saw at once "the deep purposefulness and true nobility" of her father. Surely this child, a Baines as much as a Johnson, would redeem her dreams and those of her father, ascending one day to the House of Representatives. Of all the first mothers, she is the closest equivalent to Joseph P. Kennedy. She not only wanted her first son to be in politics, she had already decided on the position he was destined to fill. To avoid the plebian sound of "Joe Johnson," the baby was named for a lawyer friend of Sam's, W. C. Linden, which Rebekah changed to the more "euphonious" Lyndon.

By the time he was three, little Lyndon Baines Johnson was learning everything from the alphabet to arithmetic from his mother. Even as a baby, Lyndon was so friendly and active, crawling surprisingly great distances, that he had to be constantly watched. At four, in part because of his hyperactive proclivities, he was entered in school early, but his mother always remained at the heart of his education. She even suggested to a teacher that he sit in her lap, as he did at home. Rebekah would have three other children—two girls, one named after her, and a son named Sam Houston, for both his father and the notable Texas hero. But Lyndon would always be special.

When he was five, his father gave the family a most welcome gift. They moved into a more spacious six-room Victorian-style home in Johnson City, closer to Sam's business and legislative interests in Austin. Although the amenities didn't yet include indoor plumbing, as Caro describes it, the house featured gingerbread scrollwork on its gables, surrounded by mature shade trees and wisteria. For a time Rebekah also became a kind of "Lady Bountiful," setting out on a one-woman crusade to bring enlightenment to her neighbors. She founded a literary society, directed plays, taught public speaking, encouraged the social graces, promoted temperance, and even held spelling bees and tutoring sessions for the local children. These activities were augmented by lively discourse at the Johnsons' dinner table. Lyndon Johnson recalled the atmosphere as warm and loving, his mother very much a hands-on parent, given to hugging and encouraging her children. However, she always held Lyndon to a higher standard than the others, and with him her affection was conditional. So much so that, as Kearns writes, when he fell short of her unrelenting expectations, she would shut him out of her sight until he came around. Yet increasingly she would confide in him. As he grew older, it became perplexing.

In 1918, when Lyndon was ten, his father, after a hiatus to look after business, returned to the legislature. Sam Ealy Johnson Jr. had become more temperate. He drank less, his moods were more consistent than Rebekah's had become, and his affection was more sustained. As his mother's expectations for him continued to heighten, Lyndon began to view his father as the more emotionally stable of the two.

In the legislature, Sam found new causes to champion. He fought for pensions for World War I veterans and their widows. He opposed an anti-German "loyalty bill" and the growing power of the Ku Klux Klan, becoming an advocate for tolerance. Nor did he forget his own constituents, pushing for graded roads and better schools. The "Johnson Blue Sky Law" protected consumers from unscrupulous stock salesmen. Whenever possible, there was Lyndon, up in the gallery, following every word. His father was now his closest companion. When Sam came home to campaign, Lyndon would join him in the family's Model

T, going from farm to farm, door to door, cajoling and conversing with everyone in that confidential but forceful Johnson style. It was wonderful being with his father at all his rallies and making the rounds. Lyndon later reminisced to Doris Kearns, "Sometimes I wished it could go on forever."

Sam's fall was sudden, and no one bailed him out. In 1919 the price of cotton fell so low that for the second time in his life Sam was wiped out, only now he had a family to support. He lost everything, even his home. Only the charity of relatives provided food and shelter. Deserted by his apprehensive friends and supporters, the best job he could find was as a part-time game warden. Later he was hired as a foreman on the road-building crew that graded the very highway from Austin to Fredericksburg that he had promoted in the legislature. Not surprisingly, he began to drink heavily again. Lyndon became contemptuous of both of his parents. Of what value now were his mother's pretentions and his father's high ideals? It was particularly bitter for Lyndon, a dapper dresser and president of his high school's senior class. Did he, too, lack a regard for reality?

What he needed was a kind of antidote—time to blow off steam. Asserting his independence, he took off with some friends for California, hitchhiking, for a carefree year of vagabond drifting. It also gave him time to think. On the long way home, he had what Kearns describes as a sort of epiphany. He would justify his mother's love and his father's respect. But first, to prove his physical strength, he worked as a laborer on a road-building gang. Then he finally agreed to go to college.

If it wasn't quite Harvard, in 1927 inexpensive Southwest Texas State Teachers College in San Marcos, only thirty miles away, seemed a more viable alternative. Now all Rebekah's mental wheels were again set in motion. She helped Lyndon obtain a job in a criminal lawyer's office and borrowed money from a sympathetic banker to get him started. Responding to his mother's supportive letters, Lyndon wrote, "Dearest Mother . . . You can't realize the difference in atmosphere after one of your sweet letters. . . . There is no force that exerts the power over me your letters do." Working his way through college, Lyndon also worked his way up, developing the skills he would later demonstrate in public life. He would never abandon many of the convictions of his father and grandfather, but he also was a clear-eyed realist, placing ambition above ideology. He cultivated older men who had the power to help him, starting with the president of his college.

Attracting the attention of new President Franklin Roosevelt and Texas Democratic leader Sam Rayburn in what had become his familiar fashion, Lyndon was named to run the New Deal's National Youth Administration in the Lone Star State. His goal remained elective office. In 1934 he found a second gracious, refined woman to sustain him. He married Claudia Alta Taylor, nicknamed "Lady Bird," only two months after they met. Rebekah approved.

The following year, Sam Johnson suffered his first heart attack. He was still very weak in 1937. Even as Lyndon feared for his father's life, he sought out his advice. Their incumbent district congressman had died, and a special election, sure to be hotly contested, would be held to succeed him. Although only twenty-nine, Lyndon was intent on running. There were eight other candidates, all older and more experienced. Lyndon's campaign, his "Blanco Blitz," simply outhustled them all. Although it was no more true of Johnson than of the other "eight in the dark," as he put it, his relentlessly promoted campaign theme had been suggested by his father: "A Vote for Johnson is a Vote for Roosevelt's Program!"

Despite his condition, Sam was intent on helping, reversing the roles of father and son in prior elections. He summoned sufficient strength to launch his son's campaign from his own front porch, before an audience including almost every resident of Johnson City. "My father became a young man again," Lyndon recalled, "[he] looked out into all those faces he knew so well and then he looked at me and I saw tears in his eyes as he told the crowd how terribly proud he was of me and how much hope he had for his country. . . . There was something in his voice and in his face that day that completely captured the emotions of the crowd." The applause was sustained. "I looked over at my mother and saw that she, too, was clapping and smiling. It was a proud day for the Johnson family."

Lyndon's narrow victory made it no less sweet. Ignoring severe stomach pains, he had campaigned with uncommon vigor. His appendix was removed only forty-eight hours before election day. Lyndon's mother finally had her congressman, and his father had his son back. A few weeks later, Sam had another massive heart attack. When Lyndon returned for his father's sixtieth birthday, Sam was in the hospital, under an oxygen tent, but he longed to go home. "Lyndon," he said, in words that would resonate, "I'm going back to that little house in the hills where the people know when you're sick and care when you die. You have to help me." Despite the protests of the medical staff, Lyndon took him home. Two weeks later, on October 23, 1937, Sam Ealy Johnson Jr. died. He was buried in the family graveyard, by the stream and under the trees he loved. Lyndon had to settle his father's remaining debts, but the debt *to* his father he could never fully repay—the example of a life committed to public service. In Rebekah's words, Sam Johnson was "a man who loved his fellow man."

Despite her concern for her husband of thirty years, Rebekah could not contain her emotions at her son's victory, which she tried to put into words: "My darling Boy, Beyond 'Congratulations, Congressman,' what can I say to my dear son in this hour of triumphant success? In this as in all the many letters I have written you there is the same theme: I love you; I believe in you; I expect great things of you. How happy it would have made my precious, noble father to know that the first born of his first born would achieve the position he desired! . . . How dear to me you are you cannot know, my darling boy, my devoted son, my strength and comfort."

Rebekah lived another twenty years, settling into a small house in Austin, writing a family history, and continuing to write letters to Lyndon. She witnessed his rise to majority leader of the Senate, but nothing could exceed her excitement about his first triumph, before the age of thirty. Rebekah Baines Johnson died on September 8, 1958, at the age of seventy-seven. Her son said of her, "She was quiet and shy, but she was the strongest person I ever knew." Not everyone would consider her quiet and shy, but of her strength there is no doubt. She was buried next to her husband in the Johnson family cemetery on the grounds of what came to be called the LBJ Ranch. But in her heart she was always a Baines, the daughter of a man whose dream was redeemed by her son.

Hannah Milhous and Francis Anthony Nixon

"My mother was a saint." Many of those assembled in the East Room of the White House were getting uncomfortable. They had worked for Richard Nixon, and most of them, whatever the excesses of Watergate, remained devoted to him. Flanking him up front, his family fought back tears. It must have been especially painful for them to get through Nixon's emotional, rambling farewell to his staff and cabinet on this, the final day of his presidency, August 9, 1974.

Eyes moistened when he paid tribute to his contrasting parents. "I remember my old man," Nixon went on. "I think they would have called him sort of a little man. . . . You know what he was, he was a streetcar motorman first, and then he was a farmer, and then he had a lemon ranch. It was the poorest lemon ranch in California, I can assure you. He sold it before they found oil on it. And then he was a grocer, but he was a great man. Because he did his job, and every job counts up to the hilt no matter what happens." In the end, Francis Anthony Nixon was also the most vigorous supporter of his son's political career. His mother was more concerned with his character.

What had brought two such dissimilar people together? Their families had even less in common. Stephen Ambrose writes of Nixon, "On his father's side, his progenitors were generally loud, boisterous, emotional, and Methodist. On his mother's side, they were generally quiet, restrained, unemotional, and Quaker." To Herbert Parmet, this contrast helps to explain Richard Nixon's "schizophrenic existence." He wanted to be like his mother but was fated to be more like his father, only without the bombast. In his memorable 1968 speech accepting the Republican nomination for president, Nixon recalled hearing train whistles at night as a child and dreaming of the faraway places he would like to see. Both parents were there to launch him on the journey. He revered his mother, but it wasn't in her nature to nurture the driven, calculated path of

Richard Nixon's career. His father was all bluster but bluntly honest, without a calculated bone in his body, which could hardly be said of his son. Frank Nixon was the greater influence because, as biographer Jonathan Aitken writes, he "fired up" his son. Ambrose calls Frank "the most influential teacher in Richard's life." To Parmet, Frank was "the driving force" in his family. While acknowledging that "I have never known anyone to work longer and harder," Richard Nixon stressed his father's encouragement. It impelled the youth to hurl his 140-pound body against much bigger opponents on the football field and to become a champion debater and student leader.

Ambrose adds, however, that both the Nixon and Milhous families had at least one quality in common: "a penchant for taking risks." Otherwise, neither would have found their way to the western edge of North America. Frank Nixon's forebears, Scottish and English as well as Irish, had come to America in the 1730s, settling in Delaware. Demonstrative Methodists, they were also fervent patriots. Nixons fought in both the Revolutionary and Civil Wars. Frank Nixon's grandfather was killed at Gettysburg. Eventually, like so many others, the Nixon family moved west.

Francis Anthony Nixon was born in Elk, Ohio, on December 3, 1878. His life might have been very different but for two things—his restless nature and the death of his adored mother when he was only eight. With sickness and poverty taking their toll, Frank's father, Samuel, struggled to keep two generations of his family together. He remarried, but his sons found their stepmother so indifferent that she was little short of cruel. In his early teens, Frank took off to make his own way in the world. Combativeness and independence would be lifelong characteristics. If challenged, he would fight anyone of any size, not unlike Harry Truman's father, but he craved success, however it might come.

Frank found work as a streetcar motorman in Columbus, Ohio. Exposed to the elements, he came to hate both the bitter cold and the management's indifference to their workmen's plight. Somehow he managed to organize an informal union to put pressure on a candidate for the state senate to introduce legislation to improve conditions. This first Nixonian political campaign was more successful for the constituents than for the candidate. The other motormen did eventually receive both heat and enclosure, but realizing he would be fired, Nixon hit the road again—or, more precisely, the rails. Possessing little more than his train fare, he took off for the perpetual warmth of southern California. It was 1907, and he was already twenty-eight. Once he arrived, fortunately he quickly found work again, even though his new job was still as a motorman. At least "interurban transit" was a line far more scenic and comfortable than his prior route in Columbus. It ran the twenty miles between Los Angeles and the growing town of Whittier, the major western community of the Religious Society of Friends, or Quakers. Frank decided to room in their boardinghouse near the Whittier terminus. The Quakers extended to the lonely newcomer a friendliness he had not previously experienced. Eventually, he joined their faith, in its more animated western version. He also began to frequent their rather proper parties.

His circumstances may have been humble, but Frank Nixon took pains to make himself presentable. Ambrose writes that he was not especially tall, but handsome, well groomed, and lively. He "wore his dark hair slicked down and precisely parted. He had a fine full face, and a strong but not oversized nose and jaw, deep penetrating eyes and a firm mouth." His sole suit was "very carefully" pressed. Affable but opinionated, he enjoyed conversing. His early foray into politics had reinforced his support for labor and Democratic populism, but he had rather quickly switched to the "sound money" Republicanism of William McKinley. Ambrose observes that Nixon's "good looks, cheerful grooming, and animated ways drew people to him, but unfortunately his loud and aggressive personality drove many of them away."

One person he definitely did not drive away was young Hannah Milhous, whom Frank met at a Valentine's Day party in 1909. She was fascinated, and he was captivated. As for Hannah's parents, they were neither fascinated nor captivated with this brash, penniless young man who had the look of a "black Irishman."

The inception of the roundabout Milhous journey to the New World had begun in the mid-1600s. In England, Oliver Cromwell had concluded that these independent Quakers, who relied on the "inner light" of personal guidance, were one sect he couldn't win over "either with gifts, honors, offices or places." When some of them finally began to emigrate, the authorities were relieved to be free of such dangerous nonconformists. William Penn established his "holy experiment" in 1682. After the monarchy had been restored, King Charles II was more than willing to repay the debt he owed to Penn's father by granting vast tracts of land in North America.

The Milhous family was of German descent, originally named Melhausen, and went to England to fight *for* Cromwell. Their reward was land in Ireland, in Timahoe County. Somehow, there they were converted to Quakerism, renounced their military heritage, and in 1729 sailed to Pennsylvania, where they had obtained 200 fertile acres to farm. In 1805 they moved to Ohio, and in 1854 to Indiana. They were not so much restless as open to new opportunities. Apparently, one pervasive characteristic many retained, although it seems at odds with their faith, was a rather smug self-satisfaction. As one in-law remarked, "The Milhouses thought highly of the Milhouses."

By the time he was twenty-eight, Franklin Milhous was already a widower with two young children. Within his community and his church he found a worthy second wife. At the age of thirty, an experienced schoolteacher, Almira Park Burdg had seemed destined for spinsterhood. She was plain but very bright, loved poetry, and fortunately was very fond of children. She would bear seven, six of them girls. The third of these daughters, born on March 7, 1885, was named Hannah after a Milhous aunt and the mother of Samuel in the Old Testament. At least in the eyes of most people, Hannah would be no more a beauty than her mother but was certainly her equal in learning, piety, and charity.

Through the Civil War and beyond, social issues were championed more by eastern Quakers, but Almira had no patience with equivocation. She revered Abraham Lincoln and espoused racial and religious toleration. As Richard Nixon recalled, "My grandmother set the standards for the whole family." Her husband was more fun-loving but in his own way was equally religious. Together they established lifelong values for their nine children, to be perpetuated in following generations.

Franklin Milhous had been expanding the prosperous plant nursery that he had inherited from his father but was always looking for wider opportunities. He was intrigued by a new settlement almost a continent away in California, named for Quaker poet John Greenleaf Whittier. The lure of abundant land at low prices, a beneficent climate, orange groves, and an expansive Quaker community already under way was irresistible. In 1897, when Hannah was twelve, her family moved to Whittier in a series of chartered railroad cars, taking with them virtually all of their possessions.

What they found was not quite paradise, but a Quaker church was already in place, and an academy—eventually to become Whittier College—had been founded in 1891. The Milhouses settled into a spacious Victorian house and established their new nursery behind it. In due course a stream of relatives came west to join them, recreating their Indiana community. Richard Nixon wrote of his maternal grandmother, as he would of his mother, "She was always taking care of every tramp who came along the road. . . . There were Negroes, Indians, and people from Mexico." If they didn't mind listening to a Bible verse and solemn prayer, anyone could get a square meal at the Milhous homestead.

Shy, dutiful, bright, and profoundly religious, Hannah Milhous finished grammar school with high grades and went on to the Quaker academy. Ambrose describes the teenaged Hannah as having "a dark, brooding look. Of medium height (five feet, five inches) . . . She was exceedingly slender, bony in her shoulders and face. She usually did up her long black hair in a knot. Her eyes were dark and deep-set. . . . All the photographs taken of her during her adolescence show a serious, almost forbidding face." Morris's description of the same features is a bit brighter, describing a "gentle young lady of wasp waist and serious countenance, marked by thick raven hair and eyebrows above dark, limpid eyes."

Frank Nixon had already lost his transit job due to an accident and was working as a foreman in a neighboring citrus orchard. He did not view Hannah as plain. She *was* shy, but also warm, intelligent, and altogether wonderful. As Aitken adds, Frank "saw beauty in her tranquil face, whose high cheekbones and intense, greenish-brown eyes fell away to . . . the Milhous ski-jump nose." Richard Nixon would resemble his mother in at least this feature. Frank started seeing Hannah virtually every night. Her parents were appalled. This audacious outsider offered nothing—no education, no culture, no profession, no family, no future. He seemed little more than a common laborer. But Hannah could be stubborn, and nothing would dissuade her. She had never been in love before, but she knew what it was, and brought her parents to a reluctant acceptance.

The Milhouses would always consider that Hannah had married beneath herself and her family. Forty-four years later, Frank Nixon's opinion, too, remained unaltered, affirming, "I knew I had picked the very best. And I haven't changed my mind." After only four months of what was probably as much a campaign as a courtship, on June 2, 1908, in the East Whittier Friends Church, twenty-three-year-old Hannah Milhous married twenty-nine-year-old Frank Nixon. Four months later Hannah was pregnant.

It must be said that Hannah's father, however he felt, was generous. The Milhouses invited Hannah home, and Frank was even given a job by his father-in-law. In June 1909, after a lengthy labor, Hannah gave birth to a boy whom the couple named Harold Samuel Nixon. At the end of 1911, always sensitive about living off the largess of others, Frank decided to plant his own lemon grove in the nearby town of Yorba Linda, on land owned by the Milhous family. Here, he built a sturdy clapboard house that still stands. The Nixons became a popular young couple in the town. Even with her baby to care for, Hannah was very active in the Women's Club. Frank taught Quaker Sunday School with Methodist fervor and served on the school board. Unfortunately, although the family lived as frugally as possible, there was no way to make the enterprise profitable. The soil was simply too sandy, the lemons of poor quality. Stubbornly, they persisted.

Hannah became pregnant again. On January 13, 1913, after enduring another difficult, protracted labor, she gave birth to the couple's second child, a healthy eleven-pound boy with brown eyes and black hair. They named him Richard Milhous Nixon. Soon relatives were contrasting quiet Harold with noisy Richard. The Nixons would have three more children, all boys—Francis Donald in 1914, Arthur Burdg in 1918, and Edward Calvert, rather a surprise, in 1930. When Richard was nine and toiling with his older brother and parents in the grove, his father finally gave it up.

However, there had been a close call with success. In 1919 oil was found nearby, a potential boon for the Nixons. Soon there was a small-scale boom. Speculators offered him $45,000 for his property. He turned them down—if there really was oil on his property, he wanted it. Hannah, perhaps on a hunch, suggested that they buy land at Santa Fe Springs, where oil was eventually found. Instead, they stayed put, where no oil was discovered. In 1922, when Frank finally sold out, it was for a fraction of what he had been offered three years before. For once, frugal Frank took out a loan, probably vouched for by his in-laws, and opened a gas station in a good location in Whittier. Bringing in and selling the produce of surrounding farmers led to a full-service grocery store, open for extended hours. For several years it was actually a success, but the family was rarely able even to eat together. No one worked harder than Hannah, who had once studied classical languages and literature. Now she rose before dawn to bake dozens of pies, one of the store's most popular products, and then waited on trade until dark. Everyone worked.

Sometimes Frank would become angry even with customers, or strike out suddenly with his own sons, settling the issue with his own strap. His anger would then dissipate quickly like a summer storm. Richard was rarely the victim of these outbursts. He had learned to gauge his father's moods, viewing them from a safe distance. Decades later, Nixon reflected on his father's volatility. "Perhaps my own aversion to personal confrontations," he observed, "dates back to these early recollections."

Hannah, whose strongest admonition was "hush," had a different approach, a sort of escalating nonviolence. Richard recalled that her tongue was never sharp when she was upset with a son's behavior, "but she would sit you down and she would talk very quietly. Then when you got through you had been through an emotional experience." Richard did not view her as lacking in warmth. He always, as Ambrose writes, "turned instinctively to his mother." As a boy, he "liked to have her sit with him when he read, and otherwise be with her."

Starting grade school in 1918, Richard demonstrated ability and orderly effort from the very beginning. He loved sports but lacked the talent or size to really excel at them. Encouraged by his mother, he enjoyed reading, music, and the sort of poetry he heard from her. "He was interested in things way beyond the grasp of a boy his age," she recalled. "He was thoughtful and serious. He always carried such a weight."

As they grew, Harold and Don, spontaneous and gregarious, reflected their father's more attractive qualities. Arthur, then the youngest son, a reflective loner, was more reticent to show affection. In the summer of 1925, he suddenly fell ill, suffering headaches, indigestion, and exhaustion. The eventual diagnosis was tubercular encephalitis. Neither physicians nor prayer could save him. After a sustained bedside vigil, he died. Richard had never before seen his father cry. Hannah grieved for the rest of her life. Now, according to his mother, Richard's "need to succeed became even stronger."

At his eighth-grade graduation from East Whittier School, Nixon took the spotlight as class president, "most outstanding" student, and valedictorian. Asked to compose an autobiography, his response was prescient. "My plans for the future . . . are to finish Whittier High School and College and then to take postgraduate work at Columbia University, New York. I would also like to visit Europe [and] I would like to study law and enter politics for an occupation so that I might be of some good to the people." Substituting Duke Law School for Columbia, it would unfold in much that way. The previous year, after the Teapot

Dome scandal broke, Richard had announced to his mother, "When I get big I'll be a lawyer they can't bribe."

Harold was not only the brother closest to Richard; he was perhaps the best friend he would ever have. Being so different, each respected the abilities of the other. Harold admired Richard's drive, achievements, and ambition. To Richard, Harold represented all the qualities he lacked—an effortless ease in any company, a cheerful outlook on life, and the ability to live for the moment. In 1927 Harold suddenly became terribly ill. This time the prognosis was clear from the start—tuberculosis. His parents took him to a series of private sanitariums, but his health only declined. Frank had sold land from behind his store to pay for the best in care. Then the family made a hard decision. Hannah would venture to Prescott, Arizona, to a rented cabin. She took in, cooked, and cared for four other tuberculosis patients as well, to pay for her son's treatments at the local sanitarium. The dry desert climate itself was believed to have curative powers. Frank and his other sons would continue to run the store. For two summers Richard went out to Arizona, whatever the risks to his own health. Frank made the six-hundred-mile round trip as often as he could. The strain was showing on everyone. Contagion might also affect Hannah.

In 1930 she made a welcome surprise trip back to Whittier for Christmas, informing her incredulous husband that at the age of forty-five she was again pregnant, with their fifth and final child, Edward Calvert. Finally, Harold insisted that he and his mother return for good. In 1933, despite the pleas of his parents, he returned to Whittier to pursue, for however long, as normal a life as he could sustain, around everything and everyone dear and familiar to him. He and his mother learned of the deaths, one by one, of each of the other youths she had cared for. As Richard reflected in 1974, it was like the death of four more of her own sons.

One morning, Harold felt very weak, much as Arthur had eight years before. He asked his mother to hold him tight in her arms, telling her, "This is the last time I will see you until we meet in heaven." When Richard rushed back home from Whittier College, both his parents were crying uncontrollably. Hannah witnessed her twenty-year-old son sink "into a deep, impenetrable silence. . . . From this time on, it seemed that Richard was trying to be *three* sons in one, striving even harder than before to make up to his father and me for our loss. . . . Unconsciously, too, I think Richard may have felt a kind of guilt that Harold and Arthur were dead and that he was alive."

The striving had started even before Harold's death. At high school, encouraged by his father at home and his mother in Arizona, Richard continued to excel, particularly in debating and public speaking. He was an acknowledged student leader, although more admired for his competence than truly popular with his classmates. Some even viewed him as a bit devious, and he lost a coveted election for student-body president. He would not lose again for the next thirty years. Gradually he began to unbend a bit and even started to date. As graduation neared, he seemed more genial and relaxed, but never as outgoing as his older brother had been. Harold's medical expenses had been staggering, and now Frank had another son to support, Hannah's Christmas surprise. Still, he would always retain his self-respect. When some wealthier parents offered to buy Richard a new suit for his appearance in the state finals of an oratorical contest, Frank was outraged. He wasn't about to accept charity. He bought the suit himself, although he could ill afford it. "There was never a day I wasn't proud of him," Richard reflected.

Third in his class, he received invitations to apply for full-tuition scholarships to Harvard and Yale, but Richard understood how badly he was needed at home. He would go to Whittier College, just as he had planned. A scholarship fund bequeathed by his Milhous grandfather supplied Richard's tuition. No one complained about nepotism. If Nixon felt regret at missing out on the Ivy League, it was transcended by the excitement of simply going to college.

The Great Depression hurt Frank's business but it did little to soften his temperament. As Parmet notes, he kept a loaded revolver in the cash register in the event of intruders, even as his wife welcomed one and all to the back door, however limited her larder. Like most other institutions, Whittier College was forced to cut back. Speaking on behalf of the whole student body, Richard questioned some of the cutbacks, even convincing the staid trustees to permit dances on campus. This time he was elected student-body president in a triumphant senior year. Whittier's president predicted that "Nixon would become one of America's important, if not greatest, leaders."

In an essay written for his senior religion course, Nixon had distanced himself from his birthright Quakerism, affirming that he could no longer accept the Bible as literal fact although "I still believe that God is the creator." Ambrose concludes, "Thereafter, there was nothing approaching a crisis of conscience or belief for Richard Nixon." His mother understood that he was not destined for preaching or teaching. As far back as eighth grade he had vowed it would be law leading to politics.

Nixon's graduation was capped by the award of a full-tuition scholarship to Duke Law School. He would have to scrimp and save to meet expenses, but that was nothing new. His father would help out to the extent of his ability. In the glow of graduation, Richard didn't even mind being called "Nixie" by jocular classmates. Still, he never quite convincingly became a relaxed "regular guy." In the future he would have many nicknames, from "Gloomy Gus" in law school to "Nick" in the navy. The only one he disdained was "Dick," although his father often used it.

Hannah saw her son through Duke and three years of naval service in World War II (which had made her fearful as a mother and uneasy as a pacifist). Nixon emerged as a lieutenant commander. She saw him through marriage, law, and politics—to the very cusp of his presidency. She was won over by her future daughter-in-law, Pat Ryan, when the young woman came by to help prepare the pies Hannah still baked for sale in the store. As it turned out, Pat Nixon would have need of the stoicism and willpower Hannah came to admire.

Frank Nixon was in his glory. He had always loved to follow politics and was even an avid reader of the *Congressional Record*, but his loyalties fluctuated. He favored Roosevelt in 1932 and opposed him in 1936. Frank's only permanent affiliation was to what one might call "the Richard Milhous Nixon Party." His son had run and won election to

Congress in 1946, went on to be elected to the Senate, and in 1952 was chosen as Eisenhower's vice president, his eyes already focused on the ultimate prize. But his father trusted no one, particularly politicians who might subvert his son's plans. He had hoped Richard would remain a highly publicized senator in the 1950s and then mount his own campaign for president.

Over his strenuous life, Frank Nixon had survived many ailments, including bleeding ulcers, but he appeared healthy enough, not to mention immensely proud (if uncomfortable in his tails) when he and Hannah attended the festivities at Richard's inauguration as vice president in 1953. Living for a time in retirement on a small farm in York, Pennsylvania, both had become particularly close to their two grandchildren, Julie and Tricia. Frank lived until 1956. He was hospitalized during the Republican National Convention, which that year was held in San Francisco. On August 22, the day for vice presidential balloting, Richard Nixon got a call from the Whittier hospital that his father had suffered a ruptured abdominal artery and was sinking fast. Richard and Pat rushed to see him. As Ambrose writes, "When they arrived . . . Frank Nixon was in an oxygen tent, in great pain, but still able to talk." He gasped out, "You get back there, Dick," fearful of last-minute "funny business" to deny his son's renomination. Instead, Richard stayed, and they watched it together on television.

Francis Anthony Nixon died at the age of seventy-seven on September 4, 1956. Like Lyndon Johnson's father, he had asked to be brought home from the hospital to die. During Richard's last visit, he told his son, "I don't think I'll be here in the morning." Richard replied, "Dad, you've got to keep fighting," and, of course, what he heard back was, "Dick, *you* keep fighting." At the restrained Quaker funeral service, the immediate family sat behind a curtain. No photographs were permitted. Frank Nixon might have preferred something more lively.

In his memoirs, Richard Nixon summed up his father's philosophy succinctly. Beyond his love for Hannah and their sons, it was the one constant in his life. "My father's interest in politics made him the most enthusiastic follower of my career from the beginning. My success meant to him that everything he had worked for and believed was true: that in America with hard work and determination a man can achieve anything."

Was the long marriage of Hannah and Frank Nixon happy? Some of their contemporaries suggested that they complemented each other with their different strengths, loud and soft compromising at a livable level. Morris believes that they remained "clearly in love," with Hannah's "serenity and devotion seeming to absorb her husband's volatile bent." Their marriage survived years of poverty, stress, and wrenching tragedy. Most of all, as Morris writes, "I think she probably had a decisive influence because he practically worshipped her," from the day she had accepted his overtures. He felt fortunate, a sentiment with which his Milhous in-laws would agree. He was proud of Hannah, even as their neighbors preferred her gentler, more generous nature, just as he took pride in his most successful son. He well understood his own volatility, even if he was sometimes powerless to contain it.

Perhaps the enigma of Richard Nixon is not bound up in having such different parents. In reality, he wasn't all that much like either. His loud, imprudent, outspoken father's comments might not always have stood up to logic or reason, but he was completely honest, his family's "driving force." His mother was more an inspiration than a determining influence, her family's heart. Richard admired almost everything about her, but he could do no more than try to emulate her example. She was simplicity herself, her son as complex a personality as has ever served in the presidency.

As she aged, Hannah less stringently contained her emotions, becoming her granddaughters' favorite babysitter. She was worried about the toll the stress of his office might have on her son. But, as always, she drew strength from her faith. On the day of her son's second inauguration as vice president, Hannah pressed a personal note into his hand: "You have gone far and we are proud of you always—I know you will keep your relationship with your maker as it should be for after all that, as you must know, is the most important thing in this life." Morris writes that Nixon "did not read it until he was alone later that night.

Deeply moved, he put it in his wallet and carried it throughout his political life."

Hannah Milhous Nixon did not live quite long enough to witness her son's supreme triumphs and his ultimate tragedy. She died on September 30, 1967, at the age of eighty-two. Richard Milhous Nixon was wrong. Books *would* be written about his mother, at least in the context of trying to understand her son. But he was also right. Immensely gifted yet fatally flawed, he was nonetheless the son of a saint.

CHAPTER 17

"Why Not the Best?"—Carters and Reagans

Lilly and James Earl Carter Sr.

"Are you better off now than you were four years ago?" Ronald Reagan asked of the TV audience, just before his sole debate with President Jimmy Carter concluded. With only a week remaining in the 1980 election, which was the incumbent, which the challenger? Sincere Jimmy Carter seemed almost frenetic, switching swiftly from one subject to another, as if seeking something that might actually stick. Relaxed Ronald Reagan, so recently portrayed as dangerously trigger-happy, was the picture of calm confidence, adroitly escaping every rhetorical trap, seeming the more presidential of the two.

A supposedly close race turned into a landslide. In launching what would become known as the "Reagan Revolution," the majority of those previously uncertain voters had finally decided more in terms of demeanor than ideology. After so sustained a national "malaise," with pessimism presented as realism, why not give this refreshingly upbeat optimist and his stirring patriotic message a chance? Specifics could come later.

Reagan, of course, was already established as "the great communicator," his conversational style, honed in Hollywood, ideal for television. Yet, Carter, in his own way, was also uncommonly adroit at communicating—only through the written more than the spoken word. He actually wrote his own books, most compellingly during his remarkable post-presidential career. His 1976 effort, introducing this Georgia "peanut farmer" to the greater American electorate, bore the unlikely title *Why Not the Best?* This from an ostensibly common-sense candidate with deep rural and religious roots, from below the "gnatline" of red-clay Georgia. Forty years later he would write about life at ninety. His distinctively informal campaign style could seem almost humble. He was eternally smiling and thrusting out his hand, "Hi. I'm Jimmy Carter and I'm running for president." Yet his autobiography told a fuller story, its details augmented by subsequent books such as *An Hour before Daylight: Memories of a Rural Boyhood* in 2001. As a result, we know a great deal more about Jimmy Carter and his family than of many earlier presidents. Equally compelling are accounts of the peripatetic childhood and youth of Ronald Reagan as well as those trying to penetrate his elusive persona. Moreover, the mismatched parents of each man tell us a good deal.

In Carter's case, his political career was ultimately launched by his reaction to the death of his father, resulting in an agonizing decision that almost threatened his marriage. In 1953, having run for the Georgia State Legislature, James Earl Carter Sr. was diagnosed with inoperable pancreatic cancer and was transported back from Atlanta to his home just outside of Plains. As soon as they heard the news, twenty-nine-year-old Naval Lieutenant James Earl Carter Jr. and his wife Rosalynn rushed from Schenectady, New York, where he was stationed, to his father's bedside. Sitting there by the hour, Jimmy Carter was struck by how small his father was, even shorter than himself. He had seemed a giant when he dominated the lives of his children and just about everything else in Plains.

For perhaps the first time, as father and son talked together, Jimmy discovered that the compassionate side of the man he thought he knew so well extended far beyond his own immediate family. It became clear from the endless stream of people—black as well as white—who called to pay their respects to the elder Carter, as staunch a segregationist as any other prominent Georgian in the 1950s. Yet, apparently, he was not only admired, he was loved. James Earl Carter Sr. died at home, on June 23, 1953, shortly before his fifty-ninth birthday, in the arms of a devoted black former employee named Annie Mae Hollis, who had returned from California to help the family cope. As Peter Bourne describes the funeral, Jimmy "was astonished at the hundreds of people, of both races, who came to express their concerns with an unanticipated degree of warmth and sincerity." Douglas Brinkley adds, "All of Sumter County was there."

Carter left an estate of over a quarter million dollars, a major business and agricultural enterprise, and a great many people reliant on its retention for their livelihoods. Who was to take it over now? Jimmy Carter's mother was in a state of such inconsolable depression that she had to be medicated. His siblings were hardly up to the task. What was Jimmy to do? Hadn't his father always had this older son—bright, knowledgeable, and responsible—in mind as his eventual heir, even as he had given his consent to a naval career? That career was flourishing; Jimmy had become an aide to brilliant, controversial Admiral Hyman Rickover, the nuclear submarine pioneer. Rickover became almost a surrogate, even more demanding, father figure. And lively Rosalynn, despite her husband's frequently late hours, loved their more cosmopolitan life. The last thing she desired was to return to the flat, bleak environs of Plains. As Rosalynn Smith she had grown up next door to the Carters, was the best friend of Jimmy's sister Ruth, and was the first young woman Jimmy had ever seriously dated. They were married in 1946 after his graduation, high in his class, from Annapolis. He was twenty-one, she only eighteen.

During the long drive back to Schenectady, Carter kept trying to compare his career, now "at the pinnacle of success for a young officer of my rank," with whether he must follow in his father's footsteps and become responsible for the security of all those families back home. When, days later, Jimmy finally reached his difficult decision and told his wife, Rosalynn was shocked. Later she reflected, "He did not think he could do anything in his life to have an impact on people . . . like his father's life made."

Perhaps there was also the inducement of being his own boss. Finally deciding to go back to Plains to take over the family business, a nervous

Jimmy Carter was heartened that his wife, with great reluctance, had decided to accompany him. As Senator William Fulbright would reiterate, "Carter had deep roots." Going back to them may have also led to a rediscovery of himself. When he would question in 1976, *Why Not the Best?*, didn't he really mean values more than personalities? In any case, business led to community involvement, then to politics, and by 1962 to public office. Twenty-three years after deciding to pursue this new path by returning to the past, James Earl Carter Jr. would be elected president of the United States.

The Carters had lived in southwestern Georgia, the most benighted region of a relatively benighted state, for over 150 years. However, the Carter family tree had hundreds of branches throughout the American South, from aristocratic plantation owners in Virginia to dirt-poor farmers in Appalachia. The Carters of Georgia were somewhere in between, moderately to substantially middle class.

Under the auspices of an uncle, both Earl, as he preferred to be called, and his older brother Alton, called "Buddy," attended school regularly. Buddy went on to run the town's profitable general store, the Plains Mercantile Company. Earl had bigger plans. Plains, which at its peak had only about seven hundred inhabitants, was like dozens of other dusty southern Georgia towns, but it already boasted a narrow-gauge railroad that served the surrounding farmers as well as passengers. In 1921 Plains achieved another distinction. For some reason, three prominent physicians—brothers Thaddeus, Bowman, and Samuel Wise, the "Three Wise Men"—decided this would be an ideal location to establish their regional hospital, the Wise Sanitarium. It included a nurses' training center, at which one of its earliest students was a slender, earnest young woman from Richland named Bessie Lillian Gordy. "Lilly" Gordy had dreamed of becoming a country doctor, but for a young woman at that time and place, it was simply an impossibility. Nursing would have to do, at least officially.

By his mid-twenties, energetic Earl was starting businesses that just about filled in all the commercial gaps in Plains. He opened an ice house, a dry-cleaning operation, and a grocery store down Main Street that didn't compete with Buddy's Plains Mercantile. But the key to a man's stature was still land. For the first and only time in his life, Earl borrowed money—to buy more and more farmland surrounding the town. Despite his natural shyness, which he covered with a genial demeanor, Earl Carter was clearly a young man with a future. Years later Uncle Buddy would tell Jimmy Carter about his father in those days: "Well, I worked just as hard as he did, but every time I made a dollar, Earl could make three."

The Gordys of Richland, a bit to the hilly southwest, had antecedents similar to the Carters of Plains. Emigrating from Scotland and England in the seventeenth century, the Gordys settled originally in Maryland. Taking advantage of lotteries, as the Carters did, they obtained land in Georgia and moved there in the early 1800s. Successful farmers, they held such posts as tax collectors and fought for the Confederacy in the Civil War. In the wake of defeat and reconstruction, they moved in a different direction than the Carters.

Lilly's father, handsome, mustached James Jackson Gordy, known to all as "Jim Jack," believed in education and activism more than business and also possessed a highly independent streak. Jim Jack and Mary Ida Nicholson Gordy had eight children. Lively Bessie Lillian, whom everyone called "Lilly," born in 1898, was in the middle. "I was Poppa's favorite," she recalled, "and he was my favorite." With widows and orphans from other branches of the family often in residence, there could be thirteen at the dinner table at any given time. Lilly would recall these mealtimes as part of a "nice, happy, very close family . . . with a great deal of conversation going back through the chaos." Instead of prospering through business and farming, the Gordys pursued the professions. Not only were two of Jim Jack's brothers physicians, one became a state legislator. Always intensely interested in politics, his own path led to appointive office, resulting more in a level of respectability than consistent financial security. Serving in such posts as postmaster, revenue officer, deputy marshal, and finally the ceremonial position of doorkeeper at the Georgia State Capitol, Jim Jack had to be circumspect. He cared far more about principles than parties. The values imparted to her oldest son by the woman who would one day be known to the entire nation as "Miss Lillian" came directly from her father.

Living in the midst of a thoroughly segregated society, Jim Jack believed firmly in racial justice and equality of opportunity. He felt that government on all levels should be a positive force for improving the lives of all its citizens. He affirmed the Christianity of moral example, not merely formal worship, flouting tradition by welcoming the distinguished bishop of the African Methodist Episcopal Church through his front door. Later still, Miss Lillian and her son Jimmy would be the only members of the Plains Baptist Church to stand in support of its racial integration.

The only respectable occupations for young white women to pursue in the South were teaching, with its implications of spinsterhood, and nursing, favored by Lilly Gordy. Although the Wise Sanitarium was rapidly expanding, from twelve to ninety beds, and openings for nurses training were highly coveted, Sam Wise was a good friend of Jim Jack Gordy, and after all, the two towns were close to each other. Lilly found nurses' training to be very rigorous, but her new independence also presented an opportunity to cut loose a bit. The work hard/play hard regimen of the entire Wise medical staff and their friends was the closest Plains came to the Roaring Twenties. Whether potential nurses were indeed "fast" or not, Lilly discovered that she enjoyed drinking, smoking, dancing, and partying in general. So did Earl Carter, who sought some relief from his rigorous business.

Earl stood about five-foot-eight, an inch or two taller than Lilly, and weighed a stocky 175 pounds. He had reddish hair and a face sunburned in all seasons from his work outdoors, although he would almost always wear a hat. Despite needing to wear spectacles, he loved sports of all kinds, as spectator or participant, and games, everything from baseball to poker. Earl was already well known to Lilly's classmates and was well liked as a good dancer, a fun date, and possessor of a sporty, open-topped Model T. With her long, lean face, Lilly was by no means a classical beauty. However, Jimmy would remember her when she was still relatively young as "very slender, almost gaunt . . . but pretty in her own way, with her dark hair parted in the middle, and eyes that almost seemed to sparkle." Most of all it was her free-spirited vivaciousness that made her popular.

She first met Earl on a double date, and their initial encounter was anything but promising. She found him tiresome and a show-off. By then Dr. Sam Wise, who had taken Lilly under his wing, urged her to take a second look, suggesting that, "He's a boy that has a lot more ambition than anyone in this town, and he's going to be worth a lot someday." To her surprise, her parents also liked what they'd heard about Earl. Apparently, his reaction to Lilly had been far more favorable. He asked her out, and soon they were dating steadily. In 1923, they became engaged. Lilly still had to complete her training to become a registered nurse and was obliged to go to a hospital in Atlanta for another six months. Thoroughly enamored, Earl called her every Sunday and drove up to see her twice. Finally, on September 26, 1923, the two were married by the pastor of the Plains Baptist Church in a modest ceremony in Earl's home. He was twenty-seven, she twenty-five.

Something in Earl beyond ambition had won Lilly over, at least for a time. The boisterous social life at the clinic carried over into the early years of their marriage. He also took her to plays in Americus. It turned out that they were both almost fanatical baseball fans. They weren't entirely mismatched. Their first child was born precisely nine months after their first New Year's together, at 7 a.m. on October 1, 1924, with Dr. Sam in attendance. When Lilly went into labor, Earl rushed back from one of his farms in time to get her to the Wise Sanitarium. James Earl Carter Jr., described by his mother as "a bright, happy baby who needed no special care," would be the first president of the United States to be born in a hospital. Two years later a daughter, Gloria, was born to the Carters. Two years after that it would be a second daughter they named Ruth. It would be another thirteen years until the birth of their final child, William Alton, nicknamed "Billy." Earl joked that this baby couldn't possibly be his, which Lilly didn't find particularly funny. It is difficult to discern precisely when the magic went out of the Carters' union. Lillian must have realized that, beyond their social life, she really shared few interests with her husband. They both were keenly interested in politics, but Lillian viewed Earl's concerns as limited to the local and provincial. And Earl still wanted to go out every Saturday night, long after she'd tired of it.

In the early years, although Earl was the unquestioned head of the household, Lillian's strong will exercised a great deal of influence. She supervised how the children were fed, clothed, and educated. "I think my children are individuals," she would insist. As Jimmy would later remark, "She grew in spirit and influence all her life." She had already won the coveted position of surgical nurse at the clinic, and between pregnancies she worked in the operating room or on private duty. Of course, she loved her children, but she also relished this increased opportunity to be of service and to sustain a degree of independence.

Spending more time out of the home each year, Lillian eventually limited her serious cooking to one day a week, generally a chicken dinner on Sunday. Her "quality time" had diminished to leaving separate notes on a table for each child, often about such areas as recommended reading. She started bringing her own books to the table to read while she ate and encouraged her growing children to do the same, while Earl simmered and ate in silence. Young Jimmy, who remembered taking refuge in his tree house because of the noise of his parents' parties, found the sounds of their silence even more disconcerting.

As the years went by, it was his father, despite his rigorous schedule, who took the children to school, church, and their social and athletic events and even helped them with their homework. There were rarely the warm family reunions so common to Southern families. Both parents could be soft as well as demanding, but it is easy to see why at that stage Jimmy still called his father "Daddy" but Lillian "Mother." Because Jimmy was the only boy in the household for the first thirteen years of his life, with his mother increasingly distant, he felt most fully his father's expectations and his influence. He called Earl Sr. "the center of my life and the focus of my admiration when I was a child. My daddy was the dominant personality in our family."

As Earl's land holdings increased to over 5,000 acres, worked by as many as two hundred families of black sharecroppers, Lillian finally became, in essence, the country doctor she had dreamed of being. "Miz Lillian" not only birthed their babies but also tended to all their medical concerns as well, to the neglect of her own children. After all, where was the need more urgent?

Mr. Earl early involved Jimmy in learning the rudiments of the family business and could see his potential. He called Jimmy "Hot" for "Hot Shot" when he was pleased, "Jimmy" when he was not, but he smiled a lot more than Admiral Rickover would. To Earl's credit, as Peter Bourne points out, he was not so immersed in the future of his business that he failed to remind all of his children that "there was a world to be conquered outside of Plains." However, personally he was satisfied to be the first citizen of his own community. When he moved his home, it was only three miles west to tiny Archery, to bring his farms' produce to a Seaboard Railroad Lines flag stop and be even closer to his tenants. The business headquarters remained in Plains. The only other white family in Archery was headed by a railroad foreman. In addition to peanuts, which largely replaced cotton as his staple crop in the 1920s, Carter's diversified farms now raised everything from pecans to peaches, pork to potatoes, and livestock of every kind.

Jimmy Carter's childhood and youth reflected the contrasting realities of rural Southern life in the 1920s and 1930s: idyllic yet rigorous. "My childhood world was really shaped by black women," he would recall, and virtually all his childhood companions were black, raised by the surrogates who filled in for his missing mother, their well-loved and caring Miz Lillian. Still, for Jimmy it was his daddy, the visible presence running everything who also was his "best friend." For a young boy it seemed a "Huckleberry Finn" kind of life. Jimmy even looked like Huck Finn, barefoot and shirtless, red-haired and freckle-faced, fishing for eels and catfish, swimming in the creeks, climbing trees, hunting quail, and aimlessly exploring to his heart's content a carefree, country life any boy who loved the outdoors might wish would go on forever. But it wasn't all play. As he got older, Jimmy plowed and hoed with his playmates and their parents, more each year, his tasks equal to his father's tenants but the expectations greater. Eventually, Earl gave him his own acre to be responsible for, to cultivate and make productive. He even sent the apprehensive youth into Plains, which now must have seemed like a metropolis, to sell boiled peanuts.

As Jimmy grew, however, a longer-term goal was emerging. Inspired by the colorful postcards he received from his globe-girdling uncle, navy radioman Tom Watson Gordy, in land-locked southern Georgia Jimmy began to dream about somehow attending the Naval Academy, and going on to an exciting career actually seeing the world as a naval officer. Hadn't his father talked of opportunities beyond the insular world of Plains?

Unlike less farsighted farmers, Earl had the means not only to diversify but to mechanize. He helped finance an agricultural station at the University of Georgia, and the library at Georgia Southern University is named for him. Everything was bought with cash. Hardheaded but astute, he had a Midas touch that was already the stuff of local legend. Even the Depression hardly touched Earl Carter, beyond enabling him to buy products cheaper. It had, of course, a devastating effect on many millions of others. The Carters never turned anyone away who came to the back door asking for food, often offering to work in return. What remained unpublicized was Mr. Earl's generosity to those in dire need within his own sphere, including giving medicine and supplies to his wife as she made her daily rounds. Indeed, he may have come to view her commitment with quiet pride. Hardly a New Dealer, he never forgave President Roosevelt for agricultural policies that actually involved plowing crops under, but Carter was politically moderate for his time and place, favoring rural electrification and investing to improve the standards of the separate black schools.

Earl also built Lillian her own secluded pond house by a fishing lake, where she could spend scarce leisure time playing cards with a few friends or reading and reflecting on her own. The relationship between Lillian and Earl seemed to be entering a sort of third stage. First, there was togetherness, followed by separation, and now finally a sort of mutually understood acceptance. Sometimes they still did things together, vacationing to Chicago or New York, involving the interests of both. Sharing their love of baseball, they happened to be in Brooklyn when Jackie Robinson made his major league debut. Lillian stood and cheered. Earl did not.

Jimmy had started school in Plains in 1930 at the age of six. This entrance into an all-white world represented a confusing separation from his childhood companions. He was undersized, insecure, and wanting to be liked. One can imagine him sticking out his hand to announce to his new classmates, "Hi. I'm Jimmy Carter. . . ." He did well throughout school, his imagination enhanced by learning more about those faraway places he longed to see one day. Carter was a favorite of his teachers. In the eighth grade he encountered one, Julia Coleman, who made such an impression that he mentioned her in his inaugural address as president. He spoke at graduation on "The Building of a Community," a combination of what he had learned from "Miss Julia" and his mother, who had left him all those notes on the table with recommendations for reading and reflection. His parents attended the graduation ceremonies together, after which they hosted a party for the entire class.

Carter also became more involved in the Plains Baptist Church, where he had been baptized, and began to share his mother's emphasis on the church's moral message over the rigidity of its forms. Many years later, after the galling disappointment of losing a race for governor to a crude bigot, Carter was deeply influenced by a long talk with his deeply religious sister, Ruth. It led to a transcendent experience of his own and to being "born again," the first president who would make such an affirmation.

Despite Jimmy's becoming qualified by his teens to succeed his father, Mr. Earl reluctantly agreed with his son's preference to pursue a naval career. Given his scholastic record and his father's influence, including befriending the local congressman, an appointment to the Naval Academy seemed a viable possibility. But first, the diminutive, slender Jimmy Carter had to build himself up physically, followed by two years of academic preparation at a local college and Georgia Tech. Finally admitted to Annapolis, with the acceleration of wartime demands, he graduated in three years. His mother and his new fiancée jointly pinned on his insignia. Why had Miss Lillian cried at Jimmy's departure for Annapolis, his first trip outside of Georgia? Perhaps there was some regret at not having spent more time with him at home. After twenty years of marriage and four children, Lillian and Earl drove home silently and then reflected separately—she in her small pond cottage, he fishing and drinking at a friend's house by a different pond.

Between 1947 and 1967, Rosalynn and Jimmy Carter had four children—three boys (the second, "Chip," named James Earl Carter III) and finally a welcome girl, Amy Lynn. Miss Lillian was prescient in at least one respect. All four of her own children had certainly turned out to be individuals. Gloria Carter Spann, perhaps the brightest of all, became a cross-country motorcyclist; Ruth Carter Stapleton became an evangelist; and Billy Carter, in fact quite bright and perceptive, became the prototypical presidential problem brother, trying to cash in by promoting such products as "Billy Beer" and the historical significance of Plains itself (although he was defeated for mayor). Still, when Miss Lillian was asked, "Aren't you proud of your son?" she responded, as had the mother of Dwight Eisenhower, "Which one?"

Like her son, Lillian Carter would be more appreciated later in her life. Miss Lillian seemed in her seventies to be the nation's good, gray grandmother, a bit eccentric and outspoken, but an irrepressible inspiration to everyone who affirmed civil and human rights. She had been so devastated by the premature death of Earl, a man whose ideas she may not have shared but whom she had once loved, that even her attentive children couldn't bring her out of a deep depression. She dwelled, not without cause, on how her husband "had been more an affectionate father than I was a mother." As her grandchildren grew, she took more of an appreciative interest in them than her own four children had experienced. Still, she needed more than to be a doting grandmother or babysitter. At sixty-eight, still healthy and bolstered by her experience as a nurse, she joined the Peace Corps and was sent to India, where the main thrust of her assignment was to promote family planning.

Returning after two exhausting but exhilarating years, she found that she had become something of national celebrity.

Asked about her and about his own activities, Billy was more than happy to comment, "I've got a mama who joined the Peace Corps when she was sixty-eight. I got a sister who's a Holy Roller preacher, another wears a helmet and rides a motorcycle, and my brother thinks he's going to be president. So that makes me the only sane one in the family." When Jimmy, already governor of Georgia, told his mother he was planning to run, she asked quite innocently, "For what?" Still, she played a prominent role in his "Peanut Brigade" campaign in 1976.

Speaking with candor, assurance, and humor, in old age she finally became the woman she always knew she could be. The latent charm of the increasingly visible Miss Lillian—even her bluntness—prompted the press to view her as a more authentic personality than her less spontaneous son. As Carl Anthony writes, "Instantly recognizable in her snow white pixie haircut, Miss Lillian was an eager celebrity of the late 1970s—whether cheering heartily at the World Series, playing poker on the way back from the pope's funeral, or sounding off on everything." She no longer merely watched Johnny Carson, she appeared as a favorite guest. After the election, she even represented President Carter overseas. As for the Equal Rights Amendment, Miss Lillian proclaimed, "I've been liberated all my life."

Her son also seemed to loosen up a bit, sometimes going beyond the limits of necessity, as in his famous 1976 interview with *Playboy* magazine. Relating religion to promiscuity, he declared, "Christ said, 'I'll tell you that anyone who looks on a woman with lust in his heart has already committed adultery.' I've looked on a lot of women with lust. I've committed adultery in my heart many times." Well, we've experienced a lot worse.

Carter may have learned the lessons of business success—ambition, hard work, discipline, shrewdness, even charity—from his father. But from his mother came his political credo—the positive, universal message of literal Christianity, affirmed in his uncompromising espousal of civil rights. For Jimmy Carter, as for his mother, a fuller appreciation came late. Through the Carter Center he has been able to merge faith with practicality beyond our borders, promoting conflict resolution as well as programs to combat poverty, hunger, ignorance, and intolerance.

Bessie Lillian Gordy Carter died on October 30, 1983, in her eighty-fifth year, outliving her daughter Ruth by a month. Billy also died in his fifties, in 1988, and Gloria in 1990. All died of pancreatic cancer. Jimmy was the only one of her children who did not smoke. At least his mother was spared the desolation of witnessing so much personal tragedy. She left a belated legacy transcending her earlier inability to comfort her children and ease their isolation: the enduring moral message of her first son.

Nelle and Jack Reagan

The defining moment for Ronald Reagan was not a death but a discovery. When he was eleven he came back to his modest home from the local YMCA on a blustery winter's night with snow on the ground. His mother had gone on one of her sewing jobs, and he had expected the house to be empty. Instead, as he ran up the front steps he nearly fell over a lump near the front door. It was his father, Jack, sprawled in the snow, flat on his back, his arms outstretched, snoring so loudly the neighbors must have heard him. He was dead drunk, the smell of bootleg whisky on his breath. It was still Prohibition, and unpredictable Jack Reagan was just as likely to go to a speakeasy and fall off the wagon during those rare occasions when things might actually be improving as to go on a bender when nothing seemed to be going right.

Should Ron wait for his mother to return home and take charge, as she generally did? No, he decided, not this time. He somehow laboriously dragged his father by his overcoat inside the house and into bed. He didn't tell his mother about it, but then he hardly had to. She had already explained to Ron and his older brother Neil about their father's "sickness," the addiction he struggled with but couldn't always control. "We shouldn't love him any less," Nelle would say, even when he might embarrass them. "We should remember how kind and loving he was when he wasn't addicted to drink." Indeed, it was more a sickness than a sin, and ceaselessly supportive, devout Nelle Reagan never stopped praying for his recovery.

To Lou Cannon, Ronald Reagan's action that evening, confronted by the raw reality of his father's addiction, represented the first moment of accepting responsibility. To Edmund Morris, it was the pivotal episode in his life. Through it all, Ron's regard for his mother, the constant inspiration of his life, only increased. She would teach him the value of prayer, he recalled, "how to have dreams and make them come true." It is little wonder that she had been attracted to handsome Jack Reagan and believed from the start that the constancy of her love in itself could counteract his drinking problem, which would only grow more serious with the years.

John Edward Reagan, the natural salesman whom everybody called "Jack," was bigger than his ambitions. He dreamed of having the largest shoe store in Illinois outside of Chicago. In pursuit of this goal, he took his family all over the state—from Fulton to Tampico, to Chicago itself, then to Galena and Monmouth, back to Tampico, and finally to Dixon. His pervasive humor, his salesman's patter, had always been tinged with a degree of cynicism. It is little wonder. The origins of Ronald Reagan's parents were equally humble but otherwise quite dissimilar. Nelle grew up surrounded by a large, close-knit, warm family. Jack's childhood seemed like something more out of Dickens. The O'Reagans had lived in County Tipperary, Ireland, for generations. Most often, they had worked as tenant farmers, living in abject poverty and buried in paupers' graves. In 1852, Michael O'Reagan decided he'd had enough and moved to London, married, and changed his name to simply Reagan. In 1856 the family emigrated to America, homesteading on land in Illinois. Their son, also named Michael, settled nearby, and in 1883 had a son named John Edward, who would be Ronald Reagan's father. Venturing out on his own, he worked his way up to being the star salesman at a dry-goods store in Fulton, Illinois.

Eventually, Ronald traced his father's family back to the tiny Irish town of Ballyporeen. During his European tour in 1984, Reagan made a stop in there. Reflecting on the poverty of his forebears, he hit just the right note: "Perhaps this is God's way of reminding us that we must always treat every individual with dignity and respect." Who can tell whose child or grandchild will someday rise to eminence? For such informal grace he had to thank the influence of his mother, who was neither Irish nor Catholic.

Nelle Clyde Wilson's family emigrated from England to Canada and then to the heartland of Illinois. Nelle was born in 1883, the same year as Jack Reagan, and near the same essentially rural community of Fulton. She had five brothers and sisters in her close-knit circle. She also only had an elementary school education. She and Jack met when working in the same retail establishment. She had learned the skills to become an accomplished seamstress; at twenty-three, Jack was already an experienced salesman, anxious to improve his circumstances.

He and Nelle were drawn to each other. A husky "black" Irishman, tall and handsome, he was a bard of the prairies, his gift for storytelling celebrated far beyond Fulton. He also possessed, as Morris writes, a sort of virile elegance. "One would never guess from Jack's urban manners and sartorial grace, that he came from a family of rural Irish immigrants. He was that rare type, the instinctive gentleman." Nelle, despite her sharp features, a too-strong chin, and thin lips, was striking, with beautiful auburn hair and blue eyes, a figure slender but shapely, with a natural intelligence that matched Jack's.

They were married in Fulton's Catholic Church in 1904, in deference to his heritage—although he had lapsed—and she was already inclined to a different faith. In 1906 they moved to Tampico, Illinois, where Jack had obtained what looked to be a better opportunity at the Pitney General Store. There their two sons were born—John Neil in 1908 and Ronald Wilson on February 6, 1911. Neil was nicknamed "Moon," from the early comic-strip character Moon Mullins. For Ronald, "Dutch" was the instant appellation. When he saw and heard his ten-pound son, after Nellie had endured a full day's labor, Jack could only exclaim, "Why, he looks like a fat Dutchman!" Both nicknames stuck.

For a time there was seeming stability. His Pitney store was doing well, and outgoing Jack Reagan was already something of a local leader. He served as a town councilman, assistant fire chief, member of service clubs, and finance chairman of the Catholic church he now infrequently attended. With only silent movies for competition, local amateur theatrical and musical groups flourished in small communities like Tampico. Sometimes they performed classic works, sometimes original productions or recitations. It was something that Nelle and Jack were quite good at, a precursor of their family's future. However, the store's success wouldn't last.

Meanwhile, Nelle had found increasing solace in religion. In 1910, on Easter Sunday, Nelle Wilson Reagan was baptized into the Disciples of Christ. By then, Neil believed himself to be more the son of his father, while Dutch was "always Nellie's boy." Finally, the family moved to Dixon, John's final opportunity at retailing. Like many boys who became president, Ronald Reagan insisted he was never really aware of his family's relative poverty. In part because of the length of time he spent there, he recalled his youth in Dixon, Illinois, as "sweet and idyllic as it could be." Indeed, it was a picturesque town, ten times bigger than Tampico, situated by the Rock River between wooded hills and limestone cliffs.

Ron's view of everything changed about the time he entered high school, a second life-altering experience. On a Sunday drive with his parents, sitting in the rear of the car with his brother, he happened to pick up and put on his mother's glasses, and made a startling discovery. Suddenly, he could see everything with a clarity he had never experienced before. He had never known he was nearsighted. It changed more than his vision.

In high school, coinciding with a major growth spurt, Reagan emerged seemingly overnight into a confident personality. A solid if not outstanding student, now he played football confidently and excelled at swimming. And to his mother's delight, under a particularly inspirational teacher, he eagerly participated in every dramatic production. He was elected senior class president and voted "Mr. Congeniality," while his steady girlfriend, one of the daughters of the new minister at his mother's church, was voted "Miss Brains"—a most attractive couple.

Nelle never quite gave up on Jack, but in their succession of towns, it is natural that her sons gradually supplanted him at the center of her activities. Unfortunately, the Depression arrived even sooner in towns like Dixon than on Wall Street itself. The last thing local cement plant workers and farmers needed now was a costly pair of shoes. By 1930, Jack's "grandest dream" was only a bitter memory. He needed to take to the road to seek work. Nelle stayed in Dixon, finding employment as a seamstress-clerk at a dress shop and taking in boarders. William Pemberton writes, "Nelle held the family together. . . . She stretched her limited budget to keep them fed and well clothed, drilled into her sons the value of an education, read to them at night, and took them to church several times a week."

Somehow both Neil and Ron managed to enroll at nearby Eureka College. Obtaining a "Needy Student Scholarship," Ron washed dishes and waited tables at his fraternity house. He was now over six feet tall, a hundred and seventy-five pounds, playing football more prominently but particularly enjoying dramatics, and both starring on and coaching the swimming team. Ron had worked since he was fourteen to help out at home, but by far his most cherished job was as a lifeguard for seven summers at Lowell Park, overseeing a particularly turbulent part of the river. The memory of the seventy-seven people he saved from drowning, encapsulated later by a photograph of himself as a young Adonis, would stay vivid in his mind long after much else had vanished.

At Eureka he had a third significant experience. Although only a freshman, he had been chosen by the more reluctant upperclassmen to lead a protest against the college president's plans to make drastic cuts. The heady experience, as Pemberton puts it, "was a defining moment for Reagan. He experienced for the first time the thrill of moving an audience." It was his own triumph, to be sure, but he understood how well his mother had prepared him for it.

Even in the 1920s and 1930s, both parents viewed people as individuals. Ron's two black football teammates from Eureka enjoyed a warm welcome and a good meal at the Reagan household even if no hotel in town would admit them. At his lowest ebb, after the Depression had hit home, Jack finally found work in a dingy store two hundred miles away, outside of Springfield. On a trip there he stayed in his car overnight in the middle of a blizzard, nearly catching pneumonia, because the proprietor of the only hotel in town had told him he'd be happy there—"We don't have any Jews." Reagan would say of his father, "He was the best storyteller I've ever heard and the strongest man of principle I've ever known. He believed in honesty and hard work. He was filled with a love of justice and a hatred of bigotry."

Returning to Dixon, Jack finally got a break of his own. One of the few Democrats in the area, committed to the New Deal, he landed a job setting up federal relief programs and later worked for the Works Progress Administration. It did a good deal for his self-esteem. The whole family supported Franklin Roosevelt, for whom Ronald Reagan cast his first presidential vote. He would always admire FDR, even after becoming an icon of Republican conservatism.

Graduating in 1932 with a degree in economics, Ron needed to find his own job. By then he really wanted to be an actor; but with jobs so scarce, he felt he might more readily find something in radio. Encouraged by his father, he borrowed his ancient car and took off in all directions. By tenacity and luck he finally found a job spinning records and announcing sports at a radio station in Davenport, Iowa. It led to a bigger job at sister station WHO in Des Moines, enabling him to proudly send a portion of each weekly paycheck home to help out his family. Ron also enlisted in the Army Reserve, and with the Fort Des Moines Cavalry Regiment he realized another long-held ambition, learning to ride as his heroes did in Saturday matinees.

To cover the Chicago baseball teams in 1935, Ron was assigned to tour spring training sites in Southern California. Somehow, through a convoluted series of events, the handsome young sportscaster managed to take a screen test. Warner Brothers offered him a contract at $100 a week for seven years, with the studio's option to either renew or pull out. In the studio system of the time, he went on to make thirteen "B" pictures during the first year. In all, he would eventually appear in a total of fifty-three, with several years of army service in between during World War II. Eventually, many were first-run features, and some were memorable—none more so that his portrayal of tragic football star George Gipp in *Knute Rockne—All American*, introducing that most memorable line, "Win one for the Gipper."

After Warner Brothers picked up his option, Ron felt secure enough to bring his parents out to California and finally buy them a house in their name, the only one they would ever own. "Nothing," he reflected, "has ever given me so much satisfaction." Ron asked his father to take on the job of handling his increasing fan mail. Invited to the premiere of the Rockne film on the Notre Dame campus itself, Jack said with some satisfaction, "I was there when my son became a star."

John Edward Reagan died in Hollywood of coronary thrombosis at the age of fifty-seven on May 18, 1941. Perhaps the only surprise is that his heart didn't give out sooner, after so many years of heavy drinking, chain-smoking three packs of cigarettes a day, and experiencing such continual frustration. Ron could only reflect that, although Jack never entirely overcame the curse of alcohol, "he and my mother had many years of great love together." Certainly, Nelle's satisfaction was the equal of her husband's, but hadn't she always expected it in some form? She viewed most of Ron's screen roles as "just the way he is at home." From Illinois to California, Nelle Reagan sought to be of service, taking food to the local prison and the underprivileged. Some people may have found her opinions to be as sharp as her features as she grew older, but she always looked for the best in others. Nelle Clyde Wilson Reagan died at the age of seventy-nine on June 25, 1962, the same year Ron finally became a Republican. The cause of death was a cerebral hemorrhage, hastened by years of what is now called Alzheimer's disease.

In 1940, Ron had married Jane Wyman, an established Hollywood star. It was the second of her four marriages. They had three children— Maureen, Christine (who was born prematurely and died the same day), and an adopted son, Michael. By 1949 they were divorced. After Reagan died, she issued a statement, "America has lost a great president and a great, kind, and gentle man." In the 748 pages of his 1990 autobiography, *An American Life*, Reagan devotes all of one paragraph to Jane Wyman. However, he included torrents of emotional accolades to his second wife, former actress Nancy Davis, who gave up her own career to devote herself almost excessively to Ronald Reagan's welfare after their marriage in 1952. They would have two rather independent-minded children—Patty Davis and Ron Reagan. That Reagan would become our first divorced president was no longer the impediment it had once been in American politics.

As his movie career waned, Reagan worked in television, particularly as a host for the General Electric Theatre and as a goodwill ambassador for the company. Later, he became president of the Screen Actors Guild and was increasingly active in politics. His rousing televised speech for Barry Goldwater in 1964, defining the new Republican conservatism as a renaissance of the American right, was the rhetorical highlight of that campaign. Urged to run for governor of California, Reagan won in 1966 and was reelected in 1970, to the consternation of more experienced opponents who insisted he was "only an actor." After two tentative but very visible attempts for the presidency, Reagan won both the nomination and election in 1980 and was resoundingly reelected in 1984. When he first entered the White House, he remarked, "Well, it looks like we're living upstairs from the store again."

So familiar to Americans, Reagan still remains something of a bane to biographers. He was a great storyteller, an inheritance from his father. But, as Cannon points out, "Ronald Reagan was always skilled at softening hard memories with happy stories," sometimes leaving his associates up in the air. Even before his poignant, personal farewell to the American people in 1994, confirming that he had been diagnosed with his own case of Alzheimer's disease, he was often viewed as an appealing enigma, possessed of a selective memory. Reagan himself sometimes all but supported such a view. So outwardly warm and congenial, he admitted in 1990 to an inclination from childhood "to hold back a little of myself." His dedicated wife, Nancy, who passed away in 2016, once said, "There's a wall around him. He lets me come closer than anyone else, but there are times when I feel that barrier."

Ronald Wilson Reagan died a decade after that affecting message describing the implications of his Alzheimer's, on June 5, 2004, at the age of ninety-three. As the colors fade, ideology aside, perhaps we should most appreciate him for his love of country and unmatched ability to express it, for what his "Shining City on a Hill" represents. That this very image derives from his mother's church is another indication of his—and our—debt to her, and to his father, who taught him how to paint a picture with words.

CHAPTER 18

The Name Doesn't Matter—Fords and Clintons

—◆◆◆—

Their names even *sound* presidential—Leslie Lynch King Jr. and William Jefferson Blythe III. However, because of divorce and death, we know them as Gerald Rudolph Ford Jr. and William Jefferson Clinton. Their fathers and stepfathers could hardly have been more different. The same could be said of their mothers, beyond a shared pride in the men their sons became.

Dorothy and Leslie King

The first time Leslie Lynch King hit his bride was on their honeymoon. In a hotel elevator a man tipped his hat to Dorothy, and she smiled back in acknowledgment. Once in their room, Leslie became enraged, accused his young wife of flirting or worse, and slapped her repeatedly. Their wedding, on Saturday, September 7, 1912, at Christ Episcopal Church in Harvard, Illinois, had been the highlight of the town's social season. Dorothy Ayer Gardner's father, a wealthy businessman, was a former mayor of Harvard. Her mother was descended from the old New England family that had founded the town. Dorothy, born on February 22, 1892, was bright as well as attractive. Her parents sent her to a small, select college in Illinois that King's sister Marietta also attended. "Dot" Gardner at twenty is described by James Cannon as a "fair, buxom brunette with a quick smile, enthusiasm for life and energy." She had been at the school for only one year when she encountered dashing Leslie King. Ten years older than Dorothy and described by Cannon as a "tall and handsome blond, with his big open face, blue eyes, strong jaw and muscular shoulders," he all but swept her off to the altar. It was not a protracted courtship. Reared in an Omaha mansion, Leslie fascinated Dorothy with his plans for the future. He also impressed her parents.

Things went wrong almost from the start. The wedding gift of Leslie's father, Charles King, was a leisurely, luxurious honeymoon, traveling by Pullman train throughout the West Coast and then back to Omaha. For Dorothy each stop turned into an exercise in terror, followed by an emotional reconciliation. After the couple finally got to Omaha, King not only beat his wife, he threw her out of the house. Somehow she found her way to the railroad station and back home to her horrified parents.

In a matter of weeks, Leslie appeared on their doorstep, even more contrite than before, and although she must have known better, Dorothy went back to Omaha with him. That time their home was a dingy basement apartment. By then Dorothy was pregnant. She hoped that perhaps having a child might improve their marital relationship. On July 14, 1913, Leslie Lynch King Jr. was born. It would not be his name for long. Unfortunately, Leslie only became more abusive. Dorothy wrapped her sixteen-day-old son in a blanket and fled the house. In December 1913 she obtained a divorce on the grounds of "extreme cruelty."

Whatever the circumstances, divorce in those times in a straight-laced little town in the Midwest constituted a scandal, and the Gardners moved to Grand Rapids, Michigan. Developed by thrifty, enterprising German and Dutch immigrants, in 1915 it boasted seventy furniture factories, 134 churches, and the highest rate of home ownership in the United States. One historian described it as "America at its best." In one of its more comfortable homes lived the relocated Levi and Adele Gardner, their daughter, and their grandson. The young man, initially simply called "Junie" for "Junior," as Cannon writes, "came out of the crib as a healthy, tow-headed boy with a toothy grin and boundless energy."

He would see his birth father again only twice. King remarried, moved to Wyoming, inherited some money, and ultimately became the proprietor of a large ranch. Coming to Michigan to pick up a new Lincoln, he tracked down his renamed son, then in high school and working at a diner. Announcing to the stunned sixteen-year-old, "I am your father," he unsuccessfully offered to take the boy back west with him. Working at Yellowstone one summer, his son turned the tables and visited him at his spacious spread in Wyoming, a meeting no more relaxed or productive than the first.

Leslie Lynch King Sr. died in Tucson, Arizona, on February 13, 1941, at the age of fifty-nine. The cause of his ferocity toward the mother of his son is buried in the mysteries of psychopathology. That son had cemented his judgment at their first meeting in Michigan, concluding, "Nothing could erase the image that I gained of my father that day: a carefree, well-to-do man who didn't really give a damn about the hopes and dreams of his firstborn son." His true father, the man he "loved and learned from and respected," was named Gerald Rudolph Ford.

Dorothy and Gerald Ford Sr.

At a "social" at Grace Episcopal Church, Dorothy had met this amiable young man of twenty-four and was impressed with his earnest manner. Tall and slender, he was dark and not particularly dashing, physically very little like Leslie King. That he liked Dot Gardner was obvious. Gerald Ford was a hardworking paint and varnish salesman, anxious to have his own business. Born in Grand Rapids, he had to leave school at the age of fourteen to support his mother and sisters after his father had been killed in a train accident. He was rather shy and serious, yet Cannon also cites his "ready smile" and "booming laugh."

What Dorothy also discovered was that he was a bachelor who genuinely loved children, a major consideration. There might be nothing flashy about this suitor, but there was nothing contrived about him, either. Dorothy Gardner and Gerald Ford were married where they had met, at Grace Church, on February 1, 1916. They would have three boys together—Thomas, in 1918; Richard, in 1924; and James, in 1927. The boys would know their older brother as "Jerry." His new name, Gerald Rudolph Ford Jr., was not made official until 1935, when he was twenty-two.

Even-tempered Gerald Ford Sr. also sought to be even-handed, but young Jerry was already at an age where they could be companions, go fishing together, and toss a football back and forth. Gerald Jr. also emerged as a protective role model to his younger brothers. Since Gerald Sr. was so often immersed in business and community projects, it fell to Dorothy to do most of the day-to-day parenting. "As a child," Ford recalled, rather hard to believe in terms of his later image, "I had a hot temper which Mother taught me to control—most of the time." She was a devout Episcopalian whose favorite excerpt from Proverbs was to turn away anger: "Trust in the Lord. . . . He shall direct thy paths." It is due to his mother's influence more than any other that Ford's autobiography would be aptly named *A Time for Healing*. His father's influence is reflected in his plainspoken approach to public life. "I'm a Ford, not a Lincoln," he announced when succeeding President Nixon.

Gerald Ford paid tribute to his mother as "the most selfless woman I have ever known." Her neighbors and friends in their oral biographies used words such as "wonderful," "gracious," "tireless," and "vivacious" to describe her ceaseless activity in church and community. As for Gerald Ford Sr., he had only three rules for his four sons: work hard to make something of yourself, never under any circumstances tell a lie, and come to dinner on time. Richard Ford recalled, "It was a very frank, open kind of relationship."

After Ford went into business for himself, his income rose, and the family moved to much larger and more spacious premises. It seemed almost a Norman Rockwellian setting, with Dorothy presiding over a bountiful dinner table and inviting everyone to take part. Ford fondly recalled, "Having the family together for major holidays . . . would fill her with joy and she wasn't shy about expressing it." In Buchen's opinion, "Jerry's . . . way with people I think he got from his mother, who was a very sociable woman . . . took a great interest in all Jerry's friends . . . and I'm sure gave him his warm, outgoing qualities."

If his father's warmth lay within, his mother's was displayed for all to see. During the prosperous years, energetic Dorothy Ford was involved in virtually every local activity. But she wasn't merely the customary clubwoman. She had a genuine commitment to helping others. As Ford recalled, "When she wasn't attending meetings, she was busy baking bread or sewing clothes for needy families." She also volunteered at the Well Baby Clinic, made dolls for poor children at Christmas, and was a member of the NAACP as well as the DAR. The Fords welcomed their sons' friends, black or white, into their home. When Jerry attended the University of Michigan, he saw nothing unusual about befriending the football team's only African American player and rooming with him on road trips.

Dorothy's faith motivated the involvement of every member of the household. Gerald Sr. helped form Youth Commonwealth, committed to assisting the poorest children in Grand Rapids, and was a deacon at Grace. Their sons served as acolytes and choir members and attended weekly services and Sunday school. All the boys became Eagle Scouts. As a neighbor put it, the Fords "didn't talk religion, they just lived it."

Although Jerry seemed almost effortlessly popular at school and became renowned for his athletic exploits, he had early difficulties in the classroom, having to overcome a stuttering problem and being left-handed, of some concern to his parents. By 1922 the senior Ford had more serious problems. A national recession following World War I was felt with great severity in the Midwest. Furniture sales plummeted, and so did his income. The mortgage on their house was foreclosed, and the family was obliged to move back to rented quarters. Not everything in Jerry Ford's childhood was idyllic. When it came time to choose a high school, Ford Sr. suggested to his son that he attend South High, where the poorer kids tended to go. "It will help you learn about living."

However, South High was also noted for the quality of its teaching—and its football team. Although only five-foot-eight and 130 pounds when he entered high school, gangling Jerry Ford became an all-city center on a championship team and a letter-winner in three sports. He did well enough academically but excelled in extracurricular activities. A quiet leader like his father, Ford was voted "the most popular high school senior" in Grand Rapids. The reward was an eye-opening trip to Washington, D.C. Jerry decided he wanted to be a lawyer and perhaps someday even a legislator.

The Ford Painting and Varnish Company would face its greatest challenge during the Depression of the 1930s. Ford called in his workforce of ten and told them no one would be laid off. Somehow they would get through it together. Everyone would make five dollars a week, including himself, to at least "keep in groceries." The company survived, but it was a close thing. By a combination of grants and grit, young Ford was able to enter the University of Michigan in 1931. Jerry managed to enjoy an active if frugal social life, became an all-American center on the football team, and graduated with a B average. Declining an opportunity to play professional football, Ford pursued his original goals, helping to pay his tuition at Yale Law School by serving as assistant football coach, gaining his degree, and passing the bar. It is an enduring irony that the finest athlete to serve in the presidency would later be satirized as clumsy.

One of the senior Ford's gifts to his oldest son was whetting his appetite for politics, a commitment they came to share. As his business gradually recovered, Gerald Ford Sr. became chairman of the Kent County Republican Committee, helping to launch the "home front" that eventually displaced a corrupt, locally dominant political machine.

Jerry Ford practiced law in Grand Rapids for only a year before joining the navy early in 1942. Requesting sea duty, he saw considerable action in the Pacific, rising to the rank of lieutenant commander. Returning to his law practice in 1945, he soon became involved in local politics. In his first race, for the House of Representatives in 1948, Ford—a moderate internationalist—won an uphill Republican primary against the incumbent isolationist and went on to win the general election. Again, he had emulated his father, opposing entrenched power. Before the election, his mother decided it was time to ask her thirty-four-year-old son, "When are you going to settle down?" On October 15, 1948, Gerald R. Ford Jr. married Elizabeth Ann "Betty" Bloomer, with whom he would have four children.

His true father, this unobtrusive but "marvelous family man," would share the joy of these grandchildren as well as the satisfaction of witnessing at least the inception of his oldest son's national political career. He died on January 26, 1962, at the age of seventy-two. He had slipped on the ice, receiving a concussion, but a heart attack was the immediate cause of death. It is not too much to say that Gerald Rudolph Ford Sr., memorialized by his son as "one of the truly outstanding people I ever knew in my life," was mourned by virtually the entire community. He left a modest financial legacy sufficient to provide for his wife's welfare, but his legacy to his community was hardly modest. To Gerald Rudolph Ford Jr., as Cannon writes, it was "incalculable . . . his own good name, and the example of hard work, integrity, and fair play on which Ford built his public life."

Dorothy Ford expressed enough interest in politics to urge her son, so secure in the House, not to pursue the vice presidency. "It would be nothing but headaches," she predicted, preferring that he retain the significant job he already held.

That she lived as long as she did was remarkable. She had many serious health problems—high blood pressure, diabetes, and cataracts in both eyes—and had endured a double mastectomy and other major surgeries. Most persistent had been heart trouble, resulting in two heart attacks. But she insisted, her spirits ever high, "I want to die with my boots on." In 1965, Ford had been named minority leader of the House. Two years later, as her son reconstructed the scene, Dorothy was "just sitting there in her pew" at Grace, waiting for the service to start, when her heart condition finally took her life. It was September 17, 1967. She was seventy-four. On the day she died, Dorothy Ford's appointment book was full for months to come.

In the spring of 1932, close to Mother's Day, Jerry had sent his mother an apologetic letter from his fraternity house at Michigan: "I'd like to send you flowers or candy or something but my financial condition is dreadfully insecure. So this will have to do. . . . Have a fine time and maybe next year I'll be able to do something more." One suspects she felt that he had already done more than enough—by justifying the values she had brought into their home, derived from the structure where she had spent her final hour.

Virginia and William Jefferson Blythe III

Bill Blythe could charm anyone. How many women he married, how many children he fathered, is still not certain. When nursing student Virginia Cassidy first glimpsed Blythe that night in 1941 as he came into the emergency ward at Shreveport's Tri-State Hospital, it was quite literally love at first sight, at least on her part. Unfortunately, the very tall, sandy-haired, ruggedly handsome Blythe had another young woman in tow. She needed an immediate appendectomy and was rushed into the operating room. When apprentice nurse Cassidy saw Blythe turn toward her "and his eyes met mine," as she recalled a half-century later, she almost required some resuscitation of her own. She was "stunned. . . . He smiled and the only way I can describe it is that he had a glow about him. I was weak-kneed and also embarrassed." Blythe's girlfriend at the time recovered; Virginia did not. Soon she was seeing Blythe regularly, although she was already engaged and nursing students were supposed to stay single.

Virginia brought Bill home to Hope, Arkansas, some fifty miles away, where she had been born on June 6, 1923, to meet her parents. When her exacting mother, Edith Grisham Cassidy, looked into Blythe's deep blue eyes, her initial reservations dissipated. She envisioned at least a stable future for Virginia, whom she didn't view as a model of stability. Blythe was neither wealthy nor educated, but he seemed to have a great deal of energy, and he certainly exuded charm. As for Virginia's father, Hope's genial long-time iceman, James Eldridge Cassidy, he liked just about everybody.

Blythe was on his way back home to Sherman, Texas, to enlist in the army. He had a good job in Chicago selling heavy automotive equipment, and it would be waiting for him when he came back from the service. Despite his aristocratic-sounding name, William Jefferson Blythe Jr., he was the oldest son of a poor farming family in Texas. His father had died when Bill was only in his early teens, obliging him to leave school around the eighth grade and work to support his mother and his siblings. His sales job meant being on the road a good deal, but it was a life he liked, and it paid well.

At the time, Virginia Cassidy was still a fresh-faced, spontaneous girl not long out of high school, where she had been quite popular and an excellent student. To make extra money, she worked as a waitress. She had only recently begun to emulate her mother's addiction to cosmetics and flirting. Edith Grisham Cassidy, through little more than a correspondence course, had attained a respected position as a private-duty nurse. For some reason, nothing her daughter did seemed to please her. Her mild-mannered husband, whom everyone called "Eldridge," doted on their only child, whom he fondly called "Ginger." Lighthearted Virginia didn't take this domestic trauma to school. Despite Edith's seeming disapproval, she couldn't help admiring her mother's steely determination to better herself. Virginia's goal at graduation from Hope High School, in the ominous year of 1941, was to escape to somewhere more exciting and a life more promising. She got as far as Shreveport, where she was accepted to nursing school at the Tri-State Hospital, shed her small-town inhibitions with a more active social life, and ran into engaging Bill Blythe. What she didn't know was that he had been married at least three times before, had impregnated other women, and may well have been at least technically married at the time they met. But in her smitten state, even that might not have mattered to Virginia.

The two were married by a justice of the peace in Texarkana, on the Texas-Arkansas border, on September 3, 1943. She was twenty, he twenty-five. A few weeks later, Blythe enlisted and was sent to North Africa and then to Italy, specializing in the repair of vehicles, an area he knew well. He was mustered out at the end of December 1945 as a technical sergeant, and they moved to Chicago, where he got his old job back. Virginia and Bill lived in a hotel in the Loop while they waited to take possession of a new home in suburban Forest Park. Soon she was pregnant. More than a bit lonely when Bill was on the road, she and her husband reached a difficult decision. Virginia would return to her family's home in Hope to prepare for the birth of their child. Perhaps her mother might finally treat her as a responsible adult, and it would only be for a short time, in any case. Bill Blythe, having seen the world, had no intention of settling down in a hick town of less than ten thousand like Hope, Arkansas.

The Blythes' home was ready in May, and Bill had returned from his sales trip. On a weekend, he drove south to pick up his wife, gunning straight through at a high rate of speed. Somewhere in Missouri, on May 17, 1946, one of his tires blew out, and he was tossed from the car and killed instantly. Ironically, Blythe would be buried in Rose Hill Cemetery, in the plot of his wife's family, within a town he loathed and she had sought to escape.

On August 19, 1946, the boy who was technically William Jefferson Blythe III was delivered by cesarean section, a month ahead of schedule. Suspicious tongues wagged throughout Hope that perhaps Bill Blythe was not his real father. Eventually, Virginia learned more about her husband's lurid past, but she still remained loyal to his memory, continuing to insist that she could judge Bill Blythe only by the way he had treated her. "I'll go to my grave," she wrote, "knowing I *was* the love of his life."

Virginia and Roger Clinton

Women have been fighting over the man who became Bill Clinton since the day he was born, from his maternal grandmother to, much later, his admiring high school principal. From the first, Edith Cassidy, only forty-five, viewed herself as better qualified to raise little Bill than her inexperienced daughter. Moreover, to gain her credentials as a nurse anesthetist, Virginia had to take courses in New Orleans, leaving her boy under Edith's care and influence. When bronchial problems had ended

Eldridge's career as Hope's iceman, he opened a grocery store in a poor neighborhood. Hope had gone dry in 1944, and the nearest source of alcohol was Texarkana. Under the counter of Eldridge's store was his stash of bootleg liquor, supplied by a man named Roger Clinton, who also was reputed to own the Buick dealership in town. Everyone called him "Dude," and it was easy to see why. As Virginia wrote, "He dressed to kill, with sharp-creased trousers and fine-tailored sports coats and two-toned shoes." He stood about five-foot-eleven, not quite as tall as Bill Blythe, and had dark curly hair. His eyes twinkled when he talked. He was the life of any party, and he loved partying. Virginia wrote, "Men adored him, women found him charming."

But there was also a sense of danger about Roger Clinton. He drank heavily. He gambled, sometimes recklessly. Gambling was illegal in Arkansas, but law enforcement was often influenced to look the other way, particularly in the wide-open resort city of Hot Springs. Roger's older brother, Raymond, who largely ran the lives of his four siblings, was one of the power elite in that "sin city." His major problem was Roger, who was also a notorious womanizer—Virginia must have heard about it—and when things weren't going his way, he could turn violent.

Things, however, weren't exactly going Virginia's way back home with her mother. Edith insisted that she had already discerned that young Bill possessed special gifts. It was important that he not acquire the undisciplined habits of his mother. As for Eldridge, predictably, he adored the child, just as he adored the child's mother. When Virginia had been in New Orleans and his wife was called away, Eldridge took the lively, chubby, cheerful little boy down to sit on the counter at his store. For the first time, Bill saw desegregation with his own eyes, a rarity in Hope, since his grandfather's store was frequented by both black and white customers.

Both sides of Virginia's emerging duality had been brought out in the Crescent City, its attractions enticing even as she vigorously pursued her studies. Edith was so concerned that Virginia might marry someone like Roger Clinton that she threatened to seek legal custody of the

exceptional four-year-old with limitless potential whom she now called
"Billy." He was the son she'd never had. But once again Virginia fell for
the blandishments of a fast-talking suitor. Since they had become reacquainted, Roger had been a perfect gentleman, at least around her. She
convinced herself that through her love and Roger's money, they could
provide a secure home for little Bill, beyond the influence of his excessively intrusive grandmother.

On June 19, 1950, Virginia married Roger Clinton. She was twenty-
seven, he was forty. At first, all went well. Although still in Hope, the
Clintons moved into a new home in a congenial neighborhood of other
mostly young families. Roger managed the Buick dealership, while
Virginia readily found work, although it kept her out at all hours. There
was a demand for qualified anesthesiologists, even in a small town like
Hope. A nanny was hired to look after Bill. He enjoyed playing with
other children, as long as he was the center of attention, a likely residue
of his grandmother's spoiling.

However, the domestic idyll didn't last long. All the rumors about
Roger soon turned to reality. Worse than his continuing drinking and
gambling, which ate up the paychecks Virginia dutifully gave him to help
pay the mortgage, Roger became abusive. Precisely what, he wanted to
know, was Virginia doing with all those doctors after their late-night
labors? As his alcoholism became more acute, his accusations turned to
violence. He not only hit his wife, he once fired a shot that narrowly missed
her head. She had to call the police and send her son to a neighbor's.
Invariably, after Roger sobered up, he pleaded with his wife for forgiveness
and promised to reform. Virginia always took him back, hoping this time
it might be true, but her main concern was for Bill, now terrified as well as
mystified. He was special, she told him as he grew older. She knew it, just
as her mother had known it. He was intended to do great things, and
nothing should get in the way. He learned early on how to compartmen-
talize his life to focus only on the positive and to sublimate the rest.

In 1952, ostensibly to get a new start, the family moved to Hot
Springs, into a home owned by Roger's brother. Hot Springs was nothing like Hope. Within the resort city there was an almost startling

separation, not unlike that in Las Vegas today—on one side, the luxurious hotels containing every sort of action; on the other, a settled community of neat homes, schools, and churches. Vice and virtue coexisted side by side, and sometimes overlapped. The enticing attractions of Hot Springs not only brought out the worst in Roger Clinton but also embodied the inner conflicts of his wife. She was proficient in her profession and very conscientious, but she also wanted to join the perpetual party on the other side of town. She tore around at all hours in her flashy convertible and dressed in a provocative fashion, heavily made up. Hot Springs was hardly the location for reconciliation, and the arguments between Bill's parents rarely ceased. The relationship with his grandmother had receded by this time.

Yet all this turmoil didn't inhibit Bill's progress, in or out of school. He did well everywhere, first in Catholic school, then in public school. At the age of ten he announced to the astonished pastor of Park Place Baptist Church that he planned to attend services regularly, with or without his parents. He learned to concentrate, whatever the disorder around him. In 1956 his parents presented him with quite a surprise. They had a child, and he had a younger brother named Roger Cassidy Clinton. Anxious to shield little Roger as much as possible from what he had witnessed, Bill became almost a substitute father, a "man-child," as David Maraniss puts it, the one fully functioning member of an irretrievably dysfunctional family.

In high school, Bill really came into his own. He was never formally adopted by Roger Clinton, but at the age of fifteen, Bill took his surname legally, finally becoming William Jefferson Clinton. It would avoid potential confusion and embarrassment, although Bill always insisted, "The name doesn't matter; it's the man." Except for sports, Bill excelled in just about everything at Hot Springs High. He was an excellent student, the acknowledged leader of his class. Although rather chunky, he was also quite popular with the girls. In 1963, representing Arkansas in Boys Nation, Clinton went to Washington and maneuvered himself into position to meet President Kennedy personally, resulting in a memorable photograph he treasured.

At high school, Bill also came under the influence of his third maternal figure, principal Johnnie Mae Mackey, a widow who came to see him as her surrogate son. The opposite of Virginia Clinton in every way, Mackey was the walking embodiment of propriety. They had both lost husbands, in Mackey's case her sole husband. When she had to tell Clinton that, having already headed so many other activities, he could not run for student body president, she burst into tears. However, Bill was selected to deliver the final address at his high school commencement. It was more a prayer than an oration: "And Lord, once more, make us care that we will never know the misery and muddle of a life without purpose." With that performance, Bill had done the impossible, reuniting the two other women vying for his affection. Virginia could not wait to share her joy with her one-time rival, Edith Cassidy. She wrote to her mother, "I was so proud of him I nearly died. He was truly in all his glory."

In 1959 Bill had experienced a defining moment not unlike young Ronald Reagan's decision to drag his drunken father into the house. After drinking tumblers of whiskey and screaming at Virginia as usual, Roger strode over to hit her, as he had done so many times before. Bill had seen enough of it. He intervened, grabbing his stepfather and telling him in even tones, "Hear me—never ever touch my mother again." He was already stronger than a stepfather whose health was beginning to deteriorate. His action affirmed that he was now the man of the house.

Virginia divorced Roger in 1962. Yet, despite everything, within three months she took him back. He had taken to sleeping on their front porch, now more a pathetic figure than a threatening one. The largest bedroom was now Bill's, the property his own domain, his launching pad. The first step in his rapid ascent was to attend Georgetown University.

Roger reflected on Bill and on a final opportunity for reconciliation. How could it be that such a promising young man would carry on *his* name? The transition in their relationship was remarkable, but little time remained. Roger was diagnosed with cancer in 1965, and although he underwent massive radiation treatments, he knew his time was running out. Bill came down every weekend he could to visit Roger at Duke Medical Center. When he couldn't visit, he wrote compassionate, positive letters to his "Daddy." In 1967 Roger was moved back home, with constant medical care. He died on November 8, 1967, at the age of fifty-eight. When Bill was named a Rhodes Scholar the following spring, he shed tears of sorrow that he could not share the news with the only father he had ever known.

High-spirited Virginia Dell Cassidy Blythe Clinton Dwire Kelley would marry twice after the death of Roger Clinton, but one should not be misled. William Jefferson Clinton was the man in her life. At thirty-two, only ten years after graduating from Georgetown, Bill Clinton would be elected governor of Arkansas. Fourteen years later he would be president. His mother shared it all. Yet, if her faith in him had justified her life, through her own example she also contributed to Bill Clinton in a less positive way. As Maraniss writes, "He had been reared by a mother who loved to flirt . . . and he left home just as the country was entering a new age of sexual freedom." The serial infidelities of Bill Clinton, even after becoming a husband and father and after entering the White House, rivaled those of John F. Kennedy, except for a diminution in class and an emphasis on rhetorical hair-splitting.

This ambivalence in so impressive a public figure must have had its genesis in his environment growing up. Yet fortitude is the quality he most shared with his mother. When she witnessed his announcement for the presidency, no longer surprised by anything he might accomplish, she knew she was dying of breast cancer. But she would not tell her son, not yet, not before he won. She passed away a year after his inauguration, on January 6, 1994, at the age of seventy, and was finally reunited with Bill Blythe in Rose Hill Cemetery. As her son would say, "I come from a town called Hope." In his mother's view of his progression, hope would be replaced by certainty.

Chapter 19

Continuity and Change—Bushes

Dorothy and Prescott Bush

The Bushes and Walkers who came to these shores in early colonial times from England and Scotland and who thrived in business before moving on to politics have really been most indebted to each other for their ascent. As Michael Kranish puts it, "Without the Walker money, without the extraordinary Walker devotion, there might well never have been two Presidents Bush." Prescott Bush was the first of this joined family to make the transition to running for political office. How he invested some of that money has been the source of speculation at variance with our conception of him as a formidable model of rectitude. As Senator Bush he was a favorite of President Eisenhower and might well have run for president himself.

Prescott Sheldon Bush was born not in a tony suburb of Manhattan but in Columbus, Ohio, on May 18, 1895, the only son of a remarkable man named Samuel Prescott Bush and his wife, Flora Sheldon Bush. Son of an Episcopal clergyman and trained in mechanical engineering, Samuel made his fortune producing the framework for railroad cars. A prominent community leader, Bush particularly liked sports. Among other activities, he founded and is reputed to have been the first coach of the Ohio State University football team. He was also a devoted Democrat.

Despite his wealth, Bush believed in sending his children to public schools for the lower grades before sending them to New England for boarding school. Prescott attended St. George's School in Newport, Rhode Island, and then went on to Yale, where his grandfather and uncle

had previously matriculated. An all-around athlete, he excelled in baseball and also played varsity football and golf. Somehow he managed to
be a cheerleader, as well. An excellent student, Bush was active in everything from debating to singing, serving as president of the Yale Glee
Club. He was tapped for the select secret society, Skull and Bones, a
distinction later accorded to his son and grandson.

By graduation he had reached his six-foot-four height and weighed
250 pounds, with a full head of black hair and thick eyebrows hood-
ing his blue eyes. Handsome as a movie star of the more somber sort,
he radiated strength and self-confidence. Considering his future, he
reflected, "Public service would be a wonderful thing to participate
in." But first, he must have some money of his own. World War I
intervened. After graduating in 1917, he joined the "Yale Battalion"
of the Connecticut National Guard and saw action in France late in
the conflict, emerging as a captain. Heeding the advice of a friend, he
launched his business career in 1919 with the Simmons Hardware
Company in St. Louis. He also fell in love with vivacious, athletic,
and outgoing Dorothy "Dottie" Walker.

She had been born on July 1, 1901, near Walker's Point in Maine, to
George Herbert Walker and Lucretia "Loulie" Wear Walker. Her ancestors ranged from her father's devout Catholics, who arrived on the rugged coast of Maine in the seventeenth century, to her mother's French
Huguenots, who, escaping persecution, came to America in 1700. First
moving to the more congenial colony of Maryland, the Walkers eventually settled in Missouri and intermingled with families of other denomi-
nations. Over time, most of the family accepted the Episcopal faith that
would be so firmly espoused by Dottie. The Walkers were as enterprising
and mobile as the Bushes. Their wealth originated in a dry-goods business in St. Louis. Longing to locate at the heart of commerce, Dorothy's
grandfather, George Herbert Walker, put its profits into an investment
banking firm in New York which eventually became the nation's largest
private bank, Brown Brothers Harriman. As avid a sports enthusiast as
Samuel Bush, George Herbert Walker donated golf's Walker Cup. A
singular difference—Walker was a devoted Republican.

Had she been born a generation or two later, Dorothy Walker might have had a dazzling career of her own. She was an exceptional athlete. Although sent east to Miss Porter's School in Farmington, Connecticut, for "finishing," in 1918 Dorothy was runner-up in the girls' national tennis tournament. She may have been even more talented in golf, rivaling the legendary "Babe" Didrikson Zaharias. However proud of her accomplishments, her protective parents, who still lived in St. Louis, viewed such spirited exertion as verging on the unladylike. Dorothy Walker was not to be put on public display. They preferred that their young champion be photographed by the press solely in the guise of a sedate debutante and then as a bride and hostess. A proper marriage was a priority, and the smitten Prescott Bush seemed just the right sort of candidate.

Fortunately, Dottie felt much the same way, despite their differing demeanors. The words already being used to describe Prescott were *imposing, stern,* and *commanding.* She saw more: the hidden humor, his wide interests, and his love of children. They were a handsome couple— Prescott, so dark and tall, hovering over Dorothy, so trim and fair, as they exchanged vows at the Episcopal Church of St. Ann on August 6, 1921, near the expansive Walker Point compound in Kennebunkport, Maine. She was twenty, he twenty-six. For over half a century, as Dorothy would say in 1972, Prescott gave her "the most joyous life any woman could experience."

Prescott's investment career coincided with the growth of his family. Their first son, named for his father, was born in 1922, after a frantic ride to the hospital from a softball game Dorothy was, of course, playing in. The second, named George Herbert Walker Bush, representing both families, was born on June 12, 1924, in Milton, Massachusetts, where the Bushes had settled. In the same year, Prescott's father-in-law invited him to join his investment bank, A. Harriman & Co., ultimately Brown Brothers Harriman, as vice president. There would be two more sons in the Bush household, Jonathan, in 1931, and William H. T., called "Bucky, in 1938, after a welcome girl, Nancy Walker, in 1926. As Prescott's business interests also expanded, focused on

Manhattan, the family moved to a larger, comfortably unostentatious home in Greenwich, Connecticut. Throughout the 1920s and 1930s, the companies in which he had an interest invested aggressively, including in some German firms that became linked to Fritz Thyssen, an early supporter of the National Socialists. However, no one has ever accused Prescott Bush of being a Nazi sympathizer, only a partner in a profit-minded investment house.

Despite all their evident advantages, the Bush children were raised in an environment devoid of pretention. Pamela Kilian writes, "Both Dorothy and Prescott Bush hewed to the Protestant ethic. They believed in hard work, temperate living, and daily Bible readings." Sustaining such unpretentiousness in a town like Greenwich was not easy. The children were not to be spoiled. "Whatever we wanted," George said, "we had to earn."

Certainly Prescott could be intimidating, Dorothy more accommodating, but good manners and propriety were important to both of them. As their second son put it, "Dad taught us about duty and service. . . . Mother taught us about dealing with life in an old-fashioned way of bringing up a family [with] generous measures of both love and discipline." Daughter Nancy added, "We were a close, happy family, but we had strict rules." In such a traditional household, father knew best. He expected children and grandchildren to be "on time, well-behaved, and properly attired." Conversation was initiated from the head of the table. When Prescott was working at home, Dorothy quietly ushered her children as well as guests up the back stairway so as not to disturb him. Prescott's expectations for all five of his children were also daunting. Jonathan Bush recalled, "We were all terrified of Dad." The oldest son, Prescott Jr., admitted that when his father was away, it "seemed like the Fourth of July." Yet they all loved this man. He could be tender as well as tough and was interested in everything his children did. What they really feared most was letting him down.

For over a decade Prescott Bush supplemented his business career with increasing community involvement. He all but ran the governing body of Greenwich and served on the boards of at least seven national corporations. In 1935 he headed the United States Golf Association and later was on the committee that helped create the New York Mets. Prominent Republicans began to ponder—might he not make an attractive candidate for public office, if he would just unbend a little? Why, Prescott was known to have taken his wife home from a party simply because their host told an off-color joke. He had cut off his own brother because of his messy divorce, just as he would later withdraw his support of presidential aspirant Nelson Rockefeller, with whom he agreed on major issues, for the same reason. Still, he was a man to watch.

Meanwhile, Dorothy exercised her own complementary influence. She was no status-conscious clubwoman, but being home more constantly than her husband, she became, in the words of her son George, "the beacon of our family—the center." Although while growing up she faced limitations of caste and gender, she would be described by her admiring daughter-in-law Barbara as "the most competitive living human." At the family's summer compound in Kennebunkport, Dorothy led a physical regimen not unlike the Kennedys' in Hyannis Port, while competing with all comers. Her daughter, Nancy, summed it up: "Mother is not much on houses or decorating. She didn't care about all that. She wouldn't be in the *Social Register*." She became an excellent horsewoman, for example, simply because she loved riding, not for publicity or prestige. Her formal education might have ended at a proper girls' school, but her learning did not.

Like her husband, Dorothy was less interested in social prominence than in promoting social responsibility. As Parmet writes, "Such circumstances nurtured the development of George Bush. . . . [E]verything had come to him without any grappling of right or wrong." His mother was, Parmet continues, the family's "spiritual conscience, making certain that daily readings of scripture and Sunday services at the Episcopal church were not neglected." In her children's memory, their mother is almost a figure of legend, a mix of common sense, candor, and consistency. Yet when her son George, who most inherited her athletic skill, as a boy complained about losing a tennis match because his game was "off," his mother replied, "You don't have a game. Get out and work harder and maybe someday you will." She was supportive, but didn't believe in inflating egos.

Barbara and George Bush

George had such an outstanding record at Andover—he was a fine student, an athlete, and president of the senior class—that it must have satisfied even his demanding parents. The commencement speaker in the perilous spring of 1942 was Secretary of War Henry L. Stimson, a visible reminder that World War II was uppermost in everyone's mind. At a Christmas dance in Greenwich, George had met a lively young woman from Rye, New York, named Barbara Pierce (distantly related to President Franklin Pierce). She was attending Ashley Hall in South Carolina and planned to go on to Smith College. However, she was so excited by the attentions of tall, handsome George Bush that she felt she could "hardly breathe." Through subsequent dates and correspondence, their acquaintance grew into affection, and by the time she came up to his senior prom, they considered themselves engaged. To the incredulity of their children, Barbara would always insist that George was the first boy she had ever kissed.

The war came first, however. Instead of going to Yale, as he had planned, George joined the navy. Just eighteen, bidding farewell to his parents, he saw for the first time tears in his father's eyes. George was sent to preflight school in North Carolina and eventually became the youngest bomber pilot in the naval air service. Back in Greenwich, Dorothy assiduously tended to her "victory garden," while Prescott was called upon to coordinate over six hundred relief agencies under the National War Fund Campaign while also raising money, with notable success, for the USO. George wrote as often as he could to both his parents and Barbara, who had started at Smith. Dottie enjoyed a welcome, if brief, meeting with her son and his intended in Philadelphia at the end of 1943, when the aircraft carrier on which Bush's torpedo bomber squadron was to be based was being commissioned. Barbara received Dorothy's star sapphire engagement ring and would never remove it.

In a matter of months, both women would endure agonizing uncertainty. During September 1944, on a bombing mission on the Bonin Islands, after making its run, Bush's plane was shot down by anti-aircraft fire. Parachuting into the Pacific, George found refuge on a raft and within three hours was picked up by an American submarine. For a month, however, with no word from him, he was presumed missing. When he finally returned to Pearl Harbor and telegraphed home, the joy in Greenwich matched the relief in Rye. Barbara had taken a leave of absence from Smith to plan for her wedding, originally scheduled for December 19. Meanwhile, George agonized about whether he had bailed out too soon, instead of trying to crash-land his plane; his two crew members had been killed. He was awarded the Distinguished Flying Cross and eventually flew fifty-eight missions.

Bush was finally able to return home on Christmas Eve. On January 6, 1945, at the First Presbyterian Church in Rye, Barbara Pierce became Mrs. George Herbert Walker Bush. Young Prescott, who had been married only a week before, interrupted his honeymoon to serve as his brother's best man. Their mother was involved in everything, including giving Barbara her old but still elegant long-sleeved white satin dress and veil. After a reception for 250 at the Apawamis Club and a too-brief honeymoon in Sea Island, Georgia, the couple traveled in George's 1941 Plymouth to married housing on naval bases in a succession of states. Although now a flight-training instructor, George also prepared for the final assault on Japan. They were in Virginia Beach when word came that the second atomic bomb had rendered that invasion unnecessary.

Two months after the end of the war, they were already on their way to New Haven, Connecticut. Yale had offered returning veterans an accelerated program to gain their degrees in only two and a half years. Miraculously, they found a small apartment in a building they shared with other young couples. Barbara was pregnant, and on July 6, 1946, the Bushes joined the baby boom. Although the new arrival, George Walker Bush, lacked the full name of his father, in future years he couldn't avoid being called "Junior." It would later seem somewhat ironic that the only child of George and Barbara Bush to be born outside of Texas grew into the most authentically Texan in public perception. The little family moved two more times before George graduated Phi Beta Kappa in economics in 1948. He had been quite a presence on campus during his truncated time at Yale—baseball captain, a student leader, and—like his father—tapped for Skull and Bones. Barbara might have continued her education at Connecticut College, but there was simply too much to do.

George didn't want to simply duplicate his inherited lifestyle or locale. When he was very young, a maternal Walker uncle had told him that "politics is the only occupation worth pursuing." That might one day be a goal, but there was an "oil boom" in Texas, and George ultimately decided he would learn that business. After talking it over, George and Barbara, with their little son, settled in the wilds of Odessa, Texas. "Settled" is not quite the word, however—they would be constantly on the move, with six children in thirteen years. George had written Barbara from the South Pacific in 1943, "How lucky our children will be to have a mother like you." Truth to tell, Barbara didn't really want to go, but she was determined to be supportive. Of course, she had not yet seen Odessa.

Although the Bushes would soon be joined by many other Ivy Leaguers also searching for "black gold," their move to Texas represented a departure from everything familiar. For George Bush, it wasn't quite "making it on your own." Just as his own career had been launched by his Walker in-laws, Prescott not only gave George a new Studebaker, he found him work with a subsidiary of his friend Neil Mallon's Dresser Industries. Starting as an equipment clerk, within a year George was made a salesman. By 1950, in partnership with a neighbor, Bush was able to start his own firm in oil exploration, based in Midland, and he was off and running, literally as well as financially.

At about the same time, Prescott Bush finally made his own transition. Having served as Republican finance chairman in Connecticut for three years and encouraged by party leaders, he decided to run for the United States Senate in 1950. He had already been active in terms of social issues, not all of them likely to win favor with Connecticut's substantial Catholic constituency. As early as 1942 he was involved in the American Birth Control League and was treasurer of the national capital campaign for Planned Parenthood in 1947. An early supporter of civil rights, he headed his state's branch of the United Negro College Fund in 1951. To the surprise of many, running against the equally moderate popular former advertising man William Benton, Bush ran a vigorous and innovative campaign, using a helicopter to get around compact Connecticut. He even sang on the campaign trail with other former Yale Wiffenpoofs and strummed a guitar at rallies. Of course, his outgoing, congenial wife was an immense asset. He wound up losing by only 1,102 votes out of over 860,000 cast, making a strong impression on Republican Party leaders.

Only two years later, the other Connecticut senator, Brien McMahon, died, and there was a special election to fill the remaining four years of his term. Bush contested the seat with popular Democratic congressman Abraham Ribicoff. Swept along by the Eisenhower landslide, this time Bush won, although with only 51.3 percent of the vote. In 1956, Bush won reelection handily. Not surprisingly, the personification of a reasoned, middle-of-the-road "moderate Republican," Prescott became a close friend of President Eisenhower in both political and personal terms, and the two often played golf together. Eisenhower included Prescott Bush on a handwritten list of possible candidates he favored for the 1960 presidential nomination.

In Harry Truman's phrase, Bush was "a workhorse, not a show horse," in the Senate. He espoused fiscal responsibility while supporting a strong but efficient national defense. He was a key proponent of Ike's federal highways program, both the civil rights and voting rights bills, the Polaris submarine (built in Groton, Connecticut), and President Kennedy's Peace Corps. Bush favored moderating the Taft-Hartley Labor Law and easing provisions of the McCarran Act restricting immigration. Opposing the isolationist Bricker Amendment, he was a staunch supporter of the United Nations and favored granting the president standby price controls, should he need them. No one ever doubted Bush's courage. He was an early critic of Joseph McCarthy's excesses, proposing a "code of fair procedures" clearly aimed at the Wisconsin senator. On *Face the Nation*, Bush said he hoped the GOP was still the party of Lincoln but that he had tried to merge the best of the traditions of both major parties. He would later regret not running again in 1962. Had he started too late? In 1953, Lyndon Johnson had described Prescott Bush to his son as "the best thing that had happened to the 83rd Congress."

It had been an equally eventful decade for George H. W. and Barbara Pierce Bush. In many ways, Barbara, the only woman in American history to witness both her husband and her son achieve the presidency, more resembled her outspoken mother-in-law than her own mother. With an authenticity transcending politics and contrived "image," Barbara would nonetheless be fiercely loyal to all her kin.

Barbara Pierce had always been popular. Her childhood was not without trauma, but it was hardly dominated by it. Her family was well off, if not nearly as rich as the Bushes and Walkers. However, the Pierce iron foundry in Pennsylvania had been so hard hit by the Depression of 1893 that Barbara's father, Marvin, had to make his own way. An outstanding athlete and student at Miami University of Ohio, he went on to earn engineering degrees at Harvard and M.I.T., but it was in publishing that he made his mark, working his way up to president of the McCall's Corporation in New York. At college, he met lovely Pauline Robinson, the daughter of an Ohio supreme court justice, and married her in 1918. They had four children, two boys and two girls; Barbara, born on June 8, 1925, was their third child. They had settled in a comfortable home in the upscale suburb of Rye, on Long Island Sound.

It was only in later years that Barbara came to better appreciate her rather austere mother. Pauline gravitated to her older daughter, Martha, who was as attractive and well mannered as herself. Barbara, five years younger, developed early weight problems. As Herbert Parmet writes, although Barbara inherited her mother's love of gardening, needlepoint, and dogs, the two were never close. Her dynamic, fun-loving father, however, made up for it and seemed particularly fond of Barbara.

Barbara had a tight group of friends, of whom she was the leading mischief-maker. Already five-foot-eight by the time she was in her teens, "Porky Pig," as she called herself, blossomed seemingly overnight into— if not quite a swan—a slender, attractive young woman with reddish-brown hair and large, arresting eyes, the most popular girl at Rye Country Day School. Before her junior year, however, Barbara's mother intervened and sent her to a "finishing school," Ashley Hall in Charleston, South Carolina. Barbara was terribly upset but not only made the best of it, she added lifelong friends even in its more circumscribed environment. She also won the coveted sportsmanship award at graduation. At the same time, Barbara kept in touch with her old friends in Rye, accompanying them during Christmas break of her junior year to a formal dance in Greenwich, Connecticut, where she met "the handsomest looking man you ever laid eyes on, bar none."

Odessa, Texas, must have looked as utterly foreign and desolate to Barbara Bush as the Pedernales had appeared to Rebekah Baines Johnson. Barbara may have abandoned all the comforts of home, but her sense of humor was intact. "Everything in life is relative," she said. "We had the only house with a bathroom, and a car." Barbara set out to create a real home and to make friends of everyone she met. Her transplanted son George was already turning himself into an authentic West Texan.

Having made the senior George a full-fledged salesman, Dresser Industries sent him to Compton, California. In all, the family would live in twenty-eight homes in seventeen cities. In California they moved five times in a single year, George traveling over a thousand miles a week. Barbara was seven months pregnant with her second child when alarming word came from the East. Her mother had died in a freak auto accident in Westchester County. Her father, who had been injured in the crash, urged Barbara not to risk losing her child by making a cross-country trip to attend the funeral. She agreed but later deeply regretted her decision. Her second child, named Pauline Robinson Bush for her mother, was born at the end of 1949. They called her "Robin." Barbara would have four more children in the next decade, John Ellis, called "Jeb"; Neil Mellon; Marvin Pierce; and finally, in 1959, another girl, Dorothy Walker, called "Doro."

Sent back to Midland, Texas, George decided to go into the oil business himself. He formed an independent development company in partnership with a neighbor, largely financed by his uncle, Herbert Walker, trading in oil leases and mineral rights. George wasn't selling drilling bits anymore. He was doing the actual drilling. It all gave him an ulcer, but it also made him a millionaire. For Barbara, the venture was equally intensive. As J. H. Hatfield writes, "She nursed young Jeb, played with Robin, and watched the kid everyone still called 'Junior' try to become the next Willie Mays." When George Sr. arrived for special weekends, coaching Little League, sometimes exhibiting his own skill with bat and glove, and hosting immense neighborhood barbecues, the Bush home became the center of activity for the entire neighborhood. That's where the action was, abetted by Barbara's hospitality. During the week, however, it was largely a one-parent household. As Jeb would recall it, "Dad was the chief executive officer, but Mother was the chief operating officer," the parent in place.

Young George loved all sports, especially if he was captain, but he didn't deal gracefully with losing. At Sam Houston Elementary School, he was bright but somewhat incorrigible. His embarrassed mother was too often called in to talk things over with the principal. Even for no-nonsense Barbara, George was quite a challenge. George adored his father but saw him too rarely, a precursor of problems to come.

Four-year-old Robin was a lovely child and had always been active. It was Barbara who first noticed her unaccustomed lethargy and the bruises on her legs. Their doctor gave her blood tests, then struggled to break the heartrending news that Robin had leukemia, so advanced that it could not be treated. Her parents tenderly took her home and told no one. Over the next seven months, an attempt was made to treat Robin with a new drug at a New York research hospital. Early every morning, George, who had rushed back to Midland, went to church to pray. Barbara, who accompanied Robin to New York, rarely left her bedside. Sometimes Robin seemed to rally, but on October 11, 1953, she died. Barbara, who had tried to stay positive, was overtaken by inconsolable grief. "I felt I could cry forever." George poured out his despair to his mother, Dorothy. "We need a girl," he wrote, "her peace made me feel strong." They would indeed have another girl, their last child, but Robin's loss would always be felt.

Young George, at seven, was also deeply affected. "Why didn't you tell me?" he demanded. He had sensed that something was wrong. "A little of me died with Robin," he recalled, but he felt it was his duty to try to pull his parents out of their sorrow. After Barbara heard her son tell friends that he couldn't play because he had to stay with her to cheer her up, she began her emotional recovery, and their relationship became closer. Jodi Enda observes, "They have a way of communicating that sets them apart." As George W. himself has put it, "I've got my father's eyes and my mother's mouth." And the same style of wit. Barbara would later curb such tendencies, at least in public, but it would be harder for her son to do so. However, when George W. was sent off to Andover, he felt it to be another source of abandonment. First, his parents didn't tell him about Robin, now this. He loved Texas and his friends at home.

By 1958 George H. W. Bush's oil company was doing so well that he moved its headquarters to Houston. By 1962, their family complete, he was ready for the transition to public service that his father's example had implanted. With the Republican Party tilting to the right, away from Prescott Bush's moderation, George ran for party chairman in Harris County. His wife, as always, was supportive. As Kilian writes, "After fifteen housebound years . . . she found it a pleasure to be at her husband's side in a fast-moving campaign." George won, but when he contested for the United States Senate two years later against incumbent Democratic liberal Ralph Yarborough, he was swept away in the anti-Goldwater tide. Undaunted, he would be in public life for thirty years.

It was during the 1964 race that Barbara tried a hair rinse called "Fabulous Fawn." Her hair had turned prematurely gray the year Robin died. The results were less than fabulous, and she returned to a more comfortably natural appearance. If she looked older than her husband, what of it? When he won his race for a House seat in 1966, Barbara picked up and moved again, to Washington, where she would be as accommodating to other congressional wives as she had been to her neighbors in Texas. By then, George W. was at Yale, and Jeb was preparing for Andover. Barbara put Doro into the National Cathedral School, and her two remaining sons into St. Albans. Her husband served in a remarkable variety of capacities before achieving the presidency—two terms in the House of Representatives, ambassador to the United Nations, chairman of the Republican National Committee, chief of the United States Liaison Office to the People's Republic of China, director of the Central Intelligence Agency, and then two terms as Ronald Reagan's vice president. He often disagreed with the president but was extremely loyal in office. Traveling to over seventy countries, often to attend state funerals, he once quipped, "I'm George Bush. You die, I fly."

Over the years Barbara had developed strong views in support of such issues as women's choice and gun control. But her vigorous advice was now given to her husband in private. One on one, she was the more natural campaigner, another way in which her son resembles her. Avoiding set speeches, an acquired skill, she instinctively knew how to mix and mingle in the nature of personal politics on any level. There is still something of the deviltry of young Barbara Pierce in matronly Barbara Bush. As first lady, she insisted on putting the top ornament on the national Christmas tree, even though she'd done it eight times before, because "it's the only thing I've done more than anyone else." When her husband kissed Prime Minister Margaret Thatcher's hand in London, Barbara reciprocated by kissing a delighted Denis Thatcher's hand.

Very comfortable in small groups, on a public platform Barbara tends to be bland and brief. However, there was an eloquent exception in 1990, when she was asked to deliver the commencement address at Wellesley College, despite the opposition of many achievement-oriented students that, as someone who had not completed college, her only distinction had been attained through her husband's achievements. She responded, "At the end of your life, you will never regret not having passed one more test, winning one more verdict, or not closing one more deal. You will regret time not spent with a husband, a child, a friend, or a parent. Who knows? Somewhere out in this audience there may even be someone who will follow in my footsteps and preside in the White House as the president's spouse . . . and I wish him well."

Prescott Bush's final decade was fulfilled, as he hoped it might be, more by the achievements of others, notably his son George, who was then in New York as UN ambassador. George and Barbara were finally able to see more of his parents, to their great pleasure. By 1972, Prescott was ailing, and in September he underwent surgery for lung cancer at Sloan-Kettering Institute in New York. The cancer had spread too quickly to be contained, but Prescott still could muster a bit of humor. In one of his son's last visits to the hospital, when George told him he'd had dinner with the Russians, Prescott, although heavily sedated, asked, "Who picked up the tab?"

Prescott Sheldon Bush died on October 8, 1972, at the age of seventy-seven. As she was certain her husband would have wished, Dorothy Bush turned his funeral at Christ Episcopal Church in Greenwich into more of a celebration of his life, with bright colors, fond stories, and upbeat music, a parting that was almost a party. The grandchildren who had once feared him served as his pallbearers. Dorothy composed a poignant but incisive eulogy that was delivered by the rector. Her strength and sensitivity were evident throughout the memorial service. To George, Prescott would always be "my mentor, my hero." Over the years, he had only learned to appreciate his father more. He wrote to his children in 1974, "My dad felt strongly the firm obligation to put something into the system." Or, as George W. Bush rephrased it a quarter of a century later, "My grandfather Prescott Bush believed a person's most enduring and important contribution was hearing and responding to the call of public service," a determination that inspired a dynasty.

Dorothy Walker Bush lived for nearly two more decades, rejoicing in her son's success, in his loyal wife she viewed as so much like herself, in her other children and many grandchildren. When George described one of his parents as "heroic" and the other as "inspiring," who could discern which was which? When he headed to the People's Republic of China to run the American Liaison Office, she wanted to see it for herself. In Beijing she bicycled to the Great Hall of the People with the whole Bush family, very probably in the lead. Although aging and ailing, she would not miss his inauguration as vice president.

When her son was elected president, Dorothy would not be denied witnessing this inaugural, as well, although she had to arrive in an ambulance plane. Her will never weakened. Two weeks after he lost his bid for reelection 1992, Bush visited his ninety-one-year-old mother in Greenwich. She'd had a stroke and was slipping in and out of consciousness, but she mustered the strength to tell him she expected to be in heaven in a few hours. She passed away on the evening of November 19, 1992.

It may be that his father's defeat helped to "liberate" George W. to pursue his own political path, as Bill Minutaglio put it. Or was it his anger at Democrat Ann Richards's memorably derisive evaluation of his father, "Poor George. He can't help it. He was born with a silver foot in his mouth"? With George W.'s brother Jeb running for governor of Florida, perhaps George H. W.'s boys were finally being unleashed on the world.

Young George's rambunctious behavior had continued through Andover and then Yale, although he managed to graduate, become president of his fraternity, and continue the family tradition of being tapped for Skull and Bones. As usual, he made friends easily. To George W., the sixties, a time of such turmoil, might well have been the Roaring Twenties. He drank to excess, experimented with drugs, and was invariably the life of the party. No longer deferred during the Vietnam War, he joined the Texas Air National Guard and learned to fly jets. At least he was never reckless in the air, but later he admitted to other excesses during those "young and irresponsible" years. In a celebrated incident, at twenty-six a very drunk George W., frustrated by all the family pressure, challenged his father to go "mano a mano," and they had to be separated by Barbara. Yet, shortly afterwards, young George was admitted to Harvard's business school and managed to get his MBA in 1975, likely with an "I'll show him" chip on his shoulder. Then he went back to Midland, Texas, intending to repeat his father's success in the oil fields and in gas, but it didn't happen. The 1970s were not the boom times of the fifties. He even made a premature bid for Congress, garnering a surprising 47 percent of the vote. But after all, both his father and grandfather had also lost their first races.

At just about that time, George W. had become reacquainted with someone he had known back in grade school and was "struck by lightning." Laura Welch had not only grown up to be a bright and attractive young woman but was as centered and sensible as George had been erratic. She was now a school librarian, and in 1977 she became Mrs. George W. Bush. Reportedly after Laura's ultimatum, "Jim Beam or me," George abruptly stopped drinking and smoking and started jogging every day. Then, inspired by Dr. Billy Graham, he found religion, declared himself to be a committed born-again Christian, and became an active communicant of Laura's Methodist church. Finally, he found a job he loved. With a syndicate, he purchased the Texas Rangers baseball team. His share was only 1.8 percent, but he was the partner out front. Perhaps he could carve out his own career, as his father had done, and one day rise to be named commissioner of major-league baseball.

However, as his father's 1988 presidential campaign kicked off, he attended all the preliminary staff meetings. He bluntly asked strategist Lee Atwater, who had worked for competing candidates, "How do we know we can trust you?" Atwater replied that he ought to come to Washington and help in the campaign. Bush took him up on it, rendering for his father in 1988 the same sort of service Bobby Kennedy had provided for his brother Jack in 1960. Moreover, he thoroughly enjoyed it. "I don't mind a battle," he'd once announced, to no one's surprise. He proved to be a more natural political animal than either his father or his grandfather. When a reporter called him less well mannered than George H. W., he replied, "We are different; he grew up in Greenwich, I grew up in West Texas." Later, he added, "I was a warrior for George Bush. . . . I would run through a brick wall for my dad." They were never closer, except perhaps after September 11, 2001.

George H. W. Bush's presidential term had extraordinary highs and lows, from his foreign-policy triumphs to the economic problems that enabled Bill Clinton to defeat him in 1992. Later, he wrote to his sons George W. and Jeb, "Do not worry when you see the stories that compare you favorably to a dad for whom English was a second language and for whom the word destiny meant nothing. . . . I am content with how historians will judge my administration." On his seventy-fifth birthday, he wrote a joint letter to all his children: "Remember the old song, 'I'll

Be There When You Are.' Well, I'll be there when you are, for there's so much excitement ahead, so many grandkids to watch and grow. If you need me, I'm here."

George W. had never forgotten colorful Ann Richards's slur of his father at the 1988 Democratic National Convention. After spearheading construction of a spacious new stadium for the Texas Rangers, he sold his share of the team at a great profit and decided to run for governor of Texas in 1994, against the "unbeatable" Richards, no matter what the polls predicted. Only a few years before, George W. had introduced himself to White House visitors as "the black sheep" of the family. It had taken him into his forties to reach maturity, spiritually as well as emotionally. Richards called him all sorts of names, starting with "shrub," but Bush simply plowed ahead. As Minutaglio points out, with what his well-organized wife, Laura, called a "lesson plan," they devised and stuck with a strategy for his campaign. It sounds simple, but consistency was the key. Take nothing for granted, have a clear message, stress it from the start, never lose your cool, recognize even unpleasant realities, stick to a few key issues and hammer them home, don't make promises you may not be able to keep, "vision *does* matter," and "come out swinging."

Against all the odds, George W. Bush was elected governor of Texas in 1994. When opponents, undoubtedly for the last time, accused him of being a transplanted son of the effete Eastern establishment, Bush replied that it is true that "I was not born in Texas . . . because I wanted to be close to my mother that day." On the day of his inauguration, his father gave him a gift, accompanied by this note: "Dear George, These cufflinks are my most treasured possession. They were given to me by Mom and Dad on June 9 . . . in 1943 when I got my Navy wings at Corpus Christi. I want you to have them now. . . . You are ready for this huge challenge."

Wearing the venerable cufflinks and facing an even larger audience, George W. Bush took the presidential oath in January 2001. Laura held the Bible that an equally proud Barbara Bush had held for her husband only twelve years before. It all seems so long ago, almost a different era. If Harry Truman's assertion that it takes fifty years to determine if the legacy of a presidential administration has any validity, George W. Bush's must be the one to prove or disprove it. Elected twice by the narrowest of margins, experiencing the most devastating attack on continental American soil, engaging in costly conflicts in distant lands, enduring the most serious economic crisis since the Great Depression—to what extent was all of this under any single administration's control? All that seems clear at this juncture is that the heritage of a dedicated family, the closest to an American political dynasty, lies in the balance of history's judgment.

CHAPTER 20

Kansas to Kenya—Stanley Ann and Barack Obama Sr.

———⚬⚬⚬———

Stanley Ann Dunham, the idealistic and ambitious mother of Barack Hussein Obama II, lived in Kansas, California, Oklahoma, Texas, Washington State, Hawaii, and Indonesia. Eventually attaining a PhD in anthropology and doing notable research, she was married and divorced twice. Her first husband was an African student named Barack Hussein Obama; the second was Indonesian, named Lolo Soetoro. She had a child with each—a girl named Maya with Soetoro, and a son named for Obama, who would become the forty-third president of the United States. Despite uneasy times with both former husbands, Dunham encouraged her children to stay in touch with them and to cherish their multiracial, multicultural identities and heritage.

Although he was raised largely by his maternal grandparents in Hawaii, whom he referred to as "Toot" (based on "Tutu," the Hawaiian word for grandmother) and "Gramps," Obama credits his mother as "the dominant figure in my formative years." In his candid 1995 book, *Dreams from My Father*, Obama adds, in memoriam to his mother, "I knew she was the kindest, most generous spirit I have ever known, and that what is best to me I owe to her." As David Maraniss puts it, "Her goals . . . were not just about herself, but also about him. A mother and her only son, making their way alone, yet together." There's nothing simple about their story.

Stanley Ann Dunham was born on November 29, 1942, in Wichita, Kansas, the only child of Madelyn Lee Payne Dunham and then-corporal Stanley Armour Dunham. Her parents viewed land-locked Kansas, in the words of David Remnick, as "a place of soul-defeating dullness," and she would inherit their restlessness. In a way, the mature Barack Obama's settling in Chicago with an equally accomplished but securely rooted wife is at least in part a reaction to his own family's restlessness, even with so devoted a mother. So is his determination to provide his two daughters with as normal and stable a life as is possible in the White House, with Michelle's mother also living in the family's private quarters.

Why did the Dunhams name their daughter "Stanley"? The common assumption, as she would repeat growing up, is that her father had hoped for a son who would inherit his name, but there are other theories. This derivation of names would also be a dilemma in Obama's own search for identity. During his high-school years in Hawaii everyone called him "Barry," and carrying a middle name like "Hussein" didn't exactly enhance his political career.

The Dunham family had a variety of ethnic origins, predominantly English but also German, Swiss, Scottish, Welsh, and Irish. The Paynes' ancestry was even more varied, including the possibility of an African relative back in the seventeenth century and another relative who might have been a full-blooded Cherokee. Of course, it all pales in comparison with the plethora of potential Obama-Soetoro relationships throughout the continents and the centuries.

Ralph Waldo Emerson Dunham and his wife, Ruth Lucille Armour Dunham, owned a modest restaurant in Wichita. In 1926, when their son Stanley (Obama's future "Gramps") was only eight, Ruth committed suicide, and he had the traumatic experience of discovering her body. The newspapers ascribed her death to ptomaine poisoning. Whatever the cause, Ralph W. E. Dunham simply took off for parts unknown, leaving his sons, Stanley and young Ralph, in the care of their maternal grandparents, who lived in the attractively named town of El Dorado, Kansas. The young Barack Obama was not the first in his family to be raised by grandparents. Unfortunately, the oil boom days in El Dorado were long past, and Remnick describes Stanley's childhood as "bleak." He grew into a gregarious but outspoken and highly argumentative teenager. After riding the rails all the way to the West Coast and back while working odd jobs, somehow he managed to graduate from high school, years behind schedule. Working on a construction site in Aurora, only twenty miles from El Dorado, at one of the local haunts he ran into a quiet and studious but ambitious Aurora High School senior named Madelyn Lee Payne. She was also rather pretty, with dark brown hair and brown eyes, and slender. The mutual attraction was immediate.

Stanley Dunham was not only older but was almost entirely different from the local boys Madelyn knew. He had been all over the country and told her about his ambition to be a famous writer and the celebrities he'd already met. To her friends, he just seemed too full of himself. As they started to date, and she took Stanley to meet her parents, the response was similar. They were simply appalled, hoping this was only a temporary fascination.

The couple's family backgrounds couldn't have been more different. Madelyn's parents were temperate, literate Methodists. There was no drinking, dancing, or card playing in their modest, spotless, stable home. They were utterly devoted to their children. The Paynes were hardly wealthy, but Madelyn's father had a steady job even during the Depression, and her mother taught, as did her aunt. That is rather what they had in mind for Madelyn, perhaps on a higher level, along with a respectable, fulfilling marriage. To Madelyn, however, her future needn't be preordained. She loved her parents and didn't resent the secure home life they provided, only its limitations. She simply wanted more—to do more, to see more. And she was captivated by this boisterous, seemingly confident intruder, even if he represented a risky ticket out of the confines of dull predictability. After all, he also wrote poetry and enjoyed music. Perhaps his interests weren't entirely self-centered.

Madelyn *was* shy, but she was also sociable. Beyond the local soda shops and movies, for fun she and her friends would take off to nearby Wichita, dance to the visiting big bands, smoke, and even obtain a drink or two, although they were underage, in "dry" Kansas—a tempting glimpse of the wider world beyond. After the traditional junior-senior banquet, three weeks short of graduation, on May 5, 1940, she quietly slipped away to Wichita with Stan, and they were secretly married. Once she had graduated, she told her parents. They could only hope, and possibly pray, for the best. Stanley's family, on the other hand, took the news calmly. Perhaps what he needed was a level-headed young woman who might provide a positive influence. As soon as they could, Mr. and Mrs. Stanley Armour Dunham were off to their new life in California. It would not be for long.

Nor would it ever work out as Stanley had projected. Even on the West Coast, bustling with opportunity, bluster didn't bring success. As Stanley struggled to get started in the Bay Area, Madelyn had to support them both, initially as a clerk in a dry-cleaning store. As Maraniss writes, it may well have prepared her for the rest of her life with inconsistent Stanley Dunham. In a way, Pearl Harbor may have saved their marriage. As a married man, Stan was not obliged to serve, but he yearned to be a pilot in the Army Air Corps. After failing the color-blindness test, he took his family back to Kansas and enlisted in the army. The Dunhams' daughter, Stanley Ann, arrived six months later. After a year being stationed at a variety of stateside bases, in October 1943 Dunham sailed for England and would serve meritoriously, from being a supply sergeant to becoming, as his grandson still proudly points out with some frequency, "a member of Patton's army," although he never saw any actual action.

Meanwhile, back in her crowded home in Kansas, even with a baby to tend to and a husband in Europe, Madelyn Dunham had enough help to work full-time on the critical Boeing assembly line in Wichita. Apparently, she could learn to do almost anything. When her husband came home, reinvigorated by his successful stint under army regulations, the old itch returned to succeed on his own. He dragged his wife and little daughter back to California, this time to Berkeley on the GI Bill, hoping to gain a BA. Even with his wife writing all his papers, he still couldn't or wouldn't settle down sufficiently to earn a degree in any discipline. Madelyn was disgusted, yet she kept moving with him—to Oklahoma, Texas, back again to Kansas, and then to Washington State. In Ponca City, Oklahoma, she had a miscarriage and a hysterectomy. Their daughter would be an only child. At about the same time, and later in Seattle, Stanley finally found a job he could hold that he was actually good at—selling furniture. He was a crack salesman. If it wasn't quite the equivalent of writing screenplays or getting a degree, it was enough to buoy everyone's spirits. At least their marriage was still viable. Madelyn started her banking career in nearby Bellevue.

Little Stanley Ann, who retained that name into high school, was already showing remarkable curiosity. Fortunately, her family would stay in one general location from middle school through her high-school graduation. She went as far as eighth grade in Seattle, when her parents decided to move to the upscale suburb of Mercer Island, close to a new and highly regarded high school. It was there that her advanced ideas really took shape and her future would unfold. She made friends readily and enjoyed honors courses with some unusually innovative teachers. Remnick writes, "Ann's crowd was not socially fast, but they were engaged, political, progressive, hungry to read and learn about the world" and perhaps one day improve it. They were intent on civil rights at the earliest signs of a movement (Ann had seen bigotry in Texas beyond anything in the Midwest) and equal rights for women (before *feminism* was coined). They read everything from Karl Marx to Margaret Mead—the latter being significant for Ann's choice of a career. They went to foreign films, loved jazz, and talked things over endlessly at a local coffeehouse.

Yet Ann was hardly a budding beatnik. She had her share of fun, regularly attending every sporting event, joining in sleepovers, and participating in everything from the service club and singing groups to the yearbook staff. As Maraniss writes, "She wore plaid skirts . . . and saddle shoes and Peter Pan collars. At five-foot-six she was slightly taller than average. She had a long chin and narrow face . . . with a bright smile . . . [and a] wonderful laugh," her often sarcastic wit frequently aimed at herself. She was just a bit heavy, but it didn't seem to inhibit her budding popularity. "It is typical," Maraniss adds, "that she would look outside her set for romance. In fact, her entire life thereafter was shaped by that tenacity." Ann was only seventeen at graduation in 1960. Although she had proclaimed herself an atheist, she was full of hope. She wrote in her yearbook that her goal was to have exotic adventures around the world. With a 3.35 grade-point average and so many advanced courses, she planned to join many of her classmates at the University of Washington.

Her unpredictable father had other plans. His employer was a family partnership, and after a falling-out, one partner decided to open his own store in Hawaii. Who better to manage it than that garrulous salesman, Stan Dunham? At forty-two, he had almost surprised himself, having put in four years with the same employer. Moreover, although as impressed as everyone else with his daughter's academic achievements, he felt she was a bit young to attend the University of Washington, so distant from Mercer Island. The University of Hawaii would be close to their new home. By now often at odds with her headstrong father, Ann reluctantly agreed.

Since the islands were a polyglot combination of every racial strain, a resident like Barack Hussein Obama represented only the darker side of the equation. He had arrived two years earlier. At twenty-three, he was the first African student at the university, where he planned to stay for three years, earn his degree, and return to his native Kenya, newly independent from Great Britain but still fraught with violence and division. Then he would go on to gain advanced degrees and help such outstanding leaders as Tom Mboya guide the new nation to a seemingly impossible unity and prosperity. He had left behind a wife and infant son. Economics was Obama's specialty, and from the day he arrived, part of the first financed group of young Kenyans to visit the United States, he was a source of considerable interest to the local media. He had particularly wanted to visit Hawaii because he had read that it was the authentic melting pot of race, harmony, and mutual understanding, only recently admitted as a state.

He was interviewed frequently, invited to speak everywhere. And he had a lot to say. The natives called him "Popolo," Hawaiian for a weed called the black nightshade. Perhaps it was not all that derisive. As Neil Abercrombie, one of his many friends, put it, "So here was this coal-black guy, and there was this absolutely dynamic aura about him. A big smile. Easy to meet. Incredibly smart. And he was exotic in the land of the exotic."

In his first year at the university, in a Russian-language class, he met an intelligent young freshman with skin as pale white as his was jet black. They struck up an acquaintance and soon began seeing each other frequently, often with his many new friends. As always, Obama dominated the conversation. Ann was quiet and seemingly contented, possibly still as innocent and impressionable as her father had feared. By December, Ann was pregnant, and in February, telling no one, she and Barack flew to the island of Maui and got married. Barack Hussein Obama Jr. (frequently written as Barack Hussein Obama II) was born on August 4, 1961, at Kapi'olani Medical Center to a "Caucasian" mother.

It came as a surprise to everyone, but perhaps not so much so in Hawaii as it might have been in, say, Kansas. Neither set of parents, one thousands of miles away, was exactly pleased with the marriage, let alone the birth. Madelyn and Stanley Dunham, who espoused tolerance, had met the father and, like everyone else, found him charming, but there was just something not quite right about him. Was he *too* glib? As it turned out, he had already lied to his new wife, telling her that he had been divorced. Back in Kenya, his first wife, Kezia Obama, was already expecting a second child, but in the local Luo tribal tradition, a new wife was fine with her, particularly as her husband had been sending her so many gifts, from unknown sources of income. As for Obama's father, Hussein Onyango Obama, he was deeply upset that his gifted son would marry a *mzungu*, a white woman, sullying his family's pure blood lines. And with a new son or not, would she ever agree to come to live in Kenya? The violence had not yet stopped, with murderous and well-publicized "Mau Mau" uprisings seeming to escalate it.

But what of Ann, the inexperienced teenage mother? There she was, alone with her infant son, her husband still at school, still pursuing his prior life, drinking with his friends, seemingly oblivious to the new circumstances. Ann had been obliged to drop out of school, yet she never evidenced a sign of resentment or remorse, at least not in public. Somehow she managed to finance an extension course from the University of Washington and enrolled as a regular student in the spring of 1962. Moving to Seattle with her son, she rented an apartment and reconnected with old friends, who noted how proud she was to show off little Barack. After a year, out of funds, she returned to Hawaii, moved in with her parents, and transferred back to the University of Hawaii. For several months she received food stamps to make it all viable. However, she had another invaluable asset. Her father simply loved little Barack and became the epitome of a doting grandfather, taking the boy everywhere, from the beach to the park. It became a second, more fulfilling vocation for Stanley.

By now even Ann Dunham Obama had no illusions about Barack Sr. In June 1962, he graduated Phi Beta Kappa from the University of Hawaii. With a choice of scholarship offers, he decided to go alone to graduate school, studying economics at Harvard. After all, why not the best? He would send for them when he could. Ann and little Barack visited him in Cambridge once, but it didn't go particularly well. She and her son would not see his father again for nearly a decade. In the interim, Obama had married another white wife, whom he abused. In all, he was married at least four times and had countless affairs and an untold number of children. When Barack Jr. later labeled his father a "womanizer," it was something of an understatement.

In January 1964, Ann filed for divorce, citing "grievous mental suffering." It was not contested. Soon after, she met Lolo Soetoro, an Indonesian geologist. He was neither as dark nor as outspoken as the senior Obama, and Ann's parents were more at ease with him. But the background of his native land was no less violent. His father and brother had been killed in the revolt against Dutch colonialism, following the brutal Japanese occupation. Eventually, Lolo was able to get his undergraduate degree in Java and set off in 1962 to pursue his master's degree at the University of Hawaii. There, at the appropriately named East-West Center he met Ann, and she fell in love again. Events moved swiftly. Soetoro received his MA in geography in 1964, and he and Ann Dunham were married in 1965. In 1966 Soetoro returned to Indonesia. Unlike Obama Sr., he had neither a prior wife nor children. In August 1967, Ann Dunham finally received her BA in anthropology from the University of Hawaii, and in October of that year she moved with her son to Jakarta to rejoin her husband.

She stayed there for five years, her son for four. It was never easy, although characteristically Ann came to love the culture, with all its complexities—indeed, to become almost attached to it. She would write extensively about Indonesian traditions and possibilities, initially in her doctoral dissertation, and would return again in 1975 to do intensive research and developmental work, in concert with many international agencies. Ann and six-year-old Barack, ready for first grade and soon to be known more as "Barry," flew initially to Japan and then on to Jakarta to reunite with Lolo.

It seemed odd. In Hawaii, a relaxed Lolo, even in a foreign land, had enjoyed playing with young Obama, like a real father. Here, at home, he seemed always on edge, nervous, more distant, moody, and secretive. He often drank excessively. Ann not only made friends everywhere she could, she managed to put Barry in a reasonably reliable school. On August 15, 1970, Soetoro and Dunham had a daughter, whom they named Maya Kasandra. It seemed to heighten his spirits, as would their new neighborhood after Lolo gained a far more lucrative job as liaison with the government for Union Oil. Barry's new school was mainly Muslim, like most schools in Indonesia, but his initial school had been Catholic. He never became fluent in the Indonesian language, although he picked up a good deal. Being registered as a Muslim because it was officially his father's faith would create controversy in later years. It would have been so much simpler had his parents initially been able to afford to send him to the International School, where the instruction was in English.

With more household help in their new home, Ann was preparing for the day her son would return to be educated in Hawaii. Although she spent full days teaching English at the American embassy, she woke an extremely reluctant Barry at 4 a.m. every weekday morning to delve for three hours into English, history, and other relevant subjects. He writes retrospectively that her response to his complaints was, "This is no picnic for me, either, buster." Ironically, as her husband seemed to be becoming more Americanized, Ann became more involved in Indonesian life, constantly traveling and learning, whatever the perils, always stressing the universality of humanity. As Remnick relates, Ann surrounded her new daughter "with dolls of all ethnicities: black, Inuit, Dutch. 'It was like the United Nations.'" Not surprisingly, as Ann became more comfortable and competent in this new environment, her relationship with Lolo began to unravel. They had fewer and fewer interests in common, and she and Lolo Soetoro were divorced on November 5, 1980. He promptly remarried and had two more children. Ann's perceptive daughter observed that despite her mother's two failed marriages, she never lost her perspective. Ann simply "saw the beauty of community and kinship," wherever she might be. She had no illusions but an upbeat belief and commitment that things could and must get better. In that, "She was just *happy*."

At ten, Barry was put on a flight back to Hawaii, ready for fifth grade at an American school and filled with mixed emotions. He deeply missed his mother, but his grandparents were waiting. For a start, they got him into the best school in Hawaii, even if indirectly. Punahou looked more like a select college, its seventy-plus lush acres encompassing a complete campus, with tuition to match. Its acceptance rate was about the same as Harvard's. Obama brought little to recommend him to the prestigious school, beyond his distant mother's conviction that he was exceptional. However, he did well on the entrance exam and interviews. Moreover, Punahou had a need-based scholarship program.

The need was evident. His mother had little money. Gramps and Toot lived in reduced circumstances in a modest tenth-floor apartment. Stan Dunham had left the furniture business and was now selling life insurance. It wasn't going well, leading to the customary distractions, drinking, arguments, and grim isolation from his wife. Toot was doing much better at the Bank of Hawaii, in 1970 becoming its first female vice president, but gender equity was a distant dream. She worked much harder than her male counterparts, yet earned less. Exhausted and frustrated, she returned home each evening to do her own drinking, sometimes to excess, and then repaired to the bedroom after a silent dinner. Her hopes of exotic adventures or even a nice cottage with a picket fence had long since faded. However, both her boss and her husband's were wealthy, influential alumni of Punahou and were more than willing to lend a hand.

Before long, Barry had his "Welcome to the Punahou family" letter of acceptance. In a way, it also seemed to buck up his grandparents and invigorate his distant mother. In effect, *they* were also being accepted, as Obama writes. It was, for Toot and Gramps, "an elevation in their family status that they took great pains to let everyone know." With "no more destinations to hope for" of their own, *he* was their hope. Visiting the school with his grandson, Stanley grabbed him by the arm, "Hell, Bar," he whispered, "This isn't a school. This is heaven."

Of course, in Hawaii, including throughout the Punahou family, there were many combinations of ethnicities. Miss Hefty, Barry's amiable homeroom teacher, had previously taught in Kenya. When she asked Obama for his full Kenyan-Indonesian-American name, his classmates' titters had to be contained. Most of them had been together since kindergarten, with affluent parents who were well acquainted with each other. There was only one other technically black person in his class, a plump girl named Coretta. The adjustment to this totally new environment was not easy. What helped was his immersion in American life. Each day he walked the five blocks to school and back home, saw if there were any new comics at the newsstand, watched cartoons and sitcoms on the TV, did homework while Gramps napped, and then joined him to pick up Toot and buy ice cream, sharing the latest snack foods from a genuinely American supermarket, with dinner consumed in front of the TV. At ten Barry would go to his room and sleep to the sounds of top-forty music on the radio.

Gradually, Barry became better adjusted to his new school and made friends, blithely suggesting to them that one or both of his fathers were actually princes in their foreign lands. He began to grasp what it took to master the new environment and the curriculum in his own language, although without studying very intensely. All this was rather suddenly interrupted by a telegram his grandmother found in the mailbox: "Your father's coming to see you," she said. "Next month. Two weeks after your mother gets here. They'll both stay through New Year's. . . . I suppose we better start looking for a place for him to stay." Gramps broke into the resulting silence, "Should be one hell of a Christmas."

When Ann arrived for her visit, she tried to reduce Barry's apprehension. Despite everything, she had maintained a correspondence with Obama, and he knew a good deal about his "baby bull." Even worse, Miss Hefty had asked Obama to speak to the class, with another class invited to attend. When Barry saw his father arrive in the doorway—a very thin, tall, dark figure who walked with a limp and used a cane but still dressed like an Englishman—he seemed hardly as intimidating as anticipated.

"So, Barry," his father said, "your Grandmama has told me that you are doing very well in school. . . . It's in the blood, I think," and then came that more familiar laugh. Barry was quiet and Ann was nervous as they took the visitor downstairs to his rented apartment. But when Barry was watching a Christmas cartoon special, things broke out into the open. Obama insisted that Barry turn off the TV, go to his room, and study, and Toot exploded. Who was this intruder to barge in and bully everyone? Obama responded that his son was being spoiled, needed a firm hand, and watched too much television. Gramps replied that this was *his* house. It wasn't only the Grinch who stole Christmas that year.

The next day, Ann told her son, "You shouldn't be mad at your father, Bar. He loves you very much. He's just a little stubborn at times." How little had changed, beyond Barack Obama's appearance. Barry began counting the days until New Year's. First, though, the dreaded day arrived at school. "We have a special treat for you today," Miss Hefty began. "Barry Obama's father is here, and he's come all the way from

Kenya, in Africa, to tell us about his country." He spoke just as effortlessly as he always had, of the wild animals, of proving one's manhood by
killing a lion, of the deep traditions of his Luo elders, of Kenya's struggle
against British rule, just as in America. He talked about how people had
been enslaved for no more reason than the color of their skin, but that
we all universally continued to strive, Kenyans and Americans, for freedom and development through hard work, sacrifice, and determination.
When he finished, Miss Hefty was beaming. Everyone applauded, and
some students actually asked questions. Mr. Eldredge, the other class's
teacher, told Barry, "You've got a pretty impressive father," and then the
bell rang for lunch.

During the next two weeks, things went better. Barry and his father
exchanged gifts—a basketball for the boy, a handsome tie for the father.
They went together to a Dave Brubeck concert, spent a lot of time relax-
ing in Obama's sublet apartment, and even danced to records he had
brought of Kenyan music. They were photographed together in front of
the Christmas tree, and then he was gone. By then, Barry was sorry to
see him depart, a mixture of so many conflicting emotions. He never saw
him again.

On November 23, 1982, returning from a trip to Ethiopia, the elder
Obama stopped at an "off-license" bar, where drinks were inexpensive,
and consumed both whisky and beer. Late that night, driving very fast as
was his custom, he lost control of his vehicle, hit a pole, and was killed.
There had been continuous political turmoil. His mentor, Tom Mboya,
had been assassinated, but this had clearly been an accident. Barry was
twenty-one. His second father, Lolo Soetoro, died of liver failure on
March 2, 1987, at the age of fifty-two.

After New Year's in 1971, Ann continued her work in Indonesia, but
she returned to Hawaii with her daughter less than a year later to complete her postgraduate work at the university and spend time with her
son, who by then scarcely knew what to expect from his tireless mother,
or when she'd bring her good cheer back to his sight. The list of Ann's
achievements would fill a book of its own. After teaching English at a
variety of venues in the 1960s, she was a cofounder of the Indonesian

Heritage Society. A weaver herself, she instructed in such crafts as weaving, batik, and dyeing at Honolulu's Bishop Museum in the 1970s, while completing coursework for her MA in anthropology at the University of Hawaii at Manoa. Her graduate work was supported by grants from the Asia Foundation and other foundations. After three years together in Hawaii, Ann and Maya returned to Indonesia, urging Barry to join them. He understandably preferred to finish high school at Punahou, where he was more comfortable and had developed a crowd of his own. He went back to living with his grandparents. It was fine with them.

By then Ann was acceptably fluent in so many languages that she could switch from one to another in the same sentence. Intensely interested in rural industries, she moved throughout Java under a grant from the East-West Center, consulted with the International Labour Organization, was a consultant for USAID and the World Bank, and developed a model of microfinance for the Ford Foundation. In the 1980s she extended her activities to Pakistan as a development consultant for several banks and corporations. In the 1990s her interest in women's rights was manifested from New York to Beijing as a research and policy coordinator for Women's World Banking and the UN's Fourth World Conference on Women. Back in Hawaii, she received her PhD in anthropology through a thought-provoking 1,043-page dissertation titled *Peasant Blacksmithing in Indonesia: Surviving and Thriving against All Odds*. In it, she argued that villagers in Java have the same economic needs as Western capitalists. Distinguished anthropologist Michael Dove praised the work as a "classic," challenging popular perceptions that the roots of poverty lie with the poor themselves.

It's unlikely that Barry read all this, although he kept in touch with his mother. He was still involved in resolving his own place in the world. One morning he found his grandparents arguing. Gramps didn't want to get dressed and drive Toot to work. She normally took the bus, but the preceding day at the bus stop a very aggressive man had asked her for money. Even after she gave him a dollar, he persisted. "If the bus hadn't come," she said, "I think he might have hit me over the head." Barry suggested that his grandfather take her this time. "It's no big deal."

Gramps turned around and replied, "It *is* a big deal. . . . You know why she's so scared this time? . . . Before you came in, she told me the fella was *black*. . . . That's the real reason she's bothered." Obama writes, "The words were like a fist in my stomach." After his grandfather finally agreed to drive his wife to work, Barry sat on the edge of his bed and reflected on his grandparents. "They had sacrificed again and again for me. They had poured all their lingering hopes into my success. Never had they given me reason to doubt their love. . . . And yet I knew that man who might easily have been my brother could still inspire their rawest fears."

If not the outstanding scholar his mother and grandparents had looked forward to lauding, Barry had evolved from the "Choom Gang" ("chooming" in Hawaiian slang means smoking marijuana), a seventies norm that also extended to cocaine (which he *did* inhale) and heavy drinking. From Indonesia and on her trips home, his very concerned mother kept at him about his mediocre grades and exhorted him to start getting serious about college. He had slimmed down considerably, and his passion became basketball, not student politics. He graduated with a B average. From Punahou, that was good enough to gain admission to a choice of high-quality colleges and universities.

Obama chose scenic Occidental College in California, aided by some financial assistance. His friends there were still multiracial, but, as one with a Japanese American wife would later tell him, "Everything doesn't revolve around race." He had some good times but decided, as he began to associate with a more serious crowd, that he might want to get into public service, to help the disadvantaged in American society. At the end of his sophomore year, he transferred to Columbia, seeking a more urban environment. Before entering, in the summer of 1981, he took a three-week trip to Asia, first to Pakistan and then to Indonesia to visit his mother and sister. He also saw scenes of such severe poverty, beyond anything he would witness in New York, that they stayed with him. At Columbia, back to being "Barack," he decided to buckle down and get serious, majoring in politics and international relations. He became active in reform groups. He also found time for his first trip to Kenya, finally meeting many of his much darker-skinned relatives. Two years after getting his BA in 1983, he went to Chicago as a community organizer, initially for a Catholic church-based group encompassing a wide area.

He entered Harvard Law School in 1988, by then firmly committed to a career in public service, graduating in 1991 magna cum laude and widely publicized as the first African American president of the *Harvard Law Review*. He might have joined any number of prestigious firms and embarked on a highly lucrative career. Instead, he chose to become an associate with a more modest law firm specializing in civil rights and neighborhood economic development. He also wrote his personal memoir, *Dreams from My Father*, and moved into politics, convinced that only actual legislative action could help the impoverished. His "advisor" at his first law firm had been another exceptional Harvard Law School graduate, attractive Michelle Robinson, from a very stable, upwardly mobile South Side African American family. The rest, as they say, is history.

In 1994, Ann Dunham, still living and working intensely in Indonesia, experienced stomach pains, which at first seemed to be simple indigestion. However, she returned the next year to be examined at the Sloan-Kettering Center in New York. The grim diagnosis was uterine cancer, which had already spread to her ovaries. She moved back to Hawaii to live near her widowed mother, Barack's Toot. Her father, and the closest to a real father her son had ever known, his Gramps, had died on February 8, 1992, at the age of seventy-three. He was buried not in Kansas but in Hawaii. Barack, aware of the danger to his mother, rushed to Hawaii to see her, but he was too late. She died on November 7, 1995, twenty-two days short of her fifty-third birthday. After the memorial service, Obama and his sister scattered her ashes over the Pacific Ocean, climbing down the rocks to the shore beneath at scenic Lanai Lookout.

Her posthumous recognition went far beyond even the recognized achievements of her life—from a biography (*A Singular Woman*) to a biographical film (*Obama Mama*). Her research was the subject of symposia at universities throughout the United States. Ann Dunham was posthumously given the highest civilian award in Indonesia, and the

University of Hawaii established in her name both an endowed faculty position and graduate fellowships in concert with the East-West Foundation, a relationship she had epitomized throughout her life. In his second book, *The Audacity of Hope*, Obama tried to put her beliefs in context: "For all her professed secularism, my mother was in many ways the most spiritually awakened person that I've ever known," her faith expressed in social consciousness. His grandparents had been not very observant Baptists and Methodists. Raised by them, he had always been a Christian, but he had also been influenced by his mother's nondenominational spirituality.

Settled in Chicago, Obama was elected to the Illinois State Senate in 1996, representing a district extending over a wide area of the South Side. In office, as he had projected when a community organizer, he promoted legislation focused on healthcare, child care, tax credits for low-income workers, and bipartisan proposals aimed at averting home foreclosure and opposing racial profiling and predatory lending practices. He was reelected twice. However, he then lost a Democratic primary for a seat in the United States House of Representatives to long-time incumbent Bobby Rush.

But Obama, now that he could finally say with more authority that he was "*from* Chicago" and having waged an intensive campaign, had learned a great deal. He ran again, that time for the United States Senate in 2004, in a carefully orchestrated campaign that began with preliminary polling as early as 2002. When Obama won the Democratic primary by a surprisingly large margin, national leaders began to take notice. He was invited to deliver the keynote address at the Democratic National Convention that July. Even before he was elected to the Senate, that one televised speech made him a national figure virtually overnight, a rarity in today's politics. "The audacity of hope! In the end, that is God's greatest gift to us, the bedrock of this nation. A belief in things not seen. A belief that there are better days ahead." With his expected Republican opponent surprisingly withdrawing from the race and being replaced late, Obama won the general election with 70 percent of the vote.

Only four years later he would be a candidate for the presidency of the United States. "Yes we can!" With a supportive wife who also turned out to be a skilled campaigner, and two attractive little daughters with names little more customary than his own—Malia and Sasha (actually, Natasha)—Barack Obama set out on the campaign trail as head of a thoroughly American family, winning the nomination and then running against war hero and incumbent Republican Senator John McCain.

One day before the election, Obama learned that his grandmother had succumbed to the cancer she had fought for so long. He had interrupted his campaign to visit her in Hawaii, intent on getting there in time, as he hadn't with his mother. She died on November 2, 2008, at the age of eighty-six. Her ashes, too, were scattered off the coast of Oahu. McCain sent a letter of condolence. Speaking in Charlotte, North Carolina, on Election Eve, Obama was unusually emotional. "She's gone home," he said. "And she died peacefully in her sleep, with my sister at her side. And so there is joy as well as tears." Madelyn Lee Payne Dunham was humble and plain-spoken, he managed to add, but "one of the quiet heroes we have all across America." The three Dunhams, each so different, were united in their ultimate hope for his future.

Many Thanks

⊸⊶⊷⊸

Thanking everyone involved in this enterprise would challenge anyone's grasp of superlatives.

I cannot imagine a more tireless editor than Olga Greco, who made so many tactfully incisive suggestions. I am also indebted to everyone else at Skyhorse Publishing, including Joe Craig, Rain Saukas, Ashley Vanicek, Stacey Fischkelta, and many others. It was all set up by my exceptional agent, Roger Williams.

Assembling this book has also been something of a family affair. My wife, Betsy, has been invaluably involved in every stage of this preparation. Our son, Bill, has lent his expert counsel on marketing, and his wife, Dr. Rebecca Gullan, somehow found the time to do an extensive survey of pictorial possibilities. My experienced associate and neighbor Elsa Efran was helpful as usual, and her husband, Dr. Jay Efran, actually kept the computer functioning reasonably well.

Angelina Renee Monroe hastened our input from many separate sources. Our vital archivists have included: Vanessa Erlichman of Polaris Images; Polly Nodine and Ryan Rutkowski of the Jimmy Carter Library and Museum; Elizabeth Druga and Kenneth Hafeli of the Gerald R. Ford Presidential Library and Museum; Elizabeth Harman of the Lyndon B. Johnson Library; Elizabeth Shortt of the Woodrow Wilson Presidential

Library; Matthew C. Hanson of the Franklin D. Roosevelt Presidential Library; Herbert Ragan of the Clinton Presidential Library; Heather G. Cole of the Theodore Roosevelt Collection; Houghton Library, Harvard University; Kathy Struss of the Dwight D. Eisenhower Presidential Library and Museum; Laurie Austin, Jennifer Quan, and Kyla Ryan of the John F. Kennedy Presidential Library and Museum; John F. Fletcher of the Richard M. Nixon Presidential Library; Mary Finch of the George Bush Presidential Library Museum; Steve Branch of the Reagan Presidential Library; Dawn Bonner of Mt. Vernon's Fred W. Smith Library for the Study of George Washington; and Julie Stoner of the Library of Congress.

And, most of all, my thanks to you, the ultimate reader.

Bibliography

———

As noted through the text, biographies and memoirs of our presidents provide insights into the influence of their parents. Here is a listing of some of the books I've found helpful:

George Washington

Alden, John R. *George Washington: A Biography*. Baton Rouge: Louisiana State University Press, 1996.

Bourne, Miriam A. *First Family: George Washington and His Intimate Relations*. New York: W. W. Norton, 1982.

Brookheiser, Richard. *Founding Father: Rediscovering George Washington*. New York: Free Press, 1996.

Ferling, John E. *The First of Men: A Life of George Washington*. Knoxville: University of Tennessee Press, 1988.

Flexner, James T. *George Washington: The Forge of Experience, 1732–1775*. Boston: Little, Brown, 1965.

Freeman, Douglas S. *George Washington: A Biography*. Vol. 1, *Young Washington*. New York: Scribner's, 1976.

Jackson, Donald, ed. *The Diaries of George Washington*, Vol. I, *1748-1765*. Charlottesville: University Press of Virginia, 1976.

John Adams

Butterfield, Lyman H., ed. *The Adams Papers: Diary and Autobiography of John Adams*. Vol. 1, *1755–1770*. Cambridge, MA: Belknap Press of Harvard University, 1962.

Ellis, Joseph J. *Founding Brothers: The Revolutionary Generation*. New York: Alfred A. Knopf, 2000.

_____. *Passionate Sage: The Character and Legacy of John Adams*. New York: W. W. Norton, 1993.

Ferling, John E. *John Adams: A Life*. Knoxville: University of Tennessee Press, 1992.

McCullough, David. *John Adams*. New York: Simon and Schuster, 2001.

Shaw, Peter. *The Character of John Adams*. New York: W. W. Norton, 1977.

Shepherd, Jack. *The Adams Chronicles: Four Generations of Greatness*. Boston: Little, Brown, 1975.

Smith, Page, *John Adams*, Vol. 1. Garden City, NY: Doubleday, 1962.

Thomas Jefferson

Brodie, Fawn M. *Thomas Jefferson: An Intimate History*. New York: W. W. Norton, 1974.

Ellis, Joseph J. *American Sphinx: The Character of Thomas Jefferson*. New York: Alfred A. Knopf, 1997.

Fleming, Thomas. *The Man from Monticello: An Intimate Life of Thomas Jefferson*. New York: William Morrow, 1969.

Gardner, Joseph L, and Julian P. Boyd, eds. *Thomas Jefferson: A Biography in His Own Words*, Vol. 1. Princeton, NJ: Princeton University Press, 1974.

Malone, Dumas. *Jefferson the Virginian*. Vol. 1, *Jefferson and His Time*. Boston: Little, Brown, 1948.

Peterson, Merrill D. *Thomas Jefferson and the New Nation: A Biography*. New York: Oxford University Press, 1970.

Randall, Henry S., *Life of Thomas Jefferson*. Vol. 1. Reading, MA: Perseus Books, 1972.

Smith, Page. *Thomas Jefferson: A Revealing Biography*. New York: McGraw Hill, 1976

James Madison

Brant, Irving. *The Fourth President: A Life of James Madison*. New York: Bobbs-Merrill, 1970.

Ketcham, Ralph. *James Madison: A Biography*. New York: Macmillan, 1971.

McCoy, Drew R. *The Last of the Fathers: James Madison and the Republican Legacy*. New York: Cambridge University Press, 1984.

Moore, Virginia. *The Madisons: A Biography*. New York: McGraw-Hill, 1979.

Peterson, Merrill D., ed. *James Madison: A Biography in His Own Words*. New York: Newsweek Books, 1974.

Rutland, Robert A. *James Madison: The Founding Father*. New York: Macmillan, 1987.

James Monroe

Ammon, Harry. *James Monroe: The Quest for National Identity*. Charlottesville: University Press of Virginia, 1990.

Cresson, William P. *James Monroe*. Chapel Hill: University of North Carolina Press, 1946.

Gilman, Daniel C. *James Monroe*. Rev. ed. Boston: Houghton Mifflin, 1898.

John Quincy Adams

Adams, John Quincy. *Diary of John Quincy Adams*. Boston: Belknap Press of Harvard University, 1982.

Hecht, Marie B. *John Quincy Adams: A Personal History of an Independent Man*. New York: Macmillan, 1972.

Nagel, Paul C. *Descent from Glory: Four Generations of the John Adams Family*. New York: Oxford University Press, 1983.

_____. *John Quincy Adams: A Public Life, A Private Life*. New York: Alfred A. Knopf, 1997.

Parsons, Lynn H. *John Quincy Adams*. New York: Greenwood Press, 1993.

Andrew Jackson

Davis, Burke. *Old Hickory: A Life of Andrew Jackson*. New York: Dial Press, 1977.

James, Marquis. *The Life of Andrew Jackson*. New York: Bobbs-Merrill, 1938.

Johnson, Gerald W. *Andrew Jackson: An Epic in Homespun*. New York: Minton, Balch, 1927.

Remini, Robert V., ed. Carol Fitzgerald, *Andrew Jackson*. Westport, CT: Meckler, 1990.

_____. *The Life of Andrew Jackson*. New York: Harper and Row, 1988.

Martin Van Buren

Fitzpatrick, John, ed. *The Autobiography of Martin Van Buren*. Vol. 1. Reading, MA: Da Capo/Perseus Books, 1973. [reprint].

Hoyt, Edwin P. *Martin Van Buren*. Chicago: Reilly and Lee, 1964.

Niven, John. *Martin Van Buren: The Romantic Age of American Politics*. New York: Oxford University Press, 1983.

Wilson, Major L. *The Presidency of Martin Van Buren*. Lawrence: University Press of Kansas, 1984.

William Henry Harrison

Cleaves, Freeman. *Old Tippecanoe: William Henry Harrison and His Time*. New York: Scribners, 1939.

Eshrey, Logan, ed. *Messages and Letters of William Henry Harrison*. North Stratford, NH: Ayer, 1975. [reprint]

Hess, Stephen A. *America's Political Dynasties—From Adams to Kennedy*. Garden City, NY: Doubleday, 1966.

Sievers, Harry J., ed. *Benjamin Harrison, 1833-1901*. Dobbs Ferry, NY: Oceana, 1969.

John Tyler

Chitwood, Oliver P. *John Tyler: Champion of the Old South*. New York: Russell and Russell, 1964.

Ellett, Katherine T. *Young John Tyler*. Richmond, VA: Dietz Press, 1976.

Seager, Robert. *And Tyler Too: A Biography of John and Julia Gardiner Tyler*. New York: McGraw-Hill, 1963.

Tyler, Lyon G. *The Letters and Times of the Tylers*. Reading, MA: Da Capo/Perseus Books, 1970.

James Polk

Morrel, Martha M. *Young Hickory: The Life and Times of President James K. Polk*. New York: E. P. Dutton, 1949.

Nevins, Allan, ed. *Polk: The Diary of a President, 1845–1849*. New York: Longmans, Green, 1929.

Seigenthaler, John. *James K. Polk: 1845–1849*. New York: Times Books, 2003.

Sellers, Charles. *James K. Polk*. Vol. 1. Princeton, NJ: Princeton University Press, 1966.

Zachary Taylor

Bauer, K. Jack. *Zachary Taylor: Soldier, Planter, Statesman of the Old Southwest*. Baton Rouge: Louisiana State University Press, 1985.

Bent, Silas. *Old Rough and Ready*. New York: Vanguard, 1946.

Dyer, Brainerd. *Zachary Taylor*. Baton Rouge: Louisiana State University Press, 1946.

Farrell, J. J. *Zachary Taylor, 1784–1850*. Dobbs Ferry, NY: Oceana, 1971.

Millard Fillmore

Bare, W. L. *Life and Public Services of Millard Fillmore*. New York: Franklin, 1971. [reprint]

Crawford, John E. *Millard Fillmore*. Westport, CT: Meckler, 1988.

Farrell, John J. *Millard Fillmore, 1800-1874*. Dobbs Ferry, NY: Oceana, 1971.

Severance, Frank H., ed. *Millard Fillmore Papers*. Vol. I. Buffalo, NY: Buffalo Historical Society, 1907.

Franklin Pierce

Hawthorne, Nathaniel. *Life of Franklin Pierce*. Boston: Somerset, 1972.

Nichols, Roy F. *Franklin Pierce: Young Hickory of the Granite Hills*. Philadelphia: University of Pennsylvania Press, 1958.

James Buchanan

Curtis, George T. *The Life of James Buchanan*. Vol. 1. New York: Harper, 1883.

Hoyt, Edwin P. *James Buchanan*. Chicago: Reilly and Lee, 1966.

Klein, Philip Shriver. *James Buchanan: Bachelor Father and Family Man*. Lancaster, PA: James Buchanan Foundation, 1991.

——. *President James Buchanan: A Biography*. University Park, PA: Pennsylvania State University Press, 1962.

McFarlane, I. D. *Buchanan*. New York: Biblio, 1981.

Abraham Lincoln

Anderson, Dwight G. *Abraham Lincoln: The Quest for Immortality*. New York: Alfred A. Knopf, 1982.

Beveridge, Albert J. *Abraham Lincoln, 1809–1858*. Vol. 1. Boston: Houghton Mifflin, 1928.

Burlingame, Michael. *The Inner World of Abraham Lincoln*. Urbana: University of Illinois Press, 1994.

Current, Richard N. *The Lincoln Nobody Knows*. New York: McGraw-Hill, 1958.

Donald, David H. *Lincoln*. New York: Simon and Schuster, 1995.

Foner, Eric, and Olivia Mahoney. *A House Divided: America in the Age of Lincoln*. New York: W. W. Norton, 1990.

Guelzo, Allen C. *Abraham Lincoln: Redeemer President*. Grand Rapids, MI: Eerdmans, 1999.

Herndon, William H. *Life of Lincoln*. Reading, MA: Perseus Books, 1973. [reprint]

McPherson, James M. *Abraham Lincoln and the Second American Revolution*. New York: Oxford University Press, 1991.

Peterson, Merrill D. *Lincoln in Modern Memory*. New York: Oxford University Press, 1994.

Sandburg, Carl. *Abraham Lincoln: The Prairie Years*. Vol. 1. New York: Harcourt, Brace, 1974.

Tarbell, Ida M. *The Life of Abraham Lincoln*. Vol. 1. New York: Doubleday and McClure, 1900.

Thomas, Benjamin P. *Abraham Lincoln: A Biography*. New York: Alfred A. Knopf, 1952.

Andrew Johnson

Graf, L. P., and P. H. Bergeron, eds. *Papers of Andrew Johnson*. Knoxville: University of Tennessee Press, 1967.

Stryker, Lloyd Paul. *Andrew Johnson: A Study in Courage*. New York: Macmillan, 1936.

Thomas, Lately. *The First President Johnson*. New York: William Morrow, 1968.

Trefousse, Hans L. *Andrew Johnson: A Biography*. New York: W. W. Norton, 1991.

Ulysses S. Grant

Barber, James G. *U. S. Grant: The Man and the Image*. Carbondale: Southern Illinois University Press, 1986.

McFeely, William S. *Grant: A Biography*. New York: W. W. Norton, 1981.

Perret, Geoffrey. *Ulysses S. Grant: Soldier and President*. New York: Random House, 1997.

Simon, John Y. *The Papers of Ulysses S. Grant*. Vol. 1, *1837–1861*. Carbondale: Southern Illinois University Press, 1967.

Smith, Jean E. *Grant*. New York: Simon and Schuster, 2001.

Rutherford B. Hayes

Barnard, Harry. *Rutherford B. Hayes and His America*. New York: Bobbs-Merrill, 1954.

Bishop, A., ed. *Rutherford B. Hayes, 1822-1893*. Dobbs Ferry, NY: Oceana, 1964.

Fitzgerald, Carol B. *Rutherford B. Hayes*. Westport, CT: Meckler, 1991.

Williams, Charles R. *The Life of Rutherford Birchard Hayes: Nineteenth President of the United States*. Vol. 1. Boston: Houghton Mifflin, 1914.

James Garfield

Booraem, Hendrik, V. *The Road to Respectability: James A. Garfield and His World, 1844–1852*. Cranbury, NJ: Bucknell University Press, 1988.

Brown, Harry J., and Frederick D. Williams, eds. *The Diary of James A. Garfield*. Vol. 1. Lansing: Michigan State University Press, 1967.

McElroy, Richard L. *James A. Garfield: His Life and Times*. Canton, OH: Daring, 1986.

Peskin, Allan. *Garfield*. Kent, OH: Kent State University Press, 1978.

Smith, Theodore C. *The Life and Letters of James Abram Garfield*. New Haven, CT: Yale University Press, 1925.

Chester A. Arthur

Doenecke, Justus D. *The Presidencies of James A. Garfield and Chester A. Arthur*. Lawrence: University Press of Kansas, 1981.

Howe, George F. *Chester A. Arthur*. New York: Ungar, 1957. [reprint]

Reeves, Thomas C. *Gentleman Boss: The Life of Chester Alan Arthur*. New York: American Political Publications, 1991. [reprint]

Grover Cleveland

Brodsky, Alyn. *Grover Cleveland: A Study in Character*. New York: St. Martin's Press, 2000.

Jeffers, H. Paul. *An Honest President: The Life and Presidencies of Grover Cleveland*. New York: William Morrow, 2000.

Nevins, Allan. *Grover Cleveland: A Study in Courage*. New York: Dodd, Mead, 1938.

_____, ed. *Letters of Grover Cleveland, 1850–1908*. Boston: Houghton Mifflin, 1933.

Tugwell, Rexford G. *Grover Cleveland*. New York: Macmillan, 1968.

Benjamin Harrison

Hess, Stephen A. *America's Political Dynasties—From Adams to Kennedy*. Garden City, NY: Doubleday, 1966.

Myers, Elizabeth P. *Benjamin Harrison*. Chicago: Reilly and Lee, 1969.

Sievers, Harry J., ed. *Benjamin Harrison, 1833-1901*. Dobbs Ferry, NY: Oceana, 1969.

William McKinley

Higgins, Eva. *William McKinley: An Inspiring Biography*. Canton, OH: Daring, 1989.

Leech, Margaret. *In the Days of McKinley*. New York: Harper & Brothers, 1959.

McElroy, William L. *William McKinley and Our America*. Canton, OH: Stark County Historical Society, 1996.

Morgan, W. Wayne. *William McKinley and His America*. Syracuse, NY: Syracuse University Press, 1963.

Theodore Roosevelt

Burton, David H. *Theodore Roosevelt*. Thorndike, ME: G. K. Hall, 1973.

Collier, Peter, and David Horowitz. *The Roosevelts: An American Saga*. New York: Simon and Schuster, 1994.

Hagedorn, Hermann. *The Roosevelt Family of Sagamore Hill*. New York: Macmillan, 1954.

McCullough, David. *Mornings on Horseback*. New York: Touchstone, 1981.

Miller, Nathan. *Theodore Roosevelt: A Life*. New York: William Morrow, 1992.

Morrison, Elting E., and John Blum, eds. *The Letters of Theodore Roosevelt*. Vol. 1. Cambridge, MA: Harvard University Press, 1951.

Pringle, Henry. *Theodore Roosevelt: A Biography*. New York: Harcourt, Brace, 1931.

Renehan, Edward J., Jr. *The Lion's Pride: Theodore Roosevelt and His Family in Peace and War*. New York: Oxford University Press, 1998.

Roosevelt, Theodore. *Autobiography of Theodore Roosevelt*. Reading, MA: Perseus Books, 1985.

William Howard Taft

Anderson, Judith I. *William Howard Taft: An Intimate History*. New York: W. W. Norton, 1981.

Pringle, Henry. *The Life and Times of William Howard Taft*. Vol. 1. New York: Farrar and Rinehart, 1939.

Ross, Ishbel. *An American Family: The Tafts, 1678-1964*. Cleveland, OH: World, 1964.

Woodrow Wilson

Blum, John Morton. *Woodrow Wilson and the Politics of Morality*. Boston: Little, Brown, 1956.

Heckscher, August. *Woodrow Wilson*. New York: Scribner's, 1991.

Link, Arthur S., ed. *The Papers of Woodrow Wilson*. Vol. 1. Princeton, NJ: Princeton University Press, 1966.

Mulder, John M. *Woodrow Wilson: The Years of Preparation*. Princeton, NJ: Princeton University Press, 1978.

Osborn, George. *Woodrow Wilson: The Early Years*. Baton Rouge: Louisiana State University Press, 1968.

Warren Harding

Downes, Randolph. *The Rise of Warren Gamaliel Harding, 1865–1920*. Columbus: Ohio State University Press, 1970.

Mee, Charles L., Jr. *The Ohio Gang: The World of Warren G. Harding*. New York: M. Evans, 1981.

Russell, Francis. *The Shadow of Blooming Grove: Warren G. Harding in His Times*. New York: McGraw-Hill, 1968.

Calvin Coolidge

Coolidge, Calvin. *The Autobiography of Calvin Coolidge*. New York: Cosmopolitan, 1929.

Fuess, Claude. *Calvin Coolidge: The Man from Vermont*. Boston: Little, Brown, 1940.

Sobel, Robert. *Coolidge: An American Enigma*. Washington, D.C.: Regnery, 1998.

White, William A. *A Puritan in Babylon: The Story of Calvin Coolidge*. New York: Macmillan, 1938.

Herbert Hoover

Burner, David. *Herbert Hoover: A Public Life*. New York: Atheneum, 1984.

Hoover, Herbert. *The Memoirs of Herbert Hoover*. Vol. 1, *Years of Adventure, 1874–1920*. New York: Macmillan, 1951.

Nash, George H. *The Life of Herbert Hoover*. Vol. 1. New York: W. W. Norton, 1983.

Lee, Nash, ed. *Understanding Herbert Hoover: Ten Perspectives*. Stanford, CA: Hoover Institution Press, Stanford University, 1988.

Smith, Richard N. *An Uncommon Man: The Triumph of Herbert Hoover*. New York: Simon and Schuster, 1984.

Franklin D. Roosevelt

Asbell, Bernard. *The FDR Memoirs*. New York: Doubleday, 1973.

Collier, Peter, and David Horowitz. *The Roosevelts: An American Saga*. New York: Simon and Schuster, 1994.

Israel, Fred L. *Franklin D. Roosevelt*. Broomall, PA: Chelsea House, 1985.

Morgan, Ted. *FDR: A Biography*. New York: Simon and Schuster, 1986.

Parks, Lillian R., and Frances S. Leighton. *The Roosevelts: A Family in Turmoil*. New York: Prentice Hall, 1981.

Ward, Geoffrey C. *Before the Trumpet: Young Franklin Roosevelt, 1882–1905*. New York: Harper and Row, 1985.

Harry S Truman

Daniel, Margaret Truman. *Harry S. Truman*. New York: William Morrow, 1972.

Ferrell, Robert H. *Harry S. Truman: A Life*. Columbia: University of Missouri Press, 1994.

Gullan, Harold I. *The Upset That Wasn't: Harry S. Truman and the Crucial Election of 1948*. Chicago: Ivan R. Dee, 1998.

Hamby, Alonzo L. *Man of the People: A Life of Harry S. Truman*. New York: Oxford University Press, 1995.

McCullough, David. *Truman*. New York: Simon and Schuster, 1992.

Miller, Merle. *Plain Speaking: An Oral Biography of Harry S. Truman*. New York: G. P. Putnam's Sons, 1973.

Miller, Richard Lawrence. *Truman: The Rise to Power*. New York: McGraw-Hill, 1986.

Truman, Harry S. *Memoirs*. Vol. 1, *Year of Decisions*. Garden City, NY: Doubleday, 1955.

Dwight D. Eisenhower

Ambrose, Stephen E. *Eisenhower*. Vol. 1, *Soldier, General of the Army, President-Elect, 1890–1952*. New York: Simon and Schuster, 1983.

Brendon, Piers. *Ike: His Life and Times*. New York: Harper & Row, 1986.

Chandler, Alfred D., Jr., Stephen E. Ambrose, Louis Galambos, et al., eds. *The Papers of Dwight David Eisenhower*. Eleven vols. Baltimore, MD: Johns Hopkins University Press, 1970–1980.

Ferrell, Robert H., ed. *The Eisenhower Diaries*. New York: W. W. Norton, 1981.

Neal, Steve. *The Eisenhowers*. Garden City, NY: Doubleday, 1978.

John F. Kennedy

Burns, James McGregor. *John Kennedy: A Political Profile*. New York: Avon, 1960.

Davis, John H. *The Kennedys: Dynasty and Disaster, 1848–1948.* New York: McGraw-Hill, 1984.

Goodwin, Doris K. *The Fitzgeralds and the Kennedys: An American Saga.* New York: St. Martin's Press, 1987.

Hilty, James W. *Robert Kennedy: Brother Protector.* Philadelphia, PA: Temple University Press, 1997.

Kennedy, Rose Fitzgerald. *Times to Remember.* Garden City, NY: Doubleday, 1974.

Parmet, Herbert S. *Jack: The Struggles of John F. Kennedy.* New York: Dial, 1980.

Reeves, Thomas C. *A Question of Character: A Life of John F. Kennedy.* New York: Free Press, 1991.

Smith, Amanda, ed. *Hostage to Fortune: The Letters of Joseph P. Kennedy.* New York: Viking, 2001.

Whalen, Richard J. *The Founding Father: The Story of Joseph P. Kennedy.* New York: New American Library, 1964.

Lyndon Johnson

Caro, Robert A. *The Years of Lyndon Johnson: The Path to Power.* New York: Alfred A. Knopf, 1982.

Dallek, Robert. *Lone Star Rising: Lyndon Johnson and His Times, 1908–1960.* New York: Oxford University Press, 1991.

Dugger, Ronnie. *The Politician: The Life and Times of Lyndon Johnson.* New York: W. W. Norton, 1982

Harwood, Richard, and Haynes Johnson. *Lyndon.* New York: Praeger, 1973.

Kearns, Doris. *Lyndon Johnson and the American Dream.* New York: Harper and Row, 1976.

Miller, Merle. *Lyndon: An Oral Biography.* New York: G. P. Putnam's Sons, 1980.

Unger, Irwin, and Debi Irwin. *LBJ: A Life.* New York: Wiley, 1999.

Richard M. Nixon

Aitken, Jonathan. *Nixon: A Life.* Washington, D.C.: Regnery, 1993.

Ambrose, Stephen E. *Nixon: The Education of a Politician, 1913–1962.* New York: Simon and Schuster, 1987.

Brodie, Fawn M. *Richard Nixon: The Shaping of His Character.* Cambridge, MA: Harvard University Press, 1983.

Hoyt, Edwin P. *The Nixons: An American Family.* New York: Random House, 1972.

Morris, Roger. *Richard Milhous Nixon: The Rise of an American Politician.* New York: Henry Holt, 1991.

Nixon, Richard. *RN: The Memoirs of Richard Nixon.* New York: Grosset and Dunlap, 1978.

Parmet, Herbert S. *Richard Nixon and His America.* Boston: Little, Brown, 1990.

Gerald Ford

Cannon, James M. *Time and Chance: Gerald Ford's Appointment with History.* New York: Harper Collins, 1994.

Ford, Betty, with Chris Chase. *The Times of My Life.* New York: Harper & Row, 1978.

Ford, Gerald. *A Time to Heal: The Autobiography of Gerald R. Ford.* New York: Harper & Row, 1978.

Reeves, Richard. *A Ford Not a Lincoln.* New York: Harcourt Brace, 1975.

Jimmy Carter

Bourne, Peter G. *Jimmy Carter.* New York: Simon and Schuster, 1997.

Carter, Jimmy. *An Hour Before Daylight: Memories of a Rural Boyhood.* New York: Simon and Schuster, 2001.

_____. *Keeping Faith: Memoirs of a President.* New York: Bantam Books, 1983.

Mazlish, Bruce, and Edwin Diamond. *Jimmy Carter: A Character Portrait*. New York: Simon and Schuster, 1979.

Morris, Kenneth E. *Jimmy Carter: American Moralist*. Athens: University of Georgia Press, 1996.

Ronald Reagan

Cannon, Lou. *Reagan*. New York: G. P. Putnam's Sons, 1982.

Cardigan, J. H. *Ronald Reagan: A Remarkable Life*. Kansas City, MO: Andrews and McMeel, 1995.

Morris, Edmund. *Dutch: A Memoir of Ronald Reagan*. New York: Random House, 1999.

Pemberton, William E. *Exit with Honor: The Life and Presidency of Ronald Reagan*. Armonk, NY: M. E. Sharpe, 1997.

Reagan, Ronald. *An American Life: The Autobiography*. New York: Simon and Schuster, 1990.

_____. *Speaking My Mind*. New York: Simon and Schuster, 1989.

Weisberg, Jacob. *Ronald Reagan*. New York: Times Books, 2016.

George H. W. Bush

Bush, Barbara. *Barbara Bush: A Memoir*. New York: Scribner's, 1994.

Bush, George H. W. *All the Best, George Bush: My Life and Other Writings*. New York: Scribner's, 1999.

Kilian, Pamela. *Barbara Bush: A Biography*. New York: St. Martin's, 1992.

King, Nicholas. *George Bush: A Biography*. New York: Dodd, Mead, 1980.

Naftal, Timothy. *George H. W. Bush*. New York: Times Books, 2007.

Parmet, Herbert S. *George Bush: The Life of a Lone Star Yankee*. New York: Simon and Schuster, 1997.